Hands On With Google® Data Studio

A Data Citizen's Survival Guide

Lee Hurst

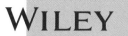

Copyright © 2020 by John Wiley & Sons, Inc., Indianapolis, Indiana

Published simultaneously in Canada

ISBN: 978-1-119-61608-5

ISBN: 978-1-119-61618-4 (ebk)

ISBN: 978-1-119-61621-4 (ebk)

Manufactured in the United States of America

For general information on our other products and services please contact our Customer Care Department within the United States at (877) 762-2974, outside the United States at (317) 572-3993 or fax (317) 572-4002.

Wiley publishes in a variety of print and electronic formats and by print-on-demand. Some material included with standard print versions of this book may not be included in e-books or in print-on-demand. If this book refers to media such as a CD or DVD that is not included in the version you purchased, you may download this material at http://booksupport.wiley.com. For more information about Wiley products, visit www.wiley.com.

Library of Congress Control Number: 2019954532

V10016770_010620

To my parents, for pursuing their interests with passion.

About the Author

Lee Hurst is a developer and occasional consultant. For the last 14 years, he has worked for Garlock Sealing Technologies, where he builds eCommerce applications, develops their global websites, and provides marketing analytics and strategy support.

Lee began working with Google Data Studio soon after its initial release in 2016. In addition to providing support through articles on his website, `helpfullee.com`, he is the creator and maintainer of the Google Data Studio Resources finder, a widely used free resource. He participates in conferences and groups, speaking on related topics, and is the organizer of the Rochester Digital Marketing meetup.

Lee has been involved with web development since the mid-1990s, when he began consulting and created the Susan B. Anthony House website in 1996. He specialized in neural networks and genetic algorithms as he worked his way through the computer science master's degree program at the Rochester Institute of Technology. He left the program to join IBM as a web applications developer in 1999.

Lee obtained a bachelor's degree in philosophy from the State University of New York (SUNY) Geneseo, and he worked a variety of jobs before finally giving in to his inner geek and pursuing further education and a career in IT. He lives with his girlfriend and two dogs in Rochester, New York, where he has provided a free community Tai Chi session every Wednesday for the last 7 years.

About the Technical Editor

Paul Roland is an online marketing expert with over 20 years of experience in providing services for both business-to-business (B2B) and business-to-consumer (B2C) companies. While at Compaq Computer Corporation during the 1990s, Paul was responsible for their server division online presence and pioneered many aspects of their web publishing process and online marketing strategy. Paul has also held marketing director roles for several marketing agencies and other energy-related corporations. These positions enabled Paul to gain deep expertise in search engine marketing solutions. Paul currently provides search engine marketing consulting services to several agencies in the Houston, Texas, area. Working with many clients that require advanced reporting led Paul to embrace Google Data Studio and actively use it over the past few years.

Acknowledgments

First, I would like to acknowledge the outstanding project team at Wiley. This book would not have happened without Devon Lewis, who contacted me on LinkedIn, suggested that I might write a book about the subject, and helped get the project approved. Gary Schwartz, my development editor, showed great patience and understanding as I went through the learning process. Along with the rest of the team, I would like to thank Barath Kumar Rajasekaran for his production work and Pete Gaughan for project management.

Next, a big shout-out to all the folks on Twitter from around the world who shared their knowledge and helped build a community. I greatly appreciate your camaraderie and support.

I also want to thank the Google Data Studio and Google Analytics teams. They have been remarkably accessible and supportive over the years. It's comforting to know that even at a giant company like Google, there are people who have a passion for their work and listen to their users.

A special thanks to my friend Allyn Evans, for not only her encouragement but also her help in arranging for the Soul Synergy Center to let me to use their real-world data for some of the examples in this book.

Finally, to Rebecca, for her boundless understanding, support, patience, advice, and love. Thank you.

Contents at a Glance

Contents

Introduction

I'll confess that when I was initially approached to write a book about Google Data Studio, I was hesitant. At the time, I was building a reputation, and some authority, on the subject. I particularly enjoyed blogging, giving presentations, and collaborating with newfound colleagues. It was exciting to explore the bounds of what was possible with each new release. But write a book on the subject? That was another matter, for sure.

I thought it might be a fool's errand to try to capture all the capabilities of such a quickly evolving platform in book form. After reading and reviewing hundreds of resources about Google Data Studio over the past few years, I had seen many "ultimate" guides published on the web, only to be outdated soon after their release. I seriously considered turning down the opportunity.

What changed my mind was a reflection on why I enjoyed working with Data Studio in the first place. It was the feeling of empowerment. I had found Data Studio to be like the Swiss Army knife of data visualization tools: although it certainly is not the best tool for every job, you can do quite a lot with it, and it is easily accessible.

Developing the ability to make sense of the tremendous amounts of data generated in our society is a challenge as well as an opportunity. Both individuals and large corporations can benefit from increased access to data if the tools to work with it are accessible and approachable. I believe that Data Studio meets these requirements and can help in the democratization of these skills.

The development of data literacy, and increasing your ability to communicate insights through visualization, is not just a set of skills to be used in a business context. Although it is becoming increasingly important for businesses to develop these skills, you can go beyond the business context and use these capabilities for your community and your personal interests.

Data Studio continues to evolve sophisticated features, but the fundamental capabilities have remained available and accessible to users at all levels. My approach to writing this book was not to provide an exhaustive detailing of features or to dive into the latest or most exotic implementations, as fun as that might be. The challenge in writing this book was to provide the reader with access to the fundamentals and guide them through the development process with examples that are relevant to their interests. The goal is to provide a foundation for those who want to explore or develop data skills.

During the writing of this book, which took several months, there were more than 20 Data Studio updates and releases. Despite all those changes, there have been only a few cosmetic updates to the examples provided. My hope, and so far, my experience, is that this book will be of value for some time to come. It is designed as a survival guide: a resource to get you started and see you safely through the challenges of working in areas that might be unfamiliar.

Beyond this book, you should find resources available to empower you to pursue your own interests even further and take advantage of new features as they become available.

Who Should Read This Book

This book is primarily designed with novices in mind. It is heavily weighted in favor of those who may be unfamiliar with the many different systems and services available. A wide range of applications are covered in this book, and chances are good that you will have an interest in several of the topics. This book should help

- Beginners looking for an accessible way to get started building skills in data visualization and analysis

- Those interested in gaining experience with data visualization tools

- Organizations looking for better ways to communicate their community involvement

- Small business owners looking to gain insight and monitor their websites and business listings

- Freelancers or small agencies looking to add better reporting capabilities for their clients

- People involved in organizations that can benefit from better reporting and communication capabilities

- People who have an interest in building their data skills and literacy for career enhancement

- Those who need to gain experience using Data Studio specifically due to business adoption

- Individuals interested in using their own data for personal growth
- People interested in analyzing and reporting on public data

What You Will Learn

This book provides a practical guide to many of the steps in the data life cycle. You'll learn how to find data, connect to data services, retrieve data, and study the basics of data preparation. We'll cover the basics of report design as well as using reports for analysis and insight discovery. And, of course, you'll learn all about using Data Studio as a tool for data visualization, analysis, and communication.

Throughout most of this book, we'll use a basic cooking analogy to guide you through the steps of creating reports and applications. We'll usually start with the finished product so that you can see the main components used in each example, and we'll then proceed to re-create the example.

For each example, I'll walk you through all the steps and not just how to create the report itself. It's important to know how and where to shop for data, how to prepare the data when necessary, and how to use the finished product.

Data Studio is a tool that can help you find your own insights from data in addition to being a medium for visual data communication. The more you work with data, the more you will build greater intuition as to where to look for insights. At the same time, your skills in analysis will grow. Again, there is no substitute for practice and experience.

It is my hope that as you work with your own data and learn to use the tools discussed in this book, you'll become more than a passive consumer of other people's work. Hopefully, you'll develop an appreciation of well-crafted communications. Also, you may develop a healthy skepticism for data presented in ways designed to promote a conclusion rather than to highlight an insight.

You have to expend a lot of mental energy in order to gain your own insights and even more energy to communicate them to an audience. I have found that working on topics and areas that interest me personally provides the motivation to expend the effort required.

My advice is to find an area of your own interest, in your personal, business, or public life, and explore that area with the tools now available.

How This Book Is Organized

Each chapter in the book has its own set of online resources. You'll find links to the live Data Studio examples, online references, and services. In addition, sample data files are provided for Part I so that you can follow along using the example data. You can access all of the online resources at www.wiley.com/go/handsondatastudio.

Part I: Data Studio Basics

This group of chapters covers the basics of working with Data Studio.

Chapter 1: Data Studio and the Data Citizen This chapter is designed to introduce users to the tools and skills that you'll be building by following the examples in this book. It explores the concepts involved in the data life cycle, the increased demand for data skills, and the roles that Data Studio can fill.

Chapter 2: Cooking with Google Data Studio This chapter will help users new to Data Studio to get up and running with the tool. Starting from scratch, we go from account setup, to personal financial data retrieval, to basic data preparation. After data preparation, we build the example report.

Along the way, you'll be introduced to basic Data Studio concepts and how to use the fundamental features of the tool. We'll cover in detail how to set up a Google Sheet with a new data connection and add that to your report. We'll also explore several of the fundamental chart visualizations and focus on configuration options that are most commonly used. Finally, you'll learn how to share the report.

Chapter 3: Enhancing Basic Graphs This chapter builds on the example created in Chapter 2. Here we cover the setup and configuration options that are important to most users, from chart visualization options to time range comparisons. I also provide an introduction to grouping concepts in order to build the updated report.

This chapter also covers how to copy Data Studio reports and reuse elements in order to save time. You'll learn more about static report design and how to use Data Studio to create password-protected PDFs for safe report sharing.

Chapter 4: Data Exploration with Interactive Elements This chapter sticks to using personal accounting data, but instead of creating static reports, we build a workbench designed for analysis. The chapter then explores the major interactive features available to Data Studio users, and it provides guidance on using various interaction options.

This chapter also introduces you to modifying and augmenting data using Data Studio functions when it is inconvenient, or impossible, to modify the source data. The last part of the chapter explores how to use the report as an analysis tool to answer specific questions.

Part II: Business and Marketing Applications

This part caters to the natural strengths of Data Studio. The focus here is on reporting for web application data, but the concepts are transferrable to other systems as well. In this set of chapters, we explore three main applications that, because of the widespread use of the web, are quite likely to be of interest to the largest set of users.

Another aspect that links these applications together is the use of data that is "live." This connection to live data sources, ones that are constantly updating and changing, lends itself well to the concept of dashboards, another major report type often developed in Data Studio.

Chapter 5: Web Data Visualization with Google Analytics   This chapter explores the major Google web measurement services, their roles, and their applications, and it dives deeper into using Data Studio with Google Analytics. Even if you don't have a web property with which to work, you'll be able to follow along by using Google's demo connectors that simulate a live website as we create the example report.

Google Analytics is one of the most widely used data collection tools globally, so naturally it is of interest to a lot of people. Although Google Analytics has its own charting capabilities, it can be difficult to create polished reports and share them with stakeholders. This chapter looks at how Data Studio can help those who report on web properties save time communicating insights as well as providing a powerful interactive platform for exploring data.

Along with making use of Google Analytics as a data source, this chapter explores working with premade templates to speed up development, applying dynamic data controls to extend the use of reports, and creating multiple-page reports.

In addition to working with an extensive data source like Google Analytics, you'll be introduced to several new chart types and some advanced interaction features such as drill-down capability.

Chapter 6: Using Google Search Console for Audience Insights   This chapter covers another widely used and important service for website owners. We take a closer look at the service and the data that it can provide about what people are searching for and how to use that information to connect to the audience for the website.

A substantial amount of this chapter is devoted to live cases of using Data Studio reports. The example reports are used to investigate a website's historical mysteries and find valuable, actionable insights for a real business.

Along the way, you'll learn how to increase the value of your data by adding your own categories and how to use hyperlinks to extend the user experience beyond your report pages.

Chapter 7: Viewing Local Organization Data from Google My Business   This chapter wraps up this section with an extensive look at Google My Business (GMB). We look at the role that GMB plays in the marketing of local businesses and organizations and its growing importance. Digging into the application, we discover why using Data Studio makes sense for users of this service.

This chapter introduces the reader to using third-party data connectors and explores the fundamentals of dashboards and mobile application design. The resulting example from this chapter is a report that works like an application on mobile phones and is designed for frequent use by busy managers.

Part III: Beyond the Office

The series of chapters explores the possibilities for using Data Studio in areas outside of standard business applications. We look at a wide variety of data sources and data visualizations. This chapter goes beyond the standard uses of Data Studio to see how it can be used by data citizens for their own personal and community interests.

Chapter 8: Getting Personal   This is a wide-ranging chapter that is devoted to creating Data Studio reports and applications for your personal use. The chapter covers self-generated, curated, and generated sources of personal data and provides examples of using each of them.

Examples in this chapter cover using direct connections as well as third-party services that can help you access your own data. This chapter details the use of several types of charts and a larger multipage Data Studio application that pulls all the personal sources together.

Chapter 9: Going Public   This chapter goes beyond business and personal applications and explores the larger arena that deals with community-oriented reporting. Although this has largely been the domain of other visualization tools, some large data organizations are providing their own Data Studio connectors to simplify the data connections process.

In this chapter, we explore how to find accessible sources of data. The examples in this chapter use major free data services and corporate sources that offer data with public access. Examples in this chapter also make use of some private data connections and teach you how to use a special Google connector with slow data sources to make your reports more responsive. You'll also find help in this chapter for working with some common data structure issues.

This chapter also explores some of the resources available to the data visualization community and how you can participate so that you can get feedback on your work and grow as a developer. Along with the standard report-building instruction, you'll find guidance for the design of embedded reports and detailed instructions showing you how to embed your reports in the pages of popular web systems.

Chapter 10: Where Do You Go from Here?   This chapter explores some directions you can take after you have mastered the basics. On the communication side, you'll find examples for annotating your reports with contextual information and instructions for your audience. This chapter provides instruction for adding videos to your reports and extending your options through the use of community visualization resources.

On the data side, this chapter covers some of the tools that Google provides for working with large volumes of data and extending your reach through data connector development.

Hardware and Software Requirements

You don't need much to create the examples in this book. To use Data Studio, you have to set up a Google Gmail account if you don't have one already, and you'll need an Internet-connected computer to work with Data Studio services.

The examples in Chapter 6 use real website data from live Google Search Console accounts. If you do not have access to that service for a real website, you can use the sample search console connectors provided by Google for most of the tasks.

The examples in Chapter 7 connect to live Google My Business accounts. At this time, there are no sample data connections available for these Google services used in that chapter.

Regardless of your ability to directly re-create the examples, you should still find value in these chapters.

How to Use This Book

If you are just starting off, I recommend that you begin by going in order through the examples in Part I. This will help you understand the fundamentals of the Data Studio tool and how to connect to sources of data.

After completing the first section, new users may want to explore the other chapters as it suits their interests. If you are interested in helping people out with their websites and other Internet properties, you'll want to go right on to Part II and work with Google Analytics and Search Console.

If you are a local business owner, or if you are involved in a local organization, you should pay particular attention to Chapter 7. Understanding and optimizing GMB listings is one of the fastest ways to increase the visibility of a business or organization. Each of these chapters offers more than just instructions for creating reports; each provides practical fundamental advice for using your reports to improve the performance of the organizations with which you are involved.

Suggestions for the More Experienced User

If you come to this book with previous Data Studio experience on the digital marketing side, I invite you to skim through Part I and Part II and go on to explore Part III in more detail. Working with personal and community-oriented applications will give you greater exposure to possibilities outside of the usual digital marketing reports. My guess is that working in some of these other areas will also spark your creativity when it comes time to get back to work.

If you are seeking career enhancement, going beyond the skills of the data citizen and pursuing growth as a citizen data scientist, focusing on any of the book sections should be helpful to you. However, I suggest that you pay extra attention to Chapter 9 and start participating in online communities in order to share your work and get support and feedback.

Whether you are a beginner or an experienced user, my hope is that you'll use the book as a guide to help you grow your communication and analytics abilities.

How to Contact the Publisher or Author

I appreciate any feedback that you have on this book. Stories of success, often from unexpected places, are one of the greatest rewards for anyone who seeks to help others. I hope you'll contact me if this book helps you and share your achievements, large or small.

You can contact me through the Helpfullee website at `https://helpfullee.com/contact`. I am also quite active on Twitter, where you can find me `@Helpfullee`.

If you believe you've found a mistake in this book, please bring it to our attention. At John Wiley & Sons, we understand how important it is to provide our customers with accurate content, but even with our best efforts an error may occur.

To submit any errata, please email our Customer Service Team at `wileysupport@wiley.com` with the subject line "Possible Book Errata Submission."

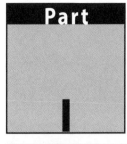

Part

I

Data Studio Basics

In This Part

Data Studio and the Data Citizen

Since you are reading this book, you probably qualify as a "data citizen." What do I mean by that term? A *data citizen* is someone who

- Has access to data in a format that can be analyzed
- Has access to the tools for data analysis
- Has a personal, business, or community interest in building their data literacy and skills
- Has some interest in deriving value from data to benefit themselves personally, their business, or their community

I'm not the first person to use the phrase "data citizen," but I found that most definitions of the term seemed too restrictive, too bound only to the interests of those working in corporate enterprises, describing their relationships to those organizations. I believe that we need to expand the concept so that it is more inclusive and focused on the individual, regardless of their business relationships.

For our purposes, being a data citizen is a recognition of your current state of meeting the criteria from the list. There is no "Data People's Republic" to enforce the rights and responsibilities of a data citizen. The only state to which you as a data citizen belong is a state of mind. It is the acknowledgment that you have the right to analyze and interpret data yourself and that you recognize the need to act responsibly with the interpretations and guidance that you provide to others.

This book is geared to those people who are ready to explore the opportunities and possibilities that come with being a data citizen. To support your growth in this area, I will be focusing on using Google Data Studio as a primary tool in your explorations. Before we get into the details, however, let's take a brief look at the factors that are creating the rise of the data citizen.

Data, Data Everywhere

You can't participate as a data citizen without data! Fortunately, we have an abundance of that resource. Data, in all its many varied forms, continues to grow at mind-boggling rates. It is currently estimated that 1.7 megabytes of data are being created for every person on Earth, every second of every day. To give that number some context, it is like every person on Earth uploading about 50 full-length movies each and every day!

Data is being generated from a large variety of sources today. Not that long ago, most information was collected by actual people. Manual data entry is still a vital part of the data collection landscape. (You're doing it whenever you fill in an online form.) The manual input of data has been augmented by data generated from software operating in virtually every aspect of business, from manufacturing to marketing.

New torrents of data are now being added by the multitude of devices that are creating measurements and logging that data, from satellites to your personal fitness tracker. In addition, we have a flood of user-generated content, from uploaded videos to Facebook posts to email to tweets. All of this digital content can be treated as data in some form or another.

In addition to the original data that we generate, there is also metadata, which is data generated about the data itself. Programs that help us classify and summarize data produce even more data!

Accessibility of Data

Another prerequisite for exercising your data citizenship is access to data. Although access to public community data, and even data generated for us at a personal level, has lagged a bit behind compared to the amount of data collected, we have more access to data than ever before.

At a personal level, we have the ability to access data generated for us from most online services—anywhere from personal banking to online music services. As concern for privacy and collection of data on our personal habits has grown, so too has some access to data generated about us.

At the community level, we also have more access to data collected by our governments and agencies. Recent trends have been for increased public access to data in an effort to make governments and organizations more transparent.

Access to this public information benefits businesses, as it gives them information that they could not afford to gather on their own.

From individual hobbyists running their own websites, to the small business and local organizations, to the largest corporations and government entities, all levels of individuals and organizations have the ability to generate data for their online properties, and all have the ability to access and analyze that data.

Deriving Value from Data

Whether or not you pursue data citizenship for your own personal or community interests, you are likely to participate in the objective of getting value from data in your business life. Working with data was once mainly the responsibility of the business analyst, but democratization of data access, visualization tools, and interpretation are pushing these responsibilities closer to the front lines of the organization.

Although there is an explosion in the volume of data, this raw material does little good sitting on the shelf. Without the process of analysis, data has only great potential, not actual value.

The Rise of the Citizen Data Scientist

Along with the growth of data, we have seen the rise of the *data scientist*. Although the concept of what a data scientist is continues to evolve, I'll summarize and say it is the job of people who create the systems designed to extract value from data. It should be noted that although the term data scientist is frequently used, most people in this field specialize in only a few aspects of the data life cycle and not the entire field of data science. There is a huge demand for data scientists, but other, less high-profile positions are filling the gap to deal with the huge opportunities that the explosion in data is providing.

A *citizen data scientist* makes use of the same concepts as the data scientist, but on a simpler and more localized scale. Using the tools for gathering, storing, enhancing, and visualizing data, they create insights and communicate information that helps drive action in organizations.

Data scientists are in demand, but most of those positions require a master's or doctorate degree, which limits the number of people going into the field. To fill the demand gap, citizen data scientists are expected to make up the shortfall. In 2018, Gartner Inc. predicted that "citizen data scientists will surpass data scientists in the amount of advanced analysis produced by 2019."

Where do citizen data scientists come from? It is unlikely that you will find job listings for citizen data scientists, as this is more of a role than a profession. Most citizen data scientists are expected to come from the regular business departments as opposed to the fields related to software engineering or mathematics.

Most of the people picking up this skillset have detailed business knowledge and can immediately use the insights provided from data analysis. Instead of being brought in from the outside, the skills are mostly developed by people already in the organization.

Before businesspeople become citizen data scientists, however, they need to develop data literacy and a practical knowledge of the data science skills needed for the role. They need to become data citizens.

The Process of Extracting Value from Data

As mentioned before, the goal of this focus on data is to get some real value out of the data to which you have access and strategically collect data that can be used later. The path to value could be described the following way:

1. **Collect data:** What we collect, or have access to, influences the rest of the process.

2. **Transform the data into information:** Data is for computers; information is for people. Aggregating and classifying data helps people comprehend it as information.

3. **Analyze the information to get insights:** Insights are aspects of information that deepen our understanding and add to knowledge. Greater understanding and knowledge have an intrinsic value.

4. **Communicate insights:** Clear communication of insights plays a major role in spreading understanding and the significance of the new information. Communication may be geared toward action.

5. **Take action from insights:** All insights may have some inherent value, but actionable insights are particularly valued. They increase your confidence that taking a specific action will move you closer to your goals. The results of the action provide impact that is of value.

Whether you are a data scientist, in the role of citizen data scientist, or acting as a private data citizen, you need tools, skills, and knowledge to extract value from data. As far as tools go, the applications developed for business are finding their way to the public, making it possible for private data citizens to extract value from data without the resources found in an organization.

While there have always been some enthusiasts working outside of organizations, their work in this area required hard-won knowledge and skills. Over time, the tools and processes needed for the individual data citizen to do meaningful work have become more accessible and easier to use.

The Roles of Visualization

One area of tools that has shown immense growth recently are those that allow us to visualize data. *Data visualization* enables us to make graphic representations of data through charts, maps, and other elements that allow us to grasp important relationships and patterns in the data that are not perceptible in the raw data. In a formal Data Science Life Cycle model, data visualization plays a role near the end of the cycle where one communicates insights found during analysis.

The communication phase has been getting increased attention over the past few years. Sophisticated analysis and brilliant insights can be wasted if the information cannot be communicated in a way in which decision makers can clearly see a connection between the information presented and a course of action to take. Recently, companies that specialize in visualization, such as Tableau and Looker, have been purchased in multi-billion-dollar acquisitions in order to help bolster the offerings of Salesforce and Google.

Data visualization can also play a role in the analysis phase. Data scientists have tools for analysis that are beyond the means of data citizens just getting started. Although technologies such as automated prediction, language analysis, and machine learning are now within the grasp of dedicated enthusiasts, it will take some time before these become entry-level services that we can use without extended study and a healthy budget.

Most of us will have to rely on our own "neural network"—that is, the organic one between our ears—to discover insights. Fortunately, our brains work quite well for many areas of insight discovery when data is presented in a way that allows us to use our innate capabilities for comparison and pattern recognition. So beyond simply communicating insights, exploration of the data using visualizations can help you discover your own insights.

The Role of Data Studio

So where does Google Data Studio fit into the toolset of a data citizen? I find that it fills many roles:

- **Data Visualization:** The most obvious function is to transform data into visualizations, charts, graphs, maps, tables, and other graphic representations. Data Studio also provides some facilities for importing visualizations that are not included in the standard set.

- **Data Access:** The Data Studio platform includes the tools needed to access the data for visualization. Google provides several data connectors, and other connectors are available through third-party vendors. In addition, Google provides a development platform for creating custom data connectors.

- **Data Processing:** Although its data processing capabilities are not extensive, Data Studio does provide fundamental facilities for modifying, grouping, and augmenting data.

- **Communication:** Data Studio provides an easy-to-access platform, both for creating and sharing reports. It provides extensive and easy-to-use media and layout capabilities, making it a great communication medium. It may not compete with presentation software, but I have seen Data Studio used at conferences in an effective way.

- **Data Exploration and Analysis:** Although analysis and insight discovery are left up to the user, the ease of creating and modifying visualizations, combined with a variety of interactive features, allows for quick data exploration and insight discovery.

Many services are available today that can fill many of these functions as well as or better than Data Studio. Tableau, for example, is one of the leaders in data visualization and the preparation of beautiful communications. Microsoft Power BI also provides extensive control over data processing as well as providing a fine array of visualization options. So, if there are other options available, what explains the popularity of Data Studio? I believe the underlying reason for the rapid adoption of Data Studio boils down to a combination of flexibility, ease of use, and accessibility.

- The combination of excellent and good-enough features makes it flexible enough to handle many tasks.

- Ease of use makes it more approachable for new users, and experienced users find it very fast to use for development.

- The accessibility of the tool is its primary strength; anyone with an Internet connection and a laptop can start developing with Data Studio immediately. No software installation or configuration is required. Anyone with an Internet connection and a browser can view Data Studio reports because no special software is required for viewing. And, of course, there is the fact that it is free, so there is little risk in trying it out!

Data Studio was initially developed for the needs of digital marketers, but this doesn't mean that its usefulness is restricted to that audience. It is a general-purpose tool, as you can see from the variety of reports shown in Figure 1.1 and it is useful for many kinds of data visualization tasks, regardless of the subject content of the data itself.

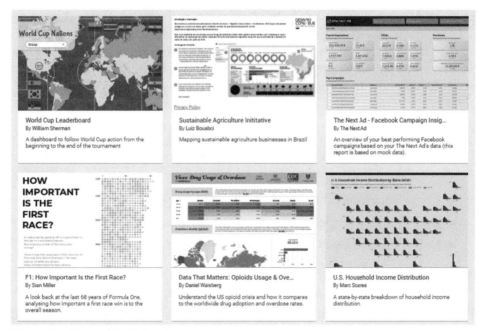

Figure 1.1: Data Studio Gallery

A Brief History of Data Studio

Data Studio is a relative newcomer in the world of data visualization. The development of the platform is a great example of rapid, Agile development, as new features have been rolled out on a nearly weekly basis for three years!

Data Studio was initially made available to users on June 2, 2016. At that time, it was released in the United States as a Public Beta, and it could be purchased by customers of the Google Analytics 360 service, a premium offering that extended the power of the standard Google Analytics package. Significantly, Google also released a Public Beta version of the product that was free to all U.S. users but limited users to creating five reports. At that time, users could only connect to six Google-based data sources. A lot has changed since then!

New capabilities being introduced on a frequent and regular basis has made this an exciting product with which you can work and grow. The Data Studio development team has done an excellent job of adding features while not breaking reports that were created using earlier versions. Fortunately, changes in the interface have been more evolutionary than revolutionary, which has given users the chance to adapt to changes a little bit at a time instead of dealing with major changes that required a lot of mental readjustment.

As of this writing, the pace of development has not slowed, and you should check the release notes frequently. These release notes are often accompanied by updated documentation. Currently, you can access the release notes at `https://support.google.com/datastudio/answer/6311467`.

The Data Studio release notes can also be used to trace the history of Data Studio development. Seeing just some of the release highlights may give you a better feel for how the product has grown.

2016 Updates

In 2016, Google focused on making Data Studio more accessible globally and provided some powerful connection options:

- Connectors were added for MySQL and Google CloudSQL.
- Data Studio was released in an additional 21 countries.
- Data Studio received ISO 27001 certification (a security standard).

2017 Updates

In 2017, Google greatly enhanced the connectivity and sharing capabilities of Data Studio. In addition, it worked on feature enhancements of the display capabilities. It was apparent that Google was actively developing the service, although it was still officially in Beta status.

- Google lifted the five-report limit, allowing users of the free version to create an unlimited number of reports. Data Studio was also made available in over 180 countries.
- More standard Google connectors were added, and developers were now able to build connectors to external services, which dramatically increased access to non-Google data sources.
- Design options were added with custom report sizes and more font choices. Links and images were made available for use in tables.
- Developers got access data file upload capability, and Google provided an option to track report usage with Google Analytics.
- Sharing options were extended to allow report viewing by the general public, and reports could now be embedded in web pages.

2018 Updates

Google got serious about Data Studio in 2018. By this I mean that Data Studio had developed a following and commercial connector support for dozens of services. Throughout 2018, the development seemed to be focused on making Data Studio a product that could be adopted by organizations, confident that it would satisfy most of their reporting needs.

In September, Google moved Data Studio from Beta to full supported product status, a significant milestone. Here are some of the major developments from 2018:

- A new Connector Gallery was made available, allowing developers to search through more than 150 free and premium connections. Community Connector development was opened to the general public, allowing people to develop their own connectors.

- Data blending capability was added. Although the capability was limited, it gave the report creator much greater power to combine data directly inside of Data Studio.

- Extract Data connectors were released that can greatly speed up report loading and interaction.

- New options available to "bookmark" a report were made available, saving the state of filters applied during a session. PDF download capabilities were also added.

- Report designers got the ability to embed external content, such as videos and Google documents, directly into reports. Chart-specific calculated field options were also made available.

- In addition to new standard chart types being made available, Google added interactive filters, allowing users to filter what is seen in the report by clicking on parts of charts and tables.

2019 Updates

During 2019, we saw Google extend the capabilities of its charts with more advanced visualization, interaction, and style options:

- Google added the ability to schedule PDF email delivery of reports. Versioning was also added, which allowed a report editor to roll back to an earlier version of a report.

- Drill-down functionality was made available in charts. This feature provided viewers with more interaction options to see different levels in a report. For example, users could now switch between country, state, and city views for data plotted on a map chart.

- Community visualizations became a standard feature, which allowed report creators to add charts not included in the standard interface.

- The ability to show minute time increments greatly increased the general utility of time-based charts.

Again, this is just a list of the *major* changes. There have been multiple releases each month with even more features and enhancements. The point here is that the sophistication and capabilities of Data Studio have been steadily and rapidly increasing. Furthermore, the pace of this development shows no signs of slowing down.

Fundamentals First

Seeing the rate of development, you might wonder how long any book featuring Data Studio will be useful. Fortunately, the core features of Data Studio and how they are used have remained constant, and the fundamental requirements of the data citizen are unlikely to change in the near future.

This book is designed as a survival guide for data citizens; it's designed to help you acquire the fundamental skills and experience with Data Studio in order to help you in your own explorations, whether they are focused on personal, business, or community application.

In order for you to develop those skills and become familiar with the tool, each chapter is focused on a different objective and each provides a separate Data Studio report as a goal. In my opinion, the best way to learn how to use Data Studio is to use it for real tasks.

Where to Go for Help

As you develop your data citizenship, you will likely need help along the way. As previously mentioned, this book's Resources page has links in each chapter to help you on your way. I recommend that you keep a small collection of other reference points to get extra help when you need it.

We already pointed out that there is an official Data Studio release page that provides information about changes in which you may be interested. You may find that there is a lag time between when Google releases new features and when detailed documentation is provided. Fortunately, there are communities of users who can help you if the official documentation does not.

My first resource in the case of problems or questions is usually Twitter. If you are a Twitter user, you can usually find help by posting with the hashtag `#DataStudio` or `#GoogleDataStudio`.

People around the globe enjoy helping to support the Data Studio community. People outside of the official Google channels often create posts and examples for new features, and they will often tweet when they publish new material on Twitter using these tags.

Asking for help directly from the various official Google entities on Twitter is usually not productive. While `@googleanalytics` and several community support people participate in Data Studio conversations on Twitter, it is not an official support channel. Google would much prefer that you use the official support page found at `https://support.google.com/datastudio`. There you'll find a support forum, tutorial materials, and more.

Outside of Google official support channels, several online communities support Data Studio users. For instance, if you are a user of Slack, you may want to check out the `#Measure` group, where there is a very active `#DataStudio` channel. You can ask for an invitation at `https://join.measure.chat`. Reddit and the Stack Exchange Network are also popular locations to find answers to Data Studio questions.

If Facebook is more your speed, you can check out the Google Marketing Platform – Enthusiasts group. You can find this group's Facebook home page at `www.facebook.com/groups/GAGTM`.

Finally, I humbly offer my own contribution to the community, the Google Data Studio Resources finder. This has been a popular community resource, and it is itself an example of what you can do with the platform. You'll find out more about that application and how to build your own in Chapter 9, "Going Public."

Additional Readings

"Role of Citizen Data Scientist in Today's Business": `www.simplilearn.com/citizen-data-scientists-article`

"Gartner Says More than 40 Percent of Data Science Tasks Will Be Automated by 2020": `www.gartner.com/en/newsroom/press-releases/2017-01-16-gartner-says-more-than-40-percent-of-data-science-tasks-will-be-automated-by-2020`

"What is Data Science?": `https://datascience.berkeley.edu/about/what-is-data-science`

Time to Get Started!

Now that you have some context for how Data Studio fits into your role as a data citizen, it's time for you to roll up your sleeves and get some hands-on experience!

Chapter 2, "Cooking with Google Data Studio," will get you started on your journey. In that chapter, you'll work on the fundamentals of getting access to data, preparing it, and creating basic reports.

Cooking with Google Data Studio

We are going to start our exploration of Google Data Studio by diving into some reports and then deconstructing them. Showing you how to build them yourself will help you to become familiar with some basic Data Studio ways of doing things.

Although you can simply browse through this book, I recommend creating the examples as they are outlined in each chapter. For this chapter, I recommend downloading the example data CSV file and the image file so that you can follow along, creating your own Data Studio report from the example resources.

All downloadable data files, images files, and links to the live Data Studio examples can be accessed from the resources page located here: www.wiley.com/go/handsondatastudio.

Our First Example

For this first example, we will go through the basics of the full process. I will use the cooking analogy of preparing a dish from start to finish. Here is a breakdown of the first six steps that prepare us for actual report construction:

1. Select a dish to prepare: We will use the example that follows.

2. Shop for ingredients: Finding data and getting it in a usable format.

3. Unpacking the groceries: Setting up Google Drive folders and moving files.

4. Preparing the ingredients: Loading the data and doing "data cleansing."

5. Get to know the kitchen: Get familiar with the Data Studio interface and starting a new report.

6. Assemble the ingredients: Connecting the data to the report and configure the fields.

After completing the preparation, we will tackle the construction steps. Ready to start cooking? Great! Let's move on to our first example.

Step 1. Select a Dish to Prepare: Visualizing a Bank Account

In our first example, we will be working with a bank account. I know, bank accounts are boooring! I know mine is! So, instead of using my actual data, I used it as a basis for a fictional character named "Chris Cooper."

The entries in this checking account are a bit exotic—just to add interest. Although the details and amounts are fictional, they are based on my own expenses. Regardless of the actual entries, bank accounts have a very uniform structure: they are laid out as ledger entries. Each transaction has an entry in a row. Each row has columns for the date, an identifier, a description, and an amount for the payment, deposit, or withdrawal.

This is a good place to start because working with a bank account starts to open the door to bigger things—from an individual, to a department at work, to the largest corporations and nations—they all maintain some kind of ledger. Understanding where money comes from and where money goes is one of the most universal applications of data. Gaining insight through visualization can truly pay dividends here!

This basic dataset has all of the major ingredients that we seek: dates, text identifiers, categories, and numbers.

In cooking, specialty tools and new gadgets are available that can help you make a dish turn out in a particular way. However, even the most cutting-edge cooks would not be without their trusty standard pots, pans, and knives.

It's the same when we are dealing with data. A basic set of time-tested visualizations can take you far along the road to insight. Most people have learned the visual language of how to interpret the standard chart types. These chart types are like the comfort food of data visualization.

So, in this first example we will begin with something simple and build from there. Think of this as learning how to make scrambled eggs. Then we'll move on to the omelet and eventually work our way up to a full country breakfast!

When you are cooking, it helps to have an idea of what the finished dish will look like. In our example, the finished product is shown in Figure 2.1. Data Studio reports are viewed in a web browser, and no extra software is needed. Reports can be exported as PDF files, but then they lose their interactivity. We will explore how to save your reports as PDF files in later chapters.

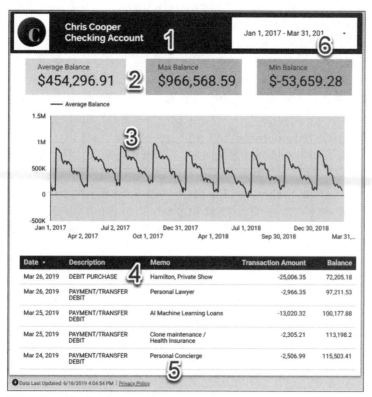

Figure 2.1: The finished product

Let's take a look at some of the details from Figure 2.1. Keep in mind that this is the "scrambled eggs" level; I didn't do a lot of formatting in order to keep it close to what we will be producing with minimal work.

1. Page header: Adding a header provides readers with a quick context for the information they are about to view and helps to set a distinctive style for the report.

Data Studio layout works a lot like presentation software, such as Microsoft PowerPoint or Google Slides. It doesn't create headers for you automatically, but you can lay out graphic elements like images, text boxes, and other elements quite easily. Here we use a simple shape to create the blue banner background, an image in the upper-left corner. In addition, there is a date selector box, but we'll come back to that later in item 6.

2. Scorecards: These are our most basic data visualization element. In this case, the boxes shown pull the numbers from the data and create summaries. Their size and prominence draw the viewer's attention and help the viewer get the "big picture" quickly. The values in these boxes come from aggregating the balance values in different ways. Aggregation is an important concept, and we will visit it in detail later on.

3. Time series: The chart shows how the account balance changes over time. Compare the insights you might get from looking at the scorecards to those shown in this chart. Though the average balance is pretty healthy overall, you can easily see that it jumps up and down in pretty regular patterns.

4. Table: Here we have a bare-bones, standard table. You will see that it looks a lot like the data found in a Google Sheet. Tables allow viewers to dive deeper into the detail should they feel a need to do so.

   Although only a few rows show on the screen, the user may scroll down the table to view any entry. Note that this table is sorted by the Date column. The user can also sort by the other columns by simply clicking on the column label.

   That may not seem exciting, but tables are the workhorse of reporting. Later on, we will add more graphic elements to the table to help the viewer find interesting details faster.

5. Report footer: This is the standard Data Studio footer. It's easy to overlook, but you will get some important information on when the data used to generate this report was extracted and a link to Google's standard privacy information policy. You do not have control over this information—it is automatically generated, and it is on every report.

6. Date range selector: One of the beauties of Data Studio is the way it allows the viewer to interact with reports. This selector is the most common and perhaps the most complex filter that can be added to a report. When this selector is on a report, viewers can change the date range themselves—for instance, to focus on the month of July 2018.

   When the user selects a new time range, as shown in Figure 2.2, all of the charts will be updated, and even the scales on the charts will automatically adjust!

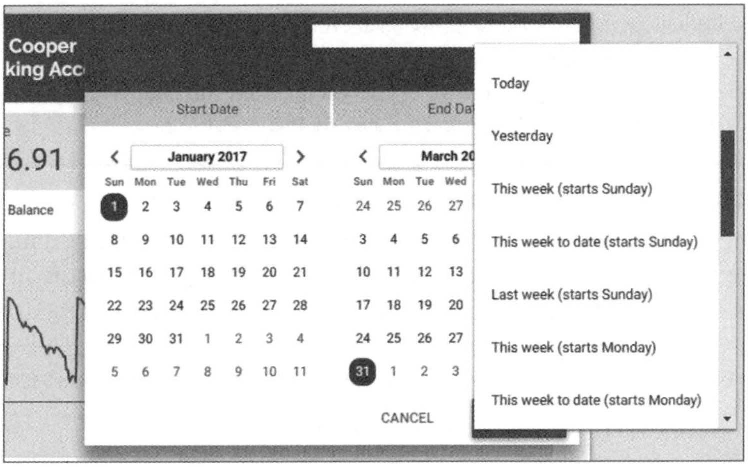

Figure 2.2: Using the date range selector

Now that you know more about the report elements, you are ready to move on to building this report. I will walk you through the process in detail for this example.

Before We Start: Things You'll Need

You can view Data Studio reports without any special setup, but to create your own reports, you must have a Google account. In addition, we will be using Google Sheets to store our data for most of the examples, which means that you will need access to Google Drive.

Don't worry! If you have personal Gmail, then you already have a Google account and everything you need. If you need an account, they are free, and you can set one up at `www.google.com/gmail`.

If you are in an organization that already uses Gmail, you can use that account also, but you may be restricted to sharing your reports only with others in your organization. In addition, access to Data Studio may be controlled by your system administrators. So far, I have found that most administrators allow access by default. If you can't access the services, you will need to check with the people in charge of administration for your organization.

Step 2. Let's Go Shopping! Getting the Data

GETTING AND PREPARING THE DATA

This book is designed to help you get started using data for your own purposes. Often, services such as online banking do not provide any visualization tools. In other cases, the charts and graphs provided by a service may not show the information in a way that is useful.

> In this section, we will go through some of the basics of how to get and prepare data so that you can create your own reports. If you would like to skip this step but still follow along, you can use our example data. All of the resources for this chapter are available here for download: `www.wiley.com/go/handsondatastudio`.

Before we start cooking, we need to get some ingredients. In culinary terms, that means we need to go to a grocery store. In the case of bank account data, it means visiting your online banking or financial service. Data export from these services is almost universal at this time, and the available formats are very uniform.

Here are the basic steps for exporting data from your bank or financial service:

1. Log into your online banking or financial service.

2. Select an account to view.

3. Choose Export.

4. Select the CSV option.

5. Download the data file.

Figure 2.3 is an example from an account to show you what to look for.

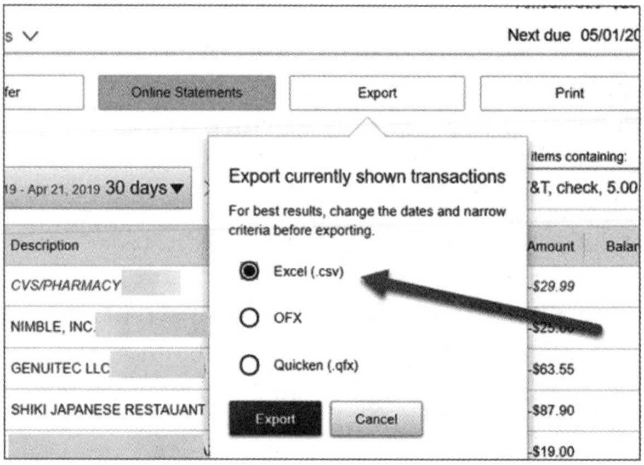

Figure 2.3: Exporting bank account data

The format that you want to select is the one marked CSV (or Excel .csv as shown in the figure). CSV stands for comma-separated values. This is a standard format that spreadsheets and databases understand. The file will download and will be called something like `export.csv` or `transactions.csv`. This is the raw data file that we will use to build the Google Sheet.

Now that we have some data, let's start organizing it. That means putting resources in a location that allows Data Studio to access it.

Step 3. Unpack the Groceries: Setting Up Google Drive

We will be storing the data from the account on Google Drive. As with most things data related, it pays to organize your materials in a thoughtful way from the start and maintain your organizational scheme. At first, this does not seem like a big deal, but as you gather more and more data and documents, it becomes increasingly difficult to find what you need.

If you are not familiar with Google Drive, it is pretty easy to get started. Your Google Drive is organized into folders and files. You can put your files in folders, and you can put your folders inside of other folders. All of this is accessible from any browser by logging into your Google account. You can see your drive by going to this location and logging in if necessary: https://drive.google.com. You should see something like the image shown in Figure 2.4.

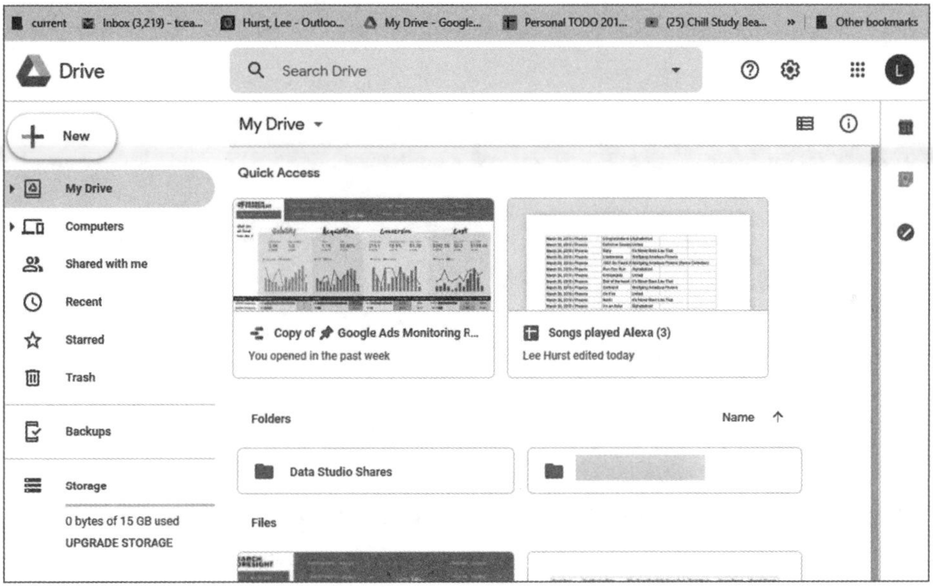

Figure 2.4: Typical Google Drive structure

1. Click the + New button and select New Folder. Name the folder `Data Studio Examples` and click Create (see Figure 2.5).

2. Find the folder in your Google Drive list, double-click to open the `Data Studio Examples` folder, and create a new folder called `Example 1`.

3. Double-click to enter that folder.

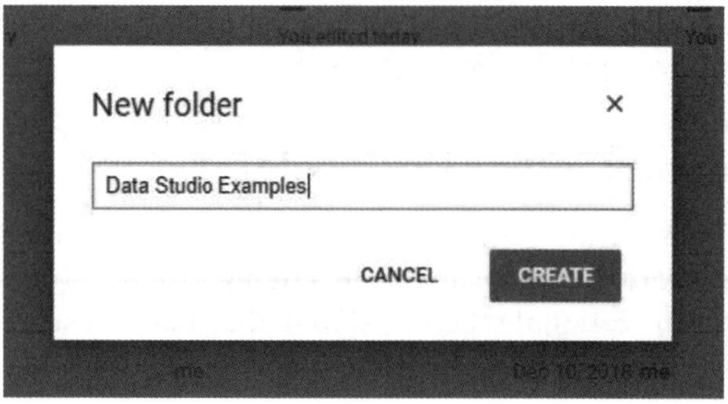

Figure 2.5: Creating a new folder

4. Upload your data file (the one ending in .csv) by dragging it into this folder, or by right-clicking and selecting Upload Files.

5. Double-click the CSV file. In this example, it is called Chapter2-AccountData .csv. A preview screen like the one shown in Figure 2.6 will appear. Click the Open With Google Sheets button as seen in in the figure. You should see a new Google Sheet on the screen.

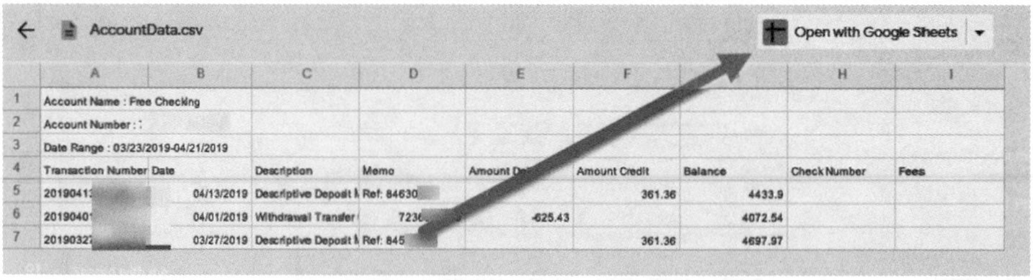

Figure 2.6: Opening a CSV file with Google Sheets

You now have a new Google Sheets document in the Example 1 folder.

Step 4. Preparing the Ingredients: Working with Google Sheets

While Data Studio can connect to a large variety of data sources, we will be using Google Sheets in this example and several others. There are a number of reasons for doing this:

■ If you have access to a Google account, you will have access to Google Sheets.

■ Google Sheets can read a variety of file types, including most Microsoft Excel spreadsheets. Google Sheets can also be connected to a variety of services.

- Google Sheets are stored on your Google Drive. Again, this makes them accessible from your standard account. You get all of the sharing and security options standard.

- If you cannot access a data source directly, it is almost always possible to get the data into Google Sheets.

- Google Sheets allows you to see your raw data and how it is organized.

If you are used to working with other spreadsheet software, like Microsoft Excel, you will find Google Sheets very familiar (although you may be annoyed by some of the differences). What is important for our purposes is not the extra features found in one tool or the other; that is, we want to get the data into a very simple row-and-column format.

Sometimes it is not possible, or even efficient, to modify the original dataset. However, when working with data in Google Sheets, it is easy to format the dataset right at the source. Later, you will see how to create new data fields directly in the Data Studio environment. For now, let's look at how to prepare the sheet for our use. We will go step by step through the cleaning process.

1. Clean the top of the sheet. Remove any descriptive rows from the top of the sheet. Select any rows above the actual column headers and delete them. Here we use a right-click to get the Delete Selected Rows option, as shown in Figure 2.7.

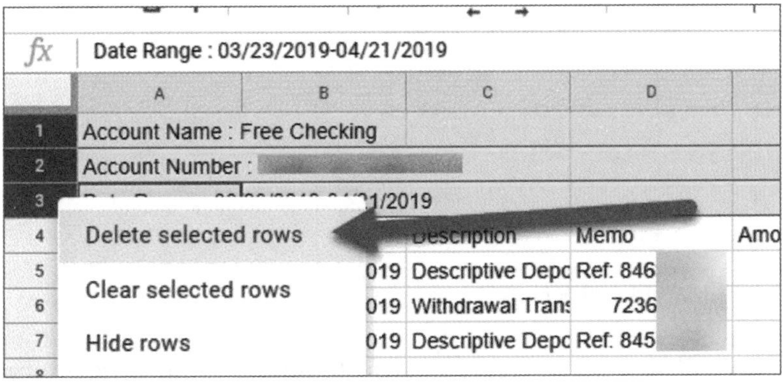

Figure 2.7: Removing descriptive rows from the sheet

2. Clean the middle of the sheet. You may find the column headers repeated further down the rows. If this is the case, remove all but the top set of column headers by selecting and deleting each duplicated row.

3. Clean the bottom of the sheet. Often, in an effort to be helpful, the export will add totals or summary rows. We want the sheet to have only simple columns and rows of data. Either remove the rows, or simply delete the contents of those cells.

4. Remove unneeded or empty columns. Simply select the column(s), right-click, and select Delete Selected Columns, as shown in Figure 2.8.

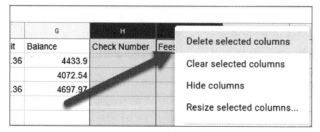

Figure 2.8: Removing unneeded columns

5. Rename any duplicated header names. You probably won't run into this when doing simple account setup, but it bears mentioning. Data Studio does not like duplicate column names, and it will not let you use the sheet as a source of data for a report if duplicate column names exist.

As part of the data preparation in Google Sheets, you may want to create new columns that will be used in a report. For instance, in our first example, we use a value for Transaction Amount. It is likely that when working with your own account data, you won't have this column. Instead, you may have separate columns for Amount Credit and Amount Debit, as shown in Figure 2.9.

	E	F	G
	Amount Debit	Amount Credit	Balance
317		361.36	4433.9
2016	-625.43		4072.54
706		361.36	4697.97

Figure 2.9: Credit and debit columns

Later, we will see how to create a new column inside the Data Studio environment without changing the original data. For now, let's create a new Transaction column in the sheet.

1. Right-click the Balance column and select Insert 1 Left. This will insert a new blank column. Set the column header to **Transaction Amount**.

2. In the first empty cell in the Transaction Amount column (G2), enter the formula **=E2+F2**. This will add the Amount Debit and Amount Credit for that row.

3. Copy the cell down the new column. A quick way to do this is to highlight the cell to be copied. Use Ctrl+C to copy the cell. Then use Ctrl+Shift+Down Arrow to select all of the cells below that one. Finally, use Ctrl+V to paste the formula. This will fill the row with the correct values, as shown in Figure 2.10.

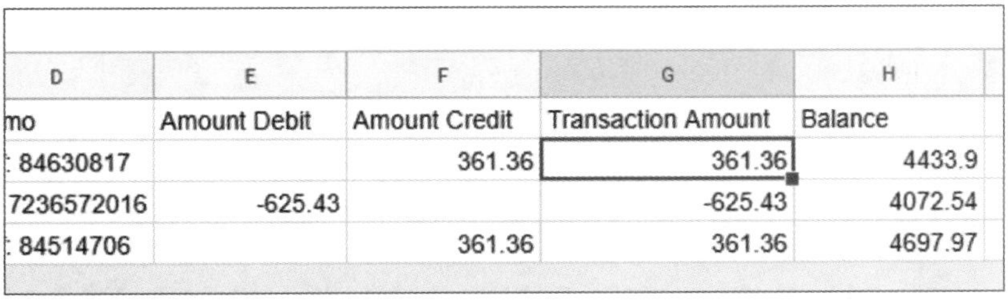

D	E	F	G	H
mo	Amount Debit	Amount Credit	Transaction Amount	Balance
84630817		361.36	361.36	4433.9
7236572016	-625.43		-625.43	4072.54
84514706		361.36	361.36	4697.97

Figure 2.10: New Transaction Amount column

Although we won't use the extra columns in this example, they don't hurt anything, so you can leave them as they are.

TIP   Check and set column data formats in your sheets! You may not need to do this with the sample data that we have provided, but it is a good idea to check the data types for each column when working with a new sheet. In this case, set the column for Date to the date format and the Transaction Amount and Balance columns to the currency format. If you are working with Sheets and find that you are getting null values in the report, this is the first area to check for problems.

Now that we have our data ready, we can move on to building the report.

Step 5. Familiarizing Yourself with the Kitchen: Data Studio Home Screen and Starting a New Report

Finally, you are ready to start working with the Data Studio services. To do this, enter this URL in your browser: `datastudio.google.com`.

If you are not logged into a Google account, you will see a product overview page. Start your session by clicking the Use It For Free button. You will be prompted to log into an account. Once you log in, you will be taken to your Data Studio home page, as shown in Figure 2.11.

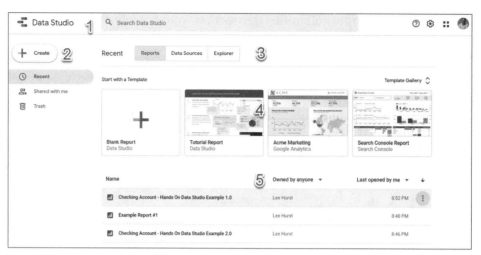

Figure 2.11: Data Studio home page

Like any good cook, we want to get a feel for our kitchen! Where is the sink? Where is the oven? When working with Data Studio, this means becoming familiar with the home page. This is where you can access all of your reports and start new ones. You will want to become familiar with some of the features here:

1. Header   You can always get back to this home screen by clicking the Data Studio symbol in the upper-left corner. The Search Data Studio field allows you to search for specific titles for reports and data sources. This is handy when you have a lot of reports, and it is another reason to use a good naming convention.

The gear symbol for User Settings lets you manage information that the Data Studio team sends to you, and it also provides some company- and region-specific acknowledgments. The question symbol will give you quick access to search for help in the documentation, articles, and help forums. The four-square symbol will show you other programs in the Google Marketing Platform. The image on the far right shows which account you have used to log in. Clicking this image allows you to log out or change user accounts.

2. Create Button and List Filters   You can use the Create button to create a new report or data source. Just below this, the Recent, Shared With Me, and Trash icons are used to filter the Reports list section.

3. Function Selection   These buttons control what shows in the Reports list section. By default, you will see Reports. Clicking the Data Sources button will switch the list to show all of your data connectors.

The Explorer option allows you to use Data Studio functionality without creating a full report. This can be useful, but the option is mostly used for Big Data applications. Using Explorer mode is beyond the scope of this book.

4. Quick Start Section   You can start a blank report here or select a pre-made template. The templates are geared to marketing reports for websites using various Google services.

5. Reports List Section   This is the main area of the Data Studio home page. By default, you will see a list of all of the reports you own and reports that you have viewed. From here, you can click a report to start editing.

The Welcome To Data Studio! report is a tutorial that will guide you through many basic screen setup options. When you have time, it's a good idea to go through it. It will take about 40 minutes to complete.

If you click the three vertical dots at the far right of a listing, you will reveal a mini menu that has shortcuts to share, rename, or remove the report or data source. If you delete a report you own, it will be removed from your main screen, but it will still be accessible in the Trash list. If you delete a report from the trash list, it will be permanently deleted.

Now that you know your way around the Data Studio home page a bit, it is time to start a new report. Click the Blank Report image in the Templates section (it has a plus sign). If it is your first time using Data Studio, you will be prompted to accept the terms of use and indicate your email preferences from the Welcome To Google Data Studio screen, shown in Figure 2.12. Click the Get Started button and accept the terms of use.

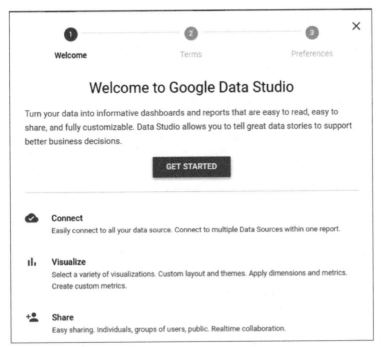

Figure 2.12: Welcome To Google Data Studio screen

After you complete the terms of use, you will be back on the home screen instead of starting the new report. This happens on your first use only. Simply click again on one of the plus symbols, and you will be transferred to the blank new report screen.

Step 6. Assemble the Ingredients: Connecting the Data to the Report

The first step to building a report is to create a new data source for the Google Sheet. A little clarification is in order here. In Data Studio terms, the Google Sheet that we are using is called a dataset, or more frequently in actual usage, a *dataset*. To link your report charts to the dataset, we need a *data connector* to create a *data source*. The *data source* maintains information on your connection credentials, and it keeps track of all the fields that are part of that connection. You can have multiple data sources connected to a dataset. You may have little need to do this in most of your work, but doing so can come in handy, as you can also share data sources with other report creators and give them different connection capabilities. More on this later.

The first thing that you will see is a blank canvas called Untitled Report, as shown in Figure 2.13. Your report is now in Edit mode. We will be reviewing the report toolbars and other features of this mode after we connect a data source to the report.

On the right side, you will see a panel that has a set of sample data sources. We will be looking at some of these in other examples. For now, you want to click the Create New Data Source button at the bottom right of the screen.

You will be presented with the connectors screen, as shown in Figure 2.14. The connector we want is the one for Google Sheets, and it is in the Google Connectors section. You may have to scroll down a bit to find it. When you hover your mouse over the block, the Select button will display, and you can click it.

If this is your first time using the Google Sheets connector with this account, you will have to go through the authorization screens that allow the connector to retrieve data from Sheets files for your account. So, click the Authorize button. You will then see another screen, as shown in Figure 2.15. Click the Allow button to give the connector access to your Google account.

Google does this regardless of whether it is to access their own service or a third-party service. You should have to do this only the first time that you create this kind of connector to your account.

Now you will be able to select your Google Sheet. Google is fairly smart here, showing you the most recently updated files from your account. If you don't see the file you need on this list, you can use the Open From Google Drive option in the leftmost column, or you can search for a spreadsheet using the magnifying glass icon in the second column.

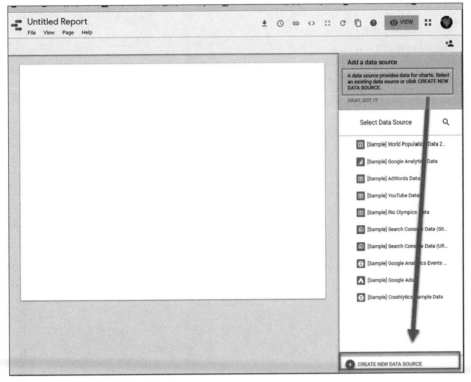

Figure 2.13: Starting with a blank canvas

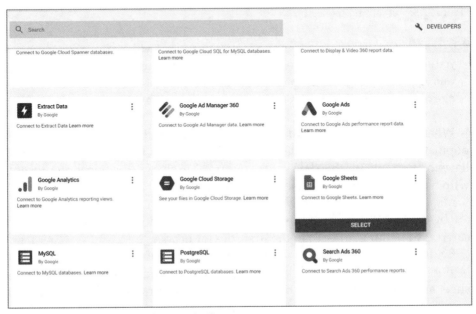

Figure 2.14: Find and select the Google Sheets connector.

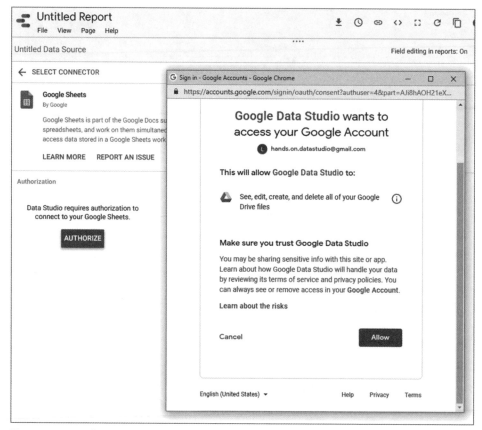

Figure 2.15: Authorizing connector

NOTE If you were just working on a new file, or you just added a file to your drive, you may not be able to find it. It takes a couple minutes for the selector to synch up with your Google Drive folders and files. I usually find that this is a good time to get a nice cup of tea or coffee. When you come back, you should be able to find your file.

When you click an item in the Spreadsheet column, the Worksheet column is populated. If there are multiple pages, or *worksheets* in Google-speak, you will have to select one for this data source. Figure 2.16 shows this selection process, with boxes to highlight the selections that you made.

Most of the time, you will want to leave the Option boxes checked, as they are by default. You do have the option to select a portion of the sheet, and you can use something other than the first row for headers.

By default, your connector will look at all of the data on the sheet, whether or not it is hidden. This is very handy, as you may want to filter the original sheet and you don't want the data changing in your reports just because you are playing with the sheet. (I haven't yet found a use for deselecting this option, but you never know!)

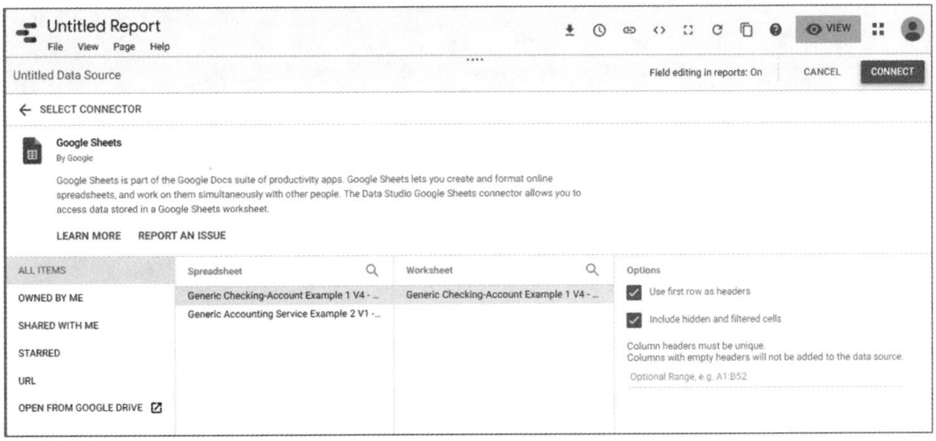

Figure 2.16: Google Sheet selection options

WARNING   Note the warning at the bottom of the Google Sheet selection options that duplicate header names are not allowed and that columns without headers will be ignored. This is often helpful if you need to put some notes or other calculations in the sheet. Just be sure to do it in an empty column, not below your regular data in a column that is being used.

Once you have everything selected, click the Connect button at the upper right. A new screen will appear, showing you the fields and their settings for this data source.

When you first create a new data source, it is a good idea to check the field settings. Fields can often be treated in different ways that will restrict how they act in charts and how their values are grouped. We will be changing the *field type* and the *aggregation method* for some of our fields.

Transaction Amount is best dealt with as a Currency field type, since it represents monetary values. By selecting Currency, then USD - US Dollar ($), we can set this field to the most appropriate type of currency.

In addition to setting the type, you need to set the aggregation method. The aggregation method tells Data Studio how to represent these values when they are grouped. In the case of Transaction Amount, we normally want to show groupings of this value by adding all of the values together. To do this, we set the aggregation method to Sum.

We will do the same for the Balance field, but in that case, we will set the aggregation method to Average. Settings for Transaction Amount and Balance are shown in Figure 2.17.

How do you know which aggregation method to set? That's a very good question, and the answer is not always clear-cut. I usually think about what this field will tell me if I had to add up all of the numbers in that field. In the case of Transaction Amount, adding up all of the values makes sense.

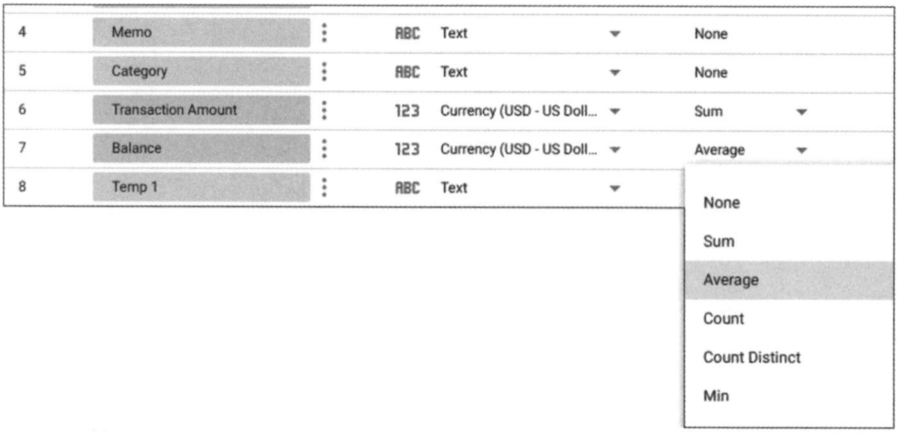

Figure 2.17: Set the field type and aggregation method for the Transaction Amount and Balance fields.

In the case of Balance, using the Sum aggregation method does not make sense. If you have $50 in an account on Monday and $60 in that account on Tuesday, adding these together doesn't mean that you magically have $110! In this case, you are better off using Average as the aggregation method, which yields an average balance of $55 over the two days. Thus, for the Balance field, we will set the aggregation method to Average.

Picking an aggregation type is trickier when there is more than one that might make sense. In the case of Transaction Amount, it might be handy to know the average transaction amount for a group of transactions in some cases and the sum of those transactions in other cases.

Fortunately, in most cases Data Studio gives us the ability to change the aggregation method when we apply the metric to an individual chart. A good rule of thumb here is to use Sum, unless it is unlikely to make sense to add the values together.

In the example data, the Transaction Number field is being treated as a number, not as text. You don't want to treat this field as numbers because adding them together doesn't provide any useful information. So, to finish the field setup, we change the Transaction Number field type to Text.

NOTE Changing the field type may change the color of the field. Data Studio classifies fields as one of two types and helps you to identify them by using color coding. The blue color coding indicates that, by default, this field is treated as a metric. Green indicates a field that is treated as a dimension. We will get into the subtleties of these later, but for now think of dimensions as answering the question "What is it?" and metrics as answering the question "How much?"

Once you have set up all the fields, you are ready to click the Add To Report button at the upper-right corner of the fields screen. Data Studio will pop up a message to confirm that you want to add this new data source to the report. Click the Add To Report button to continue. Once you do this, you will be back at the blank canvas, but you will have a new control panel on the right side.

There are a couple more setup tasks we should do before we start adding the charts to the table: naming the report and setting up the canvas.

Setting the name for the report is easy. Simply click the text "Untitled Report" in the upper-left corner and enter a new name, as shown in Figure 2.18. The name for this report is **Checking Account - Hands On Data Studio Example 1.0**.

Figure 2.18: Setting the report name

Get in the habit of good descriptive report naming right from the start! This will save you time and frustration later when you are trying to find a particular report or connector.

Next, we will change the size of the canvas for this page. On the right side of the page, you will see the Layout And Theme panel. We will look at some of the other options shown here later, but for now, we would like to change the canvas size. If you don't see the canvas size settings, just scroll down the panel a bit.

Set Width and Height to **700** in each box, as shown in Figure 2.19.

TIP   There is no save button in Data Studio. Your changes are automatically saved!

This is a good time to review the toolbar layout in Edit mode, as shown in Figure 2.20. Here is a brief description of the icons and their functions.

The top section on the right contains high-level functions for your report. We've already covered some of the standard icon functions. If you hover over these icons, they will show tooltips that describe their function. Clicking the Share drop-down shows functions for inviting others to share the report, scheduling email delivery, getting a link to the report, getting code to embed the report in a web page, and downloading the report as a PDF file. The refresh button allows you to reload data for the report, including any data that may have recently changed.

The large View button in this section is used to switch back and forth between Edit mode and View mode. View mode is the way that your users will see the report in their browser. In View mode, this button changes to Edit and has a pencil icon. You will probably find yourself switching between the Edit and View modes quite a bit while creating reports.

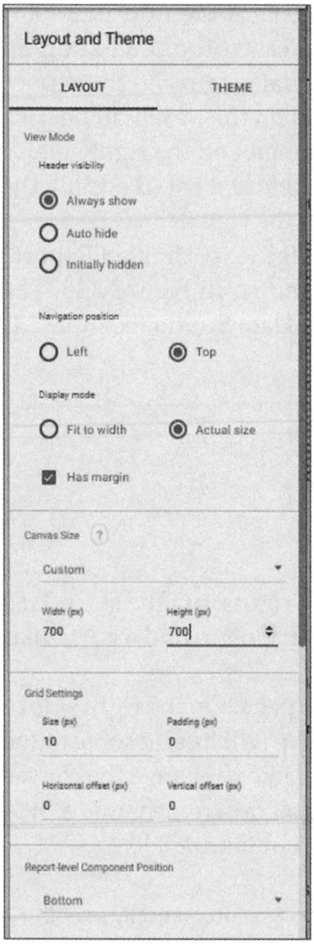

Layout and Theme

LAYOUT	THEME

View Mode

Header visibility

◉ Always show

◯ Auto hide

◯ Initially hidden

Navigation position

◯ Left   ◉ Top

Display mode

◯ Fit to width   ◉ Actual size

☑ Has margin

Canvas Size ?

Custom ▾

Width (px)	Height (px)	
700	700|	⬍

Grid Settings

Size (px)	Padding (px)
10	0

Horizontal offset (px)	Vertical offset (px)
0	0

Report-level Component Position

Bottom ▾

Figure 2.19: Setting the size of the page canvas

Figure 2.20: Edit mode menus and toolbar

Below the menus, you will find the editing toolbox. We will look at some of the functions here later. Many of the menu options are also available from the toolbar or by right-clicking report elements and opening a context menu.

The edit toolbar currently has the following functions, from left to right:

Add A Page: Data Studio reports can have multiple pages.

Selection mode: changes the tool back to a pointer for selecting components. Selecting a chart or other graphic element on the canvas will open the elements configuration tab on the right side of the canvas.

Undo and Redo: You can also undo or redo most actions using the keyboard shortcuts Ctrl+Z to undo and Ctrl+Y to redo.

Add A Chart: This drop-down shows all the chart types available to be added to the report.

Community Visualization and Components: This feature lets you bring in third-party visualization tools and other charts. This is an advanced functionality and beyond the scope of this book.

Date Range: This adds a date range selector to the report. These allow the viewer to change the time range of the report being viewed.

Filter control: Filter controls are added to the report to provide more user interaction and control. Filters are a major part of Data Studio functionality, and we will be working with these in the coming chapters.

Data control: Data Studio allows some data sources to be swapped out of the report by the viewer. This icon inserts a data control into the report.

URL Embed: Data Studio allows embedding of videos and other documents directly in the report.

Text: This inserts a text box similar to other drawing and presentation programs.

Image: This inserts an image box that can be filled by uploading a picture from your computer.

Line: This allows you to draw simple or complex lines with arrows and curves. You can connect lines to other elements for diagram drawing.

Rectangle and Circle: These provide basic shapes for visual composition and layout.

Layout And Theme: This is a shortcut to view editing options for the look and feel of the report.

Step 7. Set the Table: Adding Your First Chart

Finally, we are ready to start adding some charts! Let's start off with a basic table. Tables are always a good place to begin when creating your reports, even if they don't make it into the final version. Tables are also a good way to check that all of the data is coming through as you would expect.

To begin, click the Add A Chart drop-down menu, as shown in Figure 2.21. We will use a simple table first. The other table variations shown in the Add A Chart drop-down are modified versions of the simple table with common style attributes already applied. I find that most often it is better to start with the simple table. We will be adding our own modifications to the table in the next chapter.

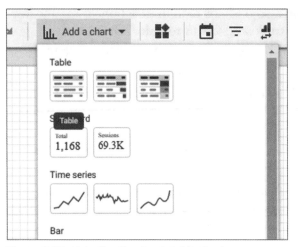

Figure 2.21: Selecting the simple table chart

Selecting the table chart floats an outline for the new table connected to the mouse pointer. To place the chart initially, left-click and drag to size the table. You don't have to get the exact position and size on the first try, as we will be moving and resizing it after it is on the canvas.

When you make a selection, Data Studio will guess at dimensions and metrics for that chart. Usually these are not exactly what you want, but it gives you a place to begin. Figure 2.22 shows how the table will likely look on the canvas after initial placement, and it also shows the Data control panel. We are going to pause here to look at how the table is positioned and controlled.

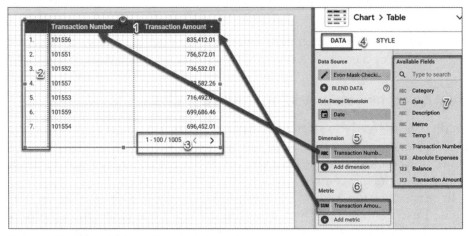

Figure 2.22: Table chart and Data control panel

1. Table selection: Once the table is placed on the canvas, it will be selected. You can tell this by the outline and the little dots, or handles, that appear on the outside of the table. When selected, the table can be moved by clicking and dragging with your mouse, or you can use the arrow keys to position it on the canvas.

   You can use the mouse to click and drag any of the handles to resize the table. If you pull the table down from the bottom, more rows will appear.

TIP Using the keyboard arrow keys while an element is selected will move the table to the next location on the background grid. This is helpful, but if you need to tweak the position just a little, hold down the Shift key when using the arrows. This will move the selected item a pixel at a time and allow for precise positioning.

Also, it's a good idea to get all of your page elements roughly in place first and do any detailed positioning at the end of page layout. You'll save yourself a lot of rework this way.

2. Number column: Data Studio will add a Number column by default. While this is sometimes useful, the Number column is something that you will often want to remove. Unfortunately, there is no way to get rid of this default behavior.

3. Paging control: By default, Data Studio puts a paging control at the bottom of tables, whether or not you need it. Again, this can be handy feature, but usually you will want to remove this control.

4. Data control panel: When you select a component, the control panel for that component appears on the right side of the screen. The control panel for charts has two tabs: Data and Style. We will look at the Style tab soon, but for now let's focus on the Data tab. The Data tab controls what goes into the table, how the table is sorted, and several other features.

5. Dimension: You may add up to 10 dimensions to a table. Dimensions answer the question "What are we measuring?" When you add more dimensions to a table, each row can get more specific. When you have more than one dimension, you can click and drag them to change the order in which they appear in the table. Dimensions always appear on the left side of tables.

6. Metric: You can add up to 20 metrics to a table. Metrics answer the question "How will we measure?" and they are numeric in nature. As with dimensions, you can click and drag them to control the order in which they appear in the table. Note, however, that metrics *always* appear to the right of the dimensions in tables.

7. Available Fields: This panel shows the fields from the data source. The fields are color coded: blue for dimensions and green for metrics. You can click and drag fields from this area to the Dimension and Metric areas of the Data tab. In this example, we do not have many fields. In other cases, such as when working with Google Analytics for websites, you may have dozens of fields. For this reason, you can use the handy search box to help you find the field you are looking for.

Now that you know the basics, let's set up our table so that it conforms to the example. Switch back to Edit mode, and click the table to select it. The Data control panel will show up on the right of the table. To get the same fields in the table as the example, drag items from the Available Fields area to add the Dimension and Metric areas.

If necessary, you can click and drag the fields for Dimension or Metric to the desired order. If you want to remove a dimension or metric, simply hover your mouse over the field and a close button (⊗) will appear. Click the close button, and the field will be removed.

There is one last item to set on the Data tab in this example. We need to change the sort order so that the items in the table appear with the most recent date at the top. You can specify how to sort the table using the Sort setting. Note that Data Studio does not currently let you drag an available field to this position. You may change it by clicking the field currently in the position, as shown in Figure 2.23. A list of available fields will appear. Select the Date field.

You will also see the drop-down option that can change the sort order to either Ascending or Descending. In the case of dates, more recent dates are considered larger, so you can leave this as Descending. If you want to see the oldest dates first, you could change this setting to Ascending.

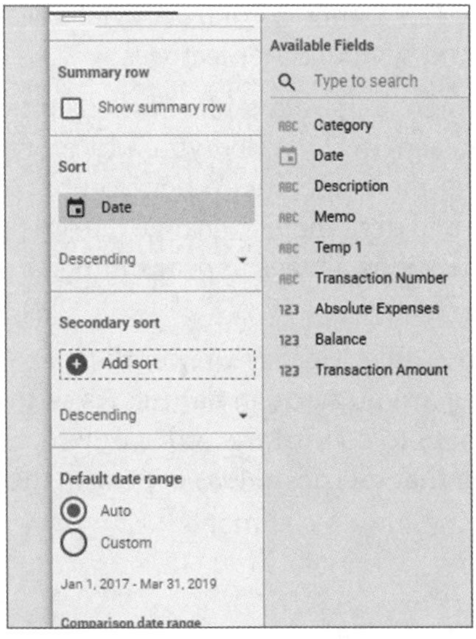

Figure 2.23: Setting the Sort field

Now we have our table on the page, but it needs some help to make it look better. First, we need to adjust the columns on the table; then we will change the style settings.

To begin, you can change the column widths individually by clicking and dragging on the dotted column lines. Although this approach is good for fine-tuning, there are two other ways of adjusting all of the columns at the same time. Try these first; then do the individual column adjustments later.

1. Hold down the Shift key and drag a column line. This will adjust all the columns at the same time.

2. Right-click the table. Select Resize Columns and choose either the Fit To Data or the Distribute Evenly option, as seen in Figure 2.24. This will resize all the columns automatically.

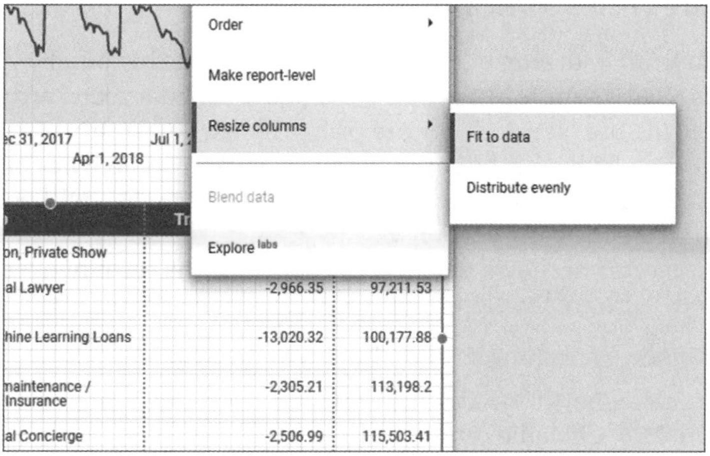

Figure 2.24: Adjusting column sizes

We have to make a couple of style adjustments to complete our table. As is often the case, we want to remove the left Number column and the pagination control at the bottom of the table. These controls are located on the Style tab.

Unless Google changes the default style options for tables in the future, you should get used to removing the numbering and pagination style settings when you first create a table.

To adjust the style, select the table with the mouse and then select the Style tab in the control panel. Scroll down the tab and deselect the boxes for Row Numbers under Table Body and Show Pagination under Table Footer, as shown in Figure 2.25.

Your table should look much neater now. If you wish to, move the table to the bottom of the canvas by clicking and dragging it with the mouse or by using the arrow keys. Click the View button to see how it looks after you move it. It should look similar to our example report.

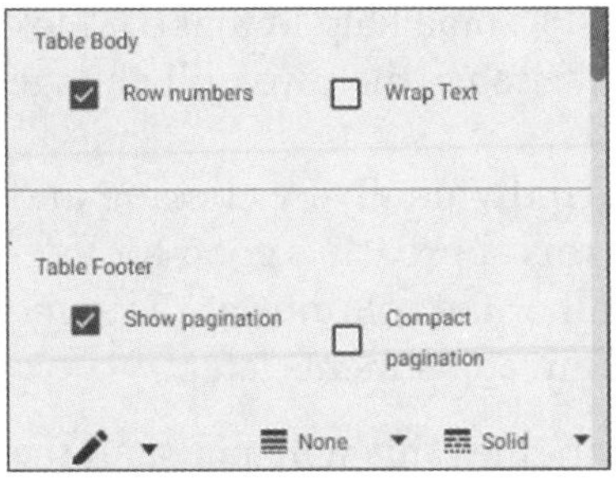

Table Body
- ☑ Row numbers
- ☐ Wrap Text

Table Footer
- ☑ Show pagination
- ☐ Compact pagination

✎ ▾ ▤ None ▾ ▦ Solid ▾

Figure 2.25: Unchecking the Row Numbers and Show Pagination settings on the Style tab

Congratulations on adding your first table! Now we are going to the top of the report to create scorecards.

Step 8. Keep Score with Scorecards

Now we are going to jump to the top of the report and look at the big numbers in the boxes. This is a very simple but useful component called a scorecard. *Scorecards* help us see the big picture. They are primarily used to summarize data over the entire time frame of the report. We will look at some ways of increasing the information power of scorecards later, but for now we will go through the steps to create the basic versions.

The *Average Balance scorecard* shows the average balance in the account over the entire time period. Here are the steps required to create this scorecard:

1. Switch to Edit mode by clicking the Edit button in the header.

2. Select the Scorecard chart from the Add A Chart drop-down menu, as shown in Figure 2.26. Click the canvas to place it.

Figure 2.26: Selecting Scorecard from the Add A Chart drop-down menu

3. On the Data tab, change the metric by dragging the Balance field to replace the Transaction Amount field, as shown in Figure 2.27.

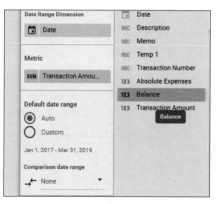

Figure 2.27: Setting the Scorecard metric

Next, we will change the text for the scorecard label. We have the correct metric for the first scorecard, but we want it to say Average Balance instead of simply Balance. To change the display label, place the mouse over the small AVG indicator on the Balance metric. The mouse pointer will change to a finger and a pencil icon will appear, as shown in Figure 2.28.

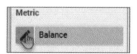

Figure 2.28: Editing a metric label in a chart

Click the pencil icon to edit the field in the chart. A new chart field attribute box will appear. Change the label to **Average Balance**, as shown in Figure 2.29. If the aggregation type Average is not selected already, select it now. Press the Enter key or click the mouse anywhere on the canvas to complete the change. The same method is used on all charts to change labels for metrics and dimensions. The changes will apply to the label only for this chart.

Next, shrink the size of the scorecard with the mouse and position the Scorecard box, as shown in Figure 2.30.

Now we will change the fill color of the scorecard. Click the Style tab on the right-side panel. Scroll down to the Background And Border section. Click the paint can icon and select the background color yellow, as shown in Figure 2.31.

The *Max Balance scorecard* shows the highest balance in the account over the entire time period. To create this card, we will take a shortcut and copy, and then modify, the Average Balance scorecard.

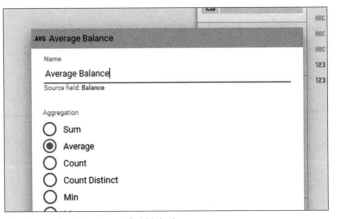

Figure 2.29: Changing a field label

Figure 2.30: Positioning the scorecard

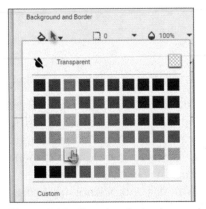

Figure 2.31: Changing the background color

> **TIP** One of the keys to creating reports faster is that if you have similar repeating elements, create one in the style and size you need, and then copy that one and modify it instead of creating new elements from scratch. This approach saves a lot of time trying to get several elements to look uniform.

1. Select the Average Balance scorecard.
2. Copy it to the clipboard using Edit ⇨ Copy, or by pressing Ctrl+C.
3. Paste the scorecard using Edit ⇨ Paste, or by pressing Ctrl+V.
4. Use the arrow keys or click and drag the scorecard with your mouse to position it on the page, as shown in Figure 2.32.

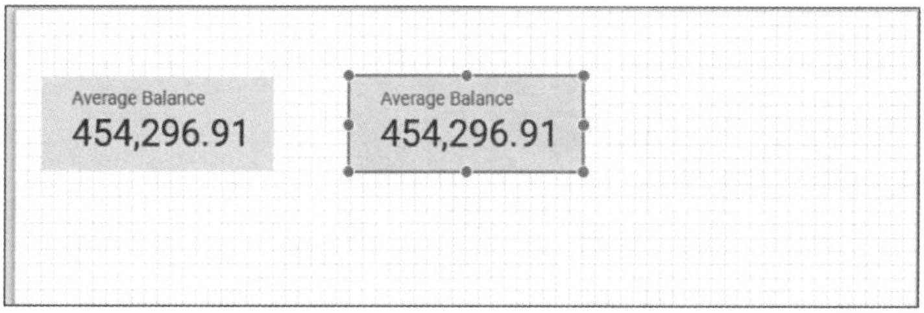

Figure 2.32: Copying and positioning the original scorecard

Next, we will change the contents of the new scorecard in the same way that we set up the original. On the Style tab, scroll down to the Background And Border section, click the paint can, and select a light green color.

Now click the Data tab. Hover your mouse pointer over the AVG label in the Average Balance field in the Metric section and click the pencil icon. Change the name to **Max Balance**, and change the Aggregation setting to Max, as shown in Figure 2.33. Press Enter or click the canvas to complete the changes.

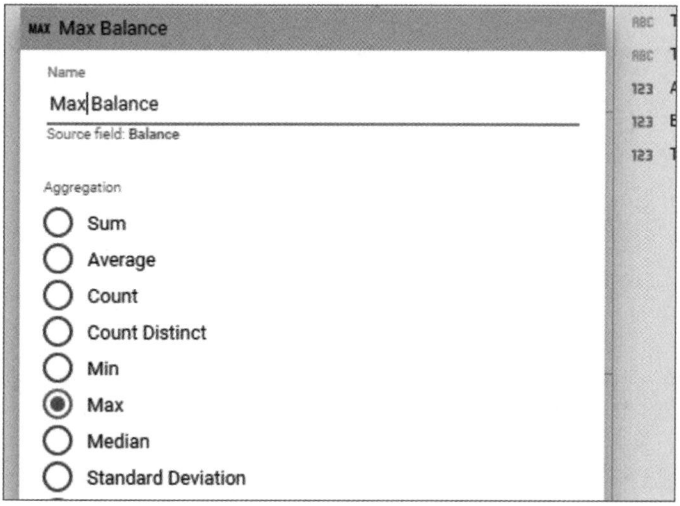

Figure 2.33: Setting the Max Aggregation type

The *Min Balance scorecard* shows the lowest balance in the account over the entire time period. To create this card, you will copy the Max Balance scorecard. Select the Max Balance scorecard. Copy it to the clipboard by using Edit ➪ Copy or by pressing Ctrl+C. Paste the scorecard by using Edit ➪ Paste or by pressing Ctrl+V.

Use the arrow keys, or click and drag with the mouse, to position the new scorecard on the page, as shown in Figure 2.34.

Figure 2.34: Positioning the copy of the Max Balance scorecard

On the Style tab, scroll down to the Background And Border section, click the paint can, and select a light red/orange color.

Switch to the Data tab. Hover your mouse pointer over the AVG label in the Average Balance field in the Metric section and click the pencil icon. Change the name to **Min Balance** and change the Aggregation setting to Min, as shown in Figure 2.35. Press the Enter key or click the canvas to complete the changes.

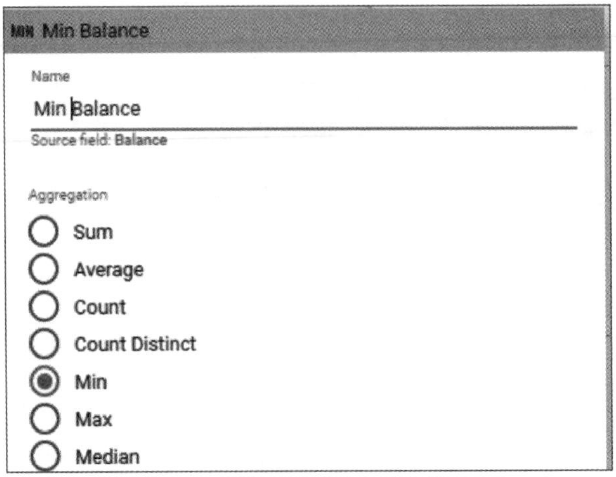

MIN Min Balance

Name

Min Balance

Source field: Balance

Aggregation

- ◯ Sum
- ◯ Average
- ◯ Count
- ◯ Count Distinct
- ◉ Min
- ◯ Max
- ◯ Median

Figure 2.35: Min Balance field settings

Switch to View mode by clicking the View button in the header. Your new report should look similar to Figure 2.36.

Congratulations on completing the scorecard setup. For the final chart, we will examine how to visualize changes over time.

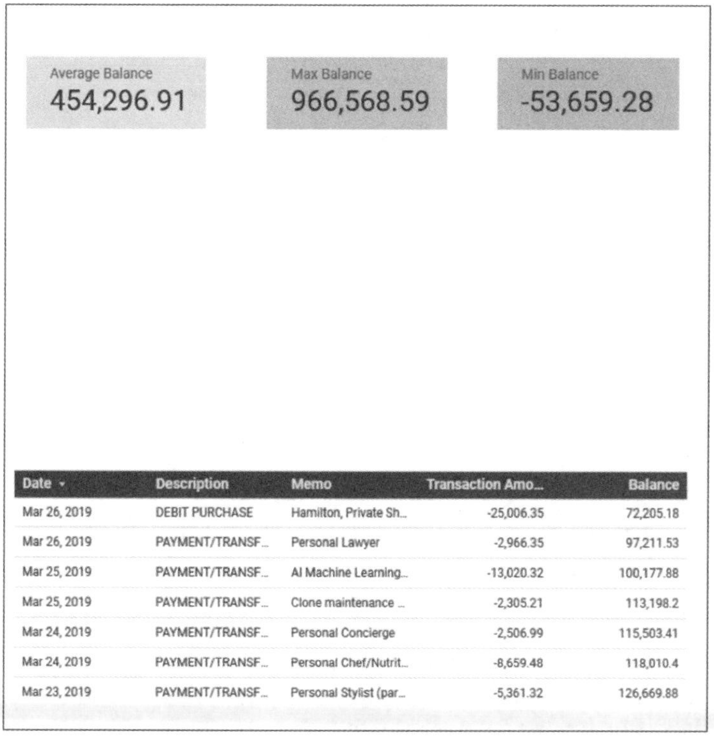

Average Balance	Max Balance	Min Balance
454,296.91	966,568.59	-53,659.28

Date ▾	Description	Memo	Transaction Amo...	Balance
Mar 26, 2019	DEBIT PURCHASE	Hamilton, Private Sh...	-25,006.35	72,205.18
Mar 26, 2019	PAYMENT/TRANSF...	Personal Lawyer	-2,966.35	97,211.53
Mar 25, 2019	PAYMENT/TRANSF...	AI Machine Learning...	-13,020.32	100,177.88
Mar 25, 2019	PAYMENT/TRANSF...	Clone maintenance ...	-2,305.21	113,198.2
Mar 24, 2019	PAYMENT/TRANSF...	Personal Concierge	-2,506.99	115,503.41
Mar 24, 2019	PAYMENT/TRANSF...	Personal Chef/Nutrit...	-8,659.48	118,010.4
Mar 23, 2019	PAYMENT/TRANSF...	Personal Stylist (par...	-5,361.32	126,669.88

Figure 2.36: Report with scorecards added

Step 9. It's About Time: Building the Time-Series Chart

Among the basic charts, the *time-series chart* is one of the most powerful. It allows us to see how things change over a period of time. This is where we make a leap from text and numbers to true visualizations. *Visualization* is truly amazing, though it is something that we often take for granted. Turning numbers into lines, bars, and other shapes allows us to use a different part of our brain to process information. This kind of mental processing is super-fast and very intuitive.

THE POWER OF VISUALIZATION

Time-series charts give the viewer a sensory way to grasp trends and patterns in a truly unique way. We can look back at the past and recognize the importance of things that were not clear to us at any particular moment. Time-series charts help us understand, in a very visceral way, the story that the data has to tell us. This is the great power of data visualization.

Of course, with great power comes great responsibility. Because the person reading a chart gets an immediate impression, it is vitally important to make sure that person sees the chart in an appropriate context.

I think of visualizations as graphic poetry or a painting: they rely on the power of analogy, and they can have great impact on the individual experiencing the visualization. However, like a painting, it is easy for the viewer to misinterpret the meaning intended by the artist. The viewer brings their own context and perception to the interpretation.

Take a look at the simple, abstract time-series chart shown in Figure 2.37. Then, gauge your emotional response to the statements that follow.

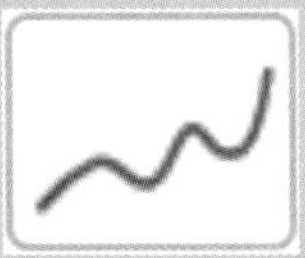

Figure 2.37: An abstract time series

1. This is the value of your retirement funds over the last 20 years.

2. This is the amount of debt your country has taken on over the last 100 years.

3. This is the average score of your favorite sports team over the last 5 years.

4. This is the unemployment rate of teenagers in your region over the last 10 years.

Even without measurements to help you understand the scale of the changes involved, I'm willing to bet that you have an immediate, strong interpretation and evaluation of what that graph is communicating to you.

"Up and to the right!" is a cliché often used for how we want investments that we make, for example, to increase in value over time. It is good to keep the following general rules in mind:

■ Time goes from left to right.

■ If things are getting better, the line should be rising; if things are getting worse, the line should be going down over time.

Any time that we break these rules, we should have good reason to do so because it makes a viewer's brain work harder to interpret what is going on.

It is also important to note that when we transform a measurement from one mode to another, we lose track of the underlying information that may have been apparent in the original. Graphic visualizations are like baked goods: they can look tasty, but you can't tell what they are made of unless you can see the ingredients.

If you share your creations, you should be sure to refer to the original sources of the data. We will get into accepted ways to reference your source data in later chapters, as it is most important when reporting on public data.

Now let's take a look at Chris Cooper's checking account balance over 27 months, as shown in Figure 2.38, and see what stands out.

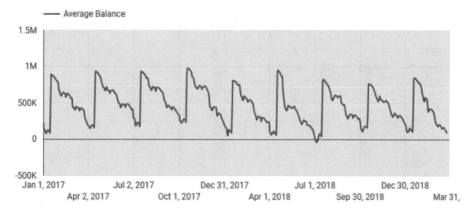

Figure 2.38: Chris Cooper's checking account balance chart

What can you conclude from this chart? What story is the graph telling you? Now compare this with the what you can say about the scorecard numbers or the rows in the table. Here are some things that come to mind for me:

- The account dipped below zero around July 1, 2018. That can't be good!

- There is a definite pattern here. The balance jumps up every couple of months, then it works its way down to low levels before jumping back up again. I think the next few months will be the same.

- There were several points where the account nearly reached zero. After the crisis point in July 2018, perhaps some changes were made. Although the account doesn't go below zero again, there are still major dips.

- The average account balance varies wildly over time!

Depending on your financial experience, you are likely to come up with many more insights that might interest Chris.

Having scorecards included on a report gives us some feel for the magnitude of the numbers involved. The time-series chart helps us see the patterns that are hidden by those summary values. If we need to, the table lets us dig deeper to see the details causing the various patterns in the chart. In the table, we can find the regular deposits provided by the Trust Fund Stock income that causes the sharp increases in the balance every quarter.

Now that we've taken some time to appreciate the power of the time-series chart, let's build one!

If you are in View mode, switch to Edit mode by clicking the Edit button. Select the simple time-series chart from the Add A Chart drop-down. In this case, we will select Smoothed Time Series Chart, as shown in Figure 2.39.

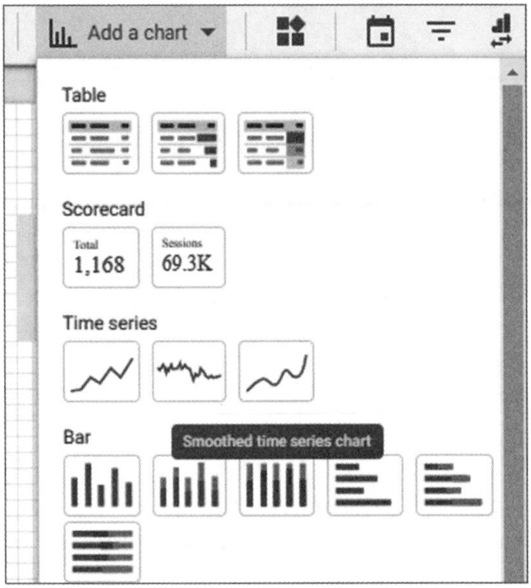

Figure 2.39: Selecting Smoothed Time Series Chart

On the Data tab, set the metric to Balance by dragging Balance from the Available Fields list, as shown in Figure 2.40.

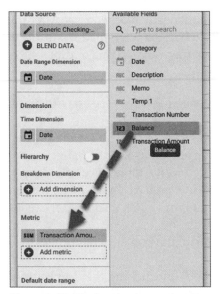

Figure 2.40: Setting the time-series chart metric

Now position and stretch the chart to fill the middle space on the canvas so that it looks like Figure 2.41.

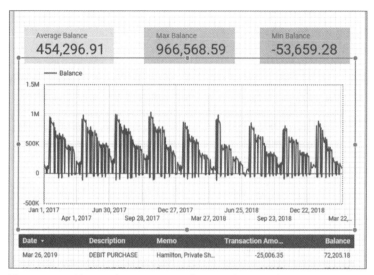

Figure 2.41: Placing the time-series chart on the page

You'll notice the current chart looks a lot busier than our example, and it appears that there are many more dips below the zero line. There are two reasons for this. First, on days when no transactions occur, there is no record of a balance either. Although there are only a few reference dates along the X-axis, the chart is trying to plot every date in the period. When a date has no entry, by default it is interpreted on the graph as a value of zero.

The other reason for the dips is due to the fact that we are using a smoothed graph. For the line to curve correctly, it sometimes dips down into the negative range to keep the line smooth and still pass through the correct values.

If you hover your mouse over the chart line at one of these points, a tooltip will appear with the value for that date. Although the line dips below zero, it will *not* show a negative balance. Again, this is just another case of Data Studio trying to fill in the curved line where there is no data.

So how do we fix these issues and maintain nice smooth lines? On the Style tab, scroll down to the General section. From the Missing Data drop-down, choose Linear Interpolation, as shown in Figure 2.42.

Doing so will connect the data smoothly where there are missing days. Just for fun, you might try selecting Line Breaks from the Missing Data drop-down so that you can see the actual gaps in the data.

In the next section, we will finish our first report by adding and adapting some graphic and interactive elements.

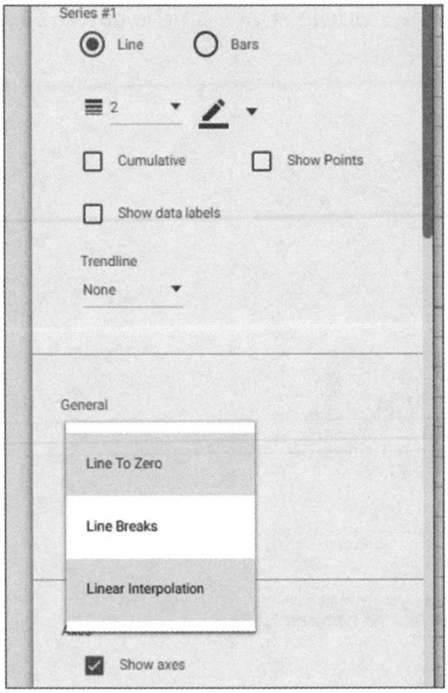

Figure 2.42: Selecting Linear Interpolation to fill in missing points

Step 10. Serving Suggestions: Finishing Touches and Sharing Your Report

Your report is almost complete. You just need a few elements to kick it up a notch. To give your report a little more style, we will build a header with some graphics. Regular graphics in Data Studio, shapes, and images work very similar to presentation software like Google Slides or Microsoft PowerPoint. Here we go!

1. Adding a header bar: Click the rectangle icon on the toolbar. Your cursor will turn into crosshairs and allow you to click and drag a rectangle shape. The default color here is blue, which is fine for our purposes. Use the arrow keys and mouse to position and size the bar as the header background. See Figure 2.43. You may need to fidget with the scorecards placement to get a thicker header in place. You do not have the ability to add text directly to rectangles and circle shapes. You will need to use a separate text box.

TIP   Reminder: Use the Shift key with the arrows to achieve fine-grained control over placement if necessary.

Figure 2.43: Placing the header bar

2. Adding a text box with the report title: Click the text box icon on the tool-bar. As with the rectangle, the pointer will turn into crosshairs, so you click and drag with the mouse to create a new text box. On the right side, you will see a Text Properties panel that lets you set the text styles.

    To set the styles to match the example, choose White for Text Color and 18 for Font Size, and set the font to Raleway. Click the Bold button to make the text boldface. These settings are shown in Figure 2.44.

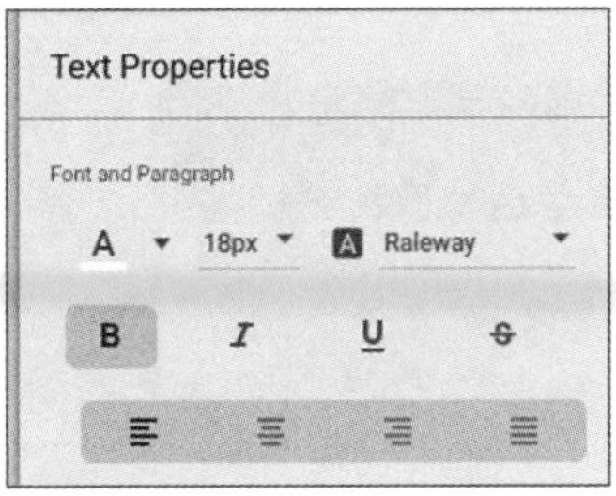

Text Properties

Font and Paragraph

A ▾ 18px ▾   **A** Raleway   ▾

B   *I*   <u>U</u>   S̶

≡   ≡   ≡   ≡

Figure 2.44: Setting text box styles

Next, click inside the text box and enter your text—in this case, **Chris Cooper Checking Account**. Since we set the color to white, you should be able to see your text on the blue background. Use the arrow keys and mouse to resize the text box and position it. When you're done, it should look like Figure 2.45.

Figure 2.45: Text box for the header

Next, we will add the logo image to the header.

TIP   You can find a link to the logo image file for this example, ChrisCooperLogo.png, **in the Chapter 2** Resources **folder. If you are following along, you may want to download and save this file to your computer for the next section.**

3. Adding a logo image: You can add images and embed other media like videos in your report. To add the log, start the process by clicking the image icon on the toolbar. As with the other graphic elements, the mouse pointer will turn into crosshairs and let you click and drag to create the new Image box.

   The Image Properties panel will appear on the right. Click the Select A File button to open a file dialog box which allows you to select any image on your computer. After a few moments, the file will upload, and it should be displayed in the image box. Adjust the size and location in the same way that you did for the other graphic elements. When you are done, it should look something like Figure 2.46.

Figure 2.46: Image added to header

4. Adding the Date Range control: As mentioned before, one of the things that makes Data Studio reports special is the manner in which they can be made interactive. This feature makes your reports much more useful and flexible than static reports. By adding a Date Range control, you ensure that your audience can select and isolate a particular time period to inspect. By default, all the charts and tables will magically recalculate based on the values in that time period.

   Start by clicking the date range icon on the toolbar and create a new Date Range box. Clicking and dragging in the same way as you did with the graphic elements, place the box as shown in Figure 2.47. As with the other elements, the configuration tabs will show up on the right side of the screen.

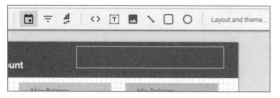

Figure 2.47: Adding a Date Range control

We need to change the Style settings to make the selector more visible when it is over the header. Select the Style tab in the configuration panel and go to the Background And Border section. Click the paint bucket icon to change the background color and set it to White. Then reposition and resize the box to fit on the right side of the header.

Finally, we need to make sure that the default date range is set. In some cases, you can leave the setting at the default, but often you will want to be very specific about the initial time period a report shows to your audience.

In this example, we will set the date range for the dates to January 1, 2018–March 31, 2019. To do this, select the DATA tab and set the default date range, as shown in Figure 2.48.

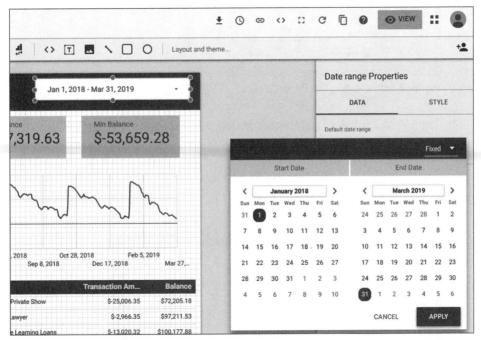

Figure 2.48: Setting the default date range

With the Date Range control in place and configured, your report is complete! Your target audience can now see your report, play with date ranges, and marvel at your work. (Unfortunately, only you, as the report owner, can view your masterpiece!)

You will have to change the report settings to share your report with individuals or the public. Fortunately, there's an easy fix. As noted earlier, one of the reasons for the rapid adoption of Data Studio is the ease with which you can share a report, and the variety of sharing and security options available.

In this case, we want to share our report so that anyone can view and use the chart. However, only the owner should be able to edit or modify it.

There are several ways to modify the Sharing settings and get a link to the report to share. Let's change the Sharing settings and get a link now by following these steps:

1. Click the Share drop-down above the toolbar next to the View button. Select Get Report Link from the menu, as shown in Figure 2.49.

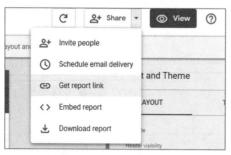

Figure 2.49: Selecting Get Report Link

2. The Get A Link To This Report dialog box will open. By default, only the owner of a report may view that report. If you use the Copy Link button on this screen before changing the Sharing options, only the owner can use the link successfully. To share this report with others, click Change Sharing Settings, as shown in Figure 2.50.

Figure 2.50: Clicking Change Sharing Settings

3. Click the Get Shareable Link icon in the upper-right corner of the screen, as shown in Figure 2.51. This will change your Sharing settings for this report and copy the link to the clipboard. You can then paste the URL into an email or share it on social media sites.

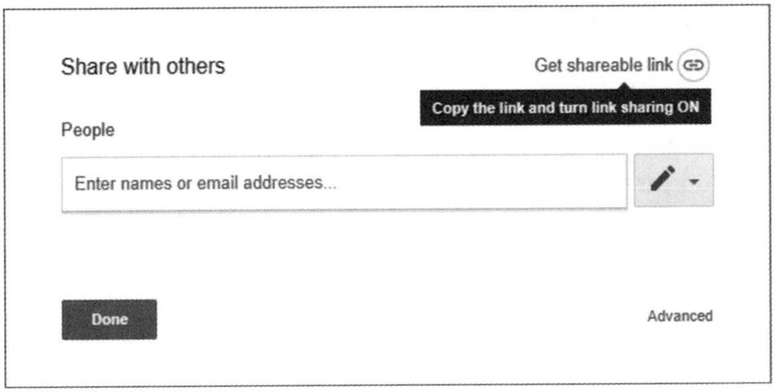

Figure 2.51: The link icon creates a shareable link.

Now that your new report is sharable, your first Google Data Studio example is complete. With the fundamentals completed, you are ready to start creating some more exciting data dishes!

Summary

In this chapter, we reviewed the basic steps that go into preparing a Data Studio report. Following the cooking analogy, we went through the following steps:

Picking a dish to prepare: In this case, we re-created a target report.

Shopping for ingredients: We explored how to retrieve data in CSV format from a personal financial service like a checking account.

Unpacking the groceries: We set up the file structures to hold our files and datasets.

Preparing the ingredients: We did some basic data cleansing to prepare our Google Sheet for access by the Data Studio connector. Some data cleansing is almost always necessary!

Checking out the kitchen: We took a quick tour of the Data Studio home page and learned how to start a new report.

Assembling the ingredients: We created a new data source using a data connector that fed data from our dataset to our report. We changed the attributes of some of the fields to make them easier to work with.

Combining the ingredients and cooking the dish: We used some of the most common Data Studio visualizations to build our report—tables, scorecards, and time-series charts.

Finishing the dish: We spruced up our report to make it more visually appealing, with header elements and an interactive date selector. We also went through the basic steps for sharing our report with the world.

After reading this chapter, I hope you were able to get up and running with Data Studio! We spent a lot of time going through basics in order to provide you with some of the fundamentals of building a rudimentary report. We will build on these fundamentals in the coming chapters.

Now that you know your way around Data Studio a bit, we can skip over some of the basics and dig into its more enticing features. In Chapter 3, "Enhancing Basic Graphs," we will build on our first example, dive deeper into dimensions, and kick your skills up a notch by adding some new ingredients to your visualizations.

Enhancing Basic Graphs

In Chapter 2, "Cooking with Google Data Studio," we went through the basics of building a simple Data Studio report. In this chapter, we'll take the report further using time comparisons and table graphing elements to allow the user to gain more insight into the data. In addition, we'll be using some time-saving methods for report creation and sharing.

You'll want to keep the purpose of the report and the needs of the user in mind when you build a new report. This new report will be designed to be saved as a PDF file and then printed. The interactive live nature of Data Studio is one of its most attractive features, but there are times when a static report is necessary.

Static Report Design

In this example, we'll replace the interactive features of the report with new components that use the same data. Since the user won't be able to interact with and explore the data, we'll enhance the charts to provide more information to the user.

The report from the previous chapter had some interactive elements that will not work on a static PDF or printed output. The Date Range control allowed the user to focus on any desired time range, and that is not an option for a printed report. We'll limit the time range to include only 2018 transactions. To provide the viewer with more context, we'll add comparisons to the previous year.

Furthermore, the detail table that allowed the user to scroll through all of the transactions and sort by different columns will be modified, since the user will not be able to see all of the transactions, or change the sort order, on a printed report. We'll modify the table so that it aggregates the transactions. Finally, to increase the value of the table, we'll add visualization elements that help the user gain more insight into the data.

PRINTING LONG TABLES

Data Studio is very good at helping us visualize large amounts of data, but it is not designed to output long, detailed reports. If you want to store a hard copy of all the transaction details, your best bet is to print a report directly from the spreadsheet or other tool designed for that purpose. Data Studio does have some export features that allow users to export the underlying data used for a table. We'll look at exporting chart data when we cover analysis in later chapters.

Figure 3.1 shows the finished report.

Figure 3.1: The finished product

Starting in the same way as we did in the last chapter. Let's examine the finished product's details and compare them with the example from Chapter 2. After that, I'll walk you through the steps to build it yourself.

Page header: We've removed the date range selector and replaced it with a text box for a description of the report.

Scorecards: Here, we'll be using a date comparison to show the value changes from 2017 to 2018.

Time-series: This chart has been updated to show the 2017 Average Balance amounts for easy comparison to 2018 values.

Table: There are lots of changes here! First, the Date field has been changed to Month. The detail fields for Description and Memo have been removed. The Transaction and Balance metric column headers have been modified to reflect that they are showing monthly figures. The Monthly Total Transactions column now has color coding to help the viewer see the relative values at a glance. Monthly Average Balance now has bar graphs along with the dollar values so that the viewer can see the relative amounts for all of the months at a glance.

Page: The page has been lengthened to accommodate the larger table and to make the report size closer to a standard printed page.

Now that you have an idea of how the new report will look, we'll use the same "cooking" process that we used in Chapter 2. This time, the steps will go much faster because we already have most of the ingredients in place!

Before Getting Started: Things You'll Need

In this example, we build on the work from the previous chapter. Go to your Data Studio home screen, and select the example report from Chapter 2 to view it.

If you skipped over the last chapter and want to follow along with this example, you'll need to access the Data Studio report, "Checking Account - Hands On Data Studio Example 1.0." You can find a link to this report in the Chapter 3 Resources section of the Resources page located here: www.wiley.com/go/handsondatastudio.

If you do not see the copy icons in the header, it means that you aren't logged into a Google account. If you log in and reload the page, you'll see the control icons in the header when viewing this report.

Because we're using an existing report and data source, you'll be able to skip over most of the preparation steps required when building a report from scratch.

To use the cooking analogy again, we'll be working with leftovers to create a new dish (which will save us a lot of time!).

Step 1. Copy the Report

When you're already the owner of a report and data source, copying a report is very simple. To begin, click the copy icon located in the upper-right side of the control header, as shown in Figure 3.2.

Figure 3.2: Click the copy icon.

Data Studio will present you with a Copy This Report screen. In this case, you should see the same data source listed for both Original Data Source and New Data Source, as shown in Figure 3.3. This is the default behavior if you own both the report and the data sources connected to it.

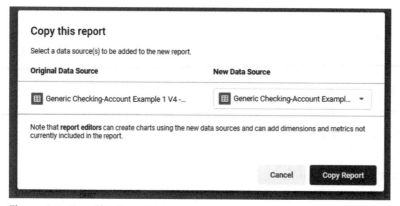

Figure 3.3: Copy This Report data source options

If you have multiple data sources for a report, each would show the original and offer a drop-down to connect a different source to replace each original in the new report.

If you were not an owner of this report, you would need to connect your own data sources at this stage . For now, all you need to do is click the Copy Report button to continue. A new tab will open on your browser, and you'll be placed into Edit mode so that you can work on your new copy.

As part of the copy process, Data Studio will rename the report and add Copy of to the beginning of the report name, as shown in Figure 3.4.

Figure 3.4: Changing the new report title

Your first task is to click in the title area to change this. For this example, change the title to **Checking Account - Hands On Data Studio Example 2.0**. Remember, there is no save button, but all changes are saved automatically. If you were to return to the Data Studio home page at this point, you'd see the new title in your list of reports along with the original.

Step 2. Modify the Header and Set the Date Range

Our new report is still controlled by the Date Range selector settings. Although we could simply change the default date range through the selector, it would be a bit out of place in a printed report. To remove the element, select the Date Range selector and click the Delete button.

Next, we will set the date range for this report page. The easiest way to do this is select the menu option Page ⇨ Current Page Settings. This will open the Current Page Settings panel on the right-side control panel. The Data tab should be selected.

Now we need to select the data source for the page. Click the dotted outline button labeled Select Data Source, as shown in Figure 3.5.

Current Page Settings	✕
DATA	STYLE

Data Source

Select Data Source

Date Range Dimension

⊕ PICK A DIMENSION

Figure 3.5: Selecting the data source for the page

This opens a new panel that displays all of the available data sources to which you have access, as shown in Figure 3.6. At the top of the list, you will see data sources that are already added to this report. Select the Generic-Checking-Account Example (or whatever data source you are currently using for this example).

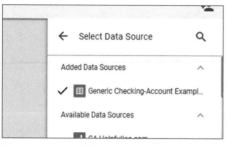

Figure 3.6: Available data sources

After selecting the data source, click the arrow at the top of the panel to return to the Page control panel. Your selection should now appear as the data source for the page. In addition, there will be new options for setting a date dimension and filters. We'll cover filtering in later chapters. For now, click the + icon next to the Pick A Dimension label.

In our example, we have only one date field named Date, and that should be the only selection available. Select Date and click the arrow at the top of the panel to return to the Page control panel.

Selecting a field for the Date Range dimension activates a new option for setting the default date range. This setting defaults to Auto, which will tell Data Studio to use the entire date range available. Since we want to limit the dates to 2018, select Custom to choose a default date range.

Selecting Custom activates another new option to select the default date range. By default, this option is set to Auto Date Range. Click the drop-down to activate the calendar picker, and then select the desired date range. In this case, Start Date is January 1, 2018, and End Date is December 31, 2018, as shown in Figure 3.7.

As soon as you make your date selection, the values on the report charts will update to reflect the shorter time frame.

We have one more change to make to the page-level settings. We want to make the report page a bit longer to accommodate the table that we will be updating.

Return to the Current Page Settings panel. Click the Style tab and change the Height (px) setting to **900**. We now have extra space at the bottom of the page.

The header looks a bit empty without the Date Range selector, so we'll add an extra text box with some information about the report. Instead of starting a new text box, it is easier to copy the existing text box, which will retain its style settings, and modify the text.

To create the new text box, select the text box containing Chris Cooper Checking Account, make a copy by pressing Ctrl+C, and paste it by pressing Ctrl+V. Click inside the new text box to edit the text, change it as shown in Figure 3.8, and move the box to the correct location.

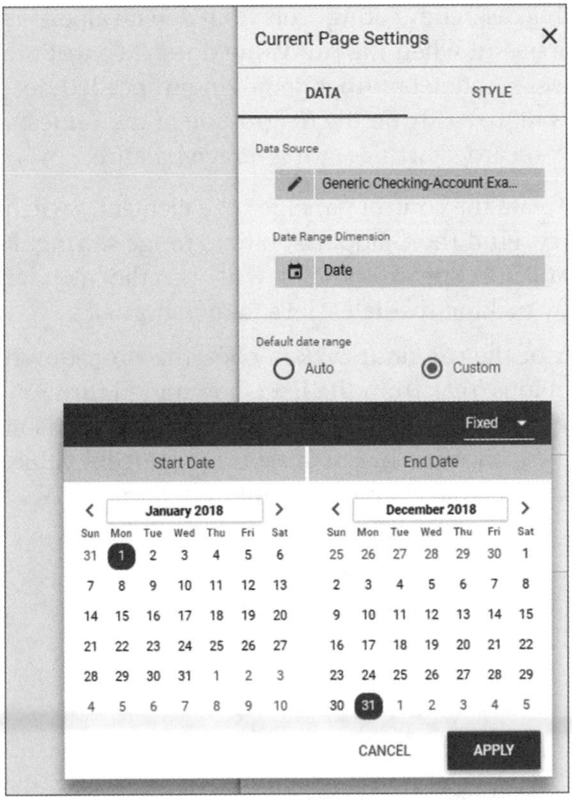

Figure 3.7: Setting the default date range

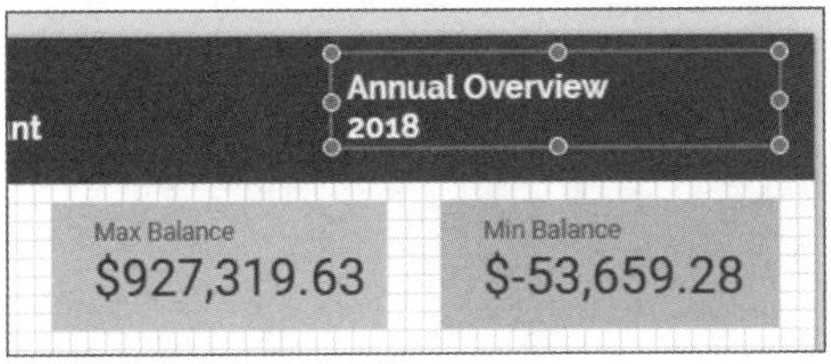

Figure 3.8: Copying and updating the new text box

Now that we have the header and the default dates taken care of, let's work our way down the report, making our configuration changes to the chart components.

Step 3. Modify Scorecards

We first want to modify the scorecards so that they show the comparison to the previous year's values. In addition, we'll modify the precision—that is, the number of decimal places to show.

Modifying the precision—in this case, eliminating cents from dollar values—is a common design decision. It is useful when the full value doesn't contribute anything significant to the viewer's understanding. Removing unneeded decimal values helps the user focus more easily on the magnitude of the values.

Follow these steps on each scorecard, starting with Average Balance:

1. Select the scorecard to activate the control panel for the element. Switch to the Data tab if necessary. Find the Comparison date range setting. It will be set to None by default. Clicking this setting will open the calendar picker. Instead of manually picking the dates, let's take a shortcut.

2. In the upper-right corner of the calendar picker, click the drop-down showing None. Select Previous Year from the list (shown in Figure 3.9), and click the Apply button. The scorecard will now show the comparison value. Note that the comparison value has defaulted to a percent value. We'll modify that to show the actual change amount in dollars.

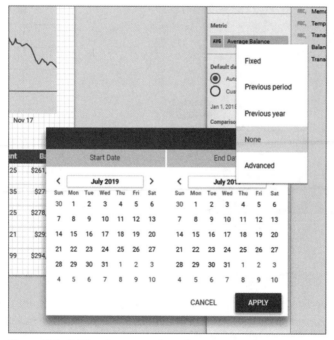

Figure 3.9: Setting the comparison date range

3. Switch to the Style tab.

4. In the Primary Metric section, change the Decimal Precision value to 0. This will round the value to the nearest dollar.

5. In the Comparison Metric section, change the Decimal Precision value to 0.

6. Click the Show Absolute Change check box. This will change the comparison value from percent values to dollar values. Figure 3.10 shows the updated style settings.

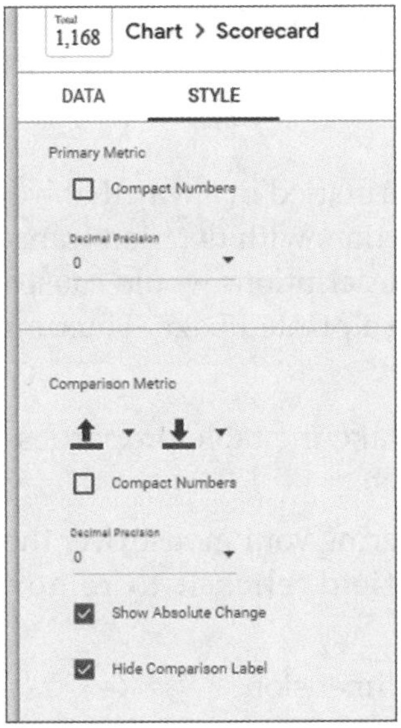

Figure 3.10: Updated style settings

7. Resize the scorecard box if necessary.

Step 4. Modify Time-Series Chart

Now that we have the scorecards updated, we can move on to adding the comparison date values to the time-series chart. We'll make the same date modifications that we made to the scorecards, but we won't have any style changes to make.

1. Select the chart to activate the control panel for the element. Switch to the Data tab if needed.

2. Find the Comparison date range setting. This will be set to None by default. Click the setting to open the calendar picker. Instead of manually picking the dates, we'll take a shortcut again. In the upper-right corner of the calendar box, click the drop-down showing None. Select Previous Year from the list, and click the Apply button.

The time-series chart will immediately update with a new line showing the 2017 values to correspond with the dates in 2018. You can see the balance patterns are very similar for both years. You can also see that the low points in the balance for 2018 are consistently lower than the low point in the balance for 2017.

Step 5. Modify the Transactions Table

We'll make some pretty big changes to the transaction details table to give the static report more value. The original table was designed for interactive use; the viewer could scroll through hundreds of transactions and sort the table in different ways. Scrolling and sorting don't make sense for a static report, so we will take the opportunity to repurpose the table and give it more meaning through aggregation and visual cues.

In the original design, we wanted the table formatted in a way that was similar to the original data set: one line per transaction, with detailed transaction information. In our new design, the notes and descriptions would cause issues because there are too many of them to show on a printed page. Thus, our first task is to remove these columns from the report.

1. While in Edit mode, select the table to make the table properties panel appear on the right side. Select the Data tab.

2. Remove the description dimension by hovering your mouse over the field. When the X symbol appears on the field, click it to remove the dimension.

3. Repeat the process to remove the Memo dimension.

When you remove these fields, the table updates. What is happening is that the metrics for Transaction Amount and Balance are recalculated for all of the transactions that occur on that day. We have now changed the table to group, or aggregate, the metrics by the single date dimension. The next step is to change the date dimension so that the metrics are aggregated by month instead of date.

1. Hover your mouse over the Date field so that the pencil icon appears.

2. Click the pencil icon, and the Properties box appears.

3. Enter **Month** in the Name field.

4. Click the Show As drop-down menu.

5. Change the value from Auto to Month, as shown in Figure 3.11.

6. As soon as these changes are made, the table updates with the new settings. Press the Enter key or click anywhere on the canvas to dismiss the Properties box.

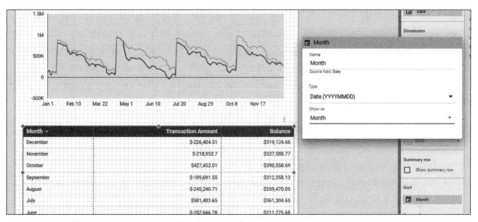

Figure 3.11: Changing Show As to display months

This looks pretty good, but we'd like to see the months in order from January to December. This is easily fixed by finding the Sort section on the Data tab and using the selector to change from Descending to Ascending. To show all of the months, click and drag the handle at the bottom of the table until all of the months are showing.

While we're still on the Data tab, let's change the column labels for the metrics:

1. Hover your mouse over the Transaction Amount metric and click the pencil icon to edit the properties.

2. Enter **Monthly Total Transactions** in the Name field and click outside the box to close it.

3. Repeat the process for the Balance metric so that it displays **Monthly Average Balance**.

To finish up our table changes, we'll add visualization elements. These elements are extremely helpful for users trying to find patterns in otherwise uniform-looking tables. Data Studio currently has two ways of doing this: *heatmaps* and *bars*.

Heatmaps allow the designer to pick a background color for the largest values in the table. As values descend, the color becomes lighter and lighter.

NOTE   Heatmaps are a very effective visualization feature, but they currently have a few limitations in Data Studio.

First, you can only define the color of the largest value, and the lighter shades are distributed by a process that you cannot control or modify. Second, it is difficult to highlight large negative values, and they will appear without color. You can see this effect when you apply the feature in this example. The ability to have more control over shading in heatmaps is a much-requested feature, and it will likely to be available in future releases.

Bars in the table are much like heatmaps in that you can select a color for the bar and Data Studio will automatically scale each bar relative to the other values in the column. Bars have a few optional settings that can extend their capability. You can show a target value that gets mapped as a line across all the bars, and you can display the scale at the bottom of the table. In our example, we'll stick to the basics.

1. To set up the table visualizations, select the Style tab in the table control column.

2. Scroll down the settings until you come to the Metrics section. Figure 3.12 shows all of the settings for the Metrics section as they were applied for the example.

Figure 3.12: Setting up the table visualizations

3. In the Column 1 section, click the drop-down. It's set to Number; change it to Heatmap. A paint bucket will appear that lets you select a color for the largest values of the heatmap. For this column, select a medium shade of green. You'll see the table update immediately with your selection.

4. In the Column 2 section, change the drop-down to Bar. Select a shade of red using the paint bucket color picker. Note that the bars now appear, but the numbers on the chart have vanished. Click the Show Number check box to make them reappear.

5. We'd like the column label to be aligned on the right side. You can make this change by selecting the align-right symbol just under the bar settings. You should see the title Monthly Average Balance slide to the right in the table header.

6. Just under the alignment section, select the Compact Numbers check box. This will change the number display in this column to show values in thousands, which is indicated by the K shown for the values in this column. This is a handy setting when you're dealing with large numbers where precision is not vital.

7. Finish the table formatting by clicking and dragging the column guides to resize your columns.

Switch to View mode to admire your newly completed report.

Step 6. Save the Report as PDF for Sharing

In this example, we purposely removed the interactive elements because we wanted the report to be effective in PDF or printed formats. Data Studio emphasizes shareability, so it was no surprise when PDF facilities were added to the tool soon after its status was changed from beta to a fully supported product in September 2018.

We'll look at more PDF functionality as we cover dynamic web reports. For now, let's generate a PDF from the report as a downloaded file. As a bonus, we'll add in password protection to keep the PDF report from prying eyes.

1. To save the report as a PDF file in View mode, first click the down arrow icon in the top control header. A Download As PDF dialog box will appear. In this case, we will select the Password Protect Report option, as shown in Figure 3.13.

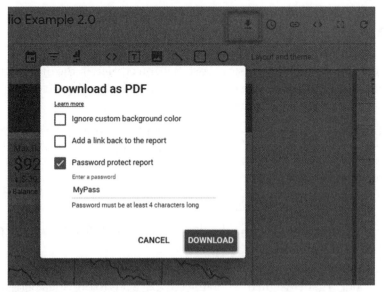

Figure 3.13: Setting the PDF options

In this case, I set the password for the report to `MyPass`.

2. Click the Download button. You'll see a message in the bottom-left corner of your browser screen notifying you that the PDF is being prepared. This usually takes only a few seconds, but times may vary depending on the size and complexity of the report. After preparation, the PDF will start downloading and the file will be named after the title of the report—in this case, `Checking_Account_-_Hands_On_Data_Studio_Example_2.0.pdf`.

This PDF file can now be stored or distributed via email. When users try to view the file, they'll be prompted to enter the password set during creation, as shown in Figure 3.14.

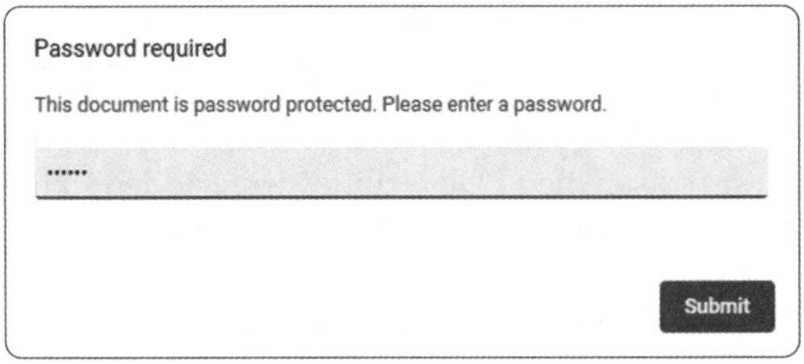

Password required

This document is password protected. Please enter a password.

•••••••

Submit

Figure 3.14: Password protection on PDF files

The PDF file from the example is available from the Resources page section for this chapter. Just remember that to view it you need to use the password MyPass.

Now that we've generated a file to share our report, the second example is complete!

Summary

In this chapter, you built on the basic report that you created in the first example, and you learned ways to repurpose existing work and extend basic graphs. We covered these Data Studio concepts in this chapter:

Design reports to be print- and PDF-friendly: Keeping the purpose of the report in mind, we removed interactive elements and modified others to be more relevant.

Copy existing reports: We used previous work as a basis for new reports. Reusing leftovers saves time!

Page-level attributes: We set the data source and date range at the page level and changed the page length.

Set and format comparison date range: We added more information for viewers to gain insight by showing comparisons to previous periods for scorecards and time-series charts.

Change aggregation groupings in a table: We modified the Date column to allow grouping and metrics totals by month.

Add table visualizations: We implemented heatmaps and bars to make it easier for the viewer to scan and grasp patterns in the table data.

Save and share as PDFs: We exported our report to a PDF file and protected the file with a password.

In Chapter 4, "Data Exploration with Interactive Elements," we'll return to using Data Studio interactive features for data exploration and finish up our work with the checking account example.

Data Exploration with Interactive Elements

This chapter returns to the cooking analogy to guide you through the steps for re-creating an example report. The first step in that process is to select a dish to cook. This step involves determining the purpose of the report, who the audience is, and what elements we'll use to communicate information about the data graphically.

In earlier chapters, we created a basic report with limited user control; then we built a more complex static report with user control removed. In this example, we want to develop a report that provides a greater degree of freedom to explore the data.

Building Our Workbench Example

Once again, we'll deal with checking account data, but this time, we'll use a new data source that adds an extra category dimension to all our transactions. This categorization is available in some banking services, and it is a standard service provided by personal finance software and services. This additional field opens up more dimensions for exploration.

The audience for this kind of report is primarily the report creator, though sometimes these reports may be shared with other analysts. The reports are not designed for presentation or printing. The purpose of this type of report is to explore a set or subset of data set rapidly in a rather free-form way.

I classify this type of report as a *workbench*. When dealing with a new set of data, I often create a set of workbenches to serve as tools to help me find interesting patterns that later become the subject of focused reports.

Data Studio is an effective tool for building this kind of workbench. It is extremely flexible for experimenting with visualization, filtering, and combining different dimensions.

On the way to building this workbench example, we'll examine ways that Data Studio lets you build your own dimensions and metrics. It's possible that you'll need to work with data sets where you are not allowed to augment the data at the source directly. This is exactly the situation in this example. We'll be creating calculated fields directly in Data Studio to overcome this obstacle.

Step 1. Selecting a Dish to Prepare: Exploration Workbench for a Bank Account

We know that our new dish will be a workbench, but what will it look like? This section looks at some of the main features and interaction points of the example. It's impractical to try to show the full functionality of highly interactive reports like workbenches in a paper format. Because of the interactive nature of this report, you should connect to the example report for this chapter and play around with it yourself.

> **NOTE**   All links to data files and live Data Studio examples for this chapter can be accessed from the Resources page located here: `www.wiley.com/go/ handsondatastudio`.

Figure 4.1 shows the default view that you'll see when you first open the report. We'll look at the main features and then some examples of how they interact with one another and the charts.

As you can see, there is a lot going on here! We widened this report to accommodate all of its functionality.

Page Header   Our standard header copied from the first example; the Date Range selector is used.

Pie Chart   At a glance, the *pie chart* shows the balance between deposits and withdrawals. This chart is also an *interactive filter*.

Bar Chart   The *bar chart* shows the relative category amounts and the transaction type in an easy-to-compare format. Interactive filtering is turned on for this chart, allowing the user to explore and isolate categories quickly.

Line Chart   The *line chart* is similar to the time-series chart in the other examples, but here we have broken out category amounts. This chart has two interaction features:

Figure 4.1: The workbench (default view)

Clicking a label on the category legend highlights the selected category and fades nonselected categories.

Clicking and dragging on the chart allows you to filter for a selected time range without using the Date Range selector.

Table   Our trusty table now shows details about transactions by memo type and category. The Transaction Type and ABS Amount columns are created from new calculated fields. Interaction has been activated on the table to allow filtering of selected memo items.

Filter Controls   We are using three common variations of the *filter control* element:

Expandable Filter Control with Search: This filter control expands when clicked to search and browse all the memo entries. The user can select or deselect any values.

Filter Control without Search   This filter allows the user to isolate deposits or withdrawals.

Filter Control with Search   This filter allows the user to see several values and scroll for selection or use the Search box to isolate values.

As you can see from the descriptions, we have a lot of interactive filtering options on this report. At first glance, some of these options may seem redundant. For example, the ability to filter for a category may be done through the bar chart or through the Category filter control. Each filter control method has some unique functions that make it a good choice for a particular design.

The interactive charts allow for quick exploration of one or two selections in an intuitive way, and they do double duty by displaying the information graphically, thus saving space. Their function may not be obvious to a casual user, however, and they suffer from one limitation: though it is easy to select a value to isolate, it is difficult to remove single items from selection.

At the same time, standard filter controls deliver much more fine-grained control over what is selected. The expandable filter for Memo, for example, allows quick searches to find and select, or deselect, any memo entry efficiently. This is a good thing because there are 241 different memo entries in our example!

We include both chart and filter controls in this example so that you can get a feel for their capabilities. Future examples will make heavy use of filtering.

SEPARATING INTERACTIVE FILTERS AND FILTER CONTROLS

In our checking account examples, there are a relatively small number of dimensions to filter and explore. When you're exploring a more complicated data set, like website data from Google Analytics, there may be dozens of dimensions, and the combination of filter possibilities grows astronomically. Thus, a workbench page trying to use both interactive charts and filter controls becomes too unwieldy.

One approach to data exploration in these cases is to create a page of bar charts with interactive filters in order to facilitate finding patterns quickly. A separate workbench page with standard filter controls allows you to remove a set of values in order to see what effect that has on the overall metrics.

Moving back and forth between graphic and filter controls, selection and deselection, allows for rapid analysis and insights.

If you are curious to see this in action, a link to a rapid analysis workbench is available from www.wiley.com/go/handsondatastudio. The report includes an embedded video showing an example of how to identify and filter out "bot" traffic hitting an actual website.

Figure 4.2 shows an example of this workbench. The Category filter control is set up to select the Housing, Royalties, and Insurance categories. I further filtered the results by clicking and dragging on the line chart to select a particular period of time. Then I removed the entries for Penthouse Rent/Timeshare by deselecting the entry in the Memo filter control.

Now that we have reviewed the workbench features and functions, let's move on to shopping for ingredients.

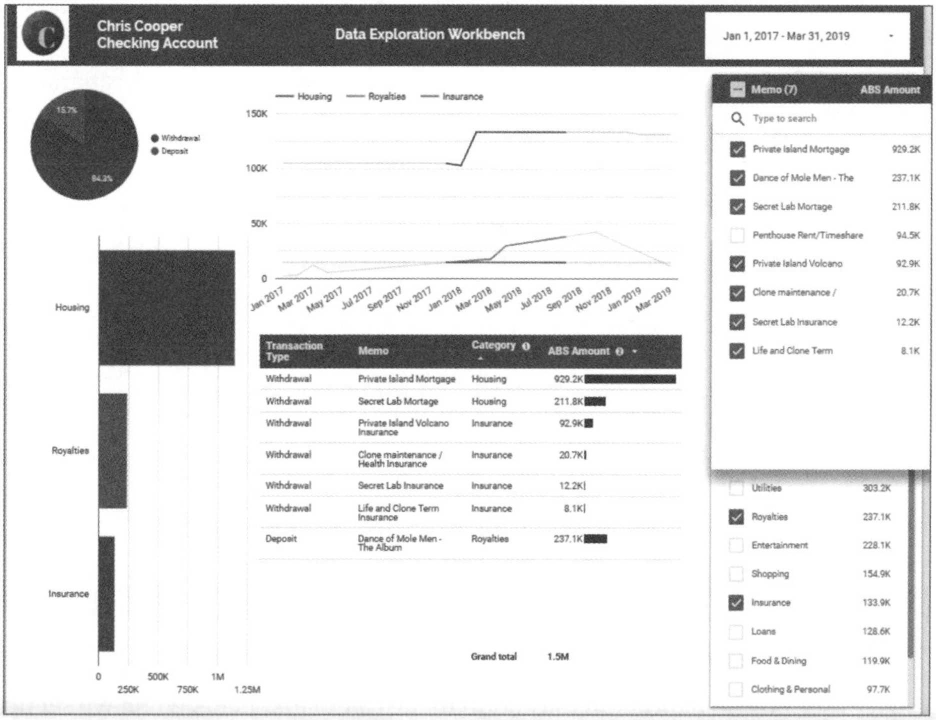

Figure 4.2: The workbench in action

Step 2. Let's Go Shopping! Getting the Data Set

It is time to get the data set for our workbench. In this scenario, our fictitious friend Chris has exported his account data from a personal finance service. This service provides the same data as in our first examples, but it also adds a category for each transaction.

Chris has already exported the CSV file, uploaded it to his Google Drive, and converted it to a Google Sheet. He created a link to the file by using the sharing method shown in Figure 4.3.

Chris sends us a link to access the file, but we only have "view" permissions and cannot edit the file. Although we could make a copy and store it in our own Google Drive folders, it makes sense to connect to Chris's copy and use it as the data set directly so that we don't have to keep track of multiple versions of the file.

This setup causes a common problem that we'll have to work around: we'd like to set up some extra columns for the report, but we cannot modify the original data set. In our case, we want to add a new dimension column for Transaction Type and a new metric column for Absolute Value.

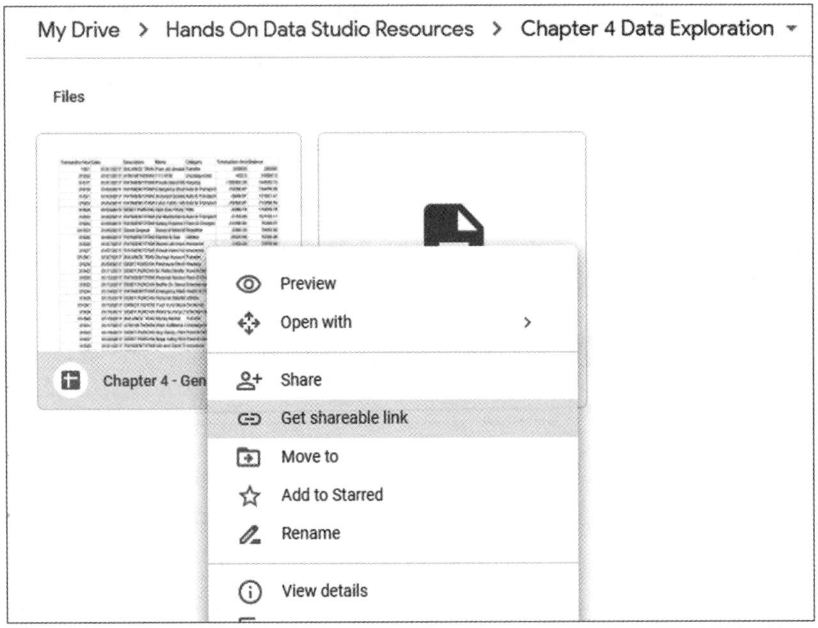

Figure 4.3: Sharing a link to a Google Sheet

We'll see how to handle this situation using calculated fields when we set up our data source. The good news is that we can skip several steps ahead in the preparation process. We won't need to "unpack the groceries" or do any data cleaning of the file.

Step 3. Assembling the Ingredients: Connecting Data to the Report

Let's begin by creating a new report in this example. To do so, open the Data Studio home screen and click Blank Report in the Start With A Template section, as shown in Figure 4.4.

We are taken to a blank report. As in previous examples, let's rename our report right away. As shown in Figure 4.5, rename the report **Data Exploration - Hands on Data Studio Example 3.0**.

With our new report named, it's now time to connect the sheet that Chris sent us. We don't have the sheet saved on our drive, and that's just fine. We want to use the data set directly without creating a copy. Let's go through the data source setup process:

1. Click Create New Data Source at the bottom of the Add A Data Source panel on the right side of the screen. The Data Connectors screen appears.

2. As in the example in Chapter 2, "Cooking with Google Data Studio," select Google Sheets as the new data connection type. This will take you to the Google Sheets selection screen.

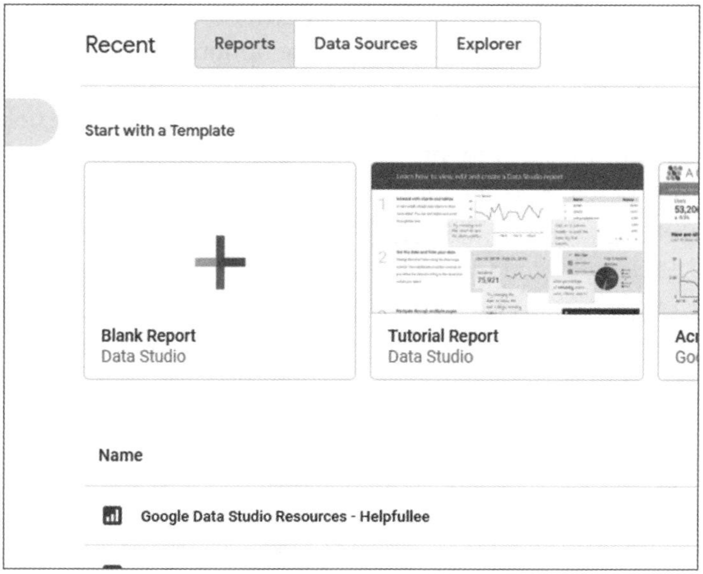

Figure 4.4: Starting a new report

Figure 4.5: Naming the report

3. The Google Sheets selection screen is the same as in our first example, but this time, the sheet we want is not shown as an option. So, select the URL option, as shown in Figure 4.6.

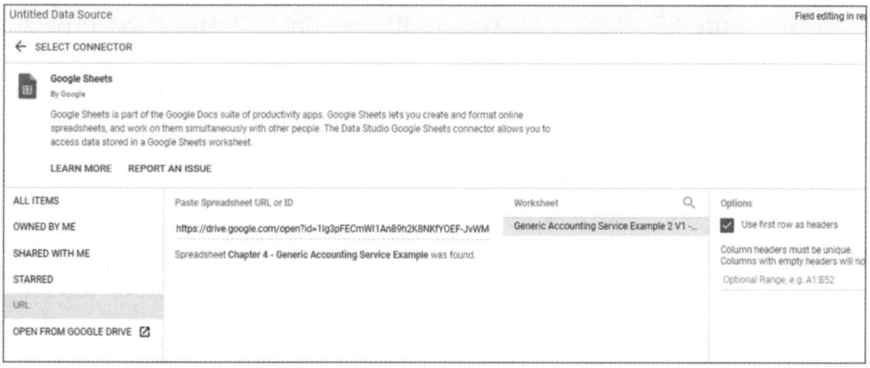

Figure 4.6: Selecting the URL option

When you paste the URL we received from Chris, the name and worksheet pages appear as selection options. Select the options shown in Figure 4.6 and accept the default settings by clicking the blue connect button on the upper-right side. This sends you to the fields setup screen. The fields for this data source are nearly identical to the ones in our first example, with the exception of the new category field.

4. Rename the data source to **GS Chris Cooper Account Example 3.0**. The GS in the name helps to identify the source as a Google Sheet.

5. Change the Type settings for Transaction Amount and Balance to Currency, US Dollars, and set the Aggregation method for Balance to Average, as shown in Figure 4.7.

GS Chris C...	Data credentials: Owner	Data freshness: 15 minutes	Community visualizations access: Off	Field editing in reports: On	

← EDIT CONNECTION						⊕ ADD A FIELD
Index	Field ↓		Type ↓	Aggregation ↓	Description ↓	🔍 Search fields
1	Transaction Number	⋮	ABC Text ▾	None		
2	Date	⋮	📅 Date (YYYYMMDD) ▾	None		
3	Description	⋮	ABC Text ▾	None		
4	Memo	⋮	ABC Text ▾	None		
5	Category	⋮	ABC Text ▾	None		
6	Transaction Amount	⋮	123 Currency (USD - US Doll... ▾	None ▾		
7	Balance	⋮	123 Currency (USD - US Doll... ▾	Average ▾		
8	Transaction Type	fx ⋮	ABC Text ▾	None		
9	ABS Amount	fx ⋮	123 Number ▾	None ▾		

Figure 4.7: Setting up the fields

Note that we leave the Aggregation method set to None for the Transaction Amount field. We'll be using this field to create a new calculated field, and aggregated metrics can be difficult to work with.

In Figure 4.7, you can see two additional fields: Transaction Type and ABS Amount. These are the new calculated fields that we'll be creating next. Calculated fields are denoted with Fx, which is the mathematical symbol for a formula.

6. Transaction Type will become a new dimension that will tell us when the transaction was a deposit or a withdrawal.

    a. Click plus symbol (+) next to Add A Field in the upper right of the Fields panel. You should now be presented with the field creation screen. On the left side are all the available fields that you can use when creating a new field display. You can drag fields over to the formula text area when needed.

    b. Now we need to give our new field a name. For this example, enter **Transaction Type**, as shown in Figure 4.8. Next, we'll enter some code in the formula box.

c. Don't worry if you're not a "coder." We'll be using what is known as a *case statement*. We'll look at case statements in much greater detail in later chapters, but for now just enter this code in the Formula box, as shown in Figure 4.8.

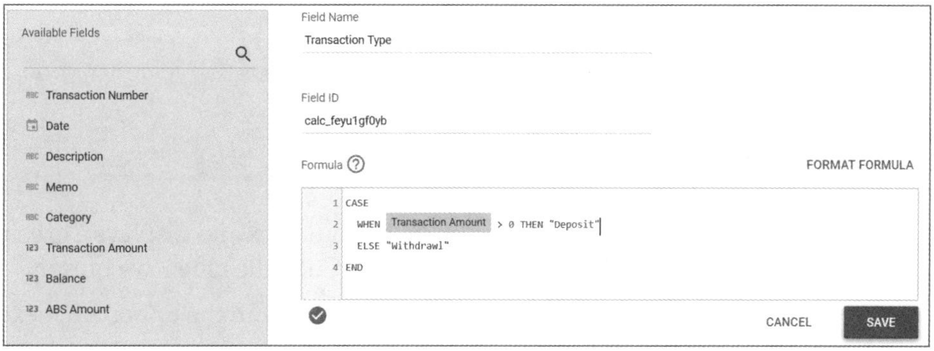

Figure 4.8: Creating the Transaction Type field

d. Data Studio evaluates the code in the Formula box and presents you with a small green check mark if the code is valid and allows you to save the new field. When the evaluation is completed, click the blue Save button.

e. After saving, return to the fields screen by clicking the arrow in the upper left, next to the text All Fields.

NOTE Data Studio can be both helpful and perplexing when creating the formula for a calculated field. The development team has been upgrading the edit box with automatic completion of field names, color coding, and a convenient Format Formula button to help make the code sections more readable. Unfortunately, when Data Studio flags a formula as invalid, it does not always give detailed information about what is wrong.

7. To create a new field, we'll follow the same steps we just went through for the calculated dimension. But because this field will provide a measurement number, it will be a new calculated metric. The formula uses the ABS() function, which takes a field value and returns it as a positive value. In simple terms, it will make sure that all the values in this field are positive. This helps us compare the different withdrawal and deposit amounts for various categories using positive numbers instead of the negative values found in the Transaction Amount field when there is a withdrawal.

a. To start, click the (+) Add A Field button again.

b. Set the Field Name to **ABS Amount**.

c. In the Formula box, add the following code as shown in Figure 4.9.

```
ABS(Transaction Amount)
```

```
Field Name
ABS Amount

Formula (?)

    1  ABS( Transaction Amount )|
```

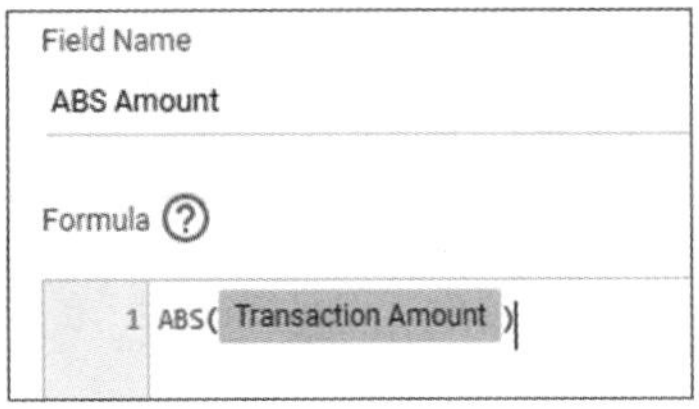

Figure 4.9: Creating the ABS Amount field

d. Data Studio evaluates the code in the Formula box and displays a green check mark to indicate the code is valid. Click the blue Save button.

e. Return to the fields screen by clicking the arrow in the upper left, next to the text All Fields.

You should now see the new calculated fields listed along with the standard fields. With the configuration of the new fields complete, you are ready to start building the report on the canvas.

To begin building the report, click the Add To Report button at the top right of the fields screen. Confirm that you want to add the data source in the confirmation dialog, and you'll be returned to the main editing view.

Adding Chart Components and Graphic Elements

Step 4. Reuse, Recycle, and Repurpose: Copying Elements from Other Reports

In Chapter 3, "Enhancing Basic Graphs," we copied the entire example report from the first chapter as a basis on which to build a new report. In this chapter, we'll look at another way to speed up development: reusing elements to which you have access in other reports.

You have seen examples of copying elements within a report when you duplicated the scorecards in Chapter 2. For this example, we'll copy the header elements from the first example so that we can keep a consistent style between the reports. We'll go step by step through this process.

> **NOTE** You may copy elements from a report only if you have edit access to that report. If you copy charts or other components that are connected to a data source instead of a simple graphic element, Data Studio will try to add the connected data source when you paste the chart into the new report. This may, or may not, be the behavior that you are seeking.

1. Load the source report in a new browser tab. The fastest way to do this is to right-click the Data Studio symbol:

   a. Right-click the Data Studio symbol in the upper-left corner of the page next to the report title. Then select Open Link In New Tab, as shown in Figure 4.10, to open the Data Studio home page in a new tab.

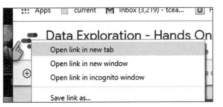

Figure 4.10: Selecting Open Link In New Tab

   b. On the home screen, select the example report from Chapter 1, "Data Studio and the Data Citizen."

2. Once the report opens, switch to editing mode by clicking the Edit button.

3. Select the header elements by clicking and dragging to select the color bar, the text boxes, and the Date Range selector, as shown in Figure 4.11. Use either Ctrl+C or the Edit menu to copy the selection to the clipboard.

Figure 4.11: Selecting header elements and copying them to the clipboard

4. Switch back to the current report browser tab and paste the selection. Clean up by closing the Source Report tab.

5. Stretch and move the new elements so that the header looks correct for the layout of the new report.

6. Select, copy, and paste the text box in the header. Change the text to read **Data Exploration Workbench**, and your header should look like Figure 4.12.

Figure 4.12: Our new header

Now that we have our header in place, we can move on to the chart elements.

Step 5. Easy as Pie! Adding a Pie Chart

We're going to add a simple pie chart to the upper-left side of the canvas. You may wonder why we haven't added such a common chart in earlier examples. The reason is that pie charts, while ubiquitous, are not usually the first choice of data visualization designers.

WHAT'S WRONG WITH PIE CHARTS?

You may not think that such a common visualization technique would stir controversy, but it does. The following graphic shows the topics Google suggests.

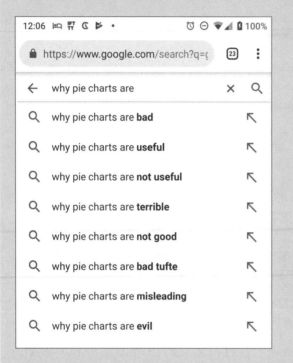

The argument against pie charts goes like this: people are very good at grasping the quantity relationships between lengths, as we see depicted in bar charts. However, we're not good at interpreting relative quantities when depicted as a function of area. Pie charts have no scale to help with accuracy, and as the number of segments and colors increases, our chances for misreading the chart increase.

Still, we're used to seeing pie charts everywhere, and in some cases, they may be expected by your audience. The circular shape of a pie chart is pleasing to the eye, and it gives us a break from all the bars and lines. So, what are we to do?

Here's my advice: pie charts are okay to use if you are dealing with a pie that has very few "slices." I set the limit to four slices and try to keep their use to a minimum. Furthermore, stay away from using multiple pie charts; use multiple bar or column charts instead.

We'll use the pie chart to show the relative value between deposits and withdrawals. Since we're using this workbench for analysis, we want to make our chart not only show values, but also operate as an interactive filter—that is, if the user selects a segment on the chart, all the other charts and filters on the page will be restricted to showing results based on that selection.

1. To begin, select the pie chart from the Add A Chart drop-down menu. Use the crosshairs to set the upper-left side of the chart, and then click and drag to size and position the new chart, as shown in Figure 4.13.

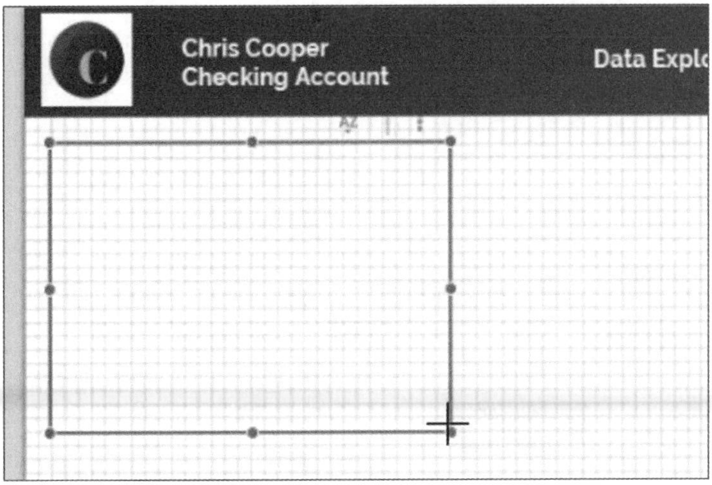

Figure 4.13: Placing the pie chart

2. Data Studio estimates values for your chart as placeholders, so we have to change those. With the pie chart selected, the Data tab is available on the right side of the screen in the Properties panel.

   a. Set the dimension to Transaction Type.

   b. Change the metric to our new field, ABS Amount. You should see the chart update to show an almost even split between deposits and withdrawals.

   c. To add interactive filtering to the chart, scroll to the bottom of the Data tab, locate Interactions, and click Apply Filter. When we add more charts, you'll see the effect of this filter setting.

Step 6. Step Up to the Bar: Adding the Bar Chart

Now we'll add another workhorse of data visualization to our workbench. The bar chart shows values, depicted graphically as bars, horizontally. Bar charts should often be your first choice if you are tempted to use another pie chart, because our brains can process the relative lengths of the bars much better than we can the relative area slices in the pie chart.

1. Select the bar chart from the Add A Chart drop-down menu, as shown in Figure 4.14. You'll see some other variations of bar charts that are available, but for now we want the basic version. Click and drag the bar chart into place.

Figure 4.14: Selecting the bar chart

2. Next we have to change the settings on the Data panel. First, set Dimension to use the Category field. The bar chart will update with the new dimension labels.

You may notice the labels for the bars are squished, cut off, or in some cases, not showing for a particular bar. We can fix this issue by making the chart larger, but that would take up too much space. We can also fix this by changing the text size in the style settings, but shrinking the text may make a chart harder to read. In this case, we'll pull the left edge of the visualization to the right to make more room for the labels.

3. With the bar chart selected, place the mouse pointer directly over the left border of the chart, just to the right of the labels. When the pointer turns into a directional symbol, right-click to grab the edge and drag it to the right, as shown in Figure 4.15. You should see the labels appear and organize themselves next to the corresponding bars.

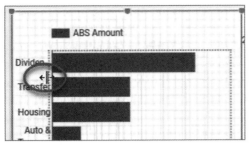

Figure 4.15: Adjusting the label area in the bar chart

Now that we have all the categories displayed, we can compare deposit categories and withdrawal categories in an intuitive way. We do have a problem, though: it is hard to distinguish withdrawals and deposit categories easily. We'll fix this by assigning a *breakdown dimension* to the chart and then assigning a consistent color scheme for deposits and withdrawals.

4. In the Data tab for the chart, you will see the Breakdown Dimension field in the Dimension section. Set this field to the Transaction Type dimension. As soon as you do this, you'll see changes to the chart. This is close to what we want, but the spacing appears to be thrown off a bit, as shown in Figure 4.16.

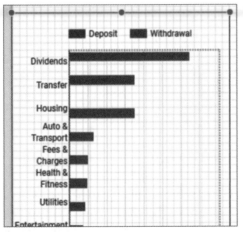

Figure 4.16: Effect of adding the breakdown dimension to the bar chart

5. We'll now apply a quick fix here to clean up the appearance of the chart by using the style settings. While the chart is selected, switch from the Data tab to the Style tab. At the top of the panel, you will see the Stacked Bars check box. Click the check box, and immediately you see the bar chart reformat into a much neater configuration.

6. Change the Number Of Bars setting from 10 to **20** to show the full range of categories.

> **TIP**   The "hack" functionality is available in the tool, but it is not readily apparent to the user. Hacks abound in the Data Studio community. Part of the fun—and challenge—of using a tool as new as Data Studio is that these kinds of workarounds are not part of well-documented patterns found in other tools. They are discovered by users and shared with the community for fame and fortune. Okay, the fame may be limited to a niche of hard-core users, and there is rarely any fortune involved!
>
> Examples for these kinds of workarounds are scattered throughout blogs and social media, and they can sometimes be hard to find. I'll share links to some of my favorite communities and people to follow at `www.wiley.com/go/handsondatastudio`.

7. Since we already have deposits and withdrawals color-coded and labeled in the pie chart, we can remove the legend above the bar chart to save some space. While on the Style tab, scroll to the bottom of the panel to the Legend section.

   Here we can make fine-tuning adjustments to the legend's appearance by changing the font size and alignment. Hovering over the small square-shaped icons reveals that they control the position of the legend in the chart, which by default is set to Top. Click the leftmost square to remove the legend, as shown in Figure 4.17.

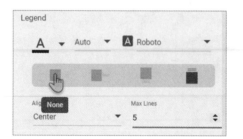

Figure 4.17: Removing the legend from the bar chart

8. Just below the Legend section are the controls for the chart header. The header is a shadowy section just above the chart. We'll visit some of the chart header functionality in later chapters. For now, change the setting from the default Show On Hover to Do Not Show.

9. Switch back to the Data tab for the chart. Set the Metric field to the ABS Amount field. Now your chart correctly shows amounts for each category.

10. Remember that we also want this chart to be interactive. Scroll to the bottom of the Data tab and select the Apply Filter check box in the Interactions section.

Keeping Dimension Colors Consistent

Our last style change will apply to all of the charts on the page: adjusting the dimension value colors. By default, the colors on charts are mapped to dimension values and assigned automatically by Data Studio. In our case, the Deposit Dimension value is set to red and the Withdrawal value is set to blue. These colors may be confusing to the viewer, as we usually associate red with danger. We want to associate the "danger" color with Withdrawals and change the Deposit color to green—generally a color that has positive connotations.

You can override these settings for a particular chart in the Style tab of most chart types by changing the settings in the Color By section, and then you will have some control over individual colors. In our example, we want to keep the charts showing colors by dimension—we just want to use different colors. To set your colors, follows these steps:

1. Select Resource ⇨ Manage Dimension Value Colors. The Dimension Value Colors panel opens at the bottom of the screen, as shown in Figure 4.18.

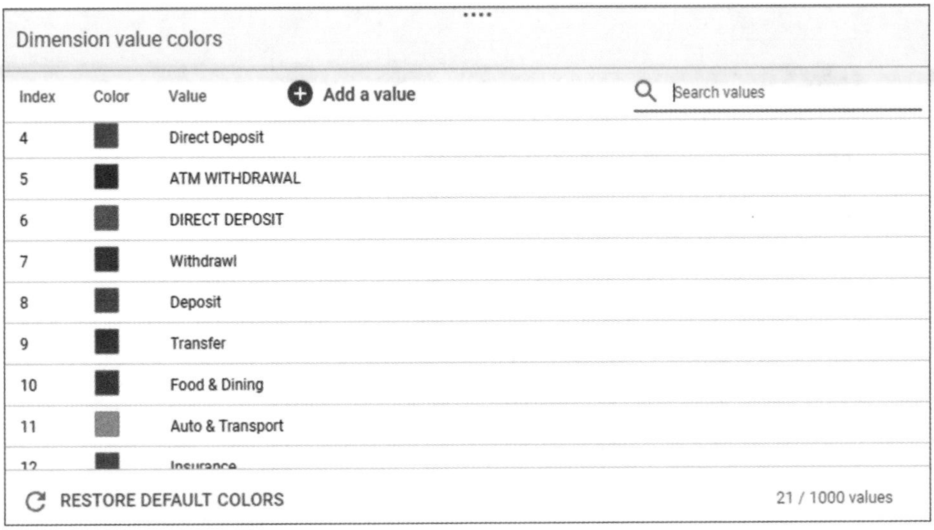

Index	Color	Value		
			⊕ Add a value	🔍 Search values
4	■	Direct Deposit		
5	■	ATM WITHDRAWAL		
6	■	DIRECT DEPOSIT		
7	■	Withdrawl		
8	■	Deposit		
9	■	Transfer		
10	■	Food & Dining		
11	■	Auto & Transport		
12	■	Insurance		

Dimension value colors

↻ RESTORE DEFAULT COLORS   21 / 1000 values

Figure 4.18: Dimension Value Colors panel

2. Although you cannot sort this list by dimension value, there is a search box to reach values quickly. Scroll down the list of values, or use the search box, to locate Deposit and click the colored box to change the color to green. Use the same procedure to set the color value for Withdrawal to red. After these selections, click the Close button in the upper-right corner of the panel.

TIP   You should perform dimension color assignment after adding some charts. It is usually easier to reassign colors after Data Studio has identified and assigned many of the dimension values. However, if you have specific colors for values in mind, you can click the Add A Value button and assign colors to values that have not yet been mapped.

With the color selections complete, we'll move on to the next chart.

Step 7. Lining Things Up: Adding the Line Chart

In Chapters 2 and 3, we used the time-series chart to show how a value changes over time. The time-series chart is a specialized type of line chart. In this example, we'll use the more general line chart type to show a complex breakdown of dimensions, but we'll still use time as our value for the x-axis of the chart. Here is the step-by-step setup for the chart:

1. Select the line chart type from the Add A Chart drop-down menu, as shown in Figure 4.19. Click and drag the new line chart to position it in the top center of the canvas. Once again, Data Studio will select some dimensions and metrics to get you started, and then we'll change them.

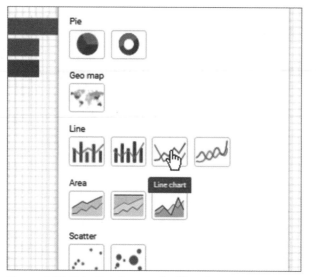

Figure 4.19: Selecting the standard line chart

2. With the line chart selected, click the Data tab and select the Date field as your dimension.

3. Modify the Date field in the dimension by hovering your mouse over the field and clicking the pencil icon. Change the Show As setting from Auto to Year Month. You should see the chart update.

4. Moving down the Data tab, set the breakdown dimension to Category. You will see the chart update with multiple colored lines corresponding to various category values.

5. Set the Metric field to ABS Amount. Again, the chart will update. It looks as if there is some useful information on the chart now! Setting the metric will probably change our sort order, however, so our dates along the bottom of the chart will be out of order.

6. Fix the date display by setting the Sort field to Year Month and changing the value from Descending to Ascending. This puts the dates in order and redraws the chart to correspond with it.

7. On the Data tab, select the Apply Filter check box in the Interactions section.

Interactions work a bit differently in a line chart than with other charts. When you are in View mode, clicking a dimension label in the legend will filter the line chart and all the other components to that dimension value. Clicking and dragging the mouse inside the table lets the user pick a range of x-axis values, which in this case are dates.

One limitation here is that you cannot use both interactive filter methods at the same time on the same chart. This is another reason to add the standard filter controls in order to make it possible to isolate specific dimension and metric values.

Onward to the table setup!

Step 8. Tables, Again!? Setting Up the Table

By now, you should be getting the hang of setting up tables. Each time we set up a chart that you have seen before, I'll provide fewer details, unless there is something new that you haven't previously experienced. If you are jumping ahead in the chapters, you may want to review the original table setup instructions in Chapters 2 and 3 if you need help.

Note the setting of the Secondary sort field in the steps that follow. This helps keep the values in descending order for each category listed.

Setting Up the Data Tab

1. Select Table from the Add A Chart drop-down menu.

2. Place the table in the lower center of the canvas.

3. Set the table dimensions: Transaction Type, Memo, and Category.

4. Set the Metric field to ABS Amount.

5. Click the Show Summary Row check box.

6. Set the Sort field to Category, Ascending.

7. Set the Secondary sort field to ABS Amount, Descending.

8. Set Apply Filter in the Interactions section.

Setting Up the Style Tab

1. Click Table Header/Wrap Text.

2. Deselect Table Body/Row Numbers and click Wrap Text.

3. Deselect Table Footer/Show Pagination.

4. Set Metrics/Column 1 type as Bar, select the dark purple color, and click the Show Number and Compact Numbers check boxes.

Now that the table is set up, we can finish the report by adding standard filter controls to its right side.

Adding and Configuring Filter Controls

Step 9. Fun with Filters: Setting Up the Standard Filter Controls

As we mentioned at the beginning of this chapter, both the interactive chart filters and the standard filter controls are extremely useful for data exploration. They nicely complement each other in terms of design, interaction, and flexibility.

> **NOTE**   Interactive chart filtering is a relatively new Data Studio feature, introduced in early November 2018. Back in the old days, we only had standard filter controls for our reports. Several clever hacks were developed to simulate some of the interactive chart functions, but they were difficult to implement and hard to replicate.
>
> Interactive charts provide more design flexibility, but as far as functionality, the standard filter controls can do everything a chart filter can do and more.

Similar to our work with the scorecards in Chapter 1, we'll start with a single filter, copy that filter, and vary it to speed up the development. We'll start with the Memo filter on the top-right side of the example report.

1. Select the Filter control from the edit toolbar, as shown in Figure 4.20. As with the other chart and graphic elements, you can click and drag it on the canvas to position it.

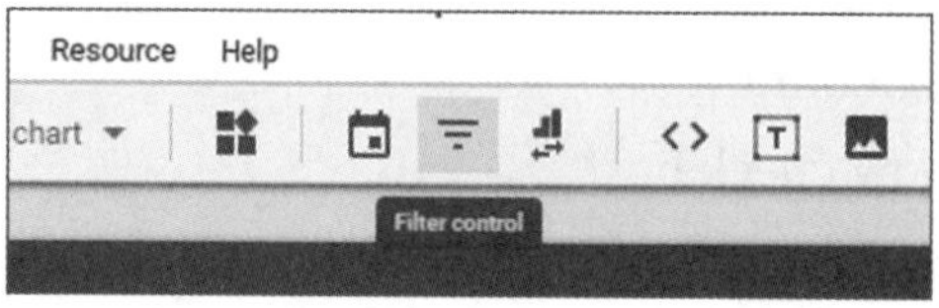

Figure 4.20: Adding a filter control component

Once you have positioned the filter, you will need to configure it in the same way charts are configured, starting with the Data tab. In this case, we don't need to make any Style adjustments.

2. Change the Dimension field to Memo.

3. Change Metric to ABS Amount.

4. Moving on to the next filter, instead of repeating the same procedure, simply highlight the Memo filter and use Ctrl+C and Ctrl+V to create a copy of the component. Use the arrow keys to position the selected control underneath the Memo filter. Continue the setup on the Data tab.

5. Set up the new control by first changing Dimension to Transaction Type.

6. Delete the Metric field. We don't need it here!

7. Select the Style tab, and in the Filter Control section, click the Fixed Size radio button and select Enable Search Box. You will see that the selector now looks more like a table than a drop-down selector.

8. Back on the canvas, drag the bottom of the Filter control down to expose the check box selections for Withdrawal and Deposits. This combination of settings is appropriate where there are a small number of potentially important values to select from. In this case, it plays the same role as our pie chart filter. Moving on, we'll create the longer filter box for Categories.

9. Press Ctrl+C to copy the filter box and paste a new copy by pressing Ctrl+V. Using the arrow keys, position the top of the new filter box just under the previous filter. Now set up the Data tab.

10. Back on the Data tab for the new filter, change Dimension to Category.

11. Set Metric to ABS Amount.

12. Switch to the Style tab, and in the Filter Control section, click the Enable Search Box check box.

13. On the canvas, drag the bottom of the Filter control down to the bottom of the report to expose more categories.

With the filters in place, our workbench is complete! Let's look at how we might share this workbench with Chris, the account owner. We want to share it specifically with Chris and allow him to modify the report if he wants to do so. Let's step through the sharing setup:

1. Click the sharing icon at the top right of the main header while in View mode. This opens the Share With Others dialog. Figure 4.21 shows the setup just before we clicked the Send button.

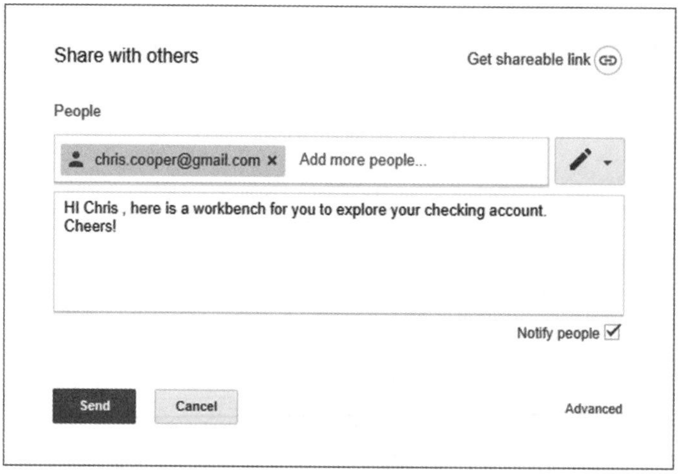

Figure 4.21: Sharing the report for editing

2. Enter Chris's email address in the People field. Note that the pencil icon is showing in the drop-down menu. We could set Sharing to View Only here, which would limit Chris to viewing the report only. Direct sharing is limited to Google accounts here, so you must enter an email that is backed by Google.

3. Enter a message for all the people with whom you are sharing, and by default, they'll receive an email message notifying them that they have been invited to share a Google Data Studio report.

4. Click the Send button to send the sharing invitation and close the dialog.

Tips for Using Interactive Filters

Filters are the primary way that users explore in Data Studio, and we'll include them in most of our examples. Data Studio is not just a new tool for creating visualizations and reporting; it is also a new medium for users to interact with data. Users will not be completely familiar with the way that interactions work in a report. In later chapters, we'll look at ways to annotate reports in order to guide the audience's attention to certain insights and to help them in their own exploration.

Let's examine some filter behavior using our new example workbench. First, the following are some high-level observations:

■ When a page loads, all filters have all items selected by default.

■ Each selector has its own check box in the header next to the dimension label.

- There is no global reset to start from scratch. The fastest way to reset all of the page is to reload it. Resetting individual selectors is a minor task in our current example, but on a workbench with dozens of filters, it is time consuming.

- By default, there is no way to save selections that you have made. Later, we'll look at how to save a set of selections for follow-up use and sharing.

- Selections made in filters affect all charts by default.

- Selections made in any filter may also affect other filters and restrict selections in those filters. This is handy in that it allows the user to "drill down." For instance, selecting Automotive on the Category filter restricts the selection in the drop-down Memo filter. However, if we select items from the Memo filter, this also restricts the categories shown, even if we reset the Category filter.

Find the Answers: Filter Challenge

Now let's look at some filtering tasks and break down how to do them with our workbench. As you go through these tasks, they become more complex. Assume that we're starting with a freshly loaded page. Remember, one way to clear all the filter values is to reload the page.

1. Using the Category filter, hover your mouse over the Transfer selection. You will see a small box pop up labeled "Only" on the right side of the selection, as shown in Figure 4.22. Clicking this box will select the single item.

Figure 4.22: Using the Only setting on a filter

2. If a single item in a list is selected, you can reset the filter by deselecting that item. If multiple items are selected, you can reset by clicking the select check box in the header of the control.

3. Using the Category filter, deselect the Housing check box. All charts and filters will be updated. Excluding items from selection cannot be done with the interactive chart filters.

4. Filter for memos containing the word "mole."

   a. First, click the Memo filter to expand it.

   b. Deselect all items using the Header check box.

   c. Type **mole** in the search box. Note that searches are not case sensitive.

   d. Click the Header check box to select all the mole items. Note that the charts and other filters are updated, and the header shows that three items are selected.

5. Filter Memos containing "dog" or "water" (or both) in the categories Pets and Shopping, and find the most expensive item.

   a. Click the Memo filter to expand it.

   b. Deselect all items using the Header check box.

   c. Type **dog** in the search box.

   d. Click the Header check box to select all the dog items, and the header will show that 11 items were selected.

   e. Clear the search box by clicking the x on the right, as shown in Figure 4.23.

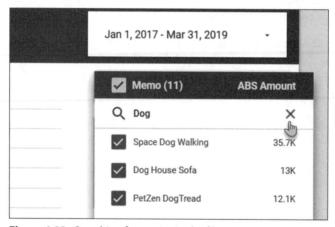

Figure 4.23: Searching for entries in the filter

   f. Enter **water** in the search box. Note that the entry for Dog Sparkling Water is already selected.

   g. Click the select button in the header to deselect all the current water entries, and you will see the total in the header change to 10.

h. Click the Header check box again to select all the water entries currently shown. The number of entries now changes to 15. Clicking the canvas will collapse the Memo Filter box.

i. Click the Pets Only selector in the Category filter.

j. Select the Shopping Category check box.

k. In the Detail table, click the column header for ABS Amount to sort the entries by value. Normally, you would think that this would bring the most expensive item to the top of the list, but you can immediately tell from the length of the bars that there must be another value that is higher than those visible.

l. Scroll down the table to find the hidden value. The largest value is hidden due to the fact that the table is first sorted by Category name and then by ABS Amount. Scrolling down the table, it is easy to see from the length of the bar that Closet Water Slide is the largest expenditure, as shown in Figure 4.24. This category ordering is primary and causes the Shopping item to go to the bottom of the list. Even when using the ABS Amount column to sort, the category sort is primary.

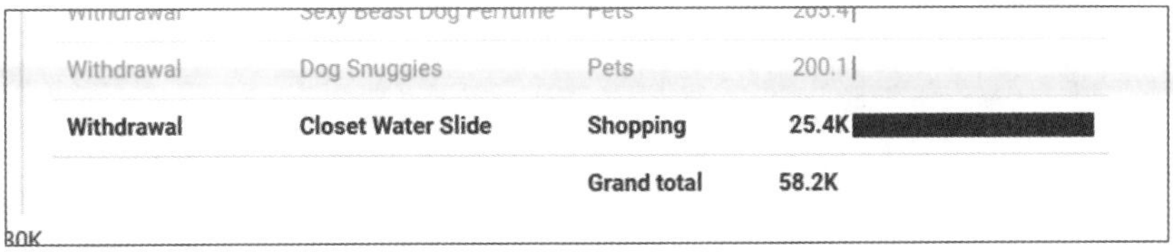

Withdrawal	Sexy Beast Dog Perfume	Pets	203.4
Withdrawal	Dog Snuggies	Pets	200.1
Withdrawal	Closet Water Slide	Shopping	25.4K
		Grand total	58.2K

Figure 4.24: Largest expenditure answer hidden at bottom of table

Summary

In this chapter, we built a "workbench," which is a Data Studio report built for data exploration with different filtering methods for interactivity. We followed the cooking analogy from Chapter 2 to build the new report with a shared file as our data set. We covered the following Data Studio concepts:

Workbenches for data exploration: We incorporated interactive elements that allow the user to filter the data in different ways.

Using a shared resource: We used a Google Sheet that was then shared to create a data source without the need to store the file on our own Google Drive.

Creating calculated fields: We added an extra dimension and metric in Data Studio without modifying the original data set.

Reusing elements: We copied header elements from earlier reports to maintain a consistent style.

New chart types: We implemented pie, bar, and line charts in our report.

Interactive chart filtering: We set up the charts to be used as filters.

Filter controls: We covered the basics of setting up and using filter controls in reports for data exploration.

In the next few chapters, you'll use what you've learned so far. We'll move away from our checking account examples using Google Sheets as data sources to explore "live" data connections and work with services that support website owners and local businesses.

Part

II

Business and Marketing Applications

In This Part

Web Data Visualization with Google Analytics

We start a new series of chapters now that will explore data visualization for website usage data. In 2019, it was estimated that more than half the world's population used the Internet (see `https://techjury.net/blog/how-many-websites-are-there`). There are millions of active websites on the Internet and even more blogs. Google, the dominant search engine in most areas of the world, states that they are aware of about 130 trillion web pages! Why look at website data?

- Almost every business has a web presence.
- Large numbers of nonbusiness organizations have websites.
- A large number of brick-and-mortar businesses and locations of interest now have Google My Business listings.
- Google Data Studio reports they are a type of web page.

We can probably agree that the web is ubiquitous and relatable. Along with all of these web pages and web users comes the desire and ability to measure digital usage. Indeed, data from Internet interactions provides an enormously rich source of information for analysis and visualization.

Google Services for Websites and Business

All websites and web pages have a purpose intended by their creators. Organizations can benefit from a better understanding of how their audience is using their web property, so insights are valuable here. Somewhat surprisingly, the smallest organization is likely to be collecting data with the same tools used by the largest enterprises to help make sense of all this data.

We'll be discussing three new sources of data in this and the upcoming chapters. Each of these sources has its own web interface for viewing and working with its own set of data but can also be used with Data Studio.

Google Analytics   *Google Analytics (GA)* is a service provided free for website owners to help them collect, store, and then view web usage data by their visitors. We'll be diving into Google Analytics data for a number of reasons:

It is estimated that GA is installed on 56 percent of websites and 85 percent of sites that use measurement software. As far as measurement services go, GA dominates the market. If you do wind up working with web data, GA is likely to be the source. See `https://w3techs.com/technologies/ overview/traffic_analysis/all`.

Although Data Studio works well with over 100 data sources, it was literally made for working with GA data. The product is managed by the Google Analytics development team. The data connectors provided by Google work extremely well.

There is a free, live sample account available for use. Every Data Studio account has access to this live connector. This fictitious account for a Google merchandise store has thousands of simulated users daily, and all of the measurements are updated in real time. The data collected is representative of a real site.

In terms of learning some of the capabilities of Data Studio, it is ideal because it is rich in dimensions and metrics.

Google Search Console   Google Analytics gets most of the attention, but Google *Search Console (SC)* provides vital services and information for website owners. Formerly known as *Webmaster Tools*, Search Console provides a direct communication link with Googles search services.

Whereas GA provides data on visitor usage while on the site, Search Console provides information about how prospective visitors are using Google Search to find the site. This is vital information for website owners as search visits often make up the largest source of traffic coming to a site. I'll cover this service in a bit more depth in the next chapter.

Google My Business   The *Google My Business* service provides control and tracking of information about "entities" on the web. *Entities* is a fancy term used to describe businesses and locations that exist somewhere. To Google, your local restaurant is an entity that has a physical location, a phone number, an address, and other characteristics, and it may fall under several categories, such as "Italian Restaurant," "Ethic Food," "Casual Dining," and so on.

As a web searcher, you see these entities in Google search or Google Maps results when you search for restaurants. Instead of just a link to the restaurant's website, a "knowledge panel" may be displayed showing the business's hours, reviews, specials, menus, and other information.

Business owners can "claim" their listing with Google by automated phone service or postcard verification. Once an owner has claimed a listing, they have some control over what is shown on it. They also get data from this service about how searchers are interacting with their listing. Again, I'll get into more detail about this increasingly important service when I cover Google My Business in Chapter 7, "Viewing Local Organization Data from Google My Business."

Consider the perspective of a manager of a small local business, say an Irish pub, which hosts live music events. The manager should be very interested in how people are searching for this business, what they see about the establishment in the knowledge panel, and the events that they can view when they visit the website.

Unfortunately for the manager, each of these tools has different, separate reporting interfaces. It's tough for larger businesses, let alone busy managers, to monitor and analyze the information that each of these holds.

Data Studio was designed to help in such cases. After going through how to generate a report with each of these tools, we'll look at a unified dashboard that could help small business owners keep up to date and take advantage of this data.

First let's jump into Google Analytics, learn a bit more about it, and see how we can leverage some experts' reports!

WHAT ABOUT SOCIAL MEDIA?

You certainly can connect to social media properties with Data Studio! I decided not to address reporting for Facebook, Instagram, Snapchat, Reddit, and so on in this book. Although you can usually pull up pretty decent information into Google Sheets from these services for analysis, there are currently no free connectors for these services. We'll look at an example using Twitter later on in the book, but that will be a special case.

Premium live connectors that work very well are available, but since this book is designed for beginners, it's unlikely that you will want to spend the money just to try them out. Reporting on social media and digital advertising is the realm of in-house marketing teams and digital marketing agencies. They are happy to spend money on premium services because it saves them so much time when reporting to clients.

Another factor besides looming deadlines and the difficulties and cost of keeping up with multiple vendors is the fact that most digital marketing applications will follow a pattern similar to the ones we'll be reviewing here. That is one of the benefits of Data Studio. It functions in very similar ways across many different data sources. If you are in a position to spend some money on connector services, you can find just about anything you need by searching the Data Studio Connectors page at `https://datastudio.google.com/data`.

A Brief Primer for Google Analytics

We use Google Analytics for reporting in this chapter, but this is not a book about Google Analytics! Still, unlike with the bank account examples, there may be concepts and terminology with which you may not be familiar. Therefore, a brief explanation of what Google Analytics does, how it works, and how it organizes data will be helpful for those not familiar with the service.

---

owner installs code
site data to Google flies
view charts insights wake!

Google Analytics Haiku, Helpfullee

If that explanation works for you, skip to the next section! If not, a slightly more expanded explanation is in order.

When you go to a website that uses Google Analytics, a small piece of special code is installed on every page. When the page loads in your browser, the code executes and causes information to be sent back to the Google Analytics measurement service. The raw data is stored in massive databases, and a unique GA ID code connects the site's account to data being prepared for use by the site owner.

If you are browsing while logged into your Google account, a non-identifying Google user ID may be sent along with the rest of the information. These IDs are used to pull general demographics like gender, age range, and even general interests.

When the site owner wants data about their website, they use the Google Analytics service. They can see only their own data for their own properties or properties to which they have been granted access to view by another Analytics account owner. A typical view of the Google Analytics service is shown in Figure 5.1.

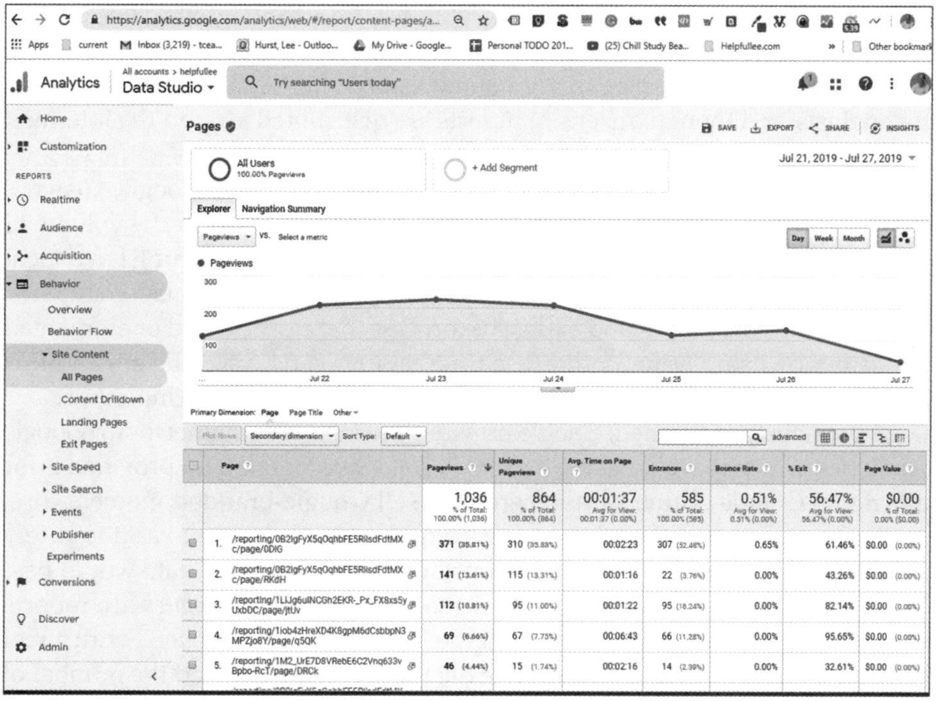

Figure 5.1: A typical Google Analytics view

What kind of information can you see? The days of the little page counter of the 1990s are long gone. There are over 500 standard dimension and metrics fields available! As you can see in Figure 5.1, dozens of reports are available in the interface. To simplify, these fields are grouped in the following areas:

Pageviews *Pageviews* is "hit"-level data. It provides information about the page viewed. There are other hit-level measures, such as events that may be collected when you click a form's Submit button. By default, when you view a web page, a lot of information gets collected from your request and browser.

Sessions A *session* is basically a group of pageviews. Analytics assigns a session ID code when you visit a site, and it can group all of the hit-level events and pageview data under a session. If you leave a site for some time and come back later, you will start a new Google Analytics session. Session-level information gives us an idea of how the user is interacting with the site at a specific time.

Users Basically, a *user* has sessions and the sessions have pageviews. The sessions are tied together with a user ID. This gives us information about how often people actually return to the site. It should be noted that Google does not allow site owners to collect *personally identifiable information (PII)* about their users through the Google Analytics data collection process.

The main purpose of the Google Analytics service is to allow site owners to see trends and patterns that let them understand the audience and the performance of the site without drowning in a sea of raw data. While Analytics is a great tool for analysis, and though dozens of reports are distributed around the interface, they are seldom used directly for reporting.

It is not practical, or advisable, to send people unfamiliar with Google Analytics into the interface to retrieve information. It is easy to get lost in the volume of reports available. Indeed, most agencies that deal in digital marketing have spent a lot of time taking the insights from GA and creating their own custom reports. This is a time-consuming and expensive process that can be eased or eliminated altogether by using Data Studio. The time savings can be significant, and this allows analysts to spend more time analyzing instead of preparing reports.

As previously mentioned, Google provides a sample data connector for Google Analytics, which is available to all users of Data Studio. The data provided is for a fictional Google online store where they sell Google-branded merchandise. Although this is "fictitious" data, it is roughly representational and is surely "live"; in other words, it is updated constantly as real website data would be.

This sample data source is used for many templates. *Templates* are reports that are shared with the public so that they can be copied and used with a real GA data source. Over time, the sample data source has increased the number of templates being shared. While individuals may want to share their reports with the general public, few organizations would want to open their data sources to public view and analysis. For the most part, using the sample account takes care of this issue.

Nonetheless, there are limitations on the sample data sources that Google provides. Though they are certainly useful, Google is the owner of these connectors and they do not provide edit control for general users. This means you cannot add calculated fields directly and reuse them as we did with the checking account examples. Once you copy a templated report and use your own data source, you are free to augment that with your own fields. We'll look at doing just that in Chapter 6, "Using Google Search Console for Audience Insights."

Using a Template to Create a New Report

One reason for the rapid adoption of Google Data Studio is because of its ability to share a report as a template. As you saw in Chapter 3, "Enhancing Basic Graphs," it is easy to copy and reuse your own template, but you can also use other people's reports.

This is particularly true for Google Analytics because everyone basically has the same set of fields with which to work. The standard Data Studio connectors provided by Google always have the same metrics and dimensions. This means that using a report with your own GA data source becomes a simple matter of copying the report and swapping your GA data source into the report.

For this example, we'll select a template report from the Data Studio Template Gallery as our starting point. Returning once again to the basic cooking analogy to set up our example report, there is not a lot of preparation to do here. This is kind of like looking in the freezer and finding a frozen pizza. We'll select the Acme Marketing template from the main Data Studio home page, as shown in Figure 5.2.

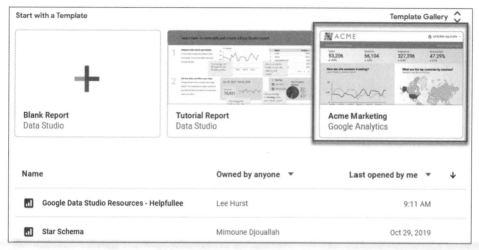

Figure 5.2: The example template on the home screen

In this case, the report is already made, and we are going to use the data connector provided with the template. The data set is the Google Analytics data from Google's demo store site.

Preparation of the ingredients has already been done. The Data Source connector for the demo account has already been created, and it is connected to the report. With the report already constructed, there is no step required to assemble the ingredients either.

After we copy the report, we'll be making changes. If you think about the cooking analogy, this might be the equivalent to adding your own toppings to a frozen pizza.

When you select the template, it will open as a report, as shown in Figure 5.3.

Before we copy and modify this report, let's take a moment to appreciate it. This was one of the first reports built by the Google Analytics team to showcase their product, and it is a prime example of how to build a quality report. Here's why:

- A lot of information is included but doesn't feel crowded.
- Colors are consistent, and only a few colors in different shades are used.
- The team used subtle background shading to keep sections distinct and easy for the eye to focus on.
- There are helpful headers explaining the sections.

Figure 5.3: The Acme Marketing template

- A variety of charts are used to highlight specific information.

- The speed at which the report loads is fantastic. The sample site has over 300,000 pageviews! That's a lot of data to summarize, but you'll notice that there was very little lag time in loading.

Let's take a look at some of the details.

Template Header   At the very top, you'll see a special header bar. The Use Template button can be added to reports using a special URL. You'll see how to use reports that are not specifically set up as templates in the next section. Don't worry, it's easy!

Report Header   You've seen the Date Range control before, so we won't dwell on that component. There is an additional component in the header called a *data control*. The data control allows the viewer to connect certain specific data sources on the fly without having to copy the report. In this case, the control extends the use of the report for *any* Google Analytics account to which the user has access. For example, Figure 5.4 shows the GA accounts that I could access when I click the selector. This is a tremendous way to extend the usability of a report. We'll look at this control in depth a bit later on.

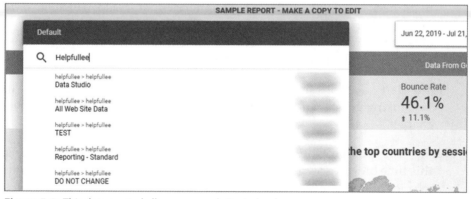

Figure 5.4: This data control allows any analytics to load.

WARNING   Note that a user must be logged into a Google account to view the data selector. If you are not logged in while viewing the report, this control does not display. If you have multiple Google accounts, this can also be confusing as the control will show only GA accounts related to the Google account under which you are logged in.

Lastly, in the header color bar, we see the title text and an indication of where the data for the report is coming from.

Scorecards   We saw these in our previous examples. In this case, they are showing gains and losses over the previous time period. As discussed in the brief explanation of how Google Analytics is used, we see Users, Sessions, Pageviews, and Bounce Rate. Each has its own measure here.

The metric called *Bounce Rate* measures the number of site visits that view only one page, do not have any interactions, and leave. Usually, a high bounce rate indicates a poor user experience, but there are exceptions.

Time Series   In this case, the chart is showing sessions over the last 30 days as compared to the previous 30 days. Note how the comparison line is not quite in sync. We'll fix this issue after we copy the report.

Bar Chart   This one shows sessions and pageviews by marketing channel. Marketing channels group different sources together. In this case, a *source* is how the visitor came to the site. For instance, if the user was on Facebook and clicked a link to the site, the source would be Facebook and the channel would be social. If the user clicks on an ad for a company and goes to the company website, that session gets logged under the channel Paid Search - Branded. Organic Search channel sessions indicate the visit came from search engine results.

Donut Chart   This is a variation of the pie chart showing a breakdown of male and female users.

Stacked Bar Chart   This is a variation of the bar chart. We saw stacking used in the hack in Chapter 4, "Data Exploration with Interactive Elements," to give each bar a different color. Here it is employed for its intended use. It breaks down each bar with a second dimension—in this case, gender—and it packs a lot of information into a small space.

World Map   Data Studio has some mapping capabilities that are helpful in visualizing geographic data. We'll be investigating some of these in this chapter.

Table   This table provides yet another way to look at sessions and pageviews, this time broken down by country. It has some additional styling options to color odd- and even-numbered rows differently in order to make it a bit easier to read.

We are going to update this report. A lot of new capabilities have been added since it was created, and we'll make use of them in our copy.

Building the Google Analytics Report

We'll step through the process of using the template and modifying it for our own use.

1. Click the Use Template button located on the upper-right side of the report to open the Copy This Report dialog. It shows you Original Data Source and New Data Source as [Sample] Google Analytics Data, as you can see in Figure 5.5. Click the Copy Report button to accept these settings.

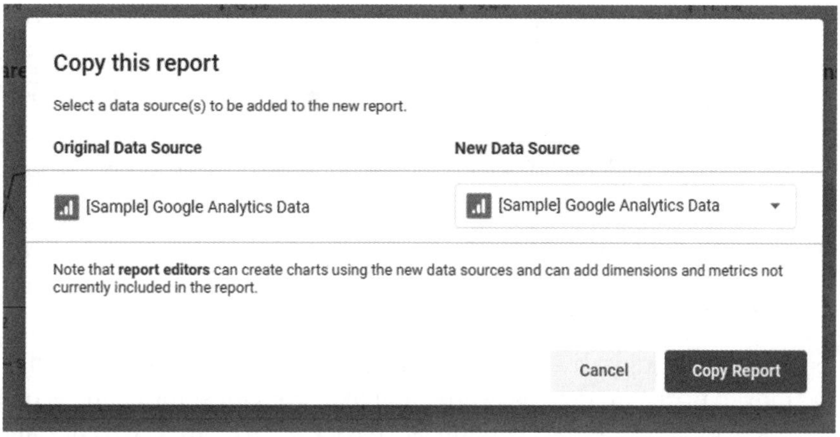

Copy this report

Select a data source(s) to be added to the new report.

Original Data Source	New Data Source
[Sample] Google Analytics Data	[Sample] Google Analytics Data ▾

Note that **report editors** can create charts using the new data sources and can add dimensions and metrics not currently included in the report.

Cancel   Copy Report

Figure 5.5: Copying a report with current settings

2. As in our previous examples, when you copy a report, the new report opens with the title changed to remind you that this is a copy. Rename the report with the title of this example: **Google Analytics - Hands On Data Studio Example 4.0**.

3. Remove some artifacts that you won't need in your copy. Click the text SAMPLE REPORT – MAKE A COPY TO EDIT to select that text box. Press the Delete key, and it will be removed. Then do the same for the light gray-colored box that was behind the text. Just select and delete it.

4. We'll keep the current light blue–colored banner, but we need to position it differently. Select the banner and position it at the top of the page. After this is in place, slide the new Data Control selector over next to the Date Range control. Select and delete the box containing "Marketing Website Summary"; you will replace it with your own title.

5. Now we'll use the copy procedure that we used in previous chapters to bring in the title box and logo from the checking account example. First, open the Data Studio home page in another tab. As you'll recall, you can do this easily by right-clicking the Data Studio icon in the upper-left part of the report next to the title and selecting Open Link In New Tab. Locate your original example report, select it, and switch to edit view if needed. Press Ctrl+right-click to select the title text and the logo, as shown in Figure 5.6.

   Copy the selection to the clipboard, switch back to your current report, and paste the elements. Since this is a web report, we'll change the title to reflect a fictitious site for Christopher Cooper. Select the text box and click inside to edit the text.

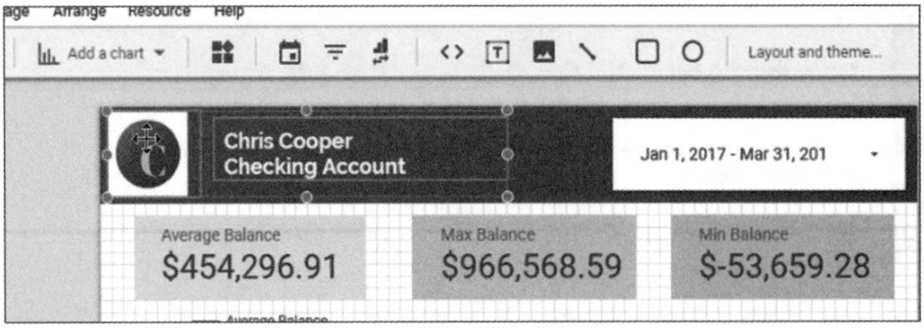

Figure 5.6: Copying elements from existing reports

6. Next, we'll adjust the location of the Scorecard group. We would like these moved up just under the header to make room for some changes that we'll make to the map chart later on. An easy way to do this is to click and drag directly through all of the scorecards to select all the cards as well as the background color box. Then, use the arrow keys to slide the entire group up into place just below the header.

Once you are done with sliding things around, you'll probably want to do some minor position tweaking to get it to look like Figure 5.7.

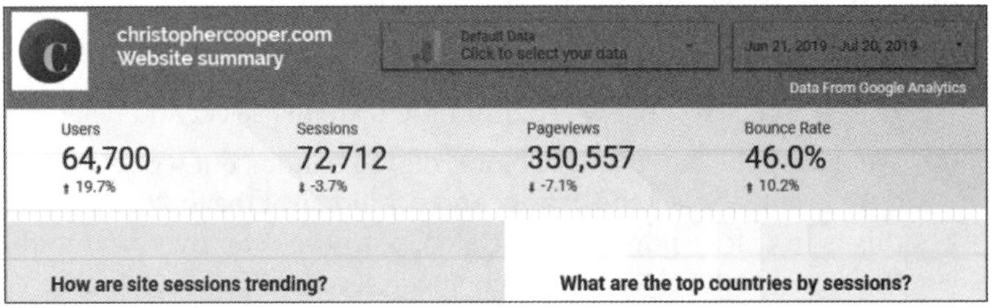

Figure 5.7: Top of report customized

Modifying the Charts

We could simply stop here with our example. We now have a customized report based on the template. Instead, let's add some new features and make this report more interactive. You can think of this as adding your own toppings to the plain frozen pizza!

We won't be making any visible changes to the time-series chart that shows sessions. However, we'd like to make this chart show the current and previous time periods lined up. Quite often, you'll find patterns in web data that follow weekly cycles where the traffic differs quite a bit from weekdays to weekend days, as seen here.

Instead of adjusting the chart itself, we'll adjust the default time period settings in the Date Range control at the top right of the page. We'll start the step-by-step chart modification with this update.

1. Select the Date Range control, and in the Data panel, you'll see that the Default Date Range drop-down menu is set to Last 30 Days (Exclude Today). Click the drop-down and change the setting to Last 28 Days and click the Apply button, as shown in Figure 5.8. You'll immediately see the lines on the chart sync up nicely. This is important, as the comparison is designed to help you see differences in the patterns, and if they are out of sync, it just becomes a distraction.

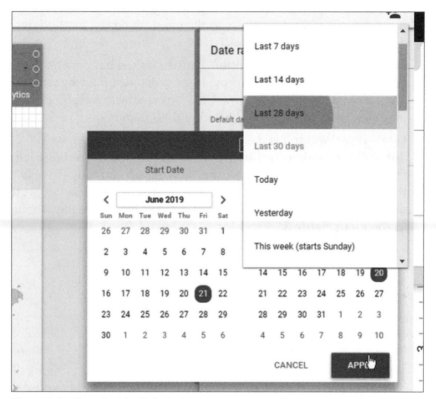

Figure 5.8: Changing the default date range

THE IMPORTANCE OF SYNCING

Comparison charts are designed to allow the user to see differences in the patterns. Synching time periods is important—if the comparison period is out of sync, the line patterns just become distracting noise.

This isn't just for looks either. I have seen several percentage point swings in sales data due to this kind of misalignment. If you find your metrics for something like sales are up one month and down the next, it's a good idea to check your comparison period alignment before reporting on the performance of your sales team!

It can take a lot of messing around in the standard Google Analytics interface to get the periods to line up correctly. The ability to fine-tune the date ranges in Data Studio is a welcome improvement.

2. Set the time-series chart to use interactive filtering. We'll make one change to the actual chart—we'll add the Interactions Filter option. As you've seen earlier, this is easy to implement. Simply select the chart, scroll down the Data panel, and select the Interactions check box for the Apply filter.

3. Moving down the left side of the report, we'll make the same minor changes to the bar chart for engagement. This chart needs no changes to speak of visually, but we'd like to add the ability to filter the other charts on the page by the channels listed here. Again, instead of adding a separate filter control, we'll add interactivity to the chart using the method described earlier.

4. Set the Interactions Filter option for the stacked bar chart showing age groups and gender. This can provide some detailed filtering when needed. We'll look more closely at how these new interactive features work, and how they work together, at the end of this chapter.

5. While we're working at the bottom-left side of the report, we'll fix up the donut chart. As you can see on your screen, the percentage labels for the different genders are not quite showing up correctly. To take care of this issue, select the donut chart and switch to its Style tab. At the top of this panel, you'll find a slider that controls the size of the "donut hole," as shown in Figure 5.9.

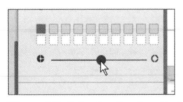

Figure 5.9: Adjusting the donut hole

Slide the control slightly to the left to fill in the hole and expose the full percentage values on the chart. To finish off the donut chart, switch to the Data tab and, as before, select the Interactions Filter option.

6. For the Country table, we'll simply select and add the Interactions Filter option as we have done for the previous charts. This will allow the table to work as a country filter.

Finally, we come to the Map graph! We are going to do some extra modifications here. Data Studio has recently added the ability to "drill down" on many charts. This means that the user has some control to narrow the focus of a chart. In the case of visualizing geographic data, this means going from a world view to a subregion like a country, and even further to a city level.

Data Studio mapping features are crude compared to many visualization tools, particularly ones that specialize in the visualization of geographic data. However, the ability to show any geographic representations of data, and the ability to drill down—even with basic implementations—opens up new avenues for the user to gain insights.

To add drill-down capabilities to the map, follow these steps:

1. We start our map manipulation by selecting the map chart. Click the Style tab, and at the very bottom of the panel, you'll find the Chart Header section. Currently, the default setting here is Show On Hover. Use the drop-down menu to change this to Always Show. This will allow the user always to see the drill-down controls once we activate some more dimensions.

2. Switch to the Data tab. You'll see that Dimension is set to Country. Note that geographic fields have the small globe icon on the left side. This means that the metric, in this case Sessions, will be displayed at a country level on the map. You can see this in action by looking at the world map where there is a color indicator that shows the United States in a much darker color, indicating more sessions.

   Before we change settings, note that Zoom Area is set to World. If you click this area, you'll get a selection of different geographic ranges from which to choose, as shown in Figure 5.10. You can use this to set a chart to a specific region. With GA data, it is possible to set this down to a region level. This will work with most countries, and for the United States, it allows you to isolate the display for a particular state. For now, we'll leave the Zoom Area setting at World.

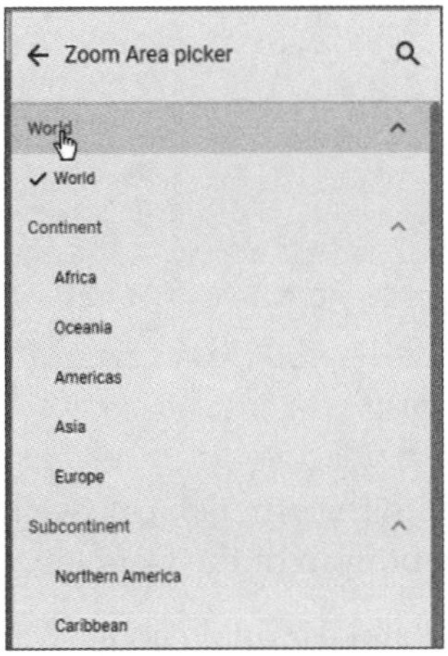

Figure 5.10: Geographic Zoom Area options

3. Return to the Dimension area to set the drill-down fields. Clicking the slide control next to the Drill Down label will cause the Continent, Sub Continent, and City fields to be added to the Dimension list. This will likely cause your chart to break and show a very nasty-looking system error message in place of the chart. This situation is shown in Figure 5.11. Don't worry about this!

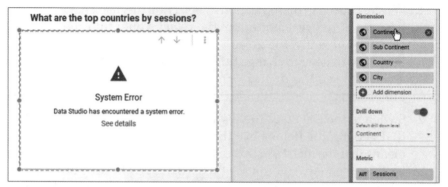

Figure 5.11: System error on the map chart

4. To fix and restore the map, remove the Continent and Sub Continent fields from the list by hovering over these fields and clicking the X symbol for each field. The default drill-down level should still be set to Country. Figure 5.12 shows the settings and the restored map chart.

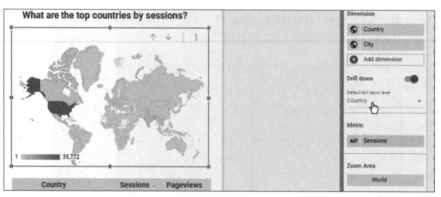

Figure 5.12: Removing the dimensions restores the map.

5. We have one last function to set here. As with the other charts, we'll turn on the chart Interactive Filter option at the bottom of the Data tab.

With the last settings in place, you may want to take a final run at tweaking the positions of charts to your satisfaction. Now we can move on and see how to make use of our new report.

Working with the New Report

Looking at your new masterpiece, you may be wondering why we made all those changes, since the report looks pretty much the same. Indeed, if this was intended as a simple monthly report, we could have left it alone and called it a day.

Adding interactivity to a report assumes enabling the user to have certain degrees of freedom to explore the data that is presented. This can be a good thing: letting users explore the data gives them a greater intuitive understanding of the relationships between the dimensions. It lets them look for areas of interest and ask their own questions. Finally, they are more likely to trust the answers when they find them on their own.

Making everything interactive, however, may provide more freedom than you want to give to a user. Too much freedom can cause users to get lost, exploring random combinations of filters and never getting much done in the way of finding useful information or gaining insight. Just because you can add more capabilities doesn't mean that you should.

If a static report is one extreme, the other is handing your audience the raw data or sending them to the Google Analytics interface and asking them to go find their own insights. In some sense, providing too much freedom is an abdication of a report creator's responsibility to guide the audience to an insight.

As the report creator, it is up to you to gauge what levels of interaction will be useful for your audience. Sometimes, a static PDF is appropriate, whereas at other times, the simple Date Range selector is enough to allow users some freedom and still keep them focused.

Another consideration to keep in mind here is that we just added a lot of interactive power to this report, but it looks essentially the same as when we started. Some people may start clicking away to explore the possibilities; others may yawn and think it's just another nice, standard-issue report. Not everyone is used to working with interactive features.

In later chapters, we'll look at ways to annotate reports to help shine a light on areas of interest and give more instructions for use.

A Real-World Example: The Effects of a Beach Party in Spain on Web Traffic

Now we'll explore using all of interactive features. To make things more interesting, I will use the data control to select my own real—not fake—Google Analytics account. I'll take you through the process of finding some insights, step by step, so that you can see how the process works.

Using Exploration to Find Patterns

1. I make sure that I am in view mode—filters are not functional in edit mode.

2. Since I am logged in, I have access to all my Google Analytics properties, so I search for my website and select it, as shown in Figure 5.13. After a moment of loading, all the charts are updated to reflect my data instead of the Sample Google store.

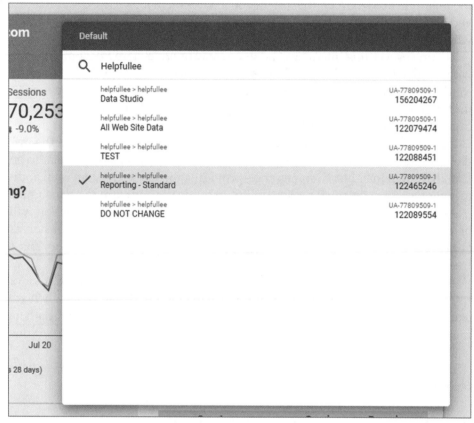

Figure 5.13: Selecting an analytics view from the data control

3. At first, the numbers do not excite me. I see minor losses in the scorecards section. I decide to get some more perspective, so I use the Date Range selector to set a longer time range—in this case, the first half of 2019, January 1 to June 31.

Changing the date range can have a dramatic effect on metrics. Looking at the last 28 days may show increases or decreases that completely disappear or reverse when you increase the time range. That's definitely the case here! See the difference in the metrics when we look at before and after increasing the time range, as shown in Figure 5.14 and Figure 5.15.

Users	Sessions	Pageviews	Bounce Rate
2,009	**2,295**	**2,760**	**80.4%**
↓ -12.3%	↓ -12.9%	↓ -17.6%	↑ 2.5%

Figure 5.14: Scorecards for last 28 days

Users	Sessions	Pageviews	Bounce Rate
11,497	**13,812**	**17,643**	**77.8%**
↑ 213.8%	↑ 201.9%	↑ 189.3%	↓ -3.7%

Figure 5.15: Scorecards for January to June 2019

In life, if you are feeling down at some moment, it's often good to take a broader view and see how far you've come! In this case, the Users comparison score increased from a drop of –12.3 percent to an increase of 213.8 percent. Woo-hoo!

4. Now the question is, "Is this increase in traffic consistent, or is it due to some one-time event?" Let's look at the time-series chart for answers. As you can see in Figure 5.16, the increase over the previous period looks pretty consistent. Some big spikes in traffic show up from the previous period, but 2019 doesn't show as much of this kind of spike.

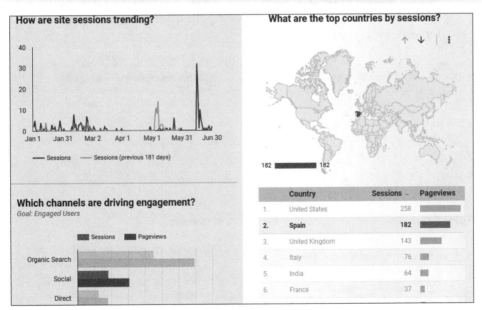

Figure 5.16: Time series for January to June 2019

> **WARNING**   This description shows the case of a *local minimum*. Local minimums without context can deceive! It is only when you are able to "zoom out" that you can see the bigger picture. Many misleading charts focus on a small period of time to show big gains or drops. This is a form of "cherry picking"—that is, the practice of selecting only data that proves your point.
>
> As a data citizen, it's your right to question these kinds of charts and your obligation to protect your audience from falling into these kinds of traps. When working with new data, I like to work with as long of a period of time as possible to see the broader trends. These help to put short-period gains and losses into perspective.

5. Now let's do some drilling down for deeper insights. As the Country table shows, there is a surprisingly high number of sessions from Spain. It's surprising because there are no Spanish pages on my site, at least not yet. Let's isolate Spanish visitors for a closer look. Clicking the Spain row on the table filters the results.

   Two things stand out here. First, there was a large traffic spike on June 15. Second, there seems to be more traffic from Social, relative to other channels.

6. Clicking each of the bars helps to show which channels are contributing to that spike. Figure 5.17 shows that Social is the major contributor, and indeed, selecting Social has moved Spain up the ranks on the country table as well.

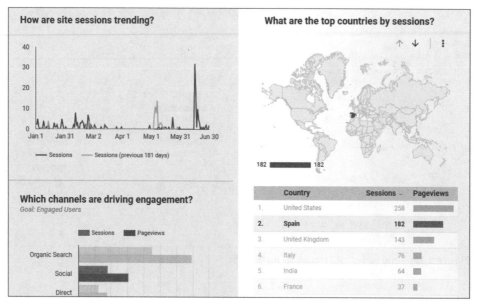

Figure 5.17: Isolating Spain and Social sessions

7. Next, I decide to drill down into Spain to see if I can find more interesting patterns that influenced this spike. Although small on the map, Spain is easy to find when it is selected from the table because it shows up in a deep blue color.

   To drill down, first I click the country on the map and then I use the header arrows to go to the city level. If you hover over the down arrow, a tooltip tells you that clicking here will "Drill down from Country to City." After I click there, the map redraws, zoomed in on Spain only, and it starts to populate city locations.

8. The circles representing locations are colored and sized by the amount of sessions originating in each location. Some locations have many circles packed together so closely that it is impossible to select a single city. Hovering over these clusters causes a magnified view of the area to make selection easier, as shown in Figure 5.18. Clicking a city circle will further filter the rest of the charts down to data associated with that city.

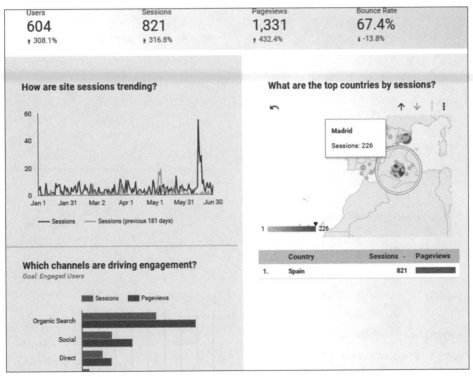

Figure 5.18: Viewing traffic from cities in Spain

9. Clicking the channels in the bar chart and consulting the map of the cities in Spain in conjunction with the time-series chart with the spike reveals a large amount of Direct, Referral, and Social traffic coming from several major cities.

10. Exploring the cities view was fun, but I found no clear patterns to explain the spike here. Next, I decide to isolate just the few days on which the spike occurred, with all of the other settings in place, to see if any other patterns yield a clue.

I could do this by using the Date Range control again, but it is such a bother to set and reset time periods using that control. There's a faster way to do this. I can use the interactive filtering on the time-series chart itself to grab just the range I want.

To do this, I click the chart and drag the mouse over the spike period on the graph. This action highlights just the spike period and filters the rest of the report for this new date range. Very handy!

Now I can immediately see that the Social channel is providing most of the impact over the isolated time range, as shown in Figure 5.19. As we saw before, this is over a larger period of time. Social does not contribute as much as Organic or Direct visits, so this is a tasty insight!

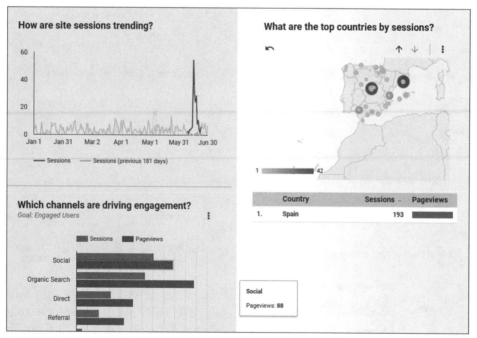

Figure 5.19: Isolating the traffic spike period

Using the Analysis to Answer Questions

After trying to filter further using the different channels, I don't find any other interesting patterns. If this were a larger workbench-style report, I would refine my questions by using even more filters. In that case, I would likely have filters for these dimensions:

Landing Page: The initial page that these people were visiting

Source: Exactly which services were sending traffic

Referral Path: Pages on other sites used to get to my site

Language: Browser default language settings

Although these would be nice, I have enough information to find the cause of the spike in this case. I'm looking for social media references about my website from Spain starting on June 15, 2019.

Searching through my Twitter account, I can see the posts on which I commented. Going back to June 15, 2019, I find the answer I was looking for! See Figure 5.20 for the evidence.

Figure 5.20: Finding the source: a beach party in Spain!

So, the source of my spike was a Spanish beach party? Well, yes, but the party was also a technical conference called SEO On the Beach. SEO is short for search engine optimization, and the conference attendees were enjoying a lovely Spanish island while taking in presentations from industry experts—lucky dogs! I was not fortunate enough be there, but I did have my site mentioned in one of the presentations, as shown in Figure 5.20, and that reference was spread around social media sites, primarily Twitter.

With this the mystery solved, I have some insights that provide opportunity for action:

- There is a sizable audience in Spain that is resonating with what I do on my site.

  Actions: Do more outreach to this community, and perhaps try translating some of my blog posts.

- There are some experts sharing my work, and this has an immediate impact on traffic.

  Actions: Thank the presenters, and investigate whether this spike turns into more steady growth in Spain.

- Much of the traffic came from social media.

  Actions: Connect with more speakers on Twitter and see if this success can be replicated.

- There's a convention on a Spanish beach!

  Action: Book my tickets!

The Limits of Demographic Data from Google Analytics

Before we take our focus away from the current report, it is a good time to check how the filters work with the demographics data charts. First, we'll switch back to the default Google Sample data source. Next, we'll set the date range to start at January 1, 2019, and end on June 30, 2019, using the date range control.

Now we turn our attention to the demographics area of the report. The donut chart for gender is pretty simple: click a segment of the chart, and the rest of the report will be filtered for the selection. In this case, you can select male or female.

The stacked bar chart, showing both age brackets and gender, is a bit more complex. Looking at Figure 5.21, we see that the largest age bracket for the data is the 25–34 range, and we can see a pretty even split between male and female users. Clicking the segment for females on this bar will filter the other tables by female and the age range at the same time.

There is something odd about the demographics data, but you may not notice it if you don't know what you are looking for. For example, hovering your mouse over the donut chart shows that females make up 31.4 percent, with a total of 299,989 members. This sounds reasonable, unless you ask the question 31.4 percent of what? The demographic charts do not say what they are measuring!

You might guess that these charts are measuring users, but the numbers don't add up to the total of the Users scorecard. In fact, the totals of males and females shown by the donut chart add up to 956,121, and this does not match any of the scorecard values.

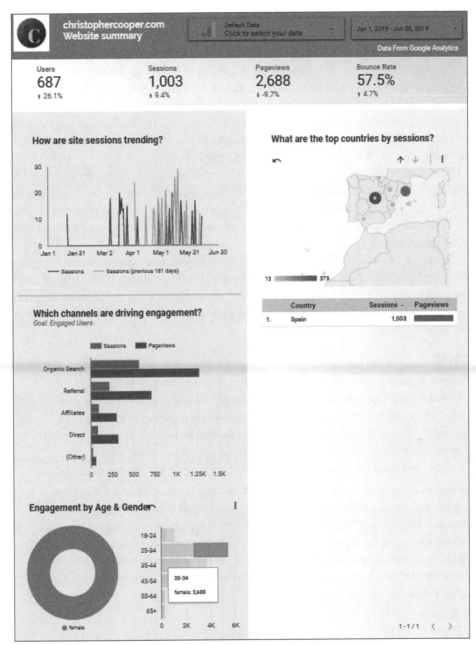

Figure 5.21: Applying an age and gender filter from the stacked bar chart

So, what's going on here? If we inspect these charts in edit mode, we find that they are measuring pageviews. So why doesn't the total of the donut chart add up to the pageviews scorecard value of 1,830,922? Why is it lower by almost 50 percent?

The reason becomes clear if you remember that demographic details like age, gender, and interests are supplemental information added by Google for logged-in users—not all users. These charts show the breakdown only for which data is available, and in this case, data is available for roughly half of the visits.

When a user clicks the bar chart segment for females age 25–34, the entire report has this additional filter applied, and it shows the metric values for only those pageviews that have been tagged with demographic data. Other pageviews may truly fall into these categories, but because the data has not been collected for them, they will not be aggregated into the results.

Therefore, how useful and accurate is this information if it is incomplete? That depends on the view of the report creator, the report viewer, and the intention of the report. If we assume that these are representative of the entire user base, then the information could be valuable to help inform marketing and advertising decisions.

This kind of information allows even small business owners some insights into demographic data about their audience. Until recently, this kind of data was expensive to obtain, and only large corporations with extensive research budgets could afford it. But now this level of analysis is within reach for any size of business.

> **TIP** As complex and far-ranging as Google Analytics appears on the surface, it does not capture all of the information about every visitor. Analytics blockers and other browser plug-ins can stop the collection of data for some users. In the case of eCommerce sites, it would be unwise to use its sales information in place of an accounting system that keeps track of sales—Google Analytics is most certainly not an accounting system! However, it is reliable and complete enough to gain valuable insights and consistent enough to make sound decisions in all but extreme cases.
>
> Privacy concerns limit how demographic information is provided, and it is against the Google terms of use to collect personally identifiable information (PII) directly through the system. This does not diminish the value of this data. Google Analytics gives you one of the clearest views as to what is happening with a web property and how visitors are interacting. Dealing with incomplete and messy data is a fact of life. We must decide how much weight we give to the data and how much we trust it, and then weigh this against its utility.

Now for a Side Dish: Adding a Page and Using Filters

The previous section showed the value of being able to explore and then narrow the focus of a report using chart filtering in a very unrestricted way. As was discussed earlier, it is sometimes appropriate to restrict users to keep them focused on a particular facet of the data. Can we do both? In this section, we'll show one way to restrict the report data in order to keep the user focused on a particular context while maintaining the flexibility of chart filtering.

To do this, we'll create a new page for the report—a side dish if you will. The new page will use the same data as our current report, but we'll restrict it to showing information about a single country, and we'll make some changes in the charts to be consistent with the new geographic boundaries.

Since we focused on Spain in the previous section, we'll use that as our focus country for the new page. Just remember that we are using Google Sample data as our default, so we are unlikely to find anything as exciting as the effect of the beach party on our traffic!

Our first setup steps are to change the data control back to the Default data source from view mode, and then switch to edit mode. Now we can create our new page.

1. Our first task is to create a new page for our focused report. We would like to keep all the charts in place for our new page, so from the main menu, select Page ⇨ Duplicate Page, as shown in Figure 5.22. We're now viewing the new page in edit mode.

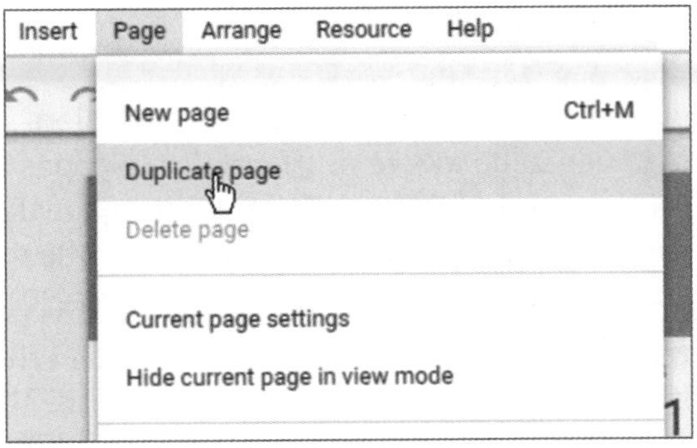

Figure 5.22: Duplicating the main report page

Adding a page to a report changes the toolbar slightly—specifically, the section originally on the far-left side and the option to add a page. It now shows which page we are currently editing. By default, the pages are named for the page number, and our starting page was named Page 1. Our new page is a duplicate of Page 1, so it is named Copy Of Page 1.

2. We would like to change the names of the pages to give users a clearer idea of what they can find on each one. To do this, click the page drop-down in the toolbar, which provides a view of all the pages. From this control, we can perform several page functions. Clicking the three vertical dots on the row for Page 1 exposes the functions Rename, Duplicate, Hide, and Remove Pages. In this case, rename Page 1 to **Summary**. Then, repeat the process to rename the second page **Focus Region - Spain**.

3. There are two position options for showing the page navigation to the report viewer: Left and Top. By default, Data Studio selects Top. In the Layout And Theme panel, select Left under Navigation Position, as shown in Figure 5.23.

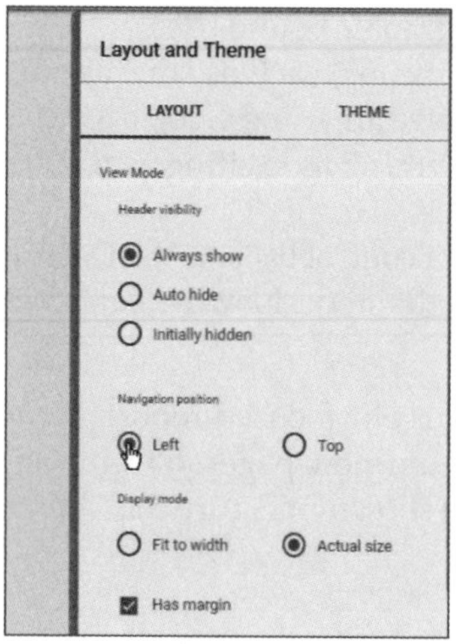

Figure 5.23: Setting the page navigation position

Which page navigation position you select is a design decision. In our example, we want the viewer to be aware of the multiple pages in the report. Top navigation is more subtle, and it takes up less screen real estate. Figure 5.24 shows the difference in the layouts when seen by the viewer.

4. Our next step is to create a filter to limit the data shown on this page to sessions identified as originating in Spain. So far, we have applied filtering through filter controls and chart interactions. In this case, we'll use a standard, noninteractive filter. Once you create a filter of this kind, it is automatically saved with the report so that it can be accessed in later editing sessions.

a. To add the new country filter, open the page control panel from the main menu by selecting Page ⇨ Current Page Settings. Here you see that the data source for our page is set to Default [Sample] Google Analytics and that we are using the Default date range. Under Filter, Page Filter, click Add A Filter (+), as shown in Figure 5.25, to open the Create Filter panel.

b. Provide a name for our new filter: **Country Spain ONLY**. As in other areas, it helps to be specific about naming things clearly. We are using only the single sample data source in our report, so by default it appears in the Data Source option.

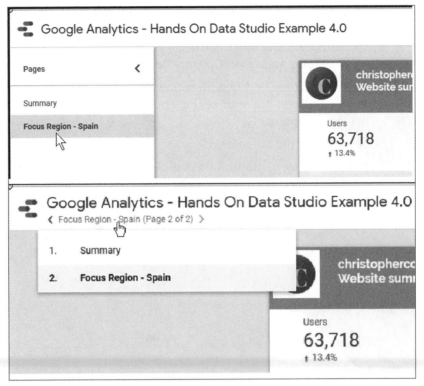

Figure 5.24: Left and top page navigation compared

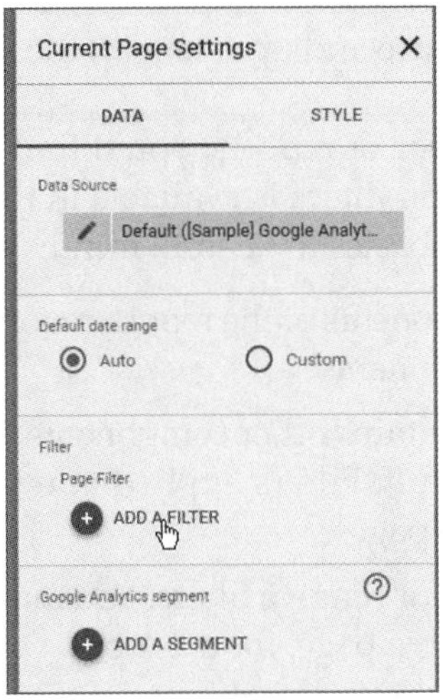

Figure 5.25: Adding a filter from the Current Page Settings panel

c. Moving down, we have the option to either include or exclude values for our filter. Excluding certain values can be very useful, but for our example, click Include.

d. Moving to the right, you'll see the field selection drop-down menu. As you know, Google Analytics contains hundreds of fields, so though you could scroll through the list, it is easier to use the search box. Here we search for and select Country on which our field should filter.

e. Next we set the Condition drop-down to Equal To (=). There are several other condition operator options here, and we'll cover some of them in other chapters.

f. Set Spain in the Value field.

g. With our filter configuration complete, as shown in Figure 5.26, click the Save button in the lower-right corner of the panel to apply the new filter.

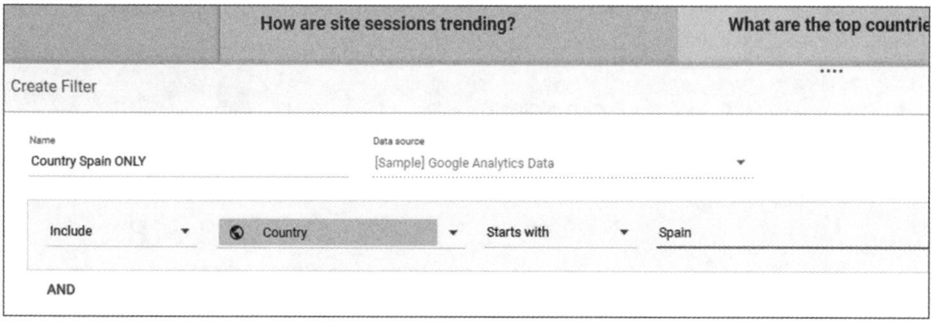

	How are site sessions trending?	What are the top countrie

Create Filter

Name
Country Spain ONLY

Data source
[Sample] Google Analytics Data ▾

Include ▾	⊘ Country ▾	Starts with ▾	Spain

AND

Figure 5.26: Configuring a filter for Spain

The report will take a moment to reconfigure and update with the new filter applied.

If you work with Data Studio on a number of reports, you'll find yourself using filters a lot. Excellent documentation on filters is available in the official Data Studio Help guides, but here are some basics to keep in mind:

▪ Filters can be applied on different components of the report: reports, pages, groups, filter controls, and chart components.

▪ A filter applied on a component that contains other components is applied to all the "child" components by default. Filters applied at report level apply to all pages and charts on those pages.

▪ Lower-level components may override or remove filters. You may remove a page-level filter for a specific chart on a page, for example.

▪ Multiple filters can be applied to a component. For instance, we could apply filters for both Spain and Social Media to a page component. The current limit for a component is 75 filters.

Now we'll make some adjustments to the report so that the charts will make more sense in our new context of using data only from Spain.

1. First, we'll adjust the table, which is set to show metrics by country. Clicking the table opens the control panel. Click the dimension field that is currently set to Country and change it to City. You'll see the table update to show cities in Spain and their metrics.

2. Select the map chart and its Data tab.

    a. Remove the Country dimension. This field is no longer needed.

    b. Slide the Drill Down switch to the left, as this functionality is no longer needed. Leaving the switch On would cause the drill up and down arrows on the chart to be still displayed, which could frustrate users since they would have no effect on the chart.

    c. You may have noticed when changing the map dimension fields that the map changes to show a detailed view of the United States. This is the default Zoom Area for cities. This is a bit unexpected but easily fixed. In the Zoom Area section of the Data tab, click the field showing the United States to open the Zoom Area picker screen. Use the search bar at the top to find and select Spain, as shown in Figure 5.27. To exit from the Zoom Area picker, click the left arrow at the top of the panel.

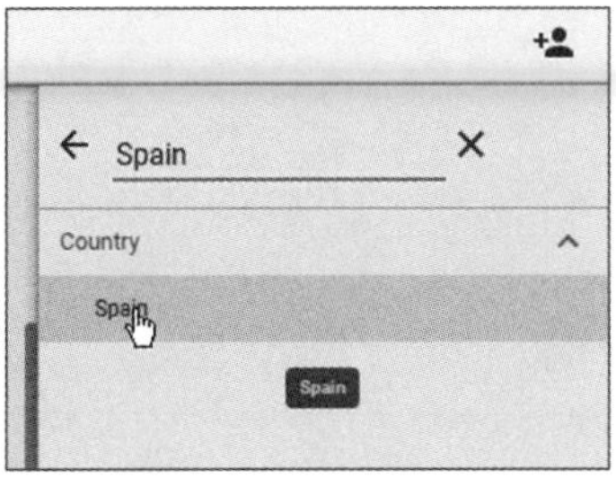

Figure 5.27: Setting Zoom Area to Spain

You should see the map of Spain start to update with city locations. The new map configuration is shown in Figure 5.28.

We'll now make some final text updates to the page. It would be appropriate to warn viewers that the demographic data is not collected for every user or session and let them know that this is a page for Spain.

1. Select the text box containing "Engagement by Age & Gender," and then click inside the box and add this note: ***Demographic data is not available for all users**.

2. Change the title in the header. Select the text box containing the `christophercooper.com` website summary. Click inside the box and add the line **Focus Region Spain**.

A final view of the new page, with the report navigation, is shown in Figure 5.29.

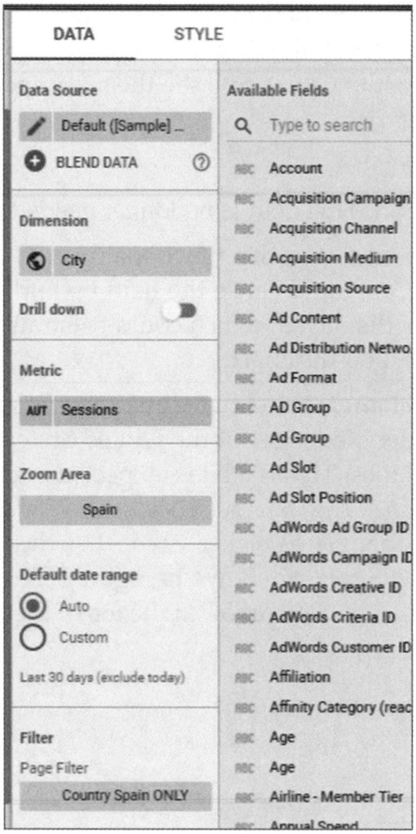

Figure 5.28: Completed update for map configuration

Summary

In this chapter, we started a new topic that covers the measurement of websites and web properties. This chapter focused on Google Analytics, a large and complex service that forms the basis for most measurement on the web today. Keeping with our cooking analogy, we looked at the premade templates as the "frozen pizza" of Data Studio reporting. We explored an actual case of finding insights from real data in a report and discussed some of the design issues balancing user control and focus, as well as some issues that we often have to deal with such as incomplete data. We covered a number of new concepts:

Web measurement data sources: Common services for measuring web property usage.

Google Analytics: The dominant web measurement platform and service.

Marketing report templates: "Plug and Play" reports ready to be copied and adapted.

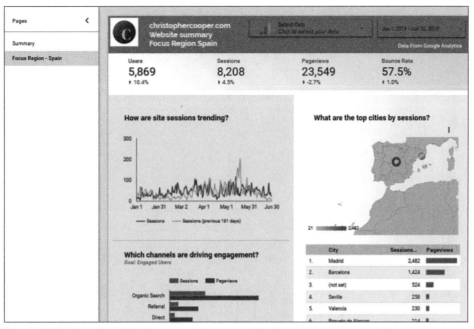

Figure 5.29: Completed Spain page and report navigation

Data controls: Selectors for common types of web reporting data sources that allow the use of a report without copying the report itself.

Donut, stacked bar, and map charts: We introduced these new frequently used chart types.

Drill down for charts: We set up our maps to show country and city on the same chart, allowing the user to explore details.

Multiple pages and navigation: You learned how to add pages to a report and how to use the basic navigation options.

Applying filters to components: We set up page filters to limit the user view to a particular segment of the data.

In the next chapter, we'll work with Google Search Console, another tool that provides a source of data for websites.

CHAPTER 6

Using Google Search Console for Audience Insights

This chapter takes a close look at the Search Console application. Search Console is another service that anyone with a Google account can access. That said, you won't see anything in the service unless you have verified that you are the owner of a site or have been added as an authorized user. This makes sense, as this information is intended for the use of site owners and it should normally not be available to the general public. Figure 6.1 shows where I can select a web property to which I have access.

In this chapter, you'll learn about some of the main functions of Search Console and why to use Data Studio instead of the standard application interface. Along

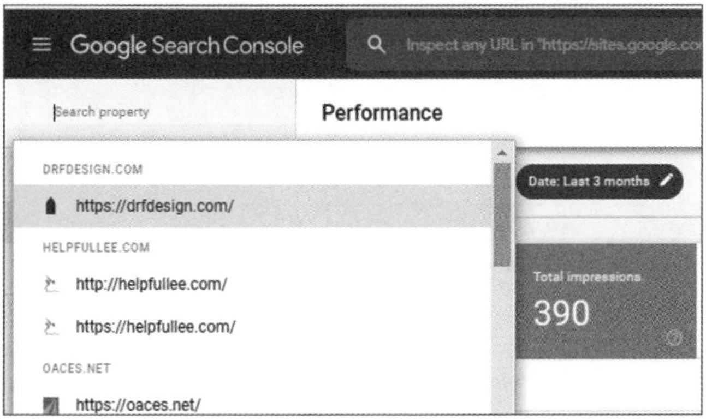

Figure 6.1: Selecting a property to view in Search Console

the way, you will get some solid advice on how to find search opportunities and get better rankings in the search result pages.

Search Console and Search Results Pages

Once a user selects a property, they have access to several services. These services help site managers understand how their site is interpreted by Google Search. Site managers can check which of their pages are being indexed by Search, how those pages are viewed by Google, how pages are linked internally and from other sites, and much more. This is an important service because most sites rely on traffic from Google Search, and this is the main access point to view and control that relationship. Figure 6.2 shows the main screen that a user sees after selecting a property to view.

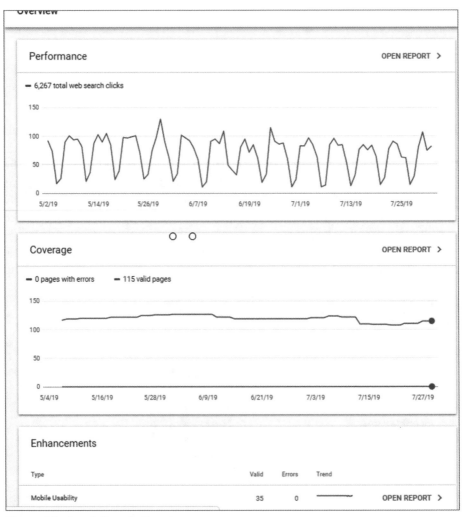

Figure 6.2: Search Console Overview screen

A lot of information is available from Search Console, but we'll focus on Google Search data for *queries* and *landing pages*. This is the most used feature of Search Console, and it provides useful information because it lets site managers understand how their pages are performing in the *Search Engine Results Pages* (*SERPs*).

So, what information do we actually get and what is the significance for a site manager? Looking at a narrow slice of information, we'll run through the rough process of how it was collected. Figure 6.3 shows the queries view for one of my websites. The chart at the top shows values for all the activity between search queries and my site over a 16-month period. The table shows the data broken down for each query.

Figure 6.3: Search Console query view

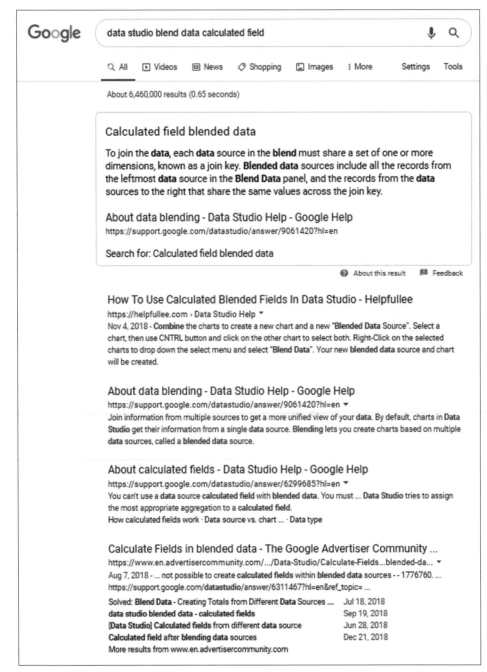

Figure 6.4: Search results for the example query

Let's go through a short story to show how the data in this table was collected for a single line of that table. First, someone has a question about a new advanced feature in Google Data Studio. They turn to Google Search to find information and type **data studio blend data calculated field** in the search box and press Enter.

This query is then sent to Google, and it performs its magic! It looks through its index for pages relevant to the search term and the possible intent of the searcher. It also gathers relevant ads for this search term and other pieces of information related to the query. Frightfully complex algorithms are applied to put these results in an order that Google thinks will be most useful to the user. It then builds the SERPs and presents the user with the first page of those results, as shown in Figure 6.4.

HOW SERPS ARE MADE

The ranking algorithms used by search engines like Google, Bing, Yahoo, Baidu, and others are closely guarded secrets and are constantly evolving. Google is by far the dominant player in this space, which is why there is so much focus on how their results are formulated. Google has stated that its algorithms take more than 200 different factors into account, and its algorithm is refined hundreds of times a year!

Because of the importance of SERPs, a whole industry has evolved that's devoted to understanding and influencing how a website shows up in these competitive listings. This is the world of search engine optimization (SEO), and those in the profession are called SEOs.

SEOs tend to be obsessed with rankings in the SERPs, as exemplified by this joke:

Question: Where should one hide a dead body?

SEO's Answer: Page 2 of the SERPs!

Although it might be wonderful if everyone had a good understanding of SEO, or the staff budget of an SEO agency, it is just not practical for most small organizations to devote the time or money to keep up with the latest tactics. Some basic principles, however, can go a long way in helping any site achieve better results:

■ Keeping in mind the purpose of your site, create content that your audience will appreciate and that is worthy of other sites linking to it.

■ Make your content easy to understand and find. Creating good titles, descriptions, and subheadings makes the content easy for users to digest and makes it easy for search engines to match your content with searches.

■ Promote your content. This doesn't mean advertising; it means using other channels like social media to let people know your content is out there and asking other sites that link to similar content to link to yours as well.

■ Listen to your audience feedback and measure results. Tools like Search Console, Analytics, and Data Studio will help give you insights on what content is working and where you might create more content to improve your SERPs.

In this case, the user sees a page from my site at the top of the results. Since the user actually saw my page in the results, Google will count this view in the Search Console data as an *impression*.

The location in the results is the site's *position*. In this case, I scored a position of 1 (hooray for me). In other searches, even for the same term, I may not be so fortunate to score so highly on the page. When multiple people search for the same term, Google calculates the *average position*. This position information is also stored in Search Console.

Now the user has a basic choice to make: click this result or continue looking. If they click my result, Google scores a click for this page with this query. The sum of all these clicks is stored in the Clicks metric.

Now if we return our attention to Figure 6.3, we can relate this information back to the results in the table. In this case, our query has 201 clicks and is the most clicked-on query for the site. We can see that there were 503 search views of our site for this term.

The next column is the number of clicks divided by the number of impressions to give the *click-through rate (CTR)*. The last column shows the site's average position for all the SERPs where a page on my site appeared for this query.

If we click on the Pages tab of this report, we'll see the same metrics but calculated for each page instead of each query. So, this is a bit different view of the data, combining all the query data for a single page instead of the entire site.

The difference here is subtle but important. Most pages will have multiple (sometimes hundreds of) different queries for which they rank. The opposite is also true; often a site may show up with multiple pages for a single query.

In the Search Console interface, you can select a single page to use as a filter, view all the query results for that page, and see the graph results that display the metrics over time, as shown in Figure 6.5.

So, with a review of the Search Console application, you can begin to understand the wealth of complex and relevant data available to anyone interested in the success of their website. You may also appreciate that, as with Google Analytics, it is possible to spend hours wandering through the data without coming up with meaningful insights that could guide a site owner to actions that might benefit their site and audience. I believe that this is one of the reasons why the tool, free to all, remains woefully underused, particularly by individuals and small organizations.

Let's see if we can remedy that situation through the use of Data Studio. Ready? Let's go back to the steps in our cooking analogy for this example and get cooking!

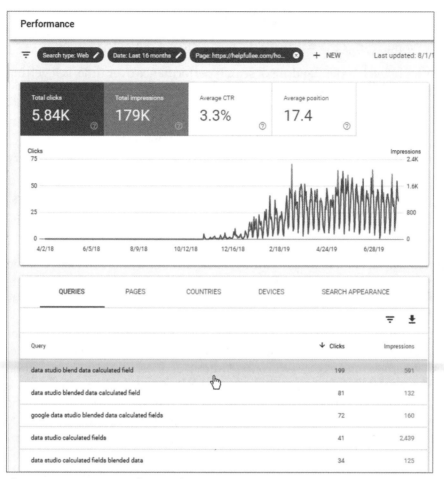

Figure 6.5: Query metrics for a single page

Creating a Search Console Report with Data Studio

As with all reports, you need to consider the audience and the purpose of the report before getting started. In this case, our audience is a small-site owner or a manager. We want to provide a report that reveals some insights without much mental work or exploration.

This is easier when you are working with a particular website where you can more easily narrow down the things to look for ahead of time. Here, because we don't have a particular site with which to work, we need a bit more flexibility and interaction to make it more generally applicable.

Step 1. Selecting the Dish to Prepare

Here are some things that we want the viewer to get out of the report:

- A high-level understanding of search performance over time. Is it getting better or worse or staying the same?
- The power to see the performance of queries and pages quickly.
- The ability to see all the queries for a single page easily.
- The ability to see how a query, page, or combination of a page and query perform over time.
- The ability to see the difference in results for desktop and mobile users.
- The power to find insights that point to changes that would benefit the site.

Although most of these insights are available through Search Console, putting them on a single page with visualizations makes the report more useful. Users can quickly explore the data as needed, without switching tabs and views as they do in the standard application.

In addition, we want to use some of Data Studio's features to group queries into categories. As you saw in Chapter 4, "Data Exploration with Interactive Elements," where we had expenses grouped into categories, this extra information can be extremely useful because it provides a level of categorization that is more relevant to the user—that is, a level between the high-level overview and the low-level detail. By using some clever organizing principles, we can provide areas that offer "low-hanging fruit"—in other words, areas where easy changes on the website can yield results.

We can also make our investigation in this report a bit easier by using a new function for the tables. Including hyperlinks extends the utility of a report by allowing users to pursue more information quickly outside of the report itself. We'll employ the hyperlink function for two uses:

Hyperlinked Queries   Clicking a query will open a new tab—a Google Search for that query. This can be extremely helpful because it allows the user to see the competing results for that query quickly and even investigate competing pages to see where they might be doing a better job of satisfying the user intent.

Hyperlinked Landing Pages   Unfortunately, Search Console data does not provide page titles in the information. Clicking the URLs will open a new tab if the user needs to inspect the actual page.

We reviewed some of the terminology specific to Search Console earlier, but a new user may not be familiar with some of the terms. To help the new user, we'll change some of the field labels to make them more relatable to a general audience. In later chapters, we'll look at ways to annotate the report to give more information to new users.

As in other chapters, we'll look at the finished product, I'll show you how to build it, and then I'll present some real-world examples of how it can be used.

Here is a breakdown of the chart components and graphic elements in this report as shown in Figure 6.6.

Header   We have reused the elements from previous reports. Again, we see the Data control and Date Range selectors here. Our date range is set to the maximum of 16 months. We have data to give an historical context, and we can see how the site is performing over time by using the Data control. We allow the user to apply the report to other Search Console web properties without copying the report. Removing the selector would restrict the report to a single property. It has some limitations in this example, as you'll see later in the chapter.

Pie Chart   The pie chart provides a quick view of how many impressions are coming from different kinds of devices. Like all the charts on this report, it has interactive filtering turned on, so clicking a segment filters the entire report for a particular device type.

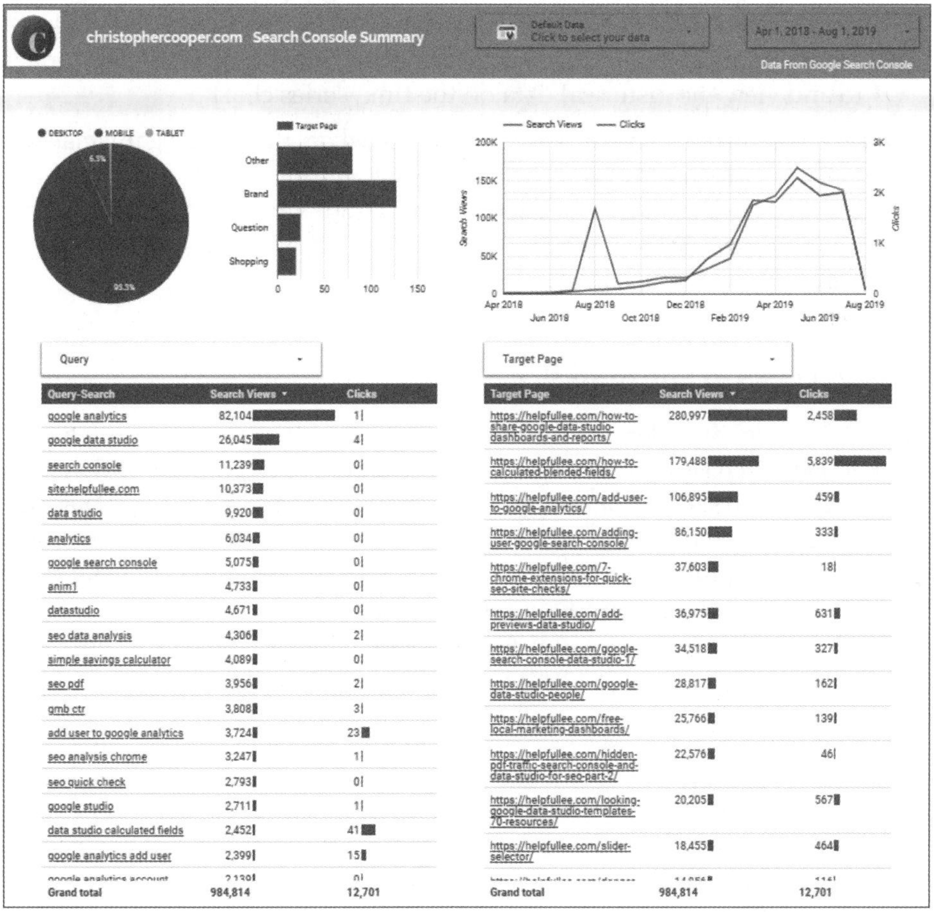

Figure 6.6: The completed Search Console report

Bar Chart   The data shown in the bar chart is coming from a new field, Search Type, that we'll create. This is our value-added field to break the queries into meaningful categories. It measures how many pages are shown for each category. Again, it is interactive, so we can investigate each of the segments more closely.

Time Series   The time-series chart shows both impressions, changed here to Search Views, and clicks. Since there is such a difference between the values for each of these metrics, we use a left axis and a right axis to get them on the same chart.

Filter Controls   We put filter controls in so that the user can select several related queries. This is very handy because sometimes we want to see how a site is performing for a group of related queries as opposed to very specific ones. We also have one for Target Pages, so it is possible to group pages arbitrarily if needed.

Query-Search Table   The Query-Search field is a new "calculated" dimension that did not exist in the original data. It shows the search query, and if the link is clicked, it will take you to an actual Google search for that query. This table is designed to spot gaps between search views and clicks. It also operates as a filter, so you can easily see which pages a query applies to and view the historical data on the time-series chart.

Target Page Table   Again, we can easily see where there are big mismatches between search views and clicks. Filtering is available here so that you can quickly see the history in the time chart and which queries are leading to views and clicks. The actual Target Page URLs are linked to the pages themselves for quick inspection.

Step 2. Let's Go Shopping!

We'll go in a slightly different direction for our data in this example. Christopher Cooper does not have a website that generates data, so that is not an option here. We could use the sample data source connectors provided by Google, but they have a serious limitation: although they are free to use, they cannot be modified. This will not work for us in this example because we are going to create some new fields that will be connected to the data source.

For this example, we need to use a live source for the connector, so I'll use my personal site as the basis for this example.

WHY THIS EXAMPLE USES REAL SITE DATA INSTEAD OF THE SAMPLE DATA

I use my own website data for the creation of many examples in this book, and occasionally I use data from other sources where I have permission. There is just no getting around the limitations of the sample connectors, and outside of the Google sample accounts, there's no alternative.

Sometimes, you may see some pretty good-looking results. I'm not trying to show off there, mind you, and in many ways what you see is not an unusual pattern of growth. I have been diligent in following the basic SEO rules, and I haven't done anything particularly exceptional.

I am somewhat embarrassed in exposing some of my own website deficiencies. At the same time, I hope others will feel free to point out opportunities that I may have missed. There are a lot of changes that I would like to make to increase the ease of use of my site and fix some technical issues. Perhaps it's very much like many sites out there after all!

As a reminder, site owners need to verify ownership of their site with Google in order to access the Search Console service for their site. This is usually not difficult, but there are several ways to get the job done. Since this is a book about Data Studio, not Search Console, instead of detailing all the ways to do this, I have included links to resources to help you connect to a site in the online resources for this chapter at www.wiley.com/go/handsondatastudio.

After a site account has been set up, other users can easily be added so that they have access and can connect with Data Studio.

It is also worth mentioning that unlike Google Analytics, with Search Console your connection is retroactive. With Google Analytics, the data starts coming in only when you set up an account and add the required tracking codes to your site. When you verify a site with Search Console, you'll have the full 16-month history of your site available within a few hours! How great is that?

As a reminder, I'll go through this example with my own site instead of using the sample Search Console data sources provided by Google. You can practice some reporting by connecting the sample connectors to a report, but you cannot build your own calculated fields using those connectors. If you're following along, you won't be able to connect to my site's Search Console. You must follow this procedure with a site to which you have access.

Our shopping for data will be fairly simple. Here are the steps:

1. On the Data Studio home screen, click the Create button in the upper-left corner of the screen and select Data Source from the drop-down, as shown in Figure 6.7.

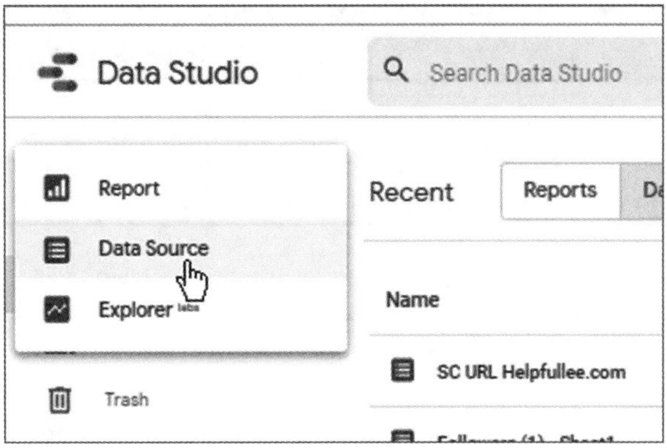

Figure 6.7: Creating a new data source

2. You'll be taken to the Data Connectors screen, where you can scroll down and select the Search Console connector. After doing this, you'll be presented with a list of all Search Console properties to which you have access. I have access to a lot of sites, so I'll use the search box to find my site. In this example, I select `https://helpfullee.com`.

> **TIP**   In this example, I have two versions available for my site: one version for HTTP and one version for HTTPS. In the past, it was fairly common, albeit confusing, when different versions of a site were available. Users were encouraged to set up profiles for every possible version of their site. Today and going forward, most sites are "secure," so they use the HTTPS version. Google has also begun to consolidate variations of a site in Search Console, so you should usually select the HTTPS version of a site if more than one selection is available.

3. Once you select a property, you'll have two options in the Tables column from which to choose. With Google's standard Search Console connectors, you can choose the Site Impression table to get data about the site in general. This data includes the field for the average ranking of search queries, but it lacks information about the target URLs. The URL Impression table gives you information about queries relating to pages, but it lacks information about how that page ranks.

   A professional analyst might want all the data included in a single connector, but the average position data is not needed for our report. So, select the URL Impression option.

4. Before leaving this screen, give the connector a descriptive name to make it easier to find in the future. I typed **Helpfullee - SC - URL 1**, indicating that this connector is for the `Helpfullee` property and is a Search Console of type URL. Finally, I give it a number just in case I make more than one

of these types of connections. All these settings are shown in Figure 6.8. After the selections and renaming, click the Connect button at the upper right. After connecting, you'll be taken to the Fields setup screen, which we'll cover in the next section.

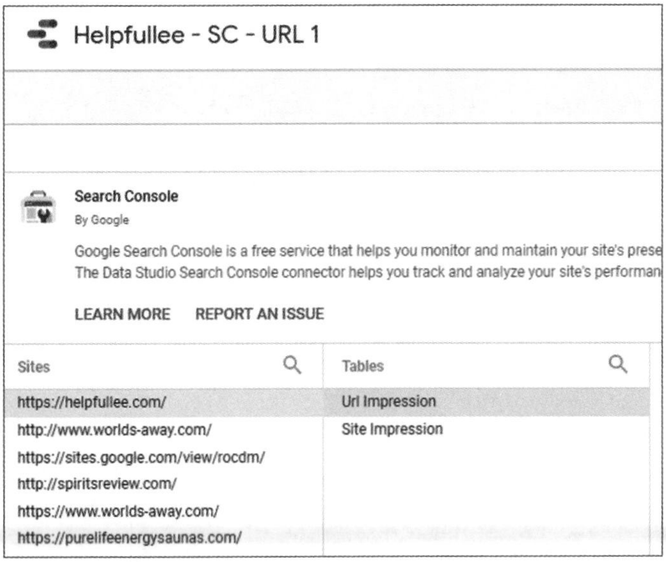

Figure 6.8: Creating a new data source

Step 3. Assemble the Ingredients

As with our other examples, we are presented with the Fields screen. For this report, we need three new fields, and we'd like to rename some of the existing fields to make their meaning a bit more relatable to new users.

> **WARNING**   Although this type of setup is ideally done at this point, you can come back and add or modify fields in the data source at any time. Just remember, if you modify an existing field in a connector that is used in multiple reports, all of those reports may be affected!
>
> This can be a double-edged sword: it means that you can upgrade multiple previous reports by changing a field, but it may also mean that those reports are now changed in ways you didn't anticipate. When in doubt about using an existing connector, set up a new one. This is also good a reason to restrict editing rights for connectors if you're sharing work with other report editors so that they won't be able to change fields without consulting other users.

Our most complex field to set up will be the Search Type field:

1. Click the Add A Field button in the upper-right corner of the Fields panel.

2. Assign the name **Search Type** to the new field.

3. Enter text in the Formula box (see Figure 6.9) and click the Update button to complete the field definition.

```
CASE
   WHEN CONTAINS_TEXT(Query, "helpfullee") THEN "Brand"
   WHEN REGEXP_MATCH(Query, ".*lee .*|.* hurst.*") THEN "Brand"
   WHEN REGEXP_MATCH(Query, ".*price.*|.*cost.*|.*buy.*|.*shop.*|.
*best.*|.*near.* " ) THEN "Shopping"
   WHEN REGEXP_MATCH(Query, ".*how .*|.*when .*|.*which
.*|.*what.*|.*who .*|.*why.*|.*where .*") THEN "Question"
   ELSE "Other"
END
```

```
1  CASE
2    WHEN CONTAINS_TEXT( Query , "helpfullee") THEN "Brand"
3    WHEN REGEXP_MATCH( Query , ".*lee .*|.* hurst.*") THEN "Brand"
4    WHEN REGEXP_MATCH( Query , ".*price.*|.*cost.*|.*buy.*|.*shop.*|.*best.*|.*near.* " )
5    THEN "Shopping"
6    WHEN REGEXP_MATCH( Query , ".*how .*|.*when .*|.*which .*|.*what.*|.*who .*|.*why.*|.*where .*")
7    THEN "Question"
8    ELSE "Other"
9  END
```
                                                                    CANCEL   **UPDATE**

Figure 6.9: Formula for the Search Type field

Anatomy of a Case Statement

Now you know why the formula box is so big! It's able to accommodate more than just a simple function definition. We're using a *case statement* here, and it's one of the features that gives Data Studio a lot of power and flexibility in creating new fields. The case statement can be thought of as a mini-program, and it is a structure found in many programming languages. If you're afraid of programming, don't worry—this is about as complex as we'll get!

Here's how the case statement works:

- Data Studio will go through each line and evaluate each WHEN clause.

- If the WHEN clause evaluates to true, the value after the THEN keyword is set as the value for the field and Data Studio stops processing.

- If the WHEN clause is not true, Data Studio moves to the next WHEN clause.

- If none of the WHEN clauses are true, Data Studio sets the field to the value after the ELSE keyword.

Let's break down each line and explain what's going on:

```
1 CASE
```

The `CASE` keyword tells Data Studio to expect the case-style formatting to follow:

```
2 WHEN CONTAINS_TEXT(Query, "helpfullee") THEN "Brand"
```

Our first `WHEN` clause is fairly simple. Data Studio now provides several useful text-checking functions. The `CONTAINS _ TEXT()` function checks the first field—in this case, the value of `Query`—and checks to see if it contains the text `"helpfullee"`.

If you start typing a function name, Data Studio will autocomplete the formula, and hovering your mouse over a formula will trigger a pop-up with a description and help for that formula, as shown in Figure 6.10. So, a human-readable translation for this line might be "When the value in a query contains `"helpfullee"`, set the value of Search Type to `"Brand"`."

```
3 WHEN REGEXP_MATCH(Query, ".*lee .*|.* hurst.*") THEN "Brand"
```

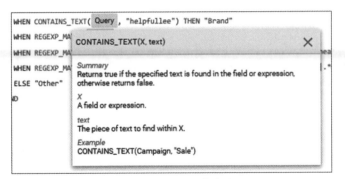

Figure 6.10: The `CONTAINS_TEXT()` help box

Sometimes the basic text functions are just not powerful enough to get the job done. This is when we turn to *regular expressions,* sometimes referred to as REGEX, and in Data Studio as REGEXP, which can be thought of as its own little language and is used in many programming languages. It defines a sequence of characters to use as a search pattern within strings of text.

The `REGEXP_MATCH()` function is a fancy version of the `CONTAINS_TEXT()` function. In this case, it checks the field `Query` for `"lee "` or `" hurst"`. It's a bit hard to tell where the spaces are here, but their placement is crucial. Here's a human-readable translation of this line: "When the value in a query field contains `lee` with a space after it OR the field contains `"hurst"` with a space before it, then set the value of Search Type to `"Brand"`."

If you're looking at the REGEXP lines and scratching your head, you're not alone. Here's a brief explanation of the symbols used in this example:

- The period (.) is a wildcard symbol. It matches any character including spaces.

- The asterisk (*) matches the character that precedes it zero or more times.

- The pipe symbol (|) means OR.

It is beyond the scope of this book to examine regular expressions in detail. We'll include some helpful references in the online resources for this chapter at www.wiley.com/go/handsondatastudio.

```
4 WHEN REGEXP_MATCH(Query, ".*price.*|.*cost.*|.*buy.*|.*shop.*|.*best.*
|.*near.* " ) THEN "Shopping"
```

The WHEN clause here works the same way as in line 3 earlier, but it matches more words. The human-readable translation for this line is, "When the value in the query field contains the word price OR cost OR buy OR shop OR best OR near, then set the value of Search Type to "Shopping"."

```
5 WHEN REGEXP_MATCH(Query, ".*how .*|.*when .*|.*which .*|.*what.*|.*who
.*|.*why.*|.*where .*") THEN "Question"
```

The human-readable translation is, "When the value in the query field contains the word how OR when OR which OR what OR who OR why OR where, then set the value of Search Type to "Question"."

```
6 ELSE "Other"
```

This one is simple! The human-readable translation is, "Set the value of Search Type to "Other"." Data Studio only sets the value from the ELSE keyword if no matches were found.

```
7 END
```

This line simply tells Data Studio that this is the end of the case statement.

So, what was the point of all this work? We now can roughly organize our queries by searcher intent. The "Shopping" and "Question" categories will work across most sites. This will give us a much better understanding of what users are seeking. You'll see how they can be used a bit later in the usage examples.

Note that the "Brand" category is specifically keyed into the helpfullee.com website. If you were to reuse this formula, you'd want to change it to match any brand terms associated with your specific site.

Of course, you can add more categories by following the basic patterns shown in this example. Just remember this: the order of the lines is important! The case statement sets the value based on the first match it finds and stops there. So, if a query is "Where can I find the best templates from helpfullee?", the search type is set to "Brand", not "Shopping" or "Question", because it matches the first WHEN clause, sets the value "Brand", and stops.

When you have updated the field, click the All Fields link in the upper-left corner of the panel to return to the Fields page. From there, you can create more fields.

Creating the Hyperlink Fields

Hyperlinks make the web work! Dark indeed were the days before hyperlinks: to access a document on the Internet, you had to know its exact location because there were no links from other documents. In this example, we'll create two new fields that use hyperlinks to let the user link to pages outside of the report.

First, let's look at the setup for the Target Page field, as shown in Figure 6.11.

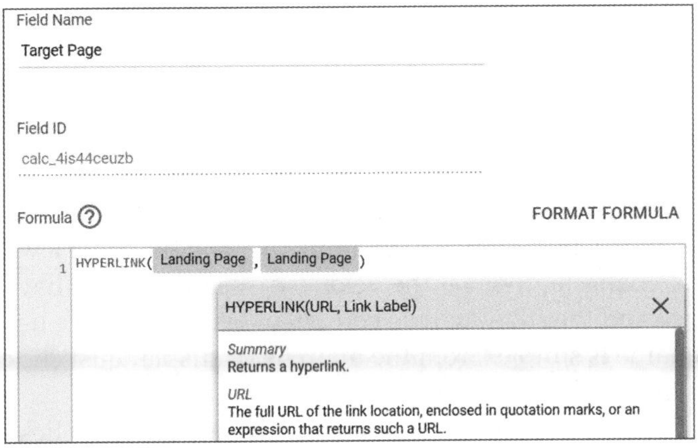

Figure 6.11: The Target page hyperlink setup

The HYPERLINK() function takes a URL as its first argument, and this is the target of the link. The second argument is the text to show the user. In this example, both of these arguments are the same. We use the value from the Landing Page field for both the text and the target of the link. After entering the formula, click the Update button and return to the Fields page.

Finally, we create a field for Query-Search, as shown in Figure 6.12.

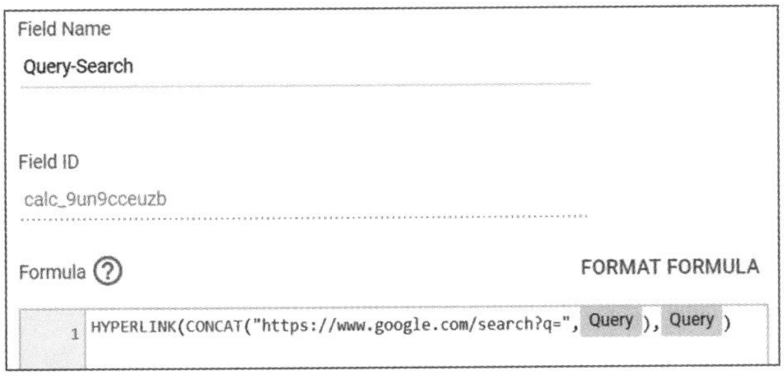

Figure 6.12: The Query-Search hyperlink setup

Here we get a little more complicated with the HYPERLINK() function. We want to create a link to show the user the search results for the query.

The solution is a bit of a hack! If you do a Google search, you can see that the results page shows the search term in the URL. For example, if you search for **a data citizens survival guide**, the resulting URL of the search results page will look something like this:

```
https://www.google.com/search?q=a+data+citizens+survival+guide&rlz=1
C1CHBF_enUS772US772&oq...
```

You clearly see the search query in the URL after `search?q=`. This is very handy! It means that you can go directly to the search results for a phrase by simply appending the phrase after the `q=` part.

In our Query-Search field, we use the `CONCAT()` function to build our target URL inside the `HYPERLINK()` function. The `CONCAT()` function simply connects two strings together; in this case, the standard Google Search URL and the value from the Query field. So, our new field will show the text from the Query field, but it will link to the search results for that phrase. We'll see more on how this works after we finish building the report.

Finishing up our field setup work, we want to change the display names of a few fields. We've seen that the labels for fields can be changed at the chart level in previous chapters, but changing them at the field level means that we have to change them only once and that they will be consistent everywhere we use them. Changing a field name is simple. From the main fields display, just click a field and you can edit the label.

Here we change the name of Impressions to **Search Views** and URL clicks to the simpler term **Clicks**.

Our final set of fields is shown in Figure 6.13. We move on to building the report by clicking the Create Report button on the upper-right side of the panel.

Index	Field		Type		Aggregation
			← EDIT CONNECTION		
1	Date	⋮	📅	Date (YYYYMMDD)	▾ None
2	Google Property	⋮	RBC	Text	▾ None
3	Landing Page	⋮	RBC	Text	▾ None
4	Device Category	⋮	RBC	Text	▾ None
5	Query	⋮	RBC	Text	▾ None
6	Clicks	⋮	123	Number	▾ Auto
7	Search Views	⋮	123	Number	▾ Auto
8	URL CTR	⋮	123	Percent	▾ Auto
9	Country	⋮	🌐	Country	▾ None
10	Search Type	fx ⋮	RBC	Text	▾ None
11	Query-Search	fx ⋮	⌘	Hyperlink	None
12	Target Page	fx ⋮	⌘	Hyperlink	None

Figure 6.13: The fields setup completed

Step 4. Setting the Table

With our preparations complete, we are ready to start building our report. When you clicked Create Report, a confirmation screen opened asking you to verify that you want to add the new data source to the report. Click the Add To Report button, and a new report canvas opens. Let's go through the steps required to build the report.

1. When you start a new report, you should see the Layout And Theme panel on the right side. Set the height of the report to **1200 px** to provide a little more room at the bottom for our tables.

2. Change the report name from Untitled Report to **Hands On Data Studio - Search Console Example 5.0**.

3. To build the report header, we'll borrow the header elements from the previous reports. Change the title in the report header to reflect that this is a **Search Console Summary**, and add a Data control, which automatically sets the Search Console properties to match our current data source type.

4. After adding the Data Range control to the page, set the default to the maximum time range for our data. Select the control and use the Data properties panel to set the default date range.

   From the drop-down, select Advanced and set the start and end dates as shown in Figure 6.14. Set Start Date to Today Minus **16** Months and set End Date to Today Minus **3** Days. Offsetting the end date by three days takes into account the two-day delay that Search Console has in providing data.

5. Now we can start adding charts. Start at the top with the pie chart. Select Pie Chart from the Charts drop-down and click and drag to put it roughly in place.

6. On the Data tab, set Dimension to Device Category and change Metric and Sort to use the Search Views field. Don't forget to click the Interactions Filter check box on the bottom of the tab!

7. We have one minor styling change to make here. Click the Style tab and scroll all the way down to the bottom to set the Legend options. We want the labels for the various device types to be on top so that the pie chart takes up less space. Click the Top box, as shown in Figure 6.15, and then resize and position the chart with your mouse.

8. Next, we'll add our bar chart showing the search types. Choose Bar Chart from the Add A Chart drop-down and click and drag it into place.

9. On the Data tab, set Dimension to Search Type and the Metric field to Landing Page. Since Landing Page is normally a dimension, the Count Unique option is applied to the values by default.

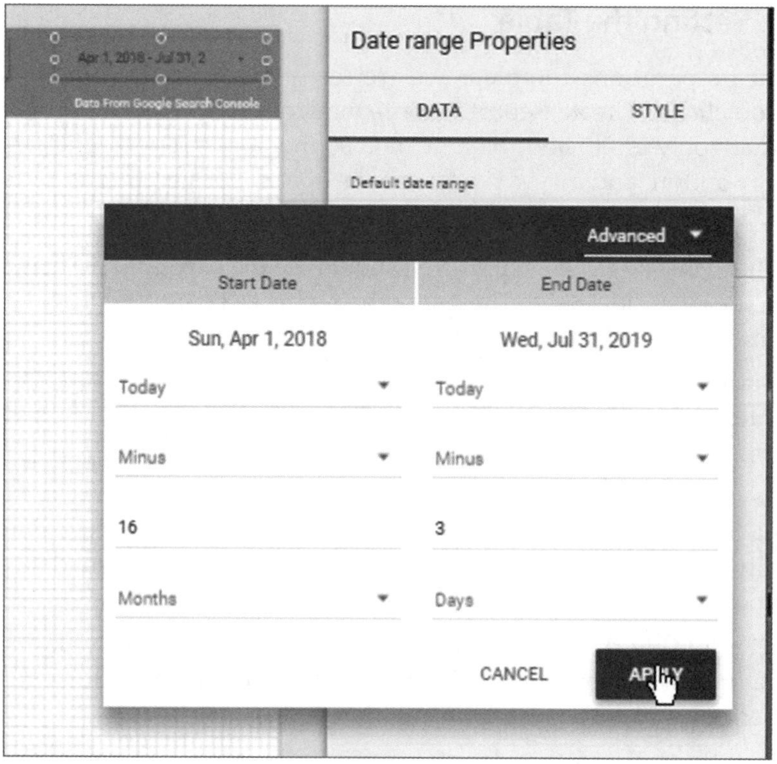

Figure 6.14: Setting the default date range

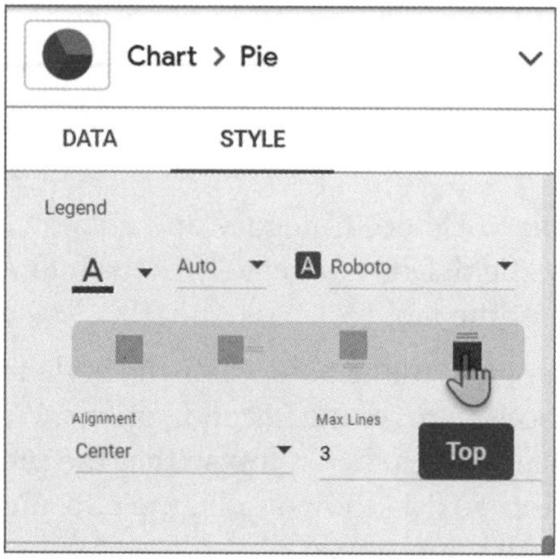

Figure 6.15: Moving the pie chart legend to the top

Please note that when you wish to use a dimension field as a metric, it does not show up as an option if you click on a field in the Metric space. To set a dimension field as a metric, *you must drag the dimension*, in this case Landing Page, from the list of Available Fields on the right side of the panel.

This gives us the number of pages that apply to each search type. We could use just about any metric here, but I find that using one that has a fairly even distribution makes it easier for the user to click the chart for filtering. We adjust some of the internal spacing of the chart to show the labels better, and we are done with this chart!

10. Select the time-series chart from the Add A Chart drop-down and click and drag it to its new size and position.

11. The completed Data tab setup is shown in Figure 6.16. By default, the chart will show the time period by date. We'll use the drill-down functionality so that users will see the chart by months initially, but they can also drill down to a weekly or daily view of the period.

   a. On the Data tab, set the Drill-Down switch to the On position. We now will have three kinds of dates in the Dimension field.

   b. Remove the Year field and replace it with another Date field. Modify the configuration of this field to Show As Year Week.

   c. Check the order of the fields and make sure the default drill -own level is set to Year Month.

   d. Add Search Views to the Metrics, so we now have both that field and Clicks in the Metrics section, with Search Views on top.

   e. Click the Interactions Apply filter check box.

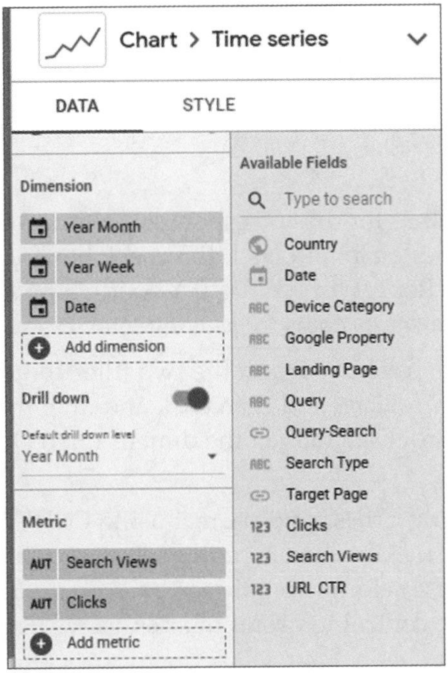

Figure 6.16: The Data tab setup for the time-series chart

12. When you have Search Views and Clicks added to the time series, you see that because the number of search views dwarfs the number of clicks, you get very little information from the Clicks line. This is often the case with Search Console. The remedy is to set up Clicks with its own scale on the right axis.

    a. Switch to the Style tab, and in the section for Series #2, select the Axis Right radio button, as shown in Figure 6.17. The chart automatically scales for clicks, and now you can see very clearly how search views and clicks have grown over time.

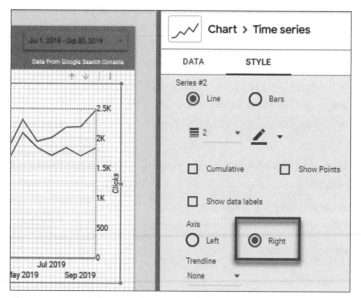

Figure 6.17: Switching Clicks to the right y-axis

    b. Let's show the metrics labels for the corresponding metric axis. Scroll a bit further down the Style tab and click the check box for the Left Y-Axis, Show Axis Title. Repeat for the Right Y-Axis, Show Axis Title check box. Now our time-series chart looks complete!

13. Working our way down the page, we'll add the two filter control drop-downs. Select the Filter Control icon and then click and drag the control into place. In the Filter Control Data tab, set the dimension to Query and the metric to Search Views.

14. Copy the Query control using Ctrl+C and paste it using Ctrl+V to create our second selector. Change the dimension for this selector to Target Page and adjust the positions of the selectors on the screen. Adding Filter controls will give us a lot more control to group queries, as we'll see in the Usage section.

15. Finally, we'll tackle the tables. Set up the left-side table first by selecting Table With Bars from the Add A Chart drop-down and clicking and dragging it into position.

16. On the Data panel, set our new field, Query-Search, as the dimension, and add Search Views and Clicks to the metrics list. Select the Show Summary Row check box and set the Interaction Filter check box so that we can click rows to filter the other charts.

17. Moving to the Style tab, deselect the Row Numbers and Show Pagination settings and click the Wrap Text check box in the Table Body section. Finally, go to each of the column configurations and click the box for Show Number so that we can see the actual values along with the bars.

18. Now that the Query-Search table is completed, copy it as the basis for our Target Page table. Use Ctrl+C and Ctrl+V to create a copy, and then slide it into place using the arrow keys for quick positioning.

19. On the Data tab, you only need to replace the Query-Search field in the dimensions with the Target Page field, and you are done!

After a quick round of tweaking the position and sizing of charts, you are ready to start getting some insights.

Bon Appetite! Using the Search Console Report

Now that everything is in place, let's see if we can find some insights based on the data from my site. Then we'll use the Data control to look at a completely different kind of site.

If you go back to Figure 6.6, you'll see the default view of this report connected to my site. Does anything jump out at you right away? For me, my eyes are drawn immediately to the big spike in search views on the time-series chart. Looking at the rest of the chart, you can see that both search views and clicks have been growing nicely over time, but that spike is really, really big! So, the first questions that come to mind are as follows:

1. What caused that spike in search views?

2. Is there something I could do to get that many views again?

DO SEARCH SPIKES HAPPEN OFTEN IN SEARCH CONSOLE?

The short answer is "No." However, I have found that most sites have some kind of unusual traffic mystery waiting to be uncovered. For example, I was looking at a furniture wholesaler's Search Console data and saw a massive spike. It appeared that tons of people were suddenly searching for a specific model lamp, but few were clicking through.

> After some quick investigation, the mystery was solved. Apparently, the lamp shared the same name as a notorious adult film star who had just released a particularly naughty film. The moral of the story is that not all exposure is good exposure!

To get a better idea of how long the spike lasted, at the month level I can tell that it affected only August 2018. By drilling down to Week and then to Day measurement, as shown in Figure 6.18, I can see that the spike was short-lived. To find out what happened that day, I can use the interactive filter on the chart, clicking and dragging over the time period, so that I see the result details only for that period.

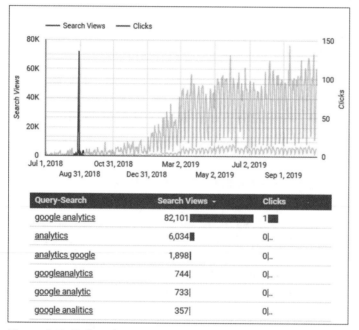

Figure 6.18: Drilling down to investigate my search view spike

You can immediately see on the Query-Search table that there were a huge number of views all related to the main term "Google Analytics." Looking at the Target Page table, we see that they were almost all getting a newly published blog post about sharing Data Studio. I can also see that almost no one actually visited my site from these views! I have a couple plausible theories about this:

- It is possible that my site was, for a brief shining moment, the top of the search results for the topic "Google Analytics." As mentioned previously, Google is constantly experimenting with the search results, and occasionally the experiments do strange things.

- I had a very nice mention of that post on Twitter from the official Google Analytics account. Often, when someone is searching for a person or business entity, recent posts from their official Twitter account will be shown in the results. It seems likely that the post, which had a link to my site, was displayed in search results for "Google Analytics."

Checking the second possibility is made simple by the addition of the hyperlink connected to Query-Search. Clicking the link for "Google Analytics" returns the result page shown in Figure 6.19.

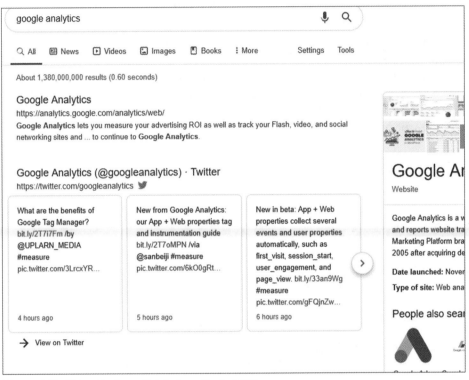

Figure 6.19: Using the hyperlink to investigate SERPs

Mystery solved! Indeed, the SERPs for the search query show some of the latest Twitter posts from the official Google Analytics account. The question now is, could we reproduce this result, and maybe more importantly, does it make any difference?

At the time of this spike, I was just getting known on Twitter for producing some good content about Data Studio. It certainly didn't hurt to get the exposure, as I was following one of the basic principles mentioned earlier: create useful content, and promote it by sharing in other channels. On the other hand, this exposure produced almost no site visits. In addition, if I was monitoring this every month, I would have noticed a huge loss in search views in September.

If I was looking at someone else's site in this situation, I'd advise them to keep sharing the content on Twitter but not to worry about trying to reproduce these results. In the future, if it happens again, I will know what to look for.

Unfortunately, that single exposure throws off most of the other results when viewed over a 16-month period. Now that the mystery is solved, I want to filter out those queries to get a more realistic view of my site.

This is the reason for including the Filter controls on the report. While I have that time period isolated, it should be easy to open the query list and deselect those terms. This turns out to not be so simple, because the page exposed not only the main terms that stand out, but also hundreds of misspellings of "Analytics"!

Fortunately, there are a couple of solutions to get rid of all of this "noisy" data. I could use the search box to view all the queries containing the string `"ana"` and click the check box to remove all of them in a single stroke, as shown in Figure 6.20. This reduces the number of different queries for that day from 1,130 down to 532. I can further reduce this number by searching for `"tic"` and delete those to get down to 400 queries. Although there is still a spike, it is not as pronounced. Once I click again on the chart to remove the filter for the dates, a bit clearer picture emerges.

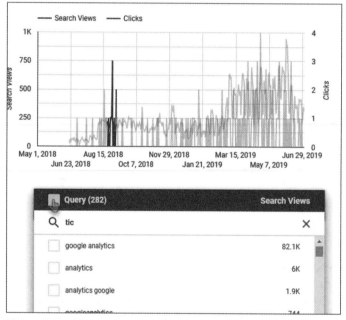

Figure 6.20: Filtering out noisy data using the Filter control

Unfortunately, I still have a bit of a problem. I did write some other posts that were focused on how to add users to Google Analytics. By using the filter, I just removed all the queries that were providing useful information about that page. A quick solution for this is to remove all the previous filtering and use the time-series chart to select data from after that date only. Although this shortens our time period, it works for our current purposes.

So, let's find an opportunity that we have more control over. By sorting the Target Page table by Clicks, we can see some "mismatches": pages that have a lot of search views, but not the same volume of clicks. Two pages stand out here, both related to adding users to Google services.

Since we are in a chapter about Search Console, we'll focus on that page. Clicking that row in the Target Pages table will filter the results of the Search Queries table so that it shows only the queries that apply to that page. Though this is somewhat helpful, because we can see mismatches now in the Query-Search table, it would help more if we could change my page to get some of this traffic.

This is where our new Search Type field comes in handy. We can get these questions quite easily by simply clicking the Question category of the bar chart. Doing this further filters our Query-Search table, so now we see only actual questions that searchers are asking.

> **TIP**   If you are in doubt about what you can add to a site to make it more appealing, look for the questions that your audience is asking and answer them! Quite often in answering the questions, you'll also pick up clicks for related queries.

As shown in Figure 6.21, we now have quite specific questions. I could easily change the title and the content of the page to reflect the language used in these queries more closely.

Specifically, I'd probably change the title to "How to Add Users to Google Search Console," and change some of the language on the page to include the terms "grant," "share," and "access" in the answer. It would also be a good idea to use the Query-Search links to check out the competing sites that were answering these queries.

An Example for Your Soul!

Soul Synergy Center (https://soulsynergycenter.com) is a business specializing in complementary healing services like yoga, massage, and Reiki. They also hold training events and feature a spiritual store. They also have one of the few Himalayan salt caves in the region at their location. Their website has a very different audience from mine. Let's put our report to the test and see if we can find insights and opportunities to make better connections with their audience.

First, it should be noted that unless we change the brand terms in our Search Types field, we won't find much insight there. Still, we can use the Query Filter control to help us filter some brand terms, and the other search types like Shopping and Question should still apply to this site.

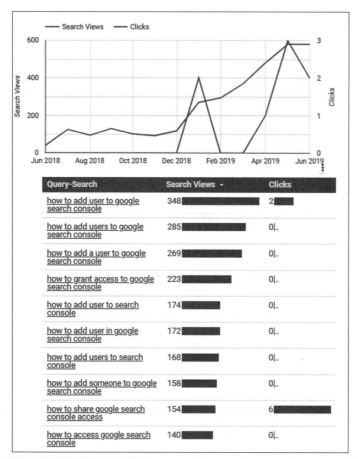

Query-Search	Search Views ▾	Clicks
how to add user to google search console	348	2
how to add users to google search console	285	0
how to add a user to google search console	269	0
how to grant access to google search console	223	0
how to add user to search console	174	0
how to add user in google search console	172	0
how to add users to search console	168	0
how to add someone to google search console	158	0
how to share google search console access	154	6
how to access google search console	140	0

Figure 6.21: Finding questions to answer

First, I reload the page to clear all the filters and start a fresh exploration session. Then I select the Soul Synergy Center site using the Data control. I am able to do this because they have added me as a user to their Search Console property. Figure 6.22 shows the initial view of their Search Console data.

When we look at the time-series chart, it is very clear that this site is either new or is missing some data. In this case, the site did a switch from `http` to the more secure `https`. If we had access to the other version of the website in Search Console, it might provide us with more context, but we'll have to make do without it.

We can see that search views peaked in December, then dropped for a bit, and then started climbing nicely. Without a longer range to view, however, it is hard to draw conclusions here about their recent increases. This is because many businesses have definite seasonal swings.

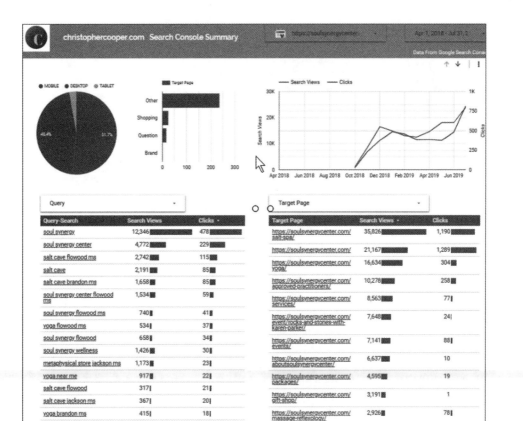

Figure 6.22: Soul Synergy initial view

We don't see any unusual spikes in the time-series chart as we did in the first example, but the relationship between search views and clicks is similar. We can also easily see that much more of their audience is using mobile devices. This is not surprising for a local business. If we click the different devices on the pie chart, we can see if the same patterns hold for each type of device.

When filtering for mobile devices, we see a steep recent climb that is not as pronounced in the desktop data. Some spikes start to appear when we use the drill-down to see weeks in the time-series chart. When we drill down to days, we can see a prominent spike clearly evident in Figure 6.23. Unlike the spike we looked at on my site, clicks follow the same pattern here, so that is promising!

If we isolate the spike period, using click and drag on the time-series chart, we can look for patterns. First, looking at the charts in the top section of Figure 6.23, we can see the searchers were heavy on the mobile side. Unfortunately, since we are not set up for Soul Synergy Center as a brand term, we don't easily see the relationship in the bar chart, but it is noticeable that there are no Questions or Shopping queries.

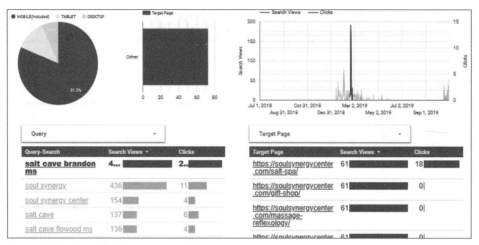

Figure 6.23: Investigating another spike

Focusing on the queries and pages tables, a couple of things stand out to me. First, the most popular page is not the home page, but the page for the salt spa. This is true even though the top search term is the business name, which would usually lead users to the home page.

Clicking a few query rows in the Query Search table reveals more information that could help produce insights. One of the things that I find interesting is not an unusual spike, but the uniformity of the search views for a number of pages for most of the top queries.

For instance, when we click on the row for `salt cave brandon ms`, we can see in Figure 6.23 that the top seven pages all had exactly 58 views! Despite the same number of views, the salt cave page is usually the winner, with the home page coming in second place for clicks. This pattern is repeated for other top search terms as well.

One more thing stands out here. The queries referring to "brandon" are unusually high, since the spa itself is in Flowood, Mississippi. Focusing only on queries with that keyword, we can see that the pattern for this town is almost all centered on the period of the spike.

So, it's time to investigate the SERPs! This is easy because we have thought-fully connected the search function to the link on the Query-Search field. We'll click the most popular query, `salt cave brandon ms`. Sadly, nothing is immediately apparent on the results page, shown in Figure 6.24, which would explain all of the data.

However, there are a few a major differences between my search and the actual searches: I am not located in Brandon, Mississippi; it is no longer February 2019; and, most importantly, I am not viewing the results from a mobile device. While I could fake my location, I don't have a time machine.

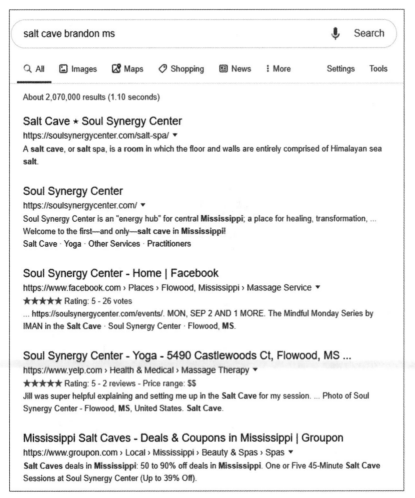

Figure 6.24: Looking for clues in the SERPs

Simulating a Mobile Device on Your Browser to Check Search Results

But I *can* easily see the search results as a mobile user if I am using one of the top three browsers. I will demonstrate this using the Google Chrome browser, but the method is similar for most browsers. The results are shown in Figure 6.25.

- Press Ctrl+Shift+I to bring up the Inspect panel. This works in all three popular browsers.
- Click the device icon to activate device emulation (see Figure 6.25, A).
- Select a mobile device to emulate (see Figure 6.25, B).
- Reload the page.

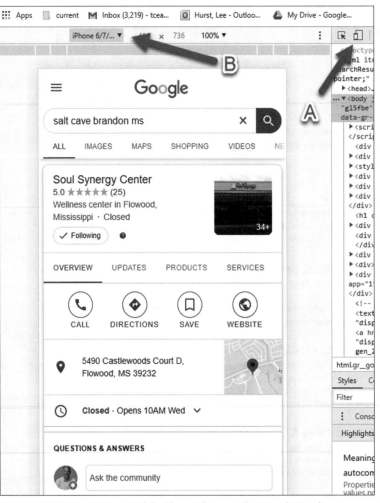

Figure 6.25: Simulating a Mobile Phone Changes the Search Results

As you can see, the results for mobile are quite different! Here we see a Google My Business (GMB) property listing. These will be the focus of our next chapter, so we won't dwell on the listings here. It is worth mentioning, however, that just like other search results, Google is constantly tinkering with GMB listings. At one time, they showed links on GMB listings for several popular pages on a site associated with that location. This could be the cause, but it is difficult to prove.

What I suspect caused this spike is this: there was an event near Brandon at that time for Soul Synergy that focused on their salt cave. Another possibility is that some media feature on TV or radio might have caused people to pull out their smartphones to find out more.

Is this a significant piece of information? Some further searching does not bring up the exact source of the traffic, so the specific source is still a mystery.

Still, whatever caused that spike, Soul Synergy might be able to do it again. Therefore, I will ask them if they know what might have caused it. Whatever it was, unlike the spike on my site, it brought with it a good number of clicks!

If we want more insights for action, we could consult the Question queries for easy content updates. Let's look at the Brand searches briefly to see how they are doing with searches for their business. As mentioned previously, we used the case statement to target `"helpfullee"` as a brand term in the Search Types field, so we can't directly use that to inspect for their brand. We can, however, simulate this segmentation through the Filter control search.

After clearing all of the filters, we click the Query Search control to expose the terms. As I showed you in Chapter 4, you can select all the desired terms quickly by deselecting the main check box, searching for a term, and then clicking the check box again. Doing this procedure with the phrase `"soul synergy"` filters for 13 unique queries.

Although there is a good upward trend, we see that mobile searches are responsible for the majority of this traffic. As before, we can filter for mobile users by clicking on the pie chart. Doing this shows a steady upward climb of search views, but clicks started to decline after February. In June, we see that clicks begin to shoot up and appear to be climbing at an increased rate, as shown in Figure 6.26.

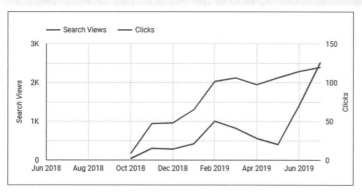

Figure 6.26: Brand search performance

When we sort the Target Pages table by clicks, we see a very productive page in the second row, but it has a strange-looking URL. Clicking this row shows that this page is responsible for a lot of traffic but that it only started appearing in June 2019.

The explanation here is fairly simple. Soul Synergy Center started focusing on their Google My Business listing at the end of May. Part of that effort included replacing the URL for the website button with a tracking link. The extra parameters on the URL starting with utm help Google Analytics determine that clicks on this URL are coming from the GMB listing button, not the regular page listing in the main results section.

Will the clicks keep climbing? We'll have to wait and see, but for now, we can report back that the efforts to update their listing are definitely paying off! This is at least some insight; we can give feedback to the business that they are making productive changes.

Searching for Actionable Insights

This is certainly good news, but we would like to give Soul Synergy Center another insight that can indicate something else with which they can work. We clear the filters again and check the Query-Search table to see if there are any mismatches between search views and clicks. Immediately, we see that the query "crystals and their meanings" has a huge mismatch: over 4,000 views and no clicks.

Maybe this is an anomaly, so we click the term to check its performance over time and the corresponding target pages. Doing this shows a steep rise in views around December. Although it is a couple months later, we see that demand is still strong and steady. Drilling down to weeks and days shows a similar consistent pattern.

Clicking the Target Page link, we see that this page is for an event on September 8, 2019, about crystals and their uses. If we had more historical information, we might see more interesting patterns. Most of the traffic is from desktop users, so it's unlikely these are just local searchers. By clicking the URL again, we release the page filter and can see all the queries leading to this page. You can see the results of this set of filters in Figure 6.27.

Query-Search	Search Views ▾	Clicks		Target Page	Search Views ▾
crystals and their meanings	4,576	0	..	https://soulsynergycenter.com/events/	10,375
stones and their meanings	332	0	..	https://soulsynergycenter.com/aboutsoulsynergycenter/	9,269
synergy meaning	329	0	..	**https://soulsynergycenter.com/event/rocks-and-stones-with-karen-parker/**	**8,905**
crystals and stones meanings	312	0	..		
stones and their meanings with pictures	286	6		https://soulsynergycenter.com/packages/	6,452
synergy 12 stones	208	0	..	https://soulsynergycenter.com/?utm_source=gmb&utm_medium=organic&utm_content=main&utm_campaign=listing	4,310
crystals meanings	204	0	..		
crystal meanings and uses	107	0	..		
stones and their meaning	101	0	..	https://soulsynergycenter.com/gift-shop/	4,033
crystals and their meaning	96	0	..	https://soulsynergycenter.com/massage-reflexology/	4,027
stones and meanings	71	0	..		
crystals meanings and uses	68	1		https://soulsynergycenter.com/event/5-element-qi-gong/	1,411
crystals stones and	68	0	..	https://soulsynergycenter	1,103
Grand total	**8,905**	**30**		**Grand total**	**197,993**

Figure 6.27: Crystal-clear interest

We see that there are a lot of similar terms that are producing views, and some that are producing clicks as well. It is the sixth page on the site in terms of views. For an event that has passed, this page is generating a lot of interest!

If we filter the queries for the term `"crystal"`, we see that there are several other event pages related to this term, some with traffic but none as exceptional as our first mismatch. If we look at the SERPs for the top crystal term, we find a lot of very visual pages on the topic.

Actions Based on Insights

Soul Synergy Center has a lot of interest from people who are intrigued by crystals: they have events and workshops, and all sell crystals and crystal jewelry in their shop. How can we help them in this area of interest?

One thing not on their website is a single, authoritative page about crystals. If they had a guide, a good one, they could build authority in that area and pass some of that authority to their other offerings.

Building a comprehensive guide is not a small task! As we saw in the SERPs, there is a lot of competition out there already, so a big guide would have to be very good indeed. Even quality content is not enough, though—you need to promote that content. Eventually, your page may rank well, and the efforts should pay off.

Narrowing the scope of the guide can help here; in this case, possibly focusing on "healing crystals and their meanings." The narrower the field, the fewer the competitors. Although it is still a fairly large pursuit to create even a narrow guide to a topic, it looks like something they should consider. This is a long-term investment. All of their current content is fairly short-lived, and this would give them a pillar to which they could connect their other content.

There is a proverb that goes something like this: "The best time to plant a tree was 20 years ago. The second-best time is now." This proverb definitely applies here.

Although this is a long-term play, we may be able to help the center further by giving them a list of terms, ranked by their popularity, related to the subject. Making sure that they include these terms in the current offerings could help draw more traffic. Fortunately, we have a source for that list, and the relative popularity of the terms is in the filtered queries table.

There is only one problem: how can we get them this data in a format they can easily use? Fortunately, this is another feature in Data Studio—the ability to export a table's data to a CSV file or a Google Sheets file. We can send them a brief explanation indicating that they should look for areas to incorporate these terms in their existing content.

To export the table, right-click a chart and select one of the export options shown in Figure 6.28. In our case, we export the table's data as a Google Table so that we can easily share a single copy with several people. This produces an easy-to-use file of terms with the same columns as our filtered source table.

Figure 6.28: Exporting the crystal-related terms

Hopefully, we have produced some valuable insights for our friends at Soul Synergy Center, in addition to a simple, but powerful, report they can use going forward.

Summary

In this chapter, we explored Search Console, a tool for website owners and managers to interface with Google Search services. Search Console plays a vital role in helping to fill in information not available from Google Analytics. It helps us better understand the relationship of a website to its audience and how that relationship is mediated by Google and other search engines.

Going back to the essentials, we followed the basic cooking analogy to build our report and followed up with actual examples of how the report could be used to gain insights that can be followed with actions to help a website be more successful pursuing its goals and audience.

We covered the following concepts and topics:

- The limits of using the sample data connectors
- A review of the Search Console interface, its uses, and fields

- Augmenting a report with your own categories using case statements
- Using hyperlink functions to connect to resources outside of the report
- How to simulate a mobile phone with your browser to check search results
- Using the report with real websites to find opportunities and insights of value to site owners and managers

Viewing Local Organization Data from Google My Business

In this chapter, we will be focused on working with local business and organization data provided by the Google My Business (GMB) service. As Google surfaces more information about local entities to the search results pages, many people are getting their first impression of an organization through the GMB listings.

We will be using Data Studio to create reports to monitor these listings, and along the way, dive into third-party data connections and mobile report design.

Google Search and the Local Organization

Google organizes entity information about people, places, and things, not just web pages. When you do a search, you often see information about these entities in a panel on the results page; this panel is referred to as a *knowledge graph*. For instance, if you search for "Albert Einstein," you get a panel with information pulled from various sources about that famous person.

Google makes assumptions about the information you want based on what it can guess about your intent and context. As an example, if you search for "pizza" on a laptop, you get completely different results from the same search on your phone, and you get different results on your phone in different locations.

Google, as well as other search engines, assumes that if you search for "pizza" on your phone, you are probably looking for a restaurant or pizza delivery, so it returns references to restaurants, not web pages about pizza in general. This behavior doesn't apply only to restaurants, or course. Google collects information about all kinds of organizations, including their physical locations, and displays knowledge panels for these organizations in the search results and on maps.

Over time, Google has surfaced more and more information about local organizations that it thinks you want to know about. If you search for "Churches near me" or simply "Churches" on your mobile device, you see these location listings. They are often shown in a small map on the search results page, as you can see in Figure 7.1. Clicking one of these listings on the map shows more detail about the organization in a knowledge panel.

Figure 7.1: A search for churches with location listings

Some of these listings are likely to be of interest to you personally or professionally, or because friends or family are involved with these organizations. Small local businesses employ a large number of people, and even if you are employed by a huge multinational corporation that does not have a local presence, you are likely to be involved with nonbusiness organizations in your community. Virtually all of these entities have knowledge graphs. When people talk about these entities and their knowledge graphs, they are referred to as *listings*.

GMB: The New Home Page in the Search Results

Unlike other kinds of Google entities, people related to an organization location may have some direct input on what shows up in the knowledge graph for a listing. *Google My Business (GMB)* is a free service that lets people associated with that organization register, update, and enhance their local search listings.

If you want to update a GMB listing, the location must be registered by someone associated with the organization at the location. While a business may register with GMB to create a new listing, in many cases these listings exist long before anyone has claimed them. Registering or claiming a location involves proving to the GMB service that you can represent the organization at the location. Some businesses that provide local services may not have a physical address, but they can still register with GMB so that their listing will show up in local searches.

Long gone are the days of simple web page links when it comes to the search results page! GMB, and other features of the search results pages, have affected the way traffic flows to websites, for better or for worse.

Although the number of searches on Google is still increasing, the percentage of searches that actually result in a user clicking on a link to a website is decreasing, particularly for mobile users. One current estimate places the number of *zero-click searches* (those that do not result in a click-through to a website) at approximately 50 percent!

> **NOTE**   For more on this topic, see https://sparktoro.com/blog/
> less-than-half-of-google-searches-now-result-in-a-click.

Similar listings are found on other search engines and social media sites, but Google's huge reach makes GMB listings extra worthy of attention from local business and other organizations. There is a popular idea in the local search engine optimization (SEO) community that GMB should be thought of as the new home page for local business instead of the actual home page of the organization's website.

Next, we'll examine some typical listings and see what information they provide to the viewer and to the location manager. Then we'll look at how Data Studio can help organizations better understand the performance of those listings.

What the User Sees in a GMB Listing

Figure 7.2 shows a GMB listing for the Baber A.M.E. Church, a well-known establishment that has been part of the Rochester, New York, community for over 50 years. I picked this listing because I was recently there to vote in a local primary election. I was impressed by the space where the voting was taking place and thought it might be a good place to hold local meetings. A few days later, I did a search for churches near me, and it showed up in the listings.

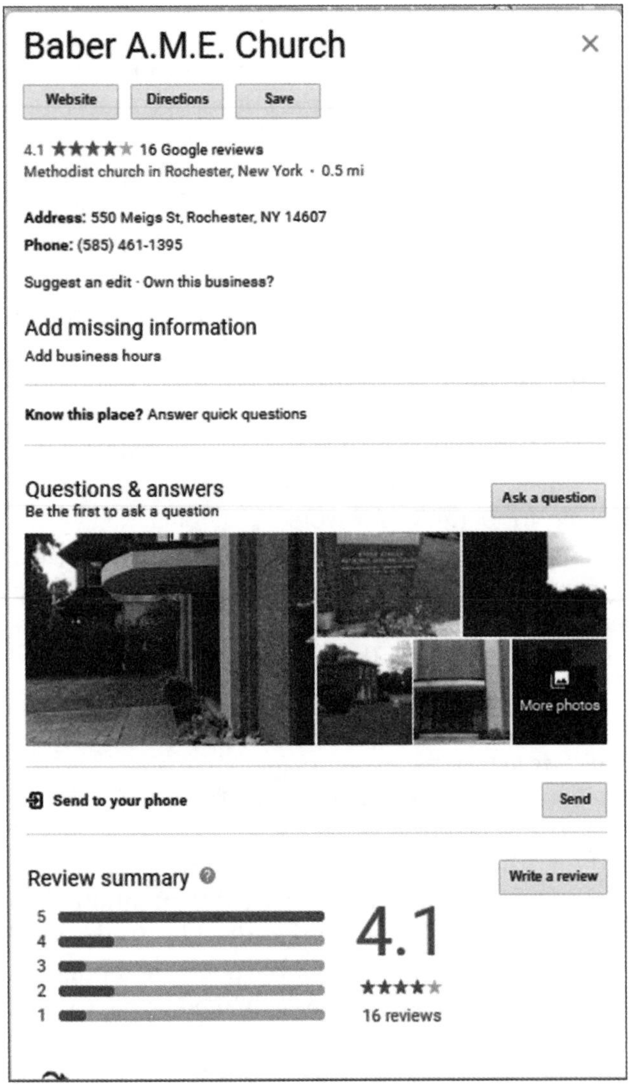

Figure 7.2: A typical GMB church listing

The main point that stands out to me, as a student of local searches, is the link to "Own this business?" This tells you that no one has yet claimed the listing. This gives us a chance to look at a listing that has not been claimed and updated by an owner. Here are the main features:

- The GMB listing includes buttons to link to their website, to get directions, and to save the listing.

- The listing contains reviews with an average rating and a link to read the actual reviews.

- The listing includes a very brief description of the organization and how far it is from me.

- On the address and phone information, the phone number is clickable, and it will trigger a call from a mobile device.

- There is a section for editing suggestions where anyone can make an editing suggestion for a listing, not just those associated with the organization.

- The GMB listing includes business hours, quick questions about the location, and a question-and-answer section. Note that there is little information added here for this listing.

- The listing includes some photos of the location posted by people who have been to this location.

- There is another review section with a breakdown by number of stars and an invitation for viewers to write their own reviews.

- Just below the image are more quotes from the reviews, a link to the church's Facebook page, and related places for which people also search.

That's quite a lot of information considering that no one from the organization has registered or is managing this listing! Although this information may be helpful if you are already familiar with the church, there is little to distinguish it from other organizations nearby. If you were new to the area and looking for a local church, you would likely pass over this listing. You don't get a sense of what might make this church special for you. There is an easy opportunity for this organization to take advantage of this listing to tell their story and why people might want to visit.

NOTE If you want to find out more about how to claim a Google My Business listing and how to manage one, I have provided some links to get you started on the Resources page for this book at www.wiley.com/go/handsondatastudio.

There are many reasons to claim and manage a GMB listing, but one of the most important is helping an organization understand how their listing is being viewed and used. Organizations that do not claim their listing have no visibility into how many people see their listing. They also do not know how many people are using their GMB listing to call, get directions, or click through to their website.

Let's take a look at another listing. This time, the listing is owned and is currently under active management, as shown in Figure 7.3. Soul Synergy Center, a wellness center and spa, is the business that we examined in Chapter 6, "Using Google Search Console for Audience Insights," when we were investigating Search Console data. Soul Synergy Center recently took a renewed interest in their listing and were kind enough to share some of their data for this book.

The GMB listing here is so long that I had to cut up the image to fit it into the page! The Soul Synergy Center listing has the same features that we looked at earlier with these additions:

More images: The site manager and visitors have added more images to the listing.

Business hours listed: Special holidays will also be listed here.

Events: Date, time, and links to upcoming events. There is also a link to view more events.

Products: A carousel shows products and prices for items from their shop and an option to view all.

Explore Collections: This provides another way to view products that they have posted on the listing.

Questions & Answers: There is only one question here now, but they have the opportunity to add more later.

Reviews from the Web: Facebook and Groupon review scores are posted here.

Popular Times: A histogram shows how busy the location is at different times.

From Soul Synergy Center: This describes the business and services provided.

Posts section: These are special messages for events, what's new, and special offers. These are similar to social media posts and can have call-to-action buttons to register for events or to find out more by going to a page on their website.

It is quite likely this listing will have more features in the near future. Currently, GMB allows businesses to show videos and add buttons for booking appointments and even message the organization directly. As with other parts of its search results, Google is constantly experimenting with new layouts and features.

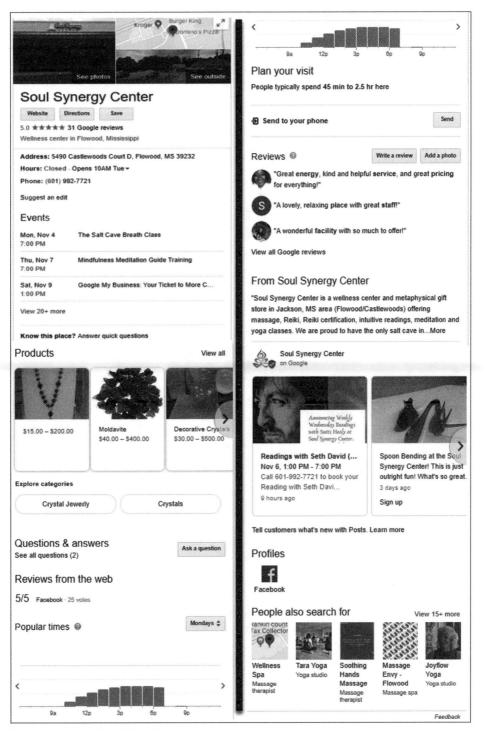

Figure 7.3: An active GMB listing

What the Owner Sees in a GMB Listing

Google My Business, like Search Console, has its own interface for the location manager, referred to as the *owner* by Google. The owner may use this interface to update information and review interaction data for the listing. This interface provides useful information and some visualizations, but these elements are scattered across different areas of the application.

Let's take a look at a GMB location from the owner's perspective. Logging into the GMB application at www.google.com/business, we see a listing of claimed locations from which to select, as shown in Figure 7.4.

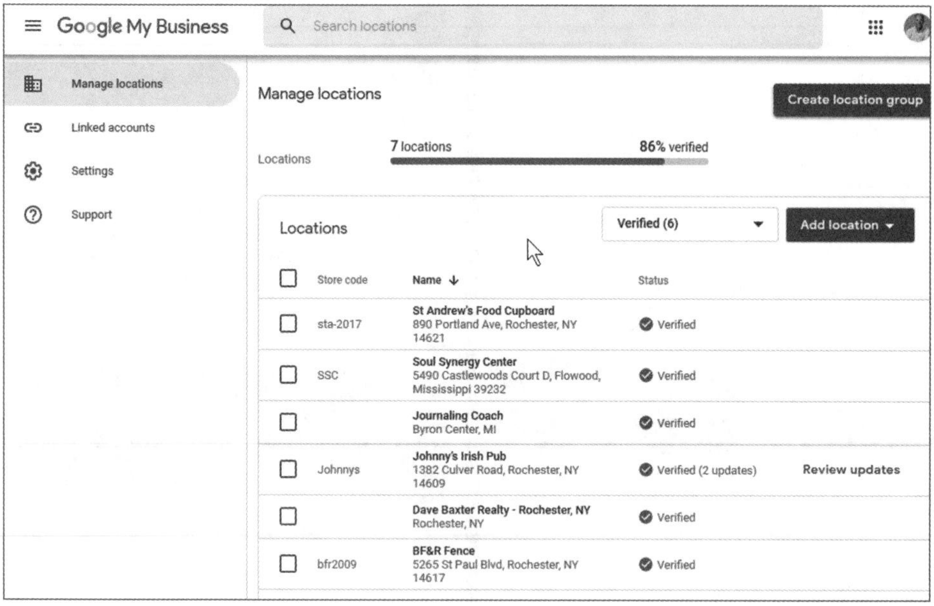

Figure 7.4: GMB locations view

On this screen, you have to select a single location you want to view. This isn't a problem if you have only one location to manage. However, businesses often have multiple locations on which they would like to report. You are limited to viewing information about single locations.

Clicking a location brings you to a home screen, as shown in Figure 7.5. This view is designed to give the manager an overview of the activity and interactions within their listing. Google provides some update suggestions and signups for associated services, as you can see in Figure 7.5. You'll see some very high-level metrics scorecards here.

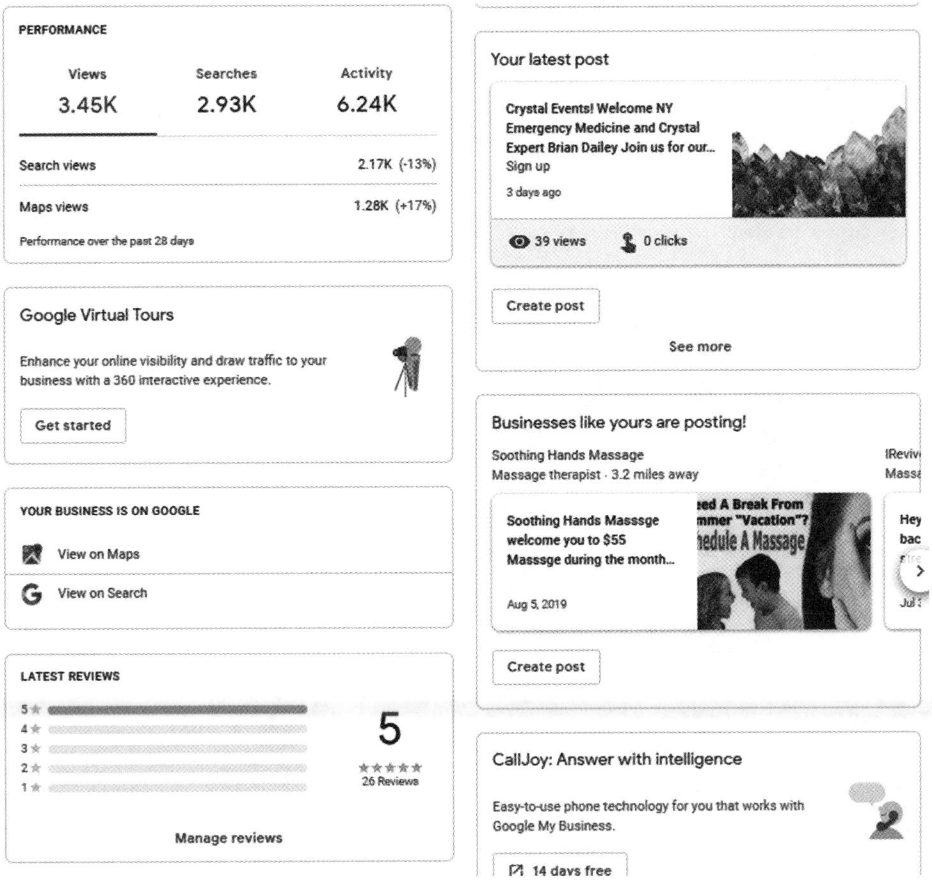

Figure 7.5: GMB home screen

Most of the information about the listing is found in the well-named Insights section. In this section, you find some information about queries used to find your location and a basic date selector. You can view charts in the GMB interface only for the most recent week, month, or quarter, as shown in Figure 7.6. Note that this feature is quite limited as compared to the Date Range selector found in Data Studio itself.

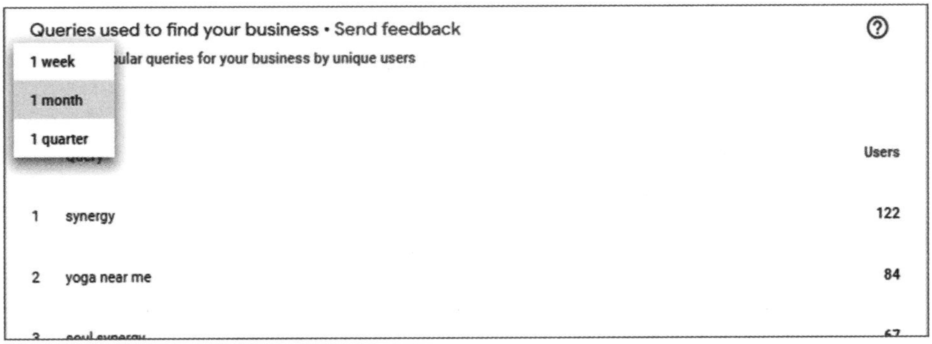

Figure 7.6: Queries and date range selection

Scroll down the page, and you see a basic breakdown of how searchers find the listing. There are three basic categories here with descriptions, a pie chart, and a breakdown of these types, as shown in Figure 7.7. Again, this is helpful, but it doesn't show you how these metrics might be changing over time, or even if they are increasing or decreasing!

Figure 7.7: Breakdown of search types

Scrolling down to the next section, you see an area chart showing the views for the listing from Google Search and on Google Maps. Although the chart may be nice to look at, it can be difficult to interpret. As shown in Figure 7.8, when we're looking at June 8, 2019, the number of search views appears to be twice the number of the Maps views. Only when you hover over the date with the mouse pointer can you see that they differ by only one view!

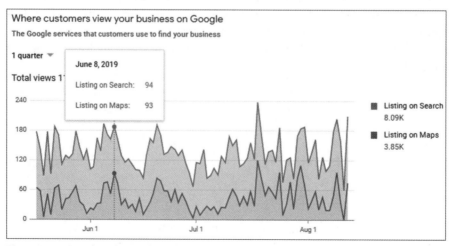

Figure 7.8: Search and Maps views

Search views are stacked on top of Maps views, making this a stacked area chart. Clicking the legend allows you to see one service at a time and to redraw the chart in order to scale that metric correctly. Again, you have no options for viewing this data in another chart format or for comparing the metrics to previous time ranges.

The next section possibly contains the most vital information for a manager: customer actions. *Customer actions* are a primary metric for GMB managers because they indicate customer interest in deeper interaction with the organization and may be counted as sales leads by a business. This section measures the following metrics:

Call You: Clicks on the Phone link

Request Directions: Clicks on the Directions button

Visit Your Website: Clicks on the Website button on the listing

As you can see in Figure 7.9, these are all shown together on another stacked area chart.

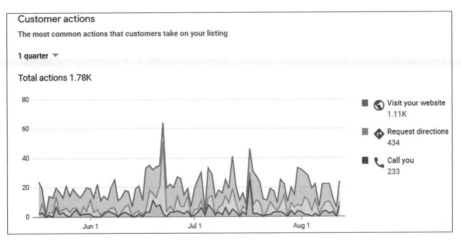

Figure 7.9: Customer Actions area chart

Again, you see the use of a stacked area chart, and once again you can compare these metrics to a previous period. Stacked area charts can be attractive, but you might prefer line charts to see the metrics independently.

Next is a section that gives a detailed breakdown of where requests for directions are originating. It goes all the way down to the zip code level and displays the metric on a Google Map, as shown in Figure 7.10. I think you'll agree that this is an impressive display, and it could render some pretty useful insights.

As of this writing, this type of chart cannot yet be reproduced in Data Studio. As good as it looks, it would be greatly improved if you could easily compare the information over a range of dates. Unless you take screenshots of this page, the information will be lost the next month, and you'll have a hard time determining whether a particular area is increasing or decreasing in requests for directions over time.

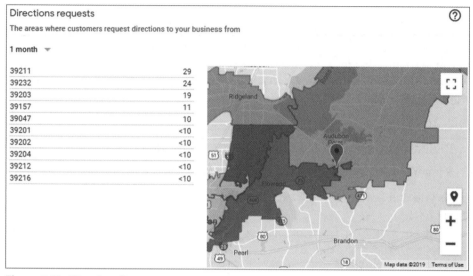

Figure 7.10: Directions Requests map

Continuing down the page, you find some useful information about phone calls and visits. There is a column chart showing the number of calls for the period, broken down by day of the week. This is useful information, and it can help managers plan for phone staffing.

Next, you may see a column chart for Popular Times if the organization has a physical location. You may also see an Average Visit Duration metric. Google doesn't know how many people have been at the location, but it can get a pretty good idea of the relative traffic on different days by tracking mobile phone locations. Again, this can be very useful information for improving staffing efficiency.

Last, you come to a chart showing photo views. This can be filtered by Owner photos or Customer photos. Although this chart suffers from some of the issues that we have seen with other charts, it does have one valuable difference: it shows how the photo views for your property are compared to "Businesses like you."

Although it may not be totally clear how Google determines which businesses are like yours, this chart still gives you a piece of competitive information that would otherwise be hard to come by. Figure 7.11 shows Customer photos for a location.

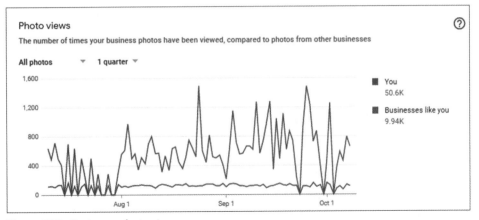

Figure 7.11: Customer photo views

Some recent studies have shown the high correlation between the number of photos posted and the number of views, so this is something over which the manager may have some control. See the Google My Business Insights Study from BrightLocal at:

```
www.brightlocal.com/research/google-my-business-insights-study/#photos
```

As mentioned earlier, GMB has more information in other sections. Reviews have their own section, where a manager can view and respond to customer comments. Regrettably, GMB does not tell you how many reviews came in over any period of time. This is unfortunate since reviews are a critical piece of information for prospective customers or visitors.

Another important GMB feature is the ability for the organization to create posts. These are similar to social media posts and can promote events, specials, products, and other messages and can contain videos. GMB provides very little information here as well. As shown in Figure 7.12, it provides post views only for the current week and some information about each post.

Why Use Data Studio for GMB?

Although the regular interface provided by GMB provides some fairly attractive charts, it is hard to tell whether a listing is doing better or worse over time for a number of important metrics. You have limited time range selections and no comparison to previous periods. The use of stacked area charts in some sections makes you work even harder to evaluate performance in many areas, and the owner has no option to view this information in a different way. If you were a location manager reporting to a business owner or to a board of directors for an organization, it would be extremely difficult to produce monthly reports and answer basic questions about performance over time or provide insights or suggestions for action.

Figure 7.12: Posts for events

GMB does have some export facilities that the owner can use to download information in a CSV format. Unfortunately, this option is not very practical for several reasons:

- Every time you download information, you must set a date range to export.
- Data is spread out among several reports.

- Although you have an extended date range and the ability to pick start and end dates from a date picker, all of the metrics for that time period are stored as aggregated totals in a single row for that location. There is no detail data by date.

The last bullet is the biggest drawback of using this method. For example, what if you want to see how many phone calls you were getting from a listing on a day-to-day basis for the last three months? You would have to download 72 separate CSV files! You could then combine these into one master worksheet, but the whole process is time consuming and certainly tedious.

Wouldn't it be easier to connect to GMB as a Data Studio data source, as we did with Google Analytics and Search Console? Here are some of the advantages of using Data Studio for GMB data:

- Automatically updated live reports
- Flexible time range selection
- Ability to share reports and even have PDFs emailed on a regular basis
- Control over the display of the charts in ways that you think best highlight the important data
- The ability to copy and modify reports with ease
- The ability to compare metrics over time easily

Of course, there is one other big advantage to using Data Studio that is not GMB related: if you are using Data Studio to report on Google Analytics, Search Console, or any other data source, you can combine all those metrics into a single report! Not only does this save time for people who need to prepare reports, it is easier for those viewing those reports to have all the information in one place in a consistent format.

Fortunately, bringing multiple data sources into a single report is simple in Data Studio. We'll look at building this kind of report in later chapters. For now, we'll stick to a report that provides information just about GMB.

So, let's go back to our cooking analogy for report creation and go through the steps required to prepare a new GMB report.

Step 1. Selecting the Dish to Prepare

For this example, our intended audience is a busy business owner or a manager in charge of marketing. We have seen several kinds of reports so far:

- Static reports designed for printing or PDF viewing

- Interactive reports with limited interactivity designed to let the viewer explore within boundaries
- Workbenches with many filters designed for exploring data and looking for patterns in data

For this report, we'll go in yet another direction. This time, the goal is to provide a report that can be frequently accessed in a very easy way. It should provide the viewer with quick-to-digest information about the general health of major metrics so that the viewer can tell whether issues exist that require attention. The report will have limited interaction in order to keep the user focused and, where possible, to be a clear guide to action. The type of report that has these features is typically called a *dashboard*.

When driving a car, the dashboard provides quick feedback at a glance so that the driver can keep their attention on the road. You frequently check some of the gauges, such as the speedometer. Other gauges, however, such as the ones for fuel and engine temperature, are not referenced as frequently, though they are still visible and important to check on a regular basis. A dashboard allows you to do a quick status check of a system, make adjustments, and see the results. It also reminds you to do important tasks, such as refueling your car.

The dashboard is in a convenient location in a car for quick glances, and we would like the same easy accessibility for our GMB report. To meet this need, we'll make this report "mobile optimized"—that is, it will be designed to be viewed on a mobile phone. This way, it can be accessed virtually anywhere and at any convenient time.

The reports we have examined so far can be viewed on any device with a browser. However, they do not have a responsive design like most web pages. To be more precise, they can be resized, but they do not reconfigure the report elements when the user switches from a large screen to a smaller one.

Although a responsive design may be ideal, we can settle for one that works reasonably well on a large screen and very well on a mobile phone. It is fairly simple to create different versions of a report for different screens. In this case, we'll design the report with the smartphone screen in mind and make it look, and respond, more like a mobile app.

With mobile screens in mind, we could make a single, very narrow and long page divided into sections so that the user could scroll through the charts. Instead of this approach, we'll use multiple pages to organize groups of metrics together.

You saw multiple page reports in Chapter 5, "Web Data Visualization with Google Analytics," where we used a separate page to focus on the region of Spain. Unfortunately, the regular page navigation methods do not scale well to small screens. We'll get around this problem by providing our own navigation buttons.

The Actions Page

Figure 7.13 shows the first page of our example report. This page is focused on GMB actions.

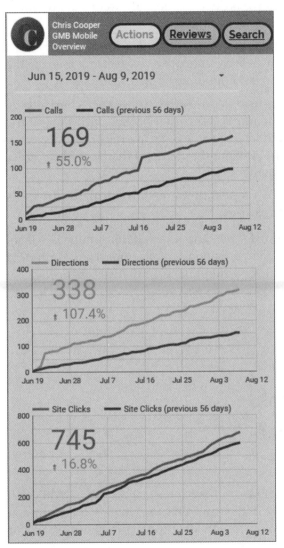

Figure 7.13: The completed report—Actions page

Here is a breakdown of the parts of this page. We use the black background with bright colors to make the display more vivid on the phone screen.

Header   Again, we see some of our familiar elements: the colored header bar, a logo image, a descriptive title, and just below that, a date range picker. To replace the standard page navigation, we have created buttons to allow the user to switch pages easily and used color to indicate which page they are on. The date range is defaulted to eight weeks to give more context than the standard four-week period.

Calls Chart   We use a standard time-series chart here, with the comparison period engaged. This chart uses the Cumulative style setting to make the changes over the last period stand out more.

Calls Scorecard   Since we are using cumulative time-series charts, there is almost always room in the upper-left corner of the chart. We put the Calls scorecard in this area to save space, and we use the same coloring to help group the related charts. We put the charts in the most likely order of importance for a small business.

Directions and Site Clicks   We repeat the same formatting as the Calls components with different coloring.

Using the Cumulative style setting for the time-series charts eliminates a lot of visual noise that makes it hard to compare periods. For comparison, Figure 7.14 shows what the chart would look like without the Cumulative setting.

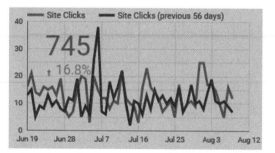

Figure 7.14: Without the Cumulative setting

Another design decision is to split the actions into separate tables. Although having the action metrics together in the same chart is visually interesting, it will be very hard for the viewer to process them with the previous periods for each metric on the same chart.

The Reviews Page

Reviews can make or break a local business, so a GMB manager needs to keep a very close eye on them. Not only do reviews affect the reputation of an organization, they also provide vital feedback from customers to the organization.

Figure 7.15 shows the layout intended to help a dashboard user keep on top of reviews.

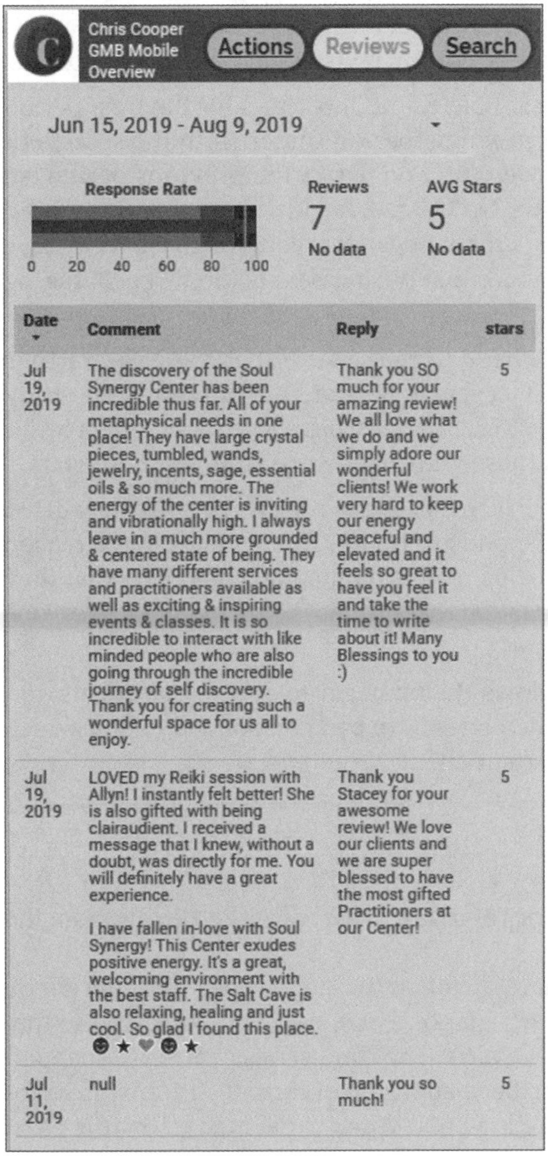

Figure 7.15: The completed report—Reviews page

This page uses the same header elements that you saw on the Actions page. The only difference is that we have removed the link and highlighted the Reviews button. Here is a quick breakdown of the rest of the page components:

Response Rate Bullet Chart   The *bullet chart* is a component we have not used before. In this case, it is showing the percentage of reviews responded to. It shows the report user immediately whether certain goal thresholds have been met. In this case, the goal of a 95 percent response rate to reviews is being met and exceeded, since all current reviews have been responded to.

Reviews Scorecard   This is a simple count of reviews for the time period with a comparison for the previous period underneath the score. For this particular case, there were no reviews in the previous period, so the comparison metric shows No Data. A healthy flow of reviews is an important ranking factor for GMB listings, and requesting visitors to leave reviews is an important practice that businesses should be encouraging and monitoring.

AVG Stars   This is a quick check to make sure that the basic ratings stay high. Surprisingly, perfect scores here are not optimal! One study (see www.locallogy.com/about-us/blog/246) has shown that perfect 5-star scores are trusted less than those with an average around 4.2–4.5 stars.

Consumers trust businesses with some negative reviews because they get to see how an organization responds to issues. Understanding the reason for a negative review also helps reassure potential customers that they are engaging with an organization that may not be a good fit for everyone but that is a good fit for them.

Reviews Table   This table allows the manager to review comments and ratings quickly, and see which ones have been responded to and which ones may need immediate attention.

The Search Page

This page holds all the other metrics of interest that we are retrieving from the listing, as shown in Figure 7.16.

This layout is similar to the chart layout on the Actions page, but the charts are smaller and easier to take in at a glance. We moved the scorecards so that they don't overlap the time-series charts. The time-series charts are stripped down so that the user can focus on the relationship of current performance compared to the previous period. Here is a breakdown of the metrics on this page:

Maps Views   This shows the number of times the listing has been viewed on Google Maps. This is an important metric for locations that require lots of visitors to be successful.

The scorecard here shows that there was moderate growth, and the time-series chart confirms that although the numbers were close for most of the period, after the midpoint this period's performance was picking up.

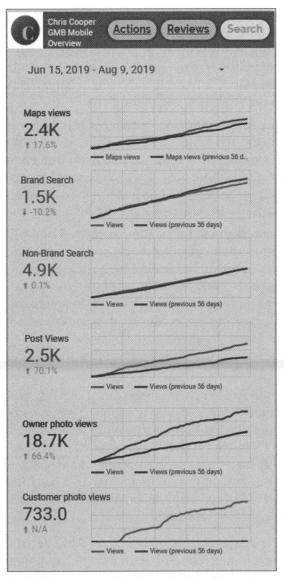

Figure 7.16: The completed report—Search page

Brand Search   This is the Direct Search metric that we saw in the GMB interface. The metric was renamed to be more relatable for the audience. Brand searches indicate queries that contain the organization name or address, which are a good indicator of the organization's reputation and other marketing efforts. In this case, we see a moderate drop-off compared to the previous period, with most of the drop occurring at the end of the period.

Non-Brand Search   This is an indication of all the views from queries that do not contain the location's name or address. This is an indication of the performance of optimizing the listing with appropriate content to catch searches as well as an indirect indicator of the search engine optimization of the website. Here we see that there is basically no change compared to the previous period, both in the scorecard and in the chart.

Post Views   Posts are often underutilized by GMB managers. Having a few posts active and updated at all times is a good practice for almost any GMB site. A quick glance at the scorecards helps put the relative volume into perspective here. There are actually more post views than either Maps or Brand Search views. In this case, the organization just restarted a consistent post program, and it looks like the efforts are paying off nicely!

Owner Photo Views   This is another area that is often neglected by GMB managers, and it is well within their control. Google suggests posting images frequently, and independent studies show a high correlation between the number of photos posted and the number of photos viewed. In the future, we might change this report so that it has some emphasis on the number of photos the business has posted during the period, and we may use a bullet chart to set a goal. In this case, the business has added about 30 images, and both the scorecard and the chart confirm the positive effect on photo views.

Customer Photo Views   These are an example of what is called *user-generated content (UGC)*. UGC also includes comments and questions. High rates of UGC being posted indicate that the location is active and that customers or members are supportive. Different types of businesses, like bars, restaurants, and hotels, naturally have more people posting pictures about their experiences at a location, so it may seem that a manager has little control over this metric. However, simply requesting visitors to share their pictures through the listing can have very positive effects.

In this case, the business just started getting customer photos. Although the performance looks good, we'll have to wait a while to see if it keeps improving. Again, we might change the format of this report to emphasize and remind managers to suggest that customers add photos of their experience with the business and track the number of customer photos uploaded.

Now that you know what the report will look when completed, we can move on to the reconstruction.

Before You Begin: What You Need to Get Started

To build a Google My Business report, you need access to a GMB property. Unfortunately, I cannot help you out with that, as there are no sample GMB listings with which you can practice or sample GMB connectors like those that we found for Google Analytics and Search Console. The next section assumes that you own a listing or that your Google account has been added by the location owner.

For those who are interested in claiming and managing a listing, we provide links in the chapter notes of the online resources page to get you started. You can find these at www.wiley.com/go/handsondatastudio.

> **TIP** If you want to get started with GMB but don't know where to begin, look to your employer or organizations to which you belong. Chances are good that they have some listings and would appreciate having reporting in return. If that is not an option, look to charitable organizations. Many small local organizations do not have the staff to maintain good listings and would welcome the help.

Step 2. Let's Go Shopping and Assemble the Ingredients

To connect your report to Google My Business, you'll need to set up a new data source connection. To do this, you start back at the Data Studio home screen, click the Create button, and select Data Source, as shown in Figure 7.17.

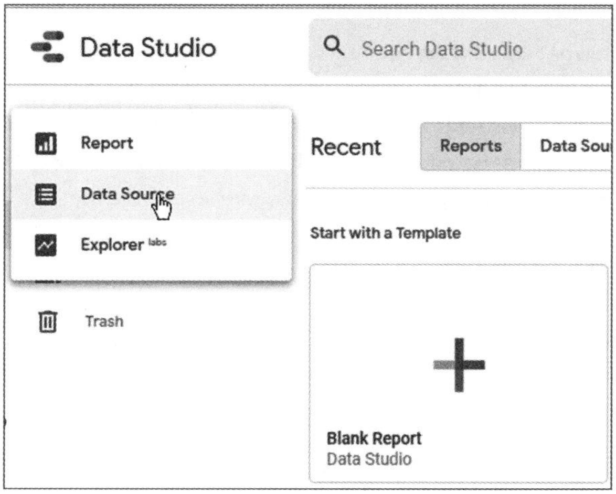

Figure 7.17: Starting the new data source setup

This will take you to the Data Source setup page, where you'll pick a connector. Here we run into a problem: there is no Google My Business connector provided by Google! Although Google may provide a GMB connector at some future date, we'll have to find a third-party provider for this connection.

Use the search box on this page to find connectors for **Google My Business**, and you see a listing of connectors for the service, as shown in Figure 7.18.

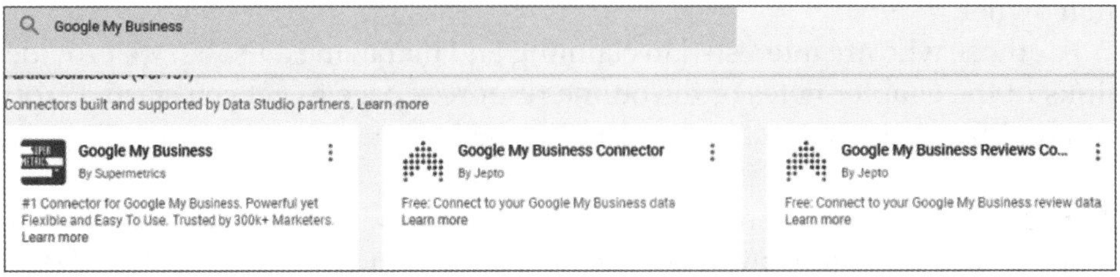

Figure 7.18: GMB connectors

For this example, we'll use two connectors provided by Jepto: the Google My Business Connector and the Google My Business Reviews Connector. Jepto (www.jepto.com), a provider of digital marketing intelligence and automation services, has created these free connectors to get more exposure for its business.

As of this writing, our only other alternatives for GMB are premium connectors that require a subscription fee to use, or you may choose to program your own connector. Although the premium connectors offer some advantages, we'll be sticking with the free options to make the example more accessible to a larger audience. Creating your own connectors is beyond the scope of this book.

> **NOTE**   If you are interested in what a premium connector can do, I provide links to another mobile-oriented example in the online chapter notes. That example uses the Supermetrics GMB Connector, which provides more dimensions and metrics than our free connector. The report shows more detailed information about posts and post views. Premium connectors are popular with digital marketing agencies, where the cost of the subscription is easily made up in time savings when reporting for several clients.

Using most third-party connectors usually requires a registration process. This is true for the Jepto connectors as well, so we'll walk through the setup process.

Setting Up the Jepto Google My Business Connector

Follow these steps to set up the Jepto GMB Connector.

1. On the Connectors screen, select the Google My Business Connector By Jepto. This will bring up the connector setup screen, as shown in Figure 7.19.

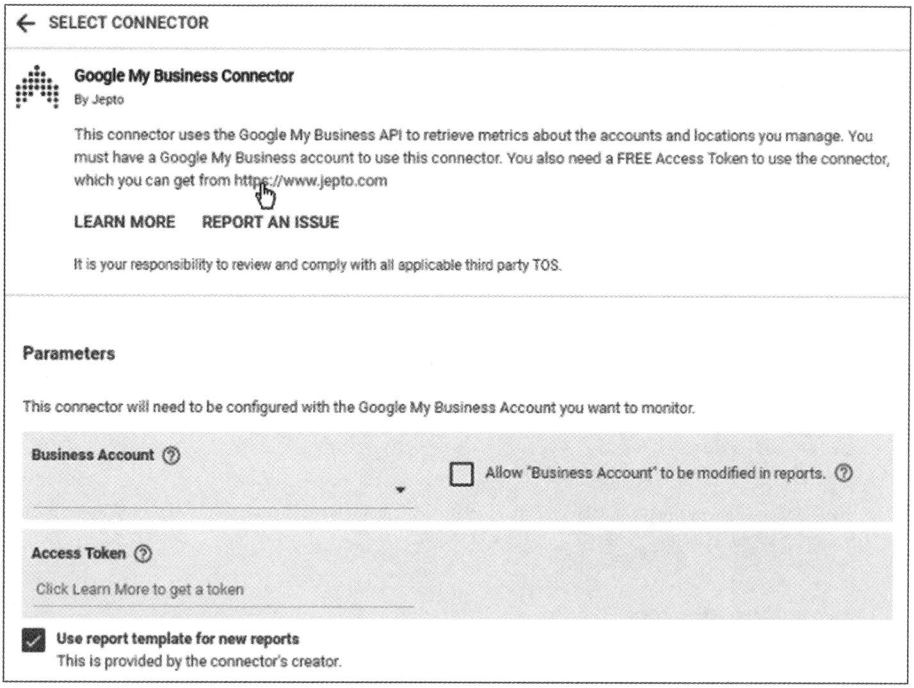
SELECT CONNECTOR
Google My Business Connector
By Jepto
This connector uses the Google My Business API to retrieve metrics about the accounts and locations you manage. You must have a Google My Business account to use this connector. You also need a FREE Access Token to use the connector, which you can get from https://www.jepto.com
LEARN MORE
REPORT AN ISSUE
It is your responsibility to review and comply with all applicable third party TOS.
Parameters
This connector will need to be configured with the Google My Business Account you want to monitor.
Business Account
Allow "Business Account" to be modified in reports.
Access Token
Click Learn More to get a token
Use report template for new reports
This is provided by the connector's creator.

Figure 7.19: Jepto connector setup screen

2. If this is your first time using Jepto connectors, you'll need to click the link in the description to get a free access token to continue the setup. You'll be taken to the Jepto home page. Scroll to the bottom of the page to find the Free Google My Business Data Studio Connector link, shown in Figure 7.20.

FREE Google My Business Data Studio Connector
No Trial. No Credit Card. Free forever.

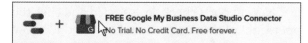

Figure 7.20: Link to access the Jepto connector

3. Click the link to open the connector access page. In addition to the connectors, Jepto provides some free Data Studio templates to get you started. We'll skip these and click the Get Access To Connectors button, as shown in Figure 7.21.

4. A registration form opens. Fill in your name, email address, and company. You should use the same Gmail account that you used to get access to

your listing as the email address. Click the Get Access button, and you should see an Access Granted page with the message that you'll receive an access token via email.

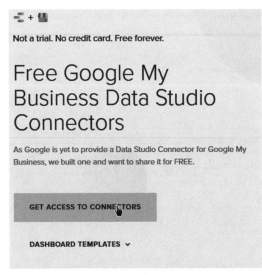

Figure 7.21: Accessing the Jepto connectors

5. Check your email for the Jepto access message. This will most likely show up in the Updates section of your Gmail account. Copy the access token code and return to the connector setup page, repeating steps 1 to 3 if needed to return to that page.

6. Select the Allow "Business Account" To Be Modified In Reports check box. Paste, or enter, the access token code into the Access Token field. Leave the Use Report Template For New Reports check box selected and click the Connect button in the upper right of the screen. You'll be asked to allow parameter sharing. Click Accept, and you are taken to the field setup screen.

7. Change the default name of the data source. In this example, we set the name to **All Sites – GMB – Business - Jepto 1.0**.

8. Modify the field labels. Changing the labels for some of the fields now will save time later when you're laying out the charts. Change the field labels listed here, and the fields setup should look like Figure 7.22. After completing these changes, click the Data Studio icon next to the title to return to the home screen.

Change Direct Searches to **Brand Search**.

Change Discovery Searches to **Non-Brand Search**.

Change Website Actions to **Site Clicks**.

Change Phone Call Actions to **Calls**.

Change Directions Actions to **Directions**.

Change Local Post Search Views to **Post Views**.

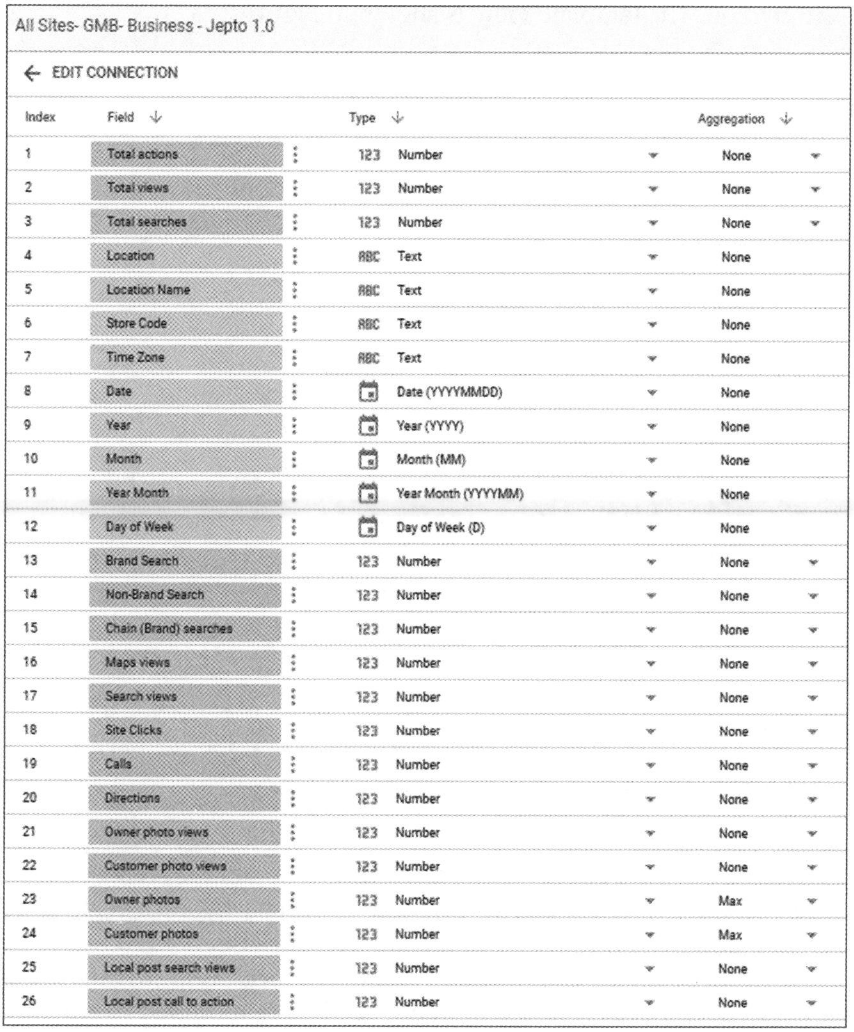

Index	Field ↓		Type ↓		Aggregation ↓	
1	Total actions	⋮	123	Number	▾	None	▾
2	Total views	⋮	123	Number	▾	None	▾
3	Total searches	⋮	123	Number	▾	None	▾
4	Location	⋮	ABC	Text	▾	None	
5	Location Name	⋮	ABC	Text	▾	None	
6	Store Code	⋮	ABC	Text	▾	None	
7	Time Zone	⋮	ABC	Text	▾	None	
8	Date	⋮	📅	Date (YYYYMMDD)	▾	None	
9	Year	⋮	📅	Year (YYYY)	▾	None	
10	Month	⋮	📅	Month (MM)	▾	None	
11	Year Month	⋮	📅	Year Month (YYYYMM)	▾	None	
12	Day of Week	⋮	📅	Day of Week (D)	▾	None	
13	Brand Search	⋮	123	Number	▾	None	▾
14	Non-Brand Search	⋮	123	Number	▾	None	▾
15	Chain (Brand) searches	⋮	123	Number	▾	None	▾
16	Maps views	⋮	123	Number	▾	None	▾
17	Search views	⋮	123	Number	▾	None	▾
18	Site Clicks	⋮	123	Number	▾	None	▾
19	Calls	⋮	123	Number	▾	None	▾
20	Directions	⋮	123	Number	▾	None	▾
21	Owner photo views	⋮	123	Number	▾	None	▾
22	Customer photo views	⋮	123	Number	▾	None	▾
23	Owner photos	⋮	123	Number	▾	Max	▾
24	Customer photos	⋮	123	Number	▾	Max	▾
25	Local post search views	⋮	123	Number	▾	None	▾
26	Local post call to action	⋮	123	Number	▾	None	▾

All Sites- GMB- Business - Jepto 1.0

← EDIT CONNECTION

Figure 7.22: The fields setup screen

In step 8, you have the option of clicking the Create Report button to go directly to a template provided by Jepto for this data source. We'll take a brief look at this report so that we can see another way our data could be presented.

The Jepto Google My Business Template

The template provided by Jepto may be fine for many uses as is, or it may provide a good place to start a new customized report. In our example, we start from scratch because our design is radically different. There are a couple of features used in this template that we won't be using in our example, so it is worth examination. The template view is shown in Figure 7.23.

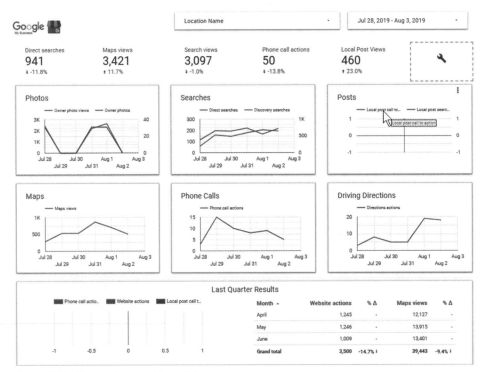

Figure 7.23: The Jepto report template

As you can see, this template creates a fairly attractive standard report. There is a row of scorecards across the top, several time-series charts, and a detail table at the bottom of the screen showing the last quarter's results.

There are a few details to note on this default report. First, this report is designed for an average user, so it will likely need to be modified to suit any specific user in a satisfactory way. In this example, one of the scorecards is broken and a few charts are empty due to a lack of data in our specific data set.

Second, we did not select a business during the data source setup, so the report is showing all of the locations' data combined by default. The report provides a filter control to allow the viewer to select a specific property when more than one exists, as shown in Figure 7.24.

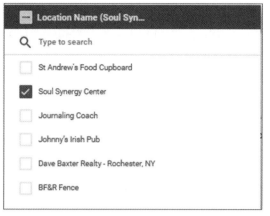

Figure 7.24: Using the location selector to filter results

Although this may be a very helpful feature if all the locations belong to the same business, it is not practical when the listings include other organization listings. When you are building reports, it is often easiest to use the selector during development and later apply a filter to limit the properties available to view for reporting to different audiences. In our example, we won't use the Location filter control; instead, we'll use a page-level filter so that the user will view information about a single location only.

Setting Up the Jepto Google My Business Reviews Connector

Our report will have a page devoted to reviews, but reviews information is not provided by the previous connector. To get the reviews data, you'll need to set up a separate Jepto GMB reviews data source. Since you already have an access token for Jepto, the process is much shorter this time.

1. Starting from the Data Studio home screen, click the Create icon and select Data Source.

2. On the connectors page, search for Jepto to find the Google My Business Reviews Connector and select it.

3. Select the Allow "Business Account" To Be Modified In Reports check box, fill in the access token field with the same code that you used earlier, and click the Connect button at the upper right of the page. Click to allow parameter sharing in the pop-up, and you should see the field setup screen.

4. Rename this data source to **All Sites – GMB - Reviews – Jepto 1.0**.

At this point, we need to create two new calculated fields. These fields will be used to create the bullet chart that shows the percentage of reviews that have been responded to. Although it may be possible to do this in a single field, we have broken them down into two fields to make the formulas simpler and clearer.

1. Click the Add A Field button at the upper right of the fields screen.

2. In the Field Name text box, type **Replied** and use the case statement for the formula, as shown in Figure 7.25.

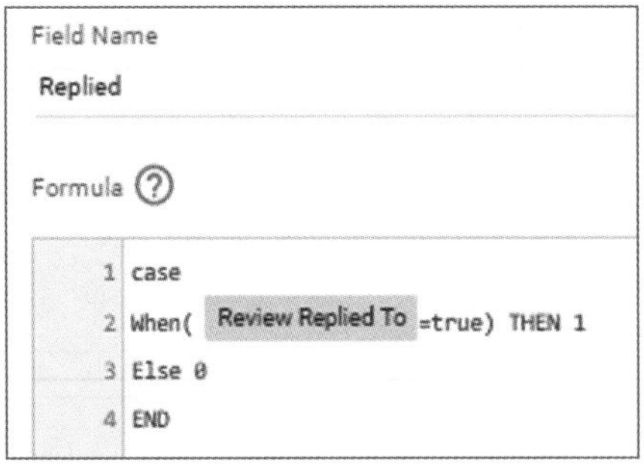

Field Name

Replied

Formula ⑦

```
1 case
2 When( Review Replied To =true) THEN 1
3 Else 0
4 END
```

Figure 7.25: Creating the Replied field

3. Click the All Fields arrow at the top left of the fields screen to return to the fields page. Click the Add A Field button.

4. In the Field Name text box, type **Replied Rate.** Enter the text as shown in Figure 7.26, and then click the Update button to continue.

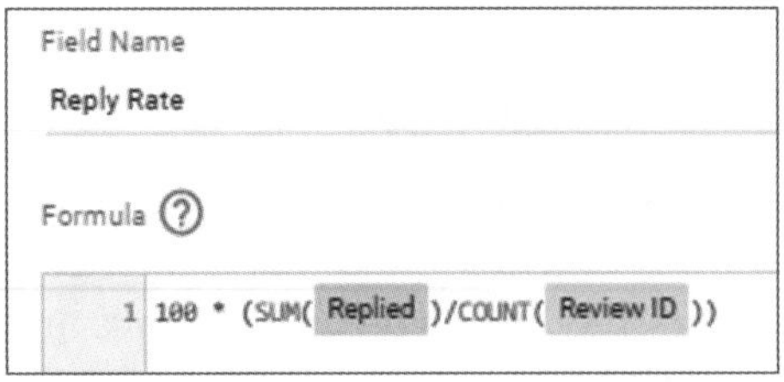

Field Name

Reply Rate

Formula ⑦

```
1 100 * (SUM( Replied )/COUNT( Review ID ))
```

Figure 7.26: Creating the Replied Rate field

5. Click the All Fields arrow at the top left of the fields screen to return to the fields page.

Now that you have the data sources set up for the report, return to the Data Studio home screen to start the report-building process.

Step 3. Setting the Table

When building a multipage report that uses a nonstandard navigation system like our example, I find it efficient to create all the pages first, get the headers and navigation in place, and then fill in the details.

The order in which you apply things like navigation may not matter much in a three-page report, but if you are working on a 20-page report, following this process will save you a lot of time!

Instead of borrowing elements from previous examples for the header section, we'll create a new one for this report that works better for the smaller mobile layout.

Report, Page, and Header Setup

We start in the usual way: from the Data Studio home screen.

1. Click the Blank Report image in the Start With A Template section. This opens a new Untitled Report.

2. Rename the report to **Hands on Data Studio – Jepto GMB Example 6.0**.

3. In the Add A Data Source panel on the right side, locate and select the All Sites – GMB – Business – Jepto 1.0 data source, and click the Add To Report button in the dialog, as shown in Figure 7.27.

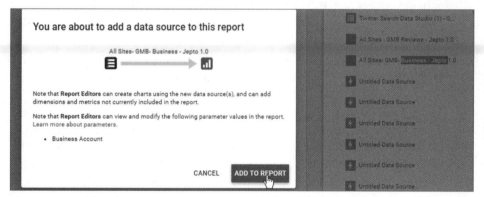

Figure 7.27: Adding the data source to the report

4. Layout and Themes should now be showing in the right panel. Change the Canvas Size settings as follows: Width = **450** and Height = **950**.

5. For the header background, click the Rectangle icon in the toolbar. Size, position, and change the color of the rectangle to match the example.

6. Add the Chris Cooper logo. This time, we'll drag and drop to add it to the screen. Locate the folder on your computer containing the image ChrisCooperLogo.png. Click and drag the file you want to add to the Data Studio report and drop it onto the canvas, as shown in Figure 7.28. Resize and position the image in the header.

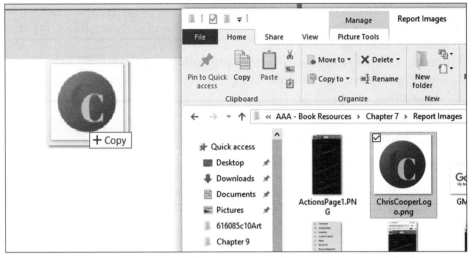

Figure 7.28: Adding the header logo

7. Create the header text by clicking the Text icon. Create a text box and enter **Chris Cooper GMB Mobile Overview** for the text. Set the text size to **14px** and the color to white by using the Text Properties panel. Resize and position the text box in the header.

8. Add the Date Range picker by selecting it on the toolbar header. Click and drag it to a position just below the colored header bar. Click the default data range in the Date Range Properties panel. Select Advanced from the drop-down and change Start Date to Today Minus 58 Days. Change End Date to Today Minus 3 Days and click the Apply button. The three-day offset is needed to take into account the data delay period for GMB data. As pointed out in earlier chapters, lining up date ranges is important for correct comparison to previous periods. This will provide us with eight weeks of results. The setup is shown in Figure 7.29.

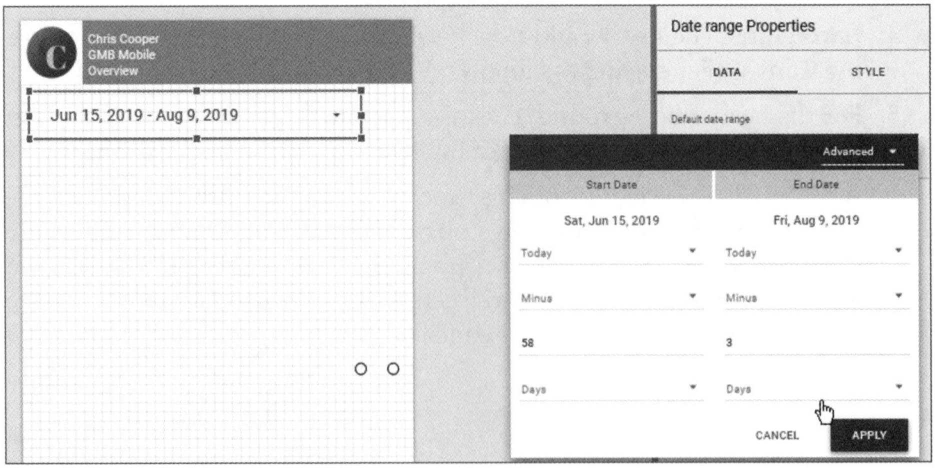

Figure 7.29: Setting the default date range

9. Set the Data Range picker to report level. *Report-level elements* are shared by a page that is added to a report, and *page-level elements* apply only to a particular page. Setting the Date Range picker, or any other control component, to report level means that when the user selects new values from the control and switches pages, those values are applied to the new page as well. In this example, if the user changes the date range in the picker and switches pages, they will not have to reset the range for the new page. You can right-click a selected item and choose Make Report-Level, as shown in Figure 7.30. Report-level elements can be set to page level in the same way.

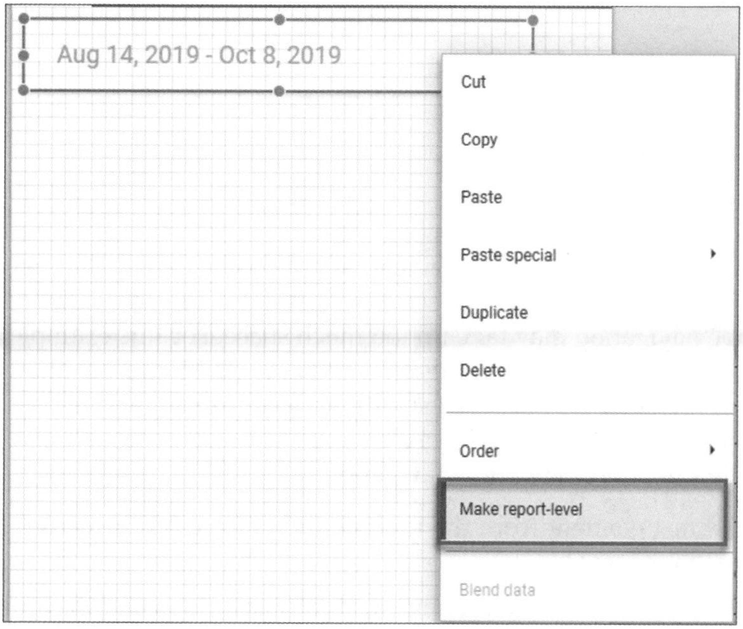

Figure 7.30: Setting Date Range picker to report level

10. Duplicate the page to create the other pages in the report. To do this, select Page ⇨ Duplicate Page. Use Duplicate Page again to create the third report page.

11. Rename the pages. You can change the names of pages, and their order in the report, by using the Show Page control on the left side of the toolbar. By default, the pages will be named Page 1, Copy Of Page 1, Copy Of Copy Of Page 1, and so on. To change the name of a page, select the vertical dots next to that page and select Rename, as shown in Figure 7.31. Rename the first page to **Actions**, the second page to **Reviews**, and the third page to **Search**.

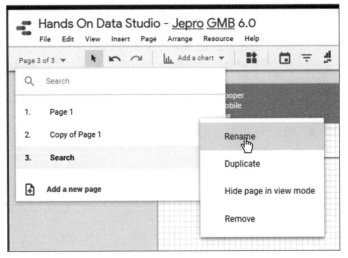

Figure 7.31: Changing page names

Page Navigation Button Setup

Data Studio provides both top and side navigation options by default, but nei-
ther of these options works very well for small screen sizes. Top navigation is
too small, and side navigation may take up too much space. For this example,
we elected to create buttons for our navigation and color the button to show
which page we are currently on. Because the buttons need to change from page
to page, we did not set these as report-level elements.

Here are the steps to build the button navigation:

1. Create a new text element from the toolbar and place it on the canvas.
   Type **Actions** in the text box.

2. Using the Text Properties panel, change the font size to **18px** and the font
   style to Raleway. Click the B icon to change the style to bold.

3. Scroll to the bottom of the Text Properties panel to the Background And
   Border section.

4. Change the background color. Use the paint can drop-down to set the
   color of the button. Set it to the light blue color. We'll set the active buttons
   to yellow in later steps.

5. We want to create rounded edges. Next to the paint can icon is the border
   radius drop-down. By default, it is set to 0. Change this setting to **100**. If
   you want square buttons, you can leave it at 0.

6. To add a border to the text box, click the pencil icon that controls the border
   color and set it to black. The icon to the right of the border color setting
   controls the line thickness. Use this drop-down to set the thickness of the
   border to **4**.

7. Just below the Background And Border section, you see the Padding section. *Padding* controls how close the text appears to the border of the text box. Use the Top drop-down to change the setting to **4px**. Figure 7.32 shows the completed configuration for the Background, Border, and Padding options.

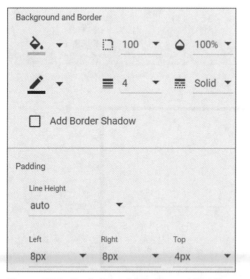

Figure 7.32: Background, Border, and Padding configuration

8. Resize the text box to the desired button shape.

9. Now that you have styled the text box as a button, you can simply copy the button to create the others quickly. Use the menu or Ctrl+C and Ctrl+V to create the copies.

10. Change the text in the copies to the correct button names, **Reviews** and **Search**.

11. Add page links to the text of each button. Start with the Actions text box. Select the text box and the text for the Actions button. Click the insert link icon in the Text Properties panel, as shown in Figure 7.33.

    Clicking the insert link icon opens the Insert Link dialog. Actions appears in the Display Text field. Click in the Paste A Link, Or Select A Page field. A drop-down selection will appear for dynamic page links. Under Pages In This Report, choose Actions, as shown in Figure 7.34. Click Apply to set the link.

12. Repeat step 11 for the other buttons to link each to the correct page.

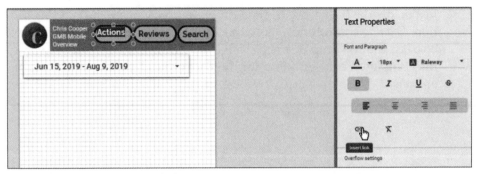

Figure 7.33: Clicking the insert link icon

Insert link

Display text

Actions

Paste a link, or select a page

Dynamic page links

First

Previous

Next

Last

Pages in this report

Actions

Reviews

Search

Cancel   Apply

Figure 7.34: Setting the link for the Actions page

13. Adjust the button location and layout.

14. Copy the buttons to the other pages. You can do so by selecting all three buttons, pressing Ctrl+C to copy them to the clipboard, switching pages, and then pasting them by pressing Ctrl+V. Use the arrow keys to position the buttons.

15. Each page should have the link removed and the button highlighted so that the user knows which page they are on. To do this on the Actions page, select the Actions text box. Select the text, and in the Text Properties

panel, click the link icon. You see a Remove Link button under the Paste A Link, Or Select A Page field, as shown in Figure 7.35. Click the button and then click Apply.

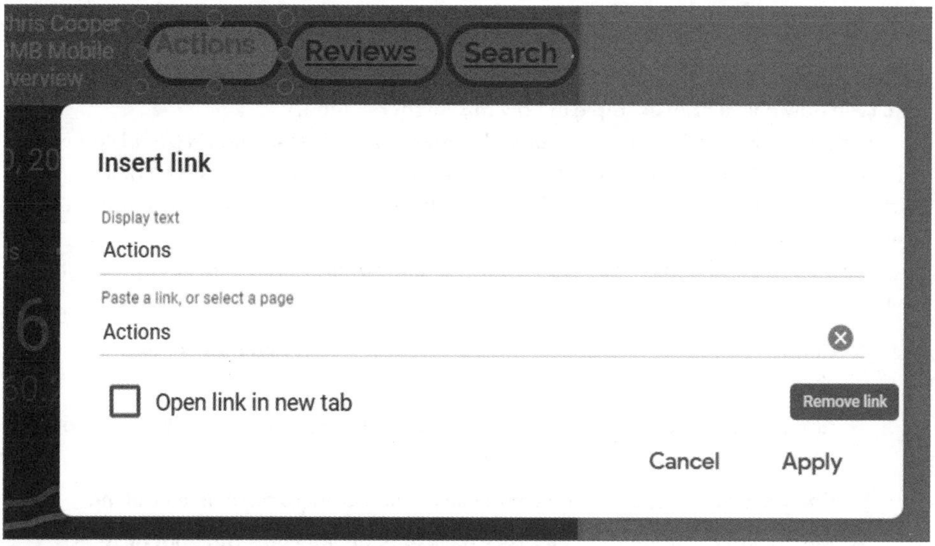

Figure 7.35: Removing the link for the Actions page

16. Repeat step 15 for all pages.

With your button navigation in place, you're ready to build the pages. Let's start with the Actions page.

Building the Actions Page

When designing this report, we decided to put the Actions page up front. These are the metrics that are the closest to actual sales for a business and interaction-type goals for other organizations. In many cases, it makes sense to calculate the estimated value of an action, such as a phone call, and create a new metric so that value can be charted as well.

This requires knowing more about a specific organization and getting the stakeholders to agree to an estimated money value for desired actions. Even if this value is estimated, it is much easier to get a business owner to take action when they see the results in terms of dollars.

Calculating value is a worthwhile exercise, but I chose to leave it out of this example because of the wide range of values that could be used, depending on the goals of a particular business or organization.

SHOW ME THE MONEY!

Just how money metrics can be used in this report would be valuable to many users, so I will now give a brief example of how this might be done.

Let's pretend that Chris Cooper runs a business that drives groups of people on all-day trips to tour craft breweries. We would like to get some estimates so that we can calculate the value of actions taken on the listing. Here is a fictitious example of what that might look like.

Most people call Chris to check pricing, and many book a tour. Some people use his website to book tours as well.

- Cooper's tours average $600, and Chris makes $400 on average for each tour they book.
- Chris knows that about 5 percent of people visiting his website will book a tour based on their Google Analytics data.
- Chris also knows that 25 percent of calls to his business result in a booking.
- Most people visiting the tour office have already booked a tour, but he does get some bookings out of walk-in business. He estimates about 10 percent of tour office visitors will end up booking a tour.

From this information, we can create some basic metrics that help measure the value of his listing. We run these by Chris, and we agree on the estimates.

Call Value

$$Calls * .25 * 400 = \$100 \text{ per Call}$$

Site Click Value

$$Site\ Clicks * .05 * 400 = \$20 \text{ per Site Click}$$

Directions Value

$$Directions * .10 * 400 = \$40 \text{ per Directions request}$$

With these estimates, it is easy to create new metrics to add to the report. The results are shown in Figure 7.36. Changing the metrics to money values and adding a new metric for the value of the listing increases Chris's incentive to pay attention to the maintenance of the GMB listing.

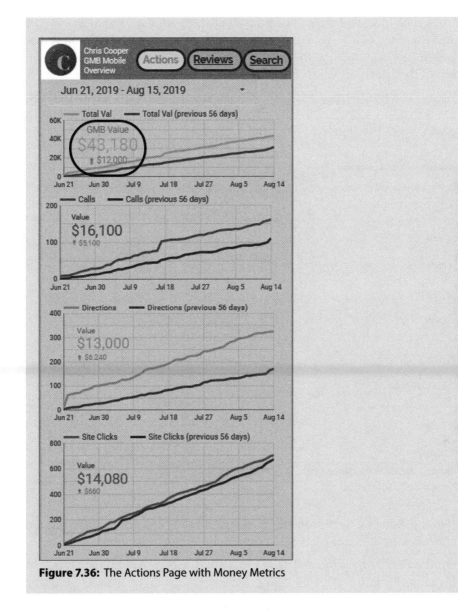

Figure 7.36: The Actions Page with Money Metrics

In setting up the Actions page, we focus on getting the position and styling set up for the time series and scorecard for calls first. After we complete that section, it's a simple matter of copying the section and changing the metrics and the color of the components. We begin on the Actions page in Edit mode.

1. Use the Add A Chart drop-down to select a new time-series chart. Click and drag the chart box to place it at the top of the page.

2. On the Data tab, set the metric to Calls. Set the comparison date range to Previous Period.

3. Click the Style tab. Under the Series #1 section, set the line thickness to **4** and the line color to gold. Select the Cumulative check box. Scroll to the Legend section and use the box icon on the far right to set the legend on top of the chart. Set Chart Header to Do Not Show.

4. Right-click the chart to bring up a menu. Choose Order ⇨ Send To Back, as shown in Figure 7.37. Doing this will ensure that other elements will go on top of the chart.

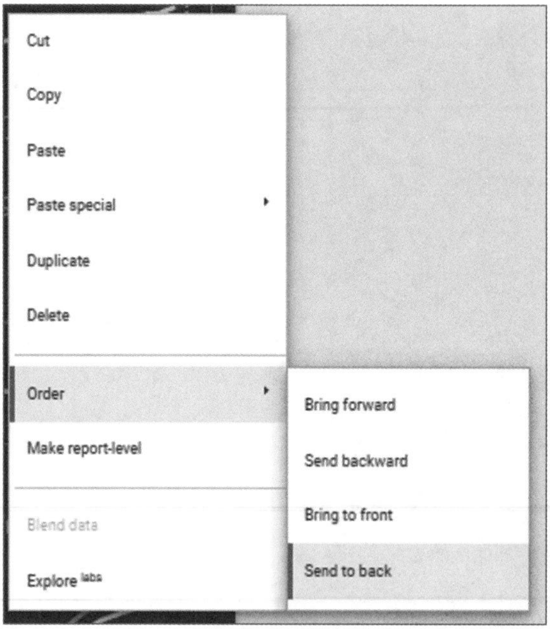

Figure 7.37: Setting the chart layer order

5. Use the Add A Chart drop-down to select Timecard. Click and drag the chart box to the upper-left area of the Calls time-series chart.

6. On the Data tab, set the metric to Calls and the comparison data range to Previous Period.

7. On the Style tab, in the Labels section, change the color to gold (the same color as the time-series chart). Select the Hide Metric Name check box. This will remove the label, which is not needed because Calls is already identified in the time-series chart legend.

8. Copy the Calls charts and paste the copy and position it. Select both charts and use copy and paste commands to create a copy of both charts. The copies will be selected, so use the arrow keys to move them as a group to the second chart position on the page.

9. Click the time-series chart to select it, and on the Data tab, set the metric to Directions. Click the Style tab and change the color of the line to purple to match the example.

10. Click the scorecard to select it, and on the Data tab, set the metric to Directions. Click the Style tab and change the color of the line to purple to match the example.

11. Repeat steps 8–11 to set up the Site Clicks charts.

12. Adjust the positions of the page elements and charts.

Creating a Location Filter for the Actions Page

We have one item left to attend to on this page. The GMB connector, by default, will pull in and aggregate data for all locations. That may be fine depending on how your GMB account is structured. In this example, however, we'll filter the report for a single location.

1. Choose Page ⇨ Current Page Settings to open the configuration panel on the right side of the screen.

2. In the Filter section, click the Add A Filter button to open the Edit Filter panel at the bottom of the screen.

3. Change the Name field value to the name of the filter. For this example, call it **Location**.

4. Set the filter parameters. We are filtering for the Soul Synergy Center location, so the settings are Include Location Name Contains Soul Synergy, as shown in Figure 7.38. Click the Save button at the bottom right of the screen. Your new filter should be added to the Current Page Settings screen, and your charts will all be updated.

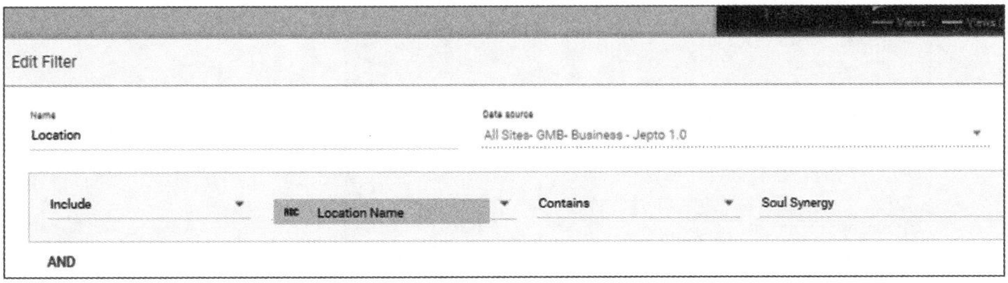

Figure 7.38: Setting the location filter

Building the Search Page

We are going to jump to the third page of the report, the Search page, because it uses the same data source as the Actions page and has similar components.

Again, we use the Cumulative setting on the charts to easily show differences over time. To start, switch to the Search page and make sure that you are in Edit mode.

1. From the Add A Chart drop-down, select the timecard. Click and drag the chart box to the upper-left area of the page.

2. On the Data tab, set the metric to Map Views. Set the comparison data range to Previous Period.

3. On the Style tab, in the Labels section, change the color to pink.

4. From the Add A Chart drop-down, select the time-series chart. Click and drag the chart box to place it at the top of the page next to the Maps Views scorecard.

5. On the Data tab, set the metric to Maps Views. Set the comparison date range to Previous Period.

6. On the Style tab, under the Series #1 section, set the line thickness to **4** and the line color to pink. Select the Cumulative check box and set Chart Header to Do Not Show.

7. Select the Maps Views charts and copy and paste them to the canvas. When you copy multiple items and paste them, the copies are selected as a group and can easily be positioned using the arrow keys. See Figure 7.39 for an example of creating a copy of the chart row.

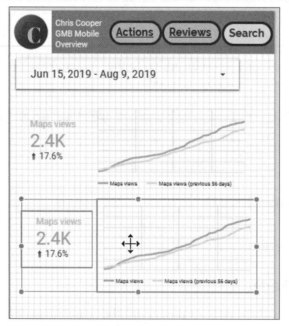

Figure 7.39: Copying a search charts row

8. Select the copied scorecard and change the metric on the Data tab to Brand Search. Switch to the Style tab and change the color to light purple.

9. Select the copied time-series charts and change the metric on the Data tab to Brand Search. Switch to the Style tab and change the line color to light purple.

10. Repeat steps 7–9 for the rest of the charts on the page (Non-Brand Search, Post Views, Owner Photo Views, and Customer Photo Views).

11. Choose Page ➪ Current Page Settings. You have already created the filter, so all that is needed here is to apply it. Click the Add A Filter button and select the Location filter for the Filter picker screen.

Building the Reviews Page

The Reviews page differs from the Search and Actions pages because it uses the Jepto Reviews data source. On this page, we'll be adding a bullet chart, a new chart type for our reports. Otherwise, this page has elements that you have seen before. We'll add that as the last step.

Start by switching to the Reviews page and making sure that you are in Edit mode.

1. Choose Page ➪ Current Page Settings. Click the data source listed in that section. Use the data source selector to find and select All Sites – GMB – Reviews – Jepto 1.0.

2. In Current Page Settings, click the Add A Filter button. Select the Location filter from the Filter picker screen. This filter works with both report data sources because the field has the same name on both data sources. The filter will limit the page to showing the reviews for this one listing.

3. Select the scorecard chart from the Add A Chart drop-down and position it on the canvas. On the Data tab, select Review ID from the Available Fields section and drag it to the Metric slot. Use the pencil icon to edit the Review ID field and rename the field to **Reviews**. Set the comparison date range to Previous Period.

4. Select the Reviews scorecard from step 3 and change the metric to Star Rating Value. Use the pencil icon to edit the metric label and change it to **AVG Stars**.

5. From the Add A Chart drop-down, select the table. Click and drag it into place on the canvas.

6. On the Data tab, set Dimensions to Creation Date, Comment, and Reply. Change the Creation Date label by using the pencil icon on the field to change the label to **Date**.

7. Set the metric to the Star Rating Value field. Use the pencil icon to edit and change the label to **Stars**.

8. On the Style tab, deselect Row Numbers and Show Pagination. Select Wrap Text in the Table Body section.

9. Adjust the table column sizes to make the comments and responses easier to view.

Creating the Bullet Chart

I think of a *bullet chart* as a thermometer turned sideways. It is most often used to show progress toward a goal. It is a bit different from most charts in Data Studio because it allows the editor to put in several values to give a metric more context. Because goal values are unique to a specific situation, you won't find them in a lot of templates because any particular settings are unlikely to satisfy the needs of most users.

In this example, the chart is used to measure the response rate to reviews and comments on the listing. Fortunately, it is widely accepted that every review should be at least acknowledged by a GMB manager in a timely fashion. We want the manager using the report to keep the response rate above 95 percent during any period of time. Soul Synergy Center has been very responsive, so the green bar goes all the way to the right. Figure 7.40 shows the same chart for another listing that is not as responsive.

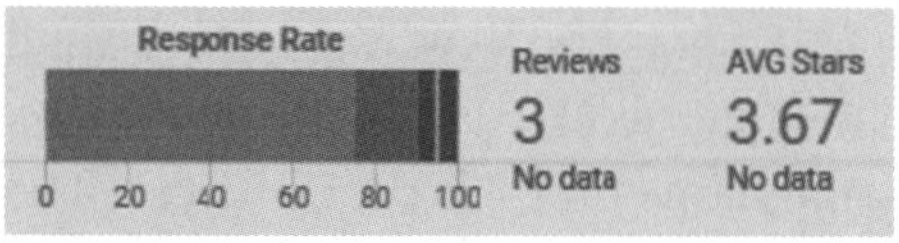

Figure 7.40: Bullet chart below goal target

Here are the steps to build the bullet chart for this example:

1. Select the bullet chart from the Add A Chart drop-down, and click and drag to place it on the screen. The configuration panel for the chart should appear on the right side.

2. On the Data tab for the chart, set the metric to Reply Rate.

3. Set Range 1 to **75**, Range 2 to **90**, and Range 3 to **100**. The range limits control the colored sections that surround the metric bar.

4. Select the Show Target check box and set Target Value to **95**. This controls the position of the black line on the chart. The values for the Data tab settings are shown in Figure 7.41.

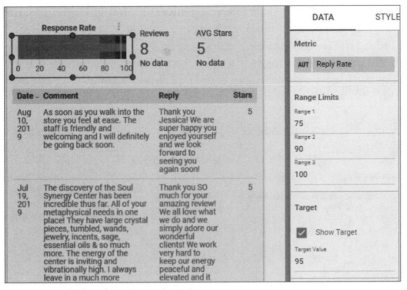

Figure 7.41: Bullet chart Data tab settings

5. Switch to the Style tab and set the bar color to green and the range color to red, as shown in Figure 7.42. Note that you can select only one color-range color.

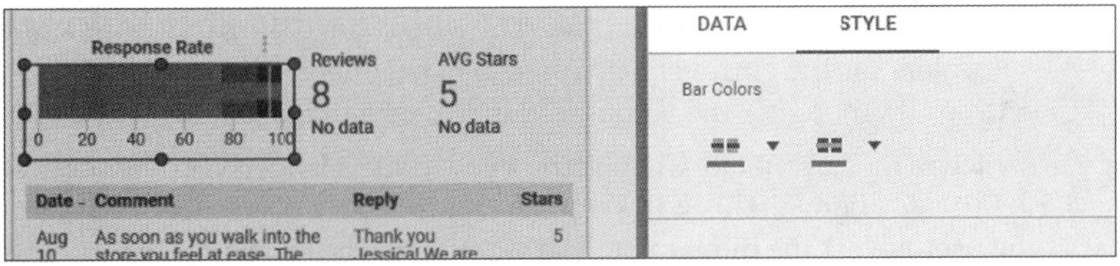

Figure 7.42: Bullet chart Style tab settings

6. Adjust the positioning of the charts on the canvas.

Changing the Layout and Theme

We have just a couple more things to do to complete this example. You may have noticed that we have been working on a white background for most of the illustrations, but for the finished report, the background is set to black. It is common for mobile applications to have black backgrounds.

The last thing we would like to do is very helpful for mobile designs. We would like to hide the report header. On a mobile device, there is not much need for the report header and it just takes up space. Removing it will give the report a feel much more like a mobile application.

We saved hiding the header bar for the last setting because only showing the header when the user hovers makes it more difficult to switch between View and Edit modes during report creation. Figure 7.43 shows mobile-phone screen captures of the report with and without the report header visible.

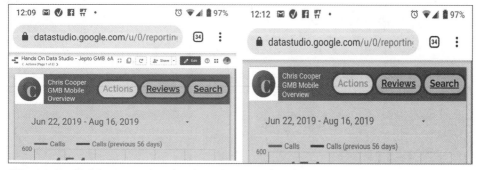

Figure 7.43: Mobile view with and without the report header

To change the Layout And Theme settings, follow these steps:

1. While in Edit mode, select Layout And Theme from the toolbar.

2. Switch to the Theme tab. Under Current Theme, change the drop-down setting from Simple to Simple Dark. This will change the background and text colors for the entire chart. You can experiment with different color settings by changing the values in the Primary and Secondary sections.

3. Switch to the Layout tab. Change the View Mode, Header Visibility option to Initially Hidden. This will keep the report header from showing unless the user hovers the mouse over the very top of the report.

Summary

This completes the series of chapters on visualizing web data with Google Data Studio. A basic knowledge of, and the ability to report from, Google Analytics, Google Search Console, and Google My Business is a vital part of measuring and guiding action for a large number of businesses and organizations.

In this chapter, we focused on Google My Business. We looked at what the GMB service does and why it is important to the success of many local businesses.

I covered these concepts and topics:

- What is Google My Business?

- Why GMB listings are important to local businesses and organizations

- The elements of a GMB listing in search results
- The GMB management interface and available reports
- Why Data Studio is a good solution for GMB reporting
- Dashboard design compared to other kinds of reports
- Considerations for dashboard and GMB report design
- Designing mobile reports with Data Studio
- Using third-party connectors for Data Studio data sources
- Dimensions and metrics available for GMB reporting
- Setting up the free Jepto GMB connectors
- Creating buttons for multipage report navigation
- Creating and using a bullet chart for measuring against a goal value
- Changing basic layout and theme settings for mobile applications

Beyond the Office

In This Part

Getting Personal

As a data citizen, you have access to much more than just business information. In this chapter and the next, we'll look at other areas where you can apply Data Studio beyond strictly business uses. This chapter will look at more personal applications, and Chapter 9, "Going Public," will cover community data sources.

What do I mean when I speak of personal applications? I think of these as Data Studio applications that promote better self-understanding, personal growth, or simply recreation. Since you need data to do data visualization, we'll look at these applications based on how the data is generated—data created directly by you, data curated by you, and data generated for you.

We'll take a look at examples in each of these areas and I'll show you how you can take control of your own data and organize and visualize it for your own purposes. Finally, I'll show you a Data Studio application that uses all three methods of data collection.

Creating Your Own Data

These days, we use a lot of applications to help us track and organize our personal data. Although these applications free us from having to measure and log things in which we are interested, they are often designed to provide information to the service provider rather than the individual. In some cases, you can retrieve your personal information, as we did in the previous checking account examples in Chapter 2, "Cooking with Google Data Studio".

You also have the option to collect and store your own information to use in ways in which you are interested. Going back to our cooking analogy, creating your own data is like growing your own ingredients, which makes the dish you prepare exceptionally satisfying!

Common examples of things you may want to measure on your own are reading lists, hobby information, personal time logs, and collections of references. There seems to be a computer or smartphone app designed to help you collect and organize nearly any kind of information. However, you don't have shop around for new tools or wait until someone builds the ideal application for your needs. You can start collecting your own information right now and connect to it with Data Studio to visualize that information.

As I've mentioned before, most data can be gathered into Google Sheets for reporting. For example, I entered information directly into a spreadsheet to keep track of my tasks at work, as shown in Figure 8.1.

Added	Description	Cat	Status	Priority	Estimate	Completec	Actual	Open Da	Notes
8/20/2019	GFIT GPT page notes from Christian - Menu changes	WEB	Working	1	0.5			6	
8/20/2019	Torque calculator updates - catchup and review	Thinkbean	Working	1	0.75			6	
8/20/2019	check garlock site deploy smartsheet? see emails	Admin	Working	1	0.25			6	
8/20/2019	Concur updates - who is the approver - Marci?	Admin	DONE	10	0.5			6	No appro
8/20/2019	project tracker notifications Project tracker? See 8/16 email	Admin	Working	1	0.25			6	
8/20/2019	8/16 email from AffiliateCmpCS - check error?	EC	Working	1	0.5			6	
8/20/2019	questions about discontinued product info on site from Matt	WEB	Working	1	0.5			6	
8/20/2019	Hartmann-Kuester,Nora need to delete duplicate upload	WEB	Working	1	0.5			6	
8/20/2019	Review august update for GPT calculator - 8/14 email	Thinkbean	Working	1	0.5			6	
8/20/2019	Weekly team meeting	Admin	DONE	10	1	8/20/2019	1	1	
8/20/2019	Google apps migration for GPT - need to check this - NOT ALLOWED?	Migration	Working	1	1			6	
8/20/2019	Reply to Tim Hurley about AMP setup.	WEB	Working	1	0.25			6	

Figure 8.1: A task list in Google Sheets

I use a Data Studio report connected to this sheet to help me easily analyze where my efforts are going. I can also analyze how I am doing at estimating the time it takes to complete tasks compared to how long it actually takes. At the end of the week, I can filter for tasks completed and easily create a list of accomplishments to send to my manager. I can also use the Data Studio report to share just some of the information instead of all the data that I am collecting.

Although it is possible to start a spreadsheet and enter your data directly, there are a couple of drawbacks to this method if you want to measure more than a task list:

- Entering data into a sheet can be cumbersome, particularly if you want to add an entry from a phone.

- Direct data entry into a spreadsheet is prone to error. It is easy to mix up things like date formats and to misspell category entries. The saying "garbage in, garbage out" applies here. In most cases you'll find it is better to restrict the entries for a field to specific options and formats so that the data will be more useful and clean. This approach requires a little thought up front, but the effort will pay dividends later when you want insights from the data you have collected.

Fortunately, there is a simple solution for entering data into a Google Sheet and keeping it clean for later reporting.

Using Google Forms to Collect Your Own Data

For most data collection tasks, a simple form will suffice. Yet using a simple form may not be the answer to all your data needs. For my task list, I needed to make frequent updates to the entries, and it is just easier to do that right on the sheet itself rather than trying to update the information in a form. However, I do find myself being inconsistent with spelling and categories, and if I used a form, at least to do the initial entry, it would solve most of those problems.

Along with Google Sheets and Data Studio, you have access to Google Forms as part of your standard Google applications. *Google Forms* is a fairly simple application that lets you build forms and share them. You can also save the form data directly into Google Sheets.

Here is an example. As I was writing this book, I wanted to track the time I spent on different tasks. My hope was to gain some insights into the time needed to complete a chapter. You can see the form that I created to do this in Figure 8.2.

Every time this form is submitted, a corresponding entry is made on a Google Sheet that allows the data to be viewed in a Data Studio report. Besides being free to use and easy to build, Google Forms has another feature that we can make use of: you can embed the forms it produces in web pages.

We're going to use the embed feature of Google Forms for our next example. If you are following along and building these examples yourself, don't worry! You won't need access to a website to try this, because you already have one. Data Studio reports *are* web pages, and one of the features now built into the tool is the ability to embed other content, including Google Forms, right in the report pages themselves.

One use of this ability to embed a form is to provide an area where users can give feedback. Although Google Forms are not the most elegant in terms of style, they provide one of the simplest mechanisms for this kind of interaction with report users. Figure 8.3 shows an example from Michael Howe-Ely. The Google Analytics report has an embedded feedback form, and the responses are shown in the report itself.

A link to this report, and to a blog post describing the setup, are included in the chapter notes in the online resources for the book at `www.wiley.com/go/handsondatastudio`.

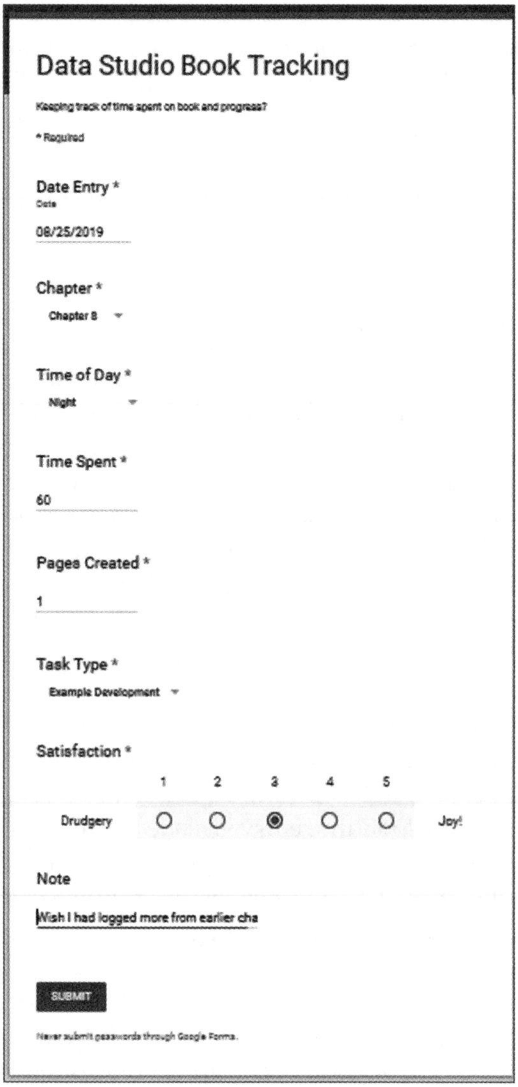

Data Studio Book Tracking

Keeping track of time spent on book and progress?

* Required

Date Entry *
Date
08/25/2019

Chapter *
Chapter 8   ▾

Time of Day *
Night   ▾

Time Spent *
60

Pages Created *
1

Task Type *
Example Development   ▾

Satisfaction *

	1	2	3	4	5	
Drudgery	○	○	◉	○	○	Joy!

Note
Wish I had logged more from earlier cha

SUBMIT

Never submit passwords through Google Forms.

Figure 8.2: A form for logging writing tasks

Embedded Google Forms Example

Next we'll go through an example to show you how to create a basic form for data capture and embed it into a report of your own. We'll build a basic form to capture information about dog walks. You may not be interested in tracking your dog walks, or even have a dog to walk, but the example can be easily modified to capture a wide variety of information.

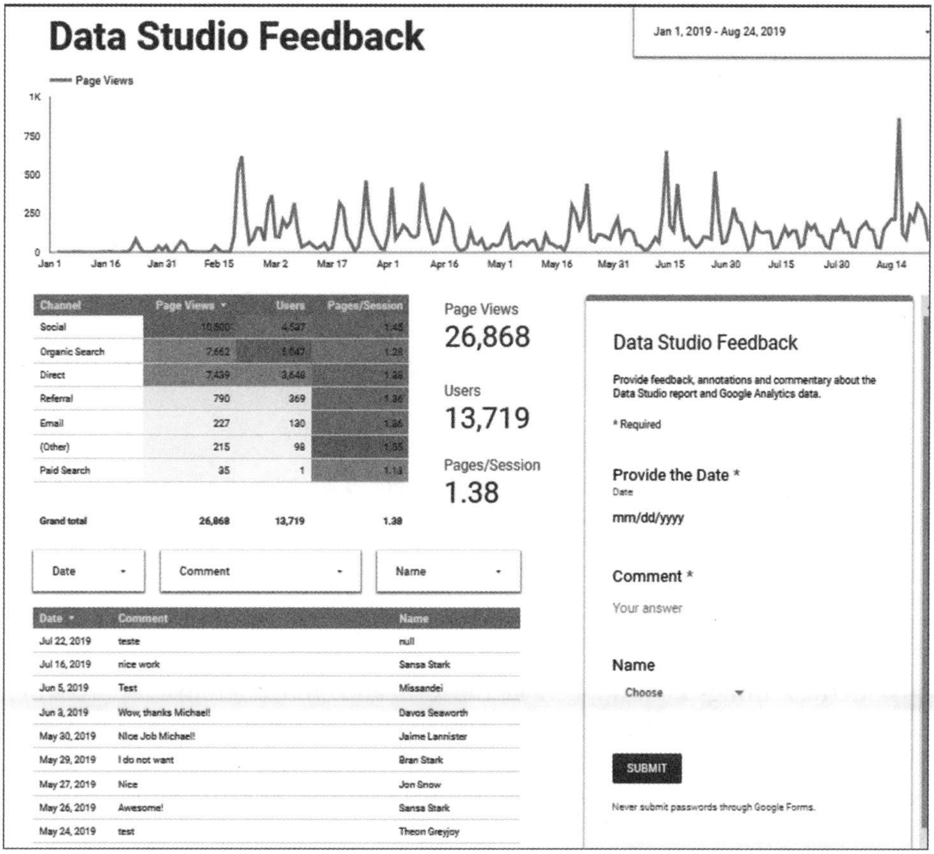

Figure 8.3: Feedback form and Comments table

Source: Google Data Studio Feedback: `http://bit.ly/31XPQDT`.

Before you start creating a form, think about the purpose of tracking information, the kind of information you want to capture, and how the data will be stored. Thinking about dog walks, I want to know how satisfying the walk was for both the dog and the walker. I am also curious to see if I can find patterns that might help me maximize the quality of future walks.

I believe a lot of factors could influence this rating, but I want to start off with a manageable number of things to measure. If you are starting off with your own personal projects, I suggest that you balance the amount of data you want to collect against the ease of collecting it. If you try to collect too much, you'll be less inclined to do the collection process. If you collect too little, you may find yourself wishing that you had more information to help you get insight after the data is collected.

I want to capture some information about the time of day, the temperature, and how long the walk was in minutes. I also want to measure the walker's satisfaction as well as estimate the dog's satisfaction. Estimating dog happiness is hardly scientific in this case, but I am free to do as I please since it is my data. If you are planning on sharing your data and insights with others, you'll want to be able to explain how the data was collected. If you are doing drug testing for a pharmaceutical company, I hope you are more rigorous!

NOTE   Obviously, the entries I created for this example are made up, but I tried to make them realistic and based on my experience as a walker with a dog. I stuck to some basic rules when entering the data, although as in real life, I made some exceptions:

- The dog is happier with longer walks.
- The dog doesn't really care what time of time of day it is.
- The dog has a mild preference for cooler weather and is not as happy in very hot weather.
- The walker prefers morning and evening walks.
- The walker prefers cooler weather and is less happy on very hot walks.
- The walker is happier with shorter walks.

With these things in mind, I create the form and embed it into a report. After some data collection, I start playing with the visualizations to see which ones give me insights about maximizing dog walk happiness. The resulting report, containing the embedded form, is shown in Figure 8.4, with a new entry ready to be added.

You may note that this report does not have our usual header. Since this is a personal report, I don't feel the need for extra graphic elements. I can always add more in the future. Data Studio makes it so simple to modify a report that I will likely change the layout and the visualizations over time. This is part of the fun of working on your personal projects. The freedom to experiment allows you to try things and build skills, which you may find can be carried over into more professional work.

Let's break this report down before we go through the steps to rebuild it.

Scorecards: A wide variety of measurements are shown here, with the most important prominently displayed at the top of the report.

Scatter Charts: We introduce a new kind of chart with several variations. *Scatter charts* help us understand the relationship between different dimensions and metrics. We'll look at some of these variations in detail.

Table: A simple table is used here to check on the data entries.

Embedded Form: On the right side of the report is the form that we use to gather the data. This form employs a variety of ways to gather information, such as short fields for gathering numbers, a drop-down for time of day, and linear selectors for getting the Happiness Rating scores. As we build the form, you'll see how validation can be set up for these elements to help make sure that we are gathering data without errors in it.

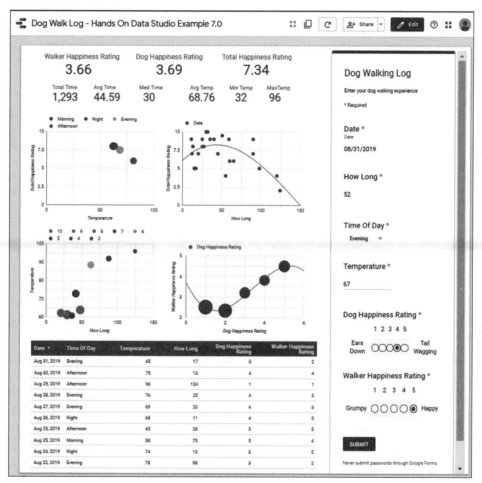

Figure 8.4: Dog Walk report with embedded form

Creating the Google Form for Data Capture

1. In Google Drive, create a new folder that will hold the new form and the new Google Sheet that will store the form data. Navigate to the new folder.

2. Click the New button on the upper-left side of the Google Drive screen. A drop-down menu will list the available applications. Click the More option to expose the menu option for Google Forms, as shown in Figure 8.5.

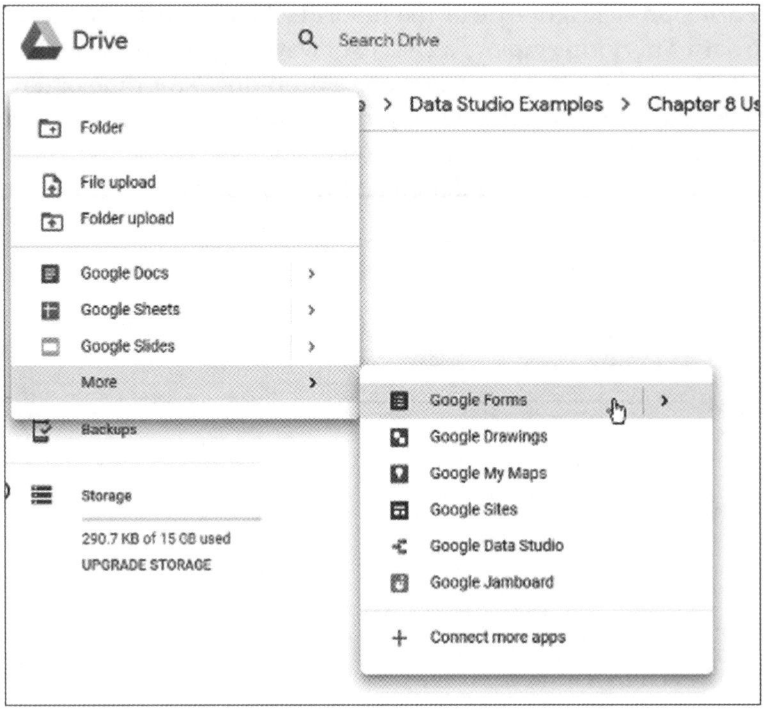

Figure 8.5: Selecting Google Forms

3. You'll be presented with a new form to set up. Initially, this form will be called Untitled. Change the name; I used **Dog Walking Log**. Just below the title is space for a description; I entered **Record your dog walking experience!**.

4. After entering the description, you'll be presented with an Untitled Question panel. Click the question type drop-down menu, which by default shows Multiple Choice, and select Date. Change the name from Untitled Question to **Date** and click the Required button at the bottom right of the panel. The Date setup should look like Figure 8.6. Click the plus button to create the next question.

5. Change the name field of the new question to **How Long**, select Short Answer from the question type drop-down menu, and click Required. Next, we'll set some data validation for the field. Click the ellipsis menu at the bottom right of the question panel to expose the options, and click Response Validation. This will open a set of validation settings. Change these to Number, Greater Than, and **10**, and for the Custom error text message, type **No Short Walks!**. This validation rule will force the user to enter a number that is greater than 10. This helps remove the possibility of errors being entered in this field. Figure 8.7 shows the completed validation setup. Click the plus button to create the next question.

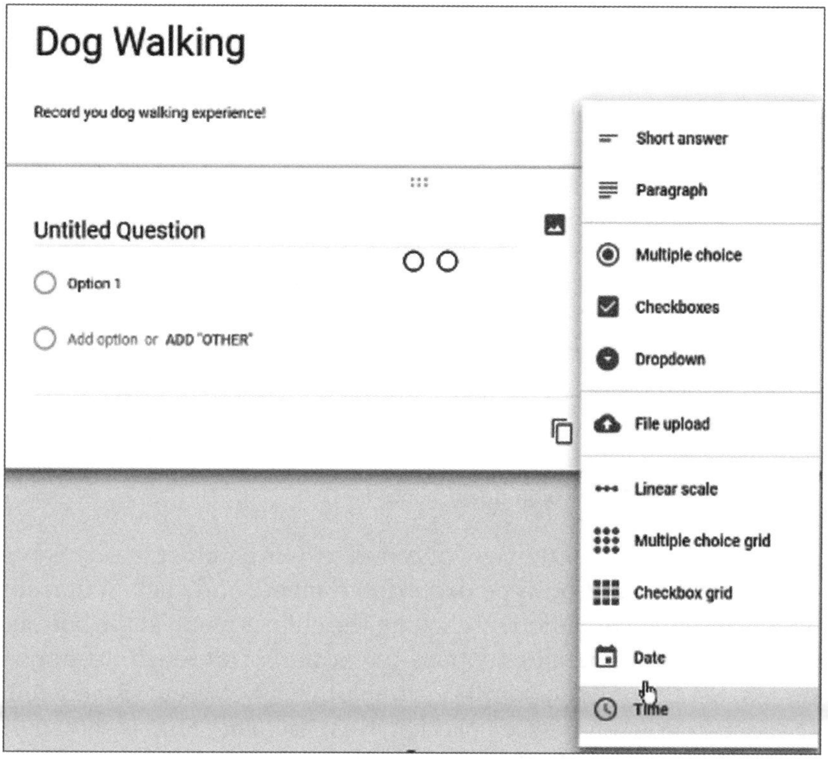

Figure 8.6: Adding a date selector for the first question

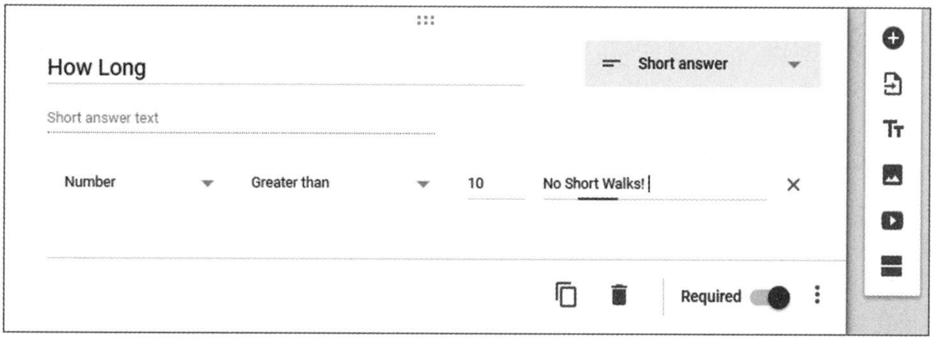

Figure 8.7: Setting a numeric validation for a question

6. Change the name field of the new question to **Time of Day** and select Dropdown from the question type menu to open the Option settings. Replace the Option 1 text in the first field with **Morning**. Google will recognize this and create a Suggestions option showing Afternoon and Evening, with an option to Add All. Click Add All, and those values are added to the list. Change Option 4 to **Night** and click Required. Figure 8.8 shows the completed setup. Click the plus button to create the next question.

Figure 8.8: Setup for the Time Of Day drop-down menu

7. Change the name field of the new question to **Temperature**, select Short Answer from the question type drop-down menu, and click Required. Set up the question validation by clicking the ellipsis menu at the bottom right of the question panel to expose the options and select Response Validation. Set the validation options to Number, Between, **-5**, and **100**. Leave the custom error message blank in this case. The setup is shown in Figure 8.9. Click the plus button to create the next question.

Figure 8.9: Setup for the Temperature question

8. Change the name field of the new question to **Dog Happiness Rating** and select Linear Scale from the question type drop-down menu. In the scale setup options, leave the defaults of 1 and 5. Change the field next to number 1 from Label (Optional) to **Ears Down**, and the field next to number 5 to **Tail Wagging**. Click Required. The setup is shown in Figure 8.10. Click the plus button to create the next question.

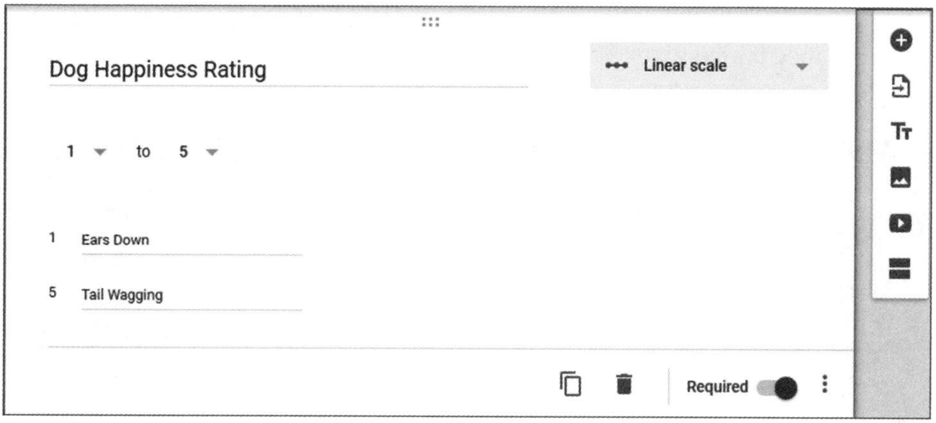

Figure 8.10: Setup for the Dog Happiness Rating question

9. Repeat step 8, setting the values for 1 to **Grumpy** and 5 to **Happy**, as shown in Figure 8.11.

Figure 8.11: Setup for the Walker Happiness Rating question

10. Now you will change the default form settings so the responses will be saved into a Google Sheet. At the top of the page, select the Responses tab. Click the Google Sheets icon, a small green and white square on the upper-right side of the tab, to Create Spreadsheet, and the Select Response Destination dialog box appears, as shown in Figure 8.12. Name the spreadsheet **Dog Walking Log (Responses)** and click Create. This opens a new tab in your browser displaying the new Sheet. This Sheet will be blank except for the column headers, which correspond to the question names. Note that there is an extra field on this sheet for Timestamp. This is different from the Date field, because that field can be set for any date and

Timestamp will record the actual date and time of any entry. This is helpful because it also gives you a unique value for each entry should you need one in your reports.

Figure 8.12: Create a Sheet for data collection

11. Preview the form. This is an important step! In order to create a data source for the Sheet, you need to have at least one row of data in the Sheet. You can delete this sample row after the connection is made between the Sheet and the report. To create an entry, click the eye icon at the top of the form page to preview the form, as shown in Figure 8.13. The form will appear in a new tab, ready to be filled in.

Figure 8.13: Previewing the form

12. Fill in the form and click Submit. The data will be stored in the Sheet, and you'll be presented with the option to submit another entry, as shown in Figure 8.14. You can now close the preview browser tab and return to the form editing browser tab.

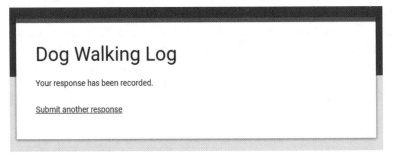

Figure 8.14: Completed form entry

13. You need a link to the form to embed it in the Data Studio report. On the form editing screen, click the Send button at the upper right of the page to open the Send form dialog box. On the Send Via line, click the link symbol. Note that there is an embed icon on this line, but that method of embedding is used for putting forms into standard web pages and is not used for embedding in Data Studio. Click Copy to copy the link to the clipboard, as shown in Figure 8.15. At this point, you may want to paste the URL into a convenient location—you'll need it in later steps.

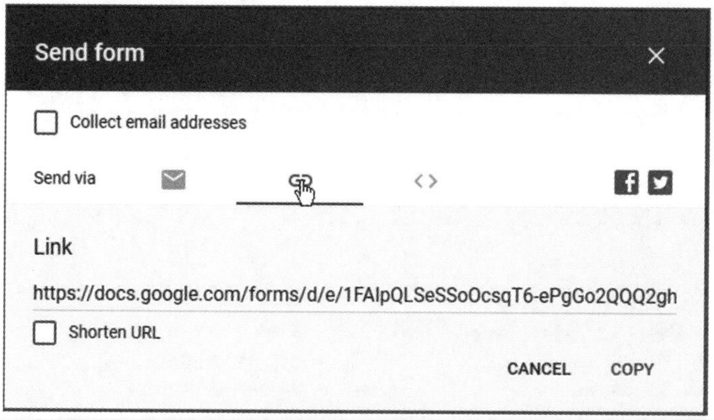

Send form   ✕

☐ Collect email addresses

Send via   ✉   GR   < >   f 🐦

Link

https://docs.google.com/forms/d/e/1FAIpQLSeSSoOcsqT6-ePgGo2QQQ2gh

☐ Shorten URL

                                                         CANCEL   COPY

Figure 8.15: Copying the Link URL for the form

Create the Data Source for the New Report

We can now create a new data source for the form response data to connect to a new report. As noted earlier, it is important to have at least one sample row in this Sheet. If the Sheet has only column headers, Data Studio will not allow you to create a new data source from the Sheet. We have covered how to create data sources from Google Sheets in earlier chapters, but we'll briefly review the procedure here for this example.

1. Start at the Data Studio home screen. Click the Create button in the upper-left corner of the screen and select Data Source, as shown in Figure 8.16.

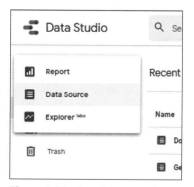

Figure 8.16: Creating a new data source

2. In the Google Connectors section, locate Google Sheets and click the Select button. This will take you to the Google Sheets connector page.

3. On the Google Sheets connector page, you should see Dog Walking Log (Responses) in the Spreadsheet list. If you don't, or you're using another Sheets file, you can use the Open From Google Drive option to locate the file. Rename the connector, select the spreadsheet, choose the Form Responses 1 Worksheet, and click the Connect button in the upper-right corner of the screen, as shown in Figure 8.17.

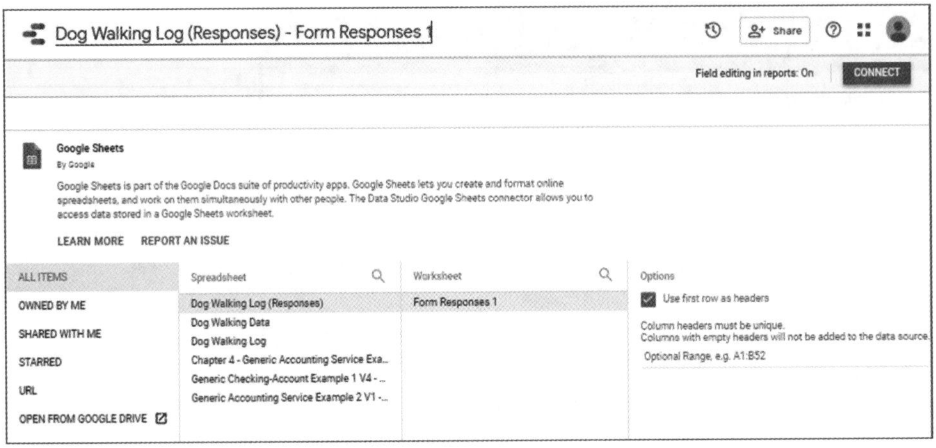

Figure 8.17: Connecting to Google Sheets

4. We would like to add a field that sums the dog and walker happiness ratings together for a total score. Click the Add A Field button in the upper-right corner of the screen and set up the new **Total Happiness** field, as shown in Figure 8.18. Return to the All Fields screen.

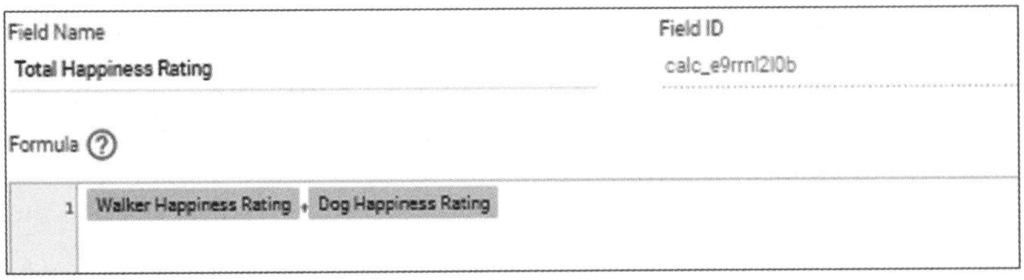

Figure 8.18: Creating the Total Happiness field

5. In the field properties, set the Total Happiness Rating Aggregation method to Average by using the drop-down for the field. Check the field types and adjust if needed. Figure 8.19 shows the completed settings. Return to the Data Studio main screen.

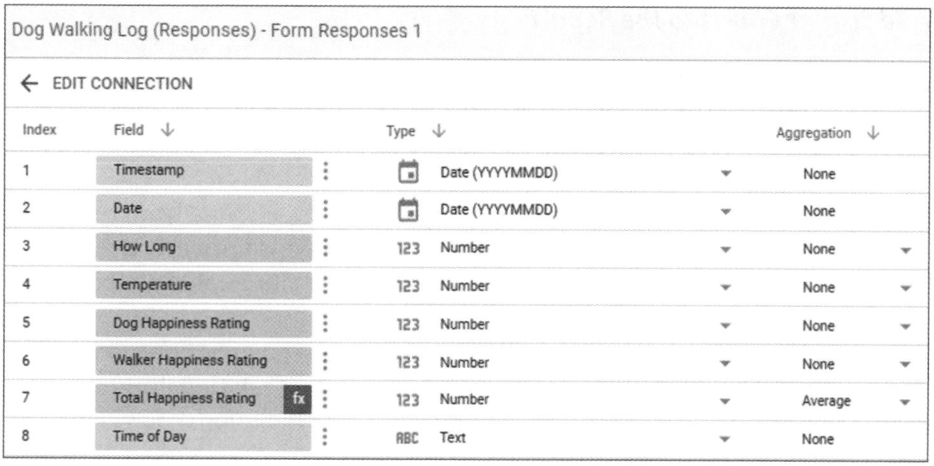

Index	Field ↓		Type ↓		Aggregation ↓	
1	Timestamp	⋮	📅 Date (YYYYMMDD)	▼	None	
2	Date	⋮	📅 Date (YYYYMMDD)	▼	None	
3	How Long	⋮	123 Number	▼	None	▼
4	Temperature	⋮	123 Number	▼	None	▼
5	Dog Happiness Rating	⋮	123 Number	▼	None	▼
6	Walker Happiness Rating	⋮	123 Number	▼	None	▼
7	Total Happiness Rating fx	⋮	123 Number	▼	Average	▼
8	Time of Day	⋮	RBC Text	▼	None	

Dog Walking Log (Responses) - Form Responses 1

← EDIT CONNECTION

Figure 8.19: Setting the field types and aggregation methods

If you are using a form to collect your own data over time, you're likely to change the report layout as you get more data and find the most appropriate ways to display it. That was the case in this example: after a full month of entries, I had a lot of options for visualizations. For this example, I chose to use some scatter charts to expose you to another useful chart type.

Create the New Report and Embed the Form

With all the ingredients in place, we're ready to bring them together in the report. Start from the Data Studio home page.

1. Click Blank Report in the Start With A Template section.

2. In the Add A Data Source panel, you should see our new data source at the top of the list. Select the data source and click Add To Report.

3. Click the URL Embed icon in the editing toolbar. Click and drag to place the embed area on the right side of the report. The URL Embed Properties panel should be on the right side of the screen. Select the Data tab and paste the URL that you saved for the form in the External Content URL field, as shown in Figure 8.20. The empty embed area should fill with the Google Form.

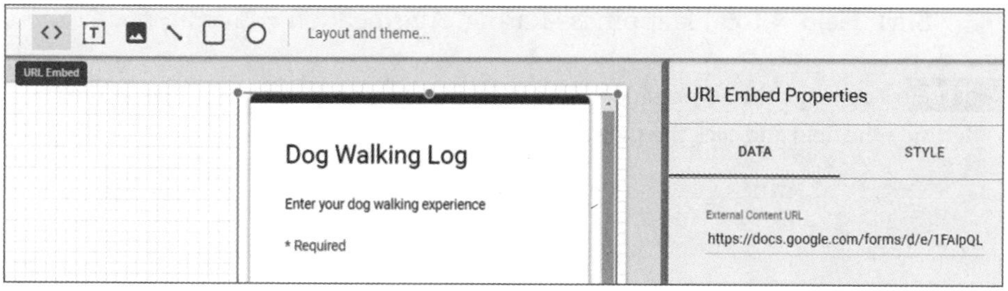

<> T ▣ ＼ ☐ ○   Layout and theme...

URL Embed

Dog Walking Log

Enter your dog walking experience

* Required

URL Embed Properties

DATA   STYLE

External Content URL
https://docs.google.com/forms/d/e/1FAIpQL

Figure 8.20: Setting the URL in the URL Embed Properties

Add Scatter Charts to the Report

We have covered how to add scorecards and tables in several sections of this book. The ones on this report are not special, so we'll skip the detailed steps to reproduce them. Here we'll focus on the setup of the scatter charts and explore some of the possibilities of this type of chart.

Although it may not seem as if we are gathering much data from our form, we have more than enough to explore the relationships between the metrics and dimensions. Scatter charts are an excellent choice for exploring these relationships.

In addition to simply plotting points on a chart, we have options to turn the scatter chart into a bubble chart. *Bubble charts* show a relationship to a third metric that sets the size of the dot on the chart. We'll explore each chart and see how it is built.

Chart 1: Total Happiness Rating vs. Temperature by Time of Day

We use a scatter chart for this component and turn it into a bubble chart simply by adding a metric for bubble size. Make sure that you are in Edit mode to begin.

1. Open the Add A Chart drop-down menu from the editing toolbar and select the scatter chart. Click and drag on the canvas to place the chart roughly into position. Don't worry about being too precise on your initial placement, as you'll usually need to do some adjustments after all the components are in place. The chart properties should appear in the right-side panel, and it should be showing the Data tab.

2. As usual, Data Studio creates the chart with valid values for dimensions and metrics, but these need to be changed. Set Date Range Dimension to Date. Set Dimension to the Time Of Day field.

3. Working your way down the Data tab, set these metrics and change their aggregation methods where necessary. Figure 8.21 shows the dimensions and metrics settings with the current state of the chart.

   Metric X: Field = Temperature, Aggregation = Average

   Metric Y: Field = Total Happiness Rating, Aggregation = Average

   Bubble Size: Field = Dog Happiness Rating, Aggregation = Average

   Sort: Field = Total Happiness Rating, Aggregation = Average

> **TIP**   To change the aggregation method for a metric, hover your mouse over the left side the field and click the pencil icon.

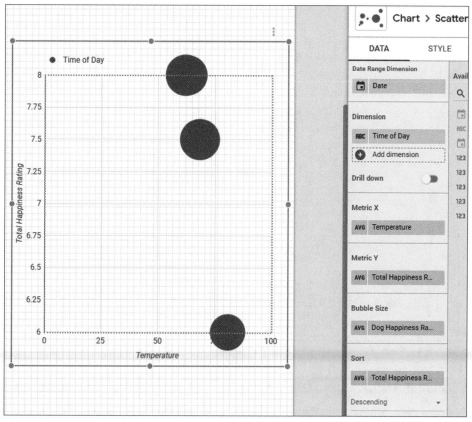

Figure 8.21: Data tab settings for Chart 1

4. Switch to the Style tab. First use the slider control to change the size of the bubbles. Then, use the Bubble Color drop-down to change the bubble color from None to Time Of Day. This causes the chart legend to show all the values, and it updates the coloring, making it easier to distinguish the different values.

5. Data Studio tries to set the scale of the chart automatically to best fit in all values, but the scale usually needs to be adjusted. Set the Left Y-Axis values for Axis Min to **0** and Axis Max to **10**. Set the X-Axis value of Axis Min to **0**. Figure 8.22 shows the Style Axis settings for the completed chart.

What can we learn from this chart? It appears that Total Happiness is higher during the time of day when the average temperature is cooler.

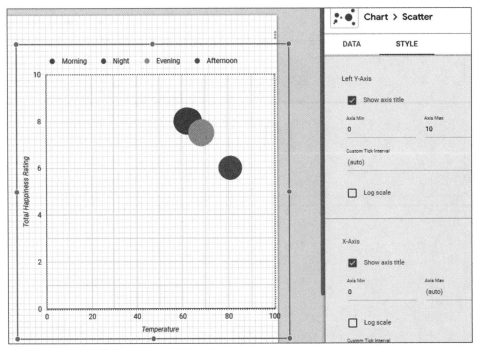

Figure 8.22: Style Axis settings for Chart 1

CORRELATION DOES NOT EQUAL CAUSATION

Please keep in mind that although correlations are very helpful in gaining insights, they do not guarantee a cause-and-effect relationship. In this case, it seems reasonable to assume that cooler temperatures are, at least in part, responsible for the Total Happiness score. However, it is only reasonable because you know a good bit about temperature and happiness already. If you were just looking at the chart values, you could have concluded that increases in happiness are causing temperatures to decrease! This seems ridiculous only because of our experience with temperature and happiness. Be careful about drawing, or accepting, conclusions based on a correlation where the underlying assumptions about cause and effect are not clear.

Chart 2: Temperature vs. How Long by Total Happiness Rating

The second bubble chart is quite similar to the first as far as construction. Again, we start from Edit mode to build this chart.

1. Add the scatter chart to the canvas.

2. Set the Date Range Dimension to Date. Set Dimension to Total Happiness Rating. Note that you can set the dimension to a metric value only, like Total Happiness Rating, by clicking and dragging the field from the

Available Fields panel to the Dimension settings. Although you can click on an existing value in the Dimension setting and get a list of fields to replace it with, this list only contains fields identified as dimensions.

3. The settings for the Data tab are as follows and are shown in Figure 8.23.

Metric X: Field = How Long, Aggregation = Average

Metric Y: Field = Temperature, Aggregation = Average

Bubble Size: Field = Total Happiness Rating, Aggregation = Average

Sort: Field = Total Happiness Rating, Aggregation = Average

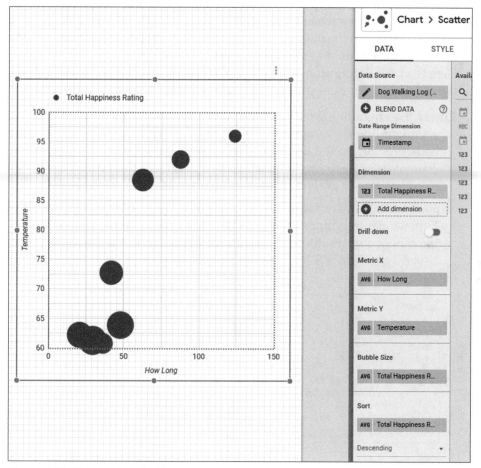

Figure 8.23: Data settings for Chart 2

4. Switch to the Style tab. First use the slider control to change the size of the bubbles. Next, use the Bubble Color drop-down to change the bubble color from None to Total Happiness Rating. Both chart axes are fine for our purposes and do not need to be updated.

What can we learn from this chart? It looks like Total Happiness is less for long walks in high temperatures, and shorter walks in cool weather score better in general.

Chart 3: Total Happiness Rating vs. How Long by Date

For this chart, bubbles showing the relative size of the date would not make sense, so we stick to the basic scatter chart. In this chart, we are making use of a *trendline* to clarify the relationship between the metrics and to help the audience estimate how a new value would be plotted.

Currently, Data Studio provides basic functions for drawing trendlines in scatter charts. Although these are helpful, there is currently no indication of how well they match the data. A chart creator is left to choose which functions seem to be a best fit for any particular chart.

Here is a brief description of the current trendline functions. To make it less abstract, let's take an example of satisfaction with the length of dog walks.

Linear: This trendline shows a simple relationship between the metrics using a straight line. Generally, we are less satisfied with longer walks. As the walk gets longer, the dog's satisfaction decreases. I could use the line to estimate how happy we'll be with a particular length of walk. The linear trendline for the graph is shown in Figure 8.24.

Exponential: This trendline shows a slightly more complex relationship. Exponential trendlines have one curve to express the trend. In this case, the exponential trendline shows little difference from the linear trendline, as shown in Figure 8.25.

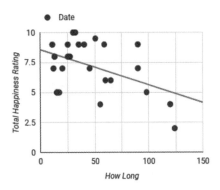

Figure 8.24: Linear trendline for Chart 3

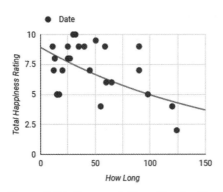

Figure 8.25: Exponential trendline for Chart 3

Polynomial: This one is used with larger data sets where there may be more factors at play influencing the relationship between the metrics. This trendline is more helpful when looking at the Total Happiness Rating, which is a complex measure made up of walker and dog satisfaction. We see that there is a rise and then a drop-off in satisfaction as length increases, as shown in Figure 8.26.

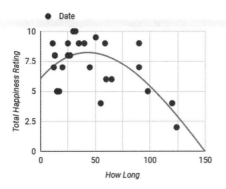

Figure 8.26: Polynomial trendline for Chart 3

Here's how to build Chart 3, starting in edit mode:

1. Add the scatter chart to the canvas.
2. Set the Date Range dimension to Date. Set Dimension to Date also. This makes the chart plot a point for every date in the records. There could be more than one walk on a specific date, so we need to make sure that the metrics are averaged.
3. Set metrics and their aggregation methods. Figure 8.27 shows the configured Data properties.

Metric X: Field = How Long, Aggregation = Average

Metric Y: Field = Total Happiness Rating, Aggregation = Average

Bubble Size: Leave this blank

Sort: Field = Total Happiness Rating, Aggregation = Average

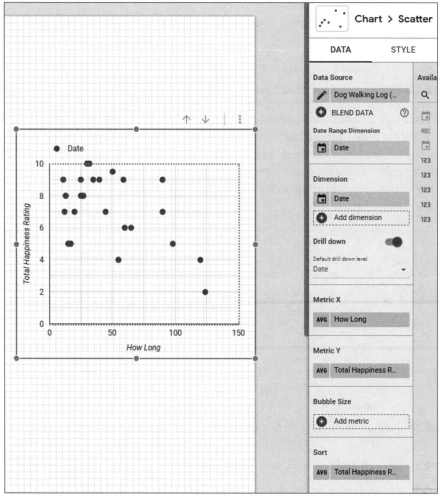

Figure 8.27: Data tab settings for Chart 3

4. Switch to the Style tab for the chart. Select Polynomial from the Trendline drop-down menu and set the desired line thickness and color, as shown in Figure 8.28.

What can we learn from this chart? The polynomial trendline helps us see that there is a peak in the relationship at about 45 minutes for walking time and that it then drops off as walks get longer. We can also see that the dots are pretty scattered on this chart, so we may not want to hold this conclusion too tightly.

Figure 8.28: Setting the trendline in the Style tab for Chart 3

Chart 4: Walker Happiness Rating vs. Dog Happiness Rating by Walker and Dog Ratings

This chart is actually two charts in the space of one! We use the drill-down feature to change the dimension being measured. This can sometimes be helpful in order to be able to flip between two dimensions on a chart. Usually, however, it is mostly used to save space on the canvas.

This is also an example of a chart that could use some explanation—even if you are the only one using it. We'll look at a way to add annotations to help remind us of what to look for in the charts at the end of this section. For now, let's build the chart and see what it can tell us.

1. Add the Scatter chart to the canvas.

2. Set the Date Range dimension to Date. Set the dimension by dragging both Dog Happiness Rating and Walker Happiness Rating from the Available Fields panel to the Dimension settings. Click the drill-down switch. Set the default drill-down level to Walker Happiness Rating.

3. Set metrics and their aggregation methods as follows:

   Metric X: Field = Dog Happiness Rating, Aggregation = Average

   Metric Y: Field = Walker Happiness Rating, Aggregation = Average

   Bubble Size: How Long, Aggregation = Average

   Sort: Field = Dog Happiness Rating, Aggregation = Average

   Figure 8.29 shows the configured Data properties.

4. Switch to the Style tab for the chart. Choose Polynomial from the Trendline drop-down menu and set the desired line thickness and color.

5. Set the left y-axis and x-axis values of Axis Min to 0. Figure 8.30 shows the Style axis settings for the completed chart.

What insights can we gain from this chart? First, we can see that Walker and Dog Happiness get better together and seem to do better with shorter walks. Second, this relationship is not exactly "symmetrical." By this I mean that the Walker score does not equal the Dog score. If it did, the string of dots would be a straight diagonal line. It is hard to tell by looking at the chart, though, what the pattern might mean.

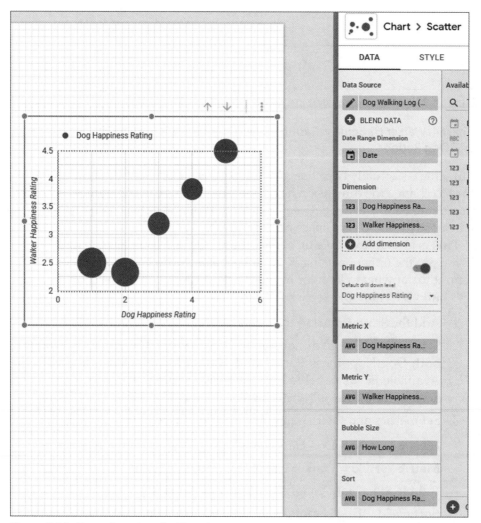

Figure 8.29: Data tab settings for Chart 4

I believe the best insights from this chart are found by hovering over the bubbles to see the actual values. Keep in mind that we are plotting the Walker rating here, and with Walker rating on the y-axis, the bubbles spacing vertically is exactly 1. On the other hand, the x-axis shows the Dog rating. When we get to the bubble plotting the Walker rating at 2, you can see that the Dog rating is much higher. By hovering over the second bubble, we can see the actual values. When the Walker rating is 2, the Dog Rating averages 2.8, as shown in Figure 8.31.

When we reach the Walker Happiness Rating of 4, we have a Dog rating of 4 to match. It seems that Dog and Walker are in sync again. When we reach the rating of Walker Happiness of 5, we can see from the bubble detail that the Dog is not sharing the Walker satisfaction and falls to a rating of 4.38, as shown in Figure 8.32.

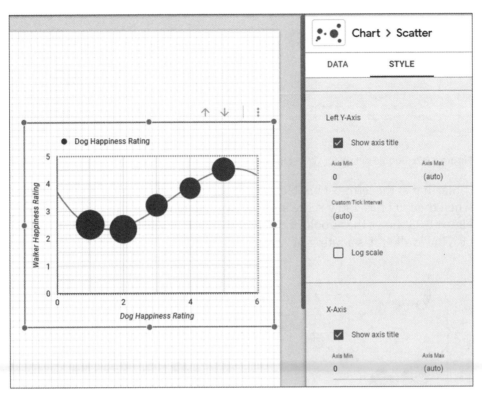

Figure 8.30: Style tab axis settings for Chart 4

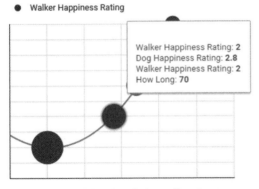

Figure 8.31: Bubble details for Walker Rating 2

It's pretty safe to say the Dog is enjoying longer walks more than the Walker, but it does not enjoy the shorter walks quite as much.

Now we turn the tables by using the drill-down feature to see this from the Dog's point of view. Using the drill up arrow in the header of the chart, switch Dimension to Dog Happiness Rating, and a new pattern takes shape. Now the bubbles will be spaced uniformly on the x-axis.

Figure 8.32: Bubble details for Walker Rating 5

Starting at the leftmost bubble, we can see the Walker rating is much higher when the Dog has a low score and the average length of these walks is long. Figure 8.33 shows the bubble detail, and we see that while the Dog has a rating of 1, the Walker has a rating of 2.5!

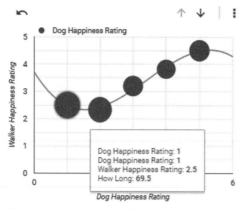

Figure 8.33: Bubble details for Dog Rating 1

As we move up the scale, the Walker rating gets more in line with the Dog, again being equal at a rating level of 4. At a Dog rating of 5, the Walker has dropped a bit to 4.5.

Curating Data from Other Sources

Now we are going to work with information that is already out there but that you collect, augment, and organize in different ways to provide more value. Whether you are collecting information privately for yourself or sharing it with others, you'll find Data Studio a great help in organizing, filtering, and displaying that data.

Just as sports fanatics collect and transform statistics about their teams and players, there seems to be a set of enthusiasts in almost any area of interest who enjoy collecting and presenting information back to their peers. Collections may also be used as features for businesses and organizations to share with their audiences.

Here is a beautiful example from Riccardo Zagaglia. Figure 8.34 shows his collection of the Best Italian Albums of 2010s. More than just a list, though, he has collected the album art, classifications of the music, and links to Spotify so that users can listen for themselves. Also included are links to the album review in the Italian music culture magazine, *SENTIREASCOLTARE*.

Figure 8.34: Data Studio collection example

This is an example of creating a valuable and entertaining resource from data that already exists. The data has been pulled together in a way that increases its value.

Another approach to curating collections is to gather new information on a topic and create a live feed. This kind of collection increases the value of the data by filtering the information and restricting it to an area of focus. This way, the user stays updated on new information on that topic, and the collection serves as a resource that can be referred to and searched. This will be the approach for our next example.

Instead of collecting information on a random topic, we'll gather information about Data Studio itself, since that is one topic in which everyone reading this book shares some interest. We'll use a service to help us collect the data on an ongoing basis. We'll always have the latest information, and we do not have to add to our collection manually.

In this example, we'll pull information from Twitter. I would like to have a collection of tweets about Data Studio. I would like this information to include the following:

- The date of the tweet
- Who tweeted on the subject
- A link to the tweet so that I can go directly to it in Twitter

Although I might be able to do a search for this topic on Twitter and export the results, I would rather keep a running log that is updated frequently. This kind of running log of tweets is particularly popular for events like conferences. You can collect all the tweets with a given event hashtag or search term. Sharing this collection allows people to keep up easily with what is going on before, during, and after an event even if they are not Twitter users.

Twitter does not provide a Data Studio connector, and though some third-party connectors are available, they do not allow searches past a certain time period. We'll start by building our own collection.

Several services are available that will let you connect to online services like Twitter and automate the collection of information. We'll use one of the most popular automation services, IFTTT. The acronym *IFTTT* stands for **IF This, Then That**, which essentially describes the recipes the service provides. Here are some of the reasons I chose to use IFTTT for this example:

- It's free.
- It connects to many major services.
- It is reasonably simple to use.
- It has been around since 2011 and runs millions of jobs every day.

In our case, the recipe is simple: if there is a new tweet containing our search term(s), then store the tweet information in a particular Google Sheet.

Setting Up IFTTT to Capture Tweets

You can sign up for IFTTT by going to `https://ifttt.com`.

This example requires that you have access to a Twitter account. These are free, but if you would prefer not to sign up for Twitter, you may want to follow along with this example and connect to some other service such as Instagram or Pinterest.

We are going to walk through, step by step, setting up the new IFTTT applet, sometimes referred to as a recipe, that will store the search tweets in a worksheet on your Google Drive. Then you'll learn how to modify the Sheet for use with Data Studio.

1. Log in to IFTTT with your user account. Click any link on the page to get more or explore.

2. In the search box, enter **Twitter**. Click the Services tab to find the Twitter service and click the Twitter box.

3. On the Twitter page, click the Connect button. You'll be taken to a screen that will let you authorize Twitter to allow IFTTT to access services on your behalf.

4. Fill in your Twitter username and password, and click the Authorize App button, as shown in Figure 8.35. You'll receive a request to validate with Twitter using a code sent to your smartphone. After you authorize, you'll be taken back to the Twitter page.

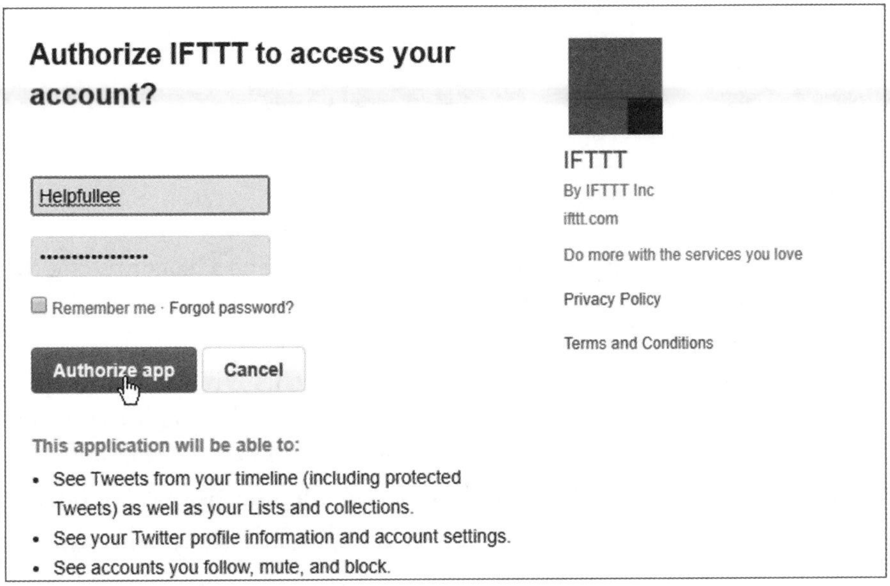

Figure 8.35: Authorizing Twitter to work with IFTTT

5. Return to the IFTTT home page and repeat these steps for Google Sheets.

Now that you have authorized IFTTT to connect to your services, you can create the applet for our example. Let's start on the IFTTT home page.

1. Click the Explore button in the upper-right corner of the page. Clicking this button will bring you to an applications discovery page.

2. In the Make Your Own Applets From Scratch row, click the plus button, as shown in Figure 8.36. Sometimes IFTTT places this option further down on the page, so you may have to scroll down a bit to find it. (I have also found that they may change their wording slightly.) This will take you to the Create Your Own Page screen.

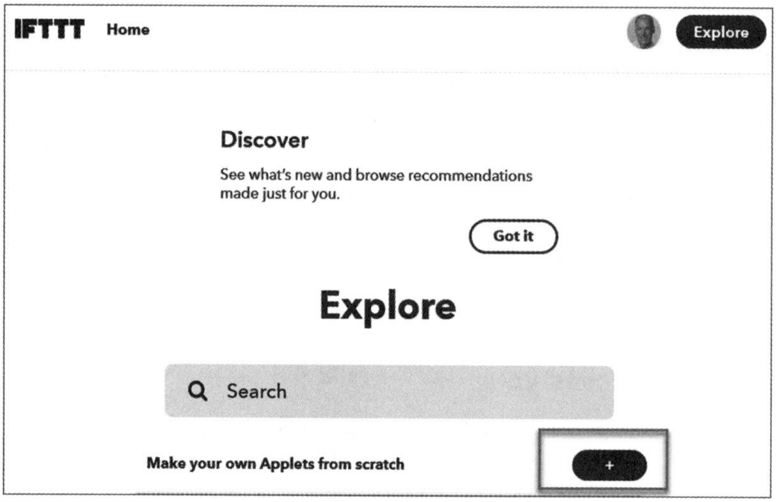

Figure 8.36: Starting the new IFTTT applet building process

3. This page does not have instructions on it, so it may be a bit confusing the first time you use the service. Click the plus button or the word This to open the Choose A Service page.

4. Search for Twitter and select the Twitter box. This will take you to the Choose Trigger page for Twitter. This is where you'll find all the things IFTTT can listen for to trigger a new action, as shown in Figure 8.37.

5. Select the New Tweet From Search option to open the Search For box.

6. Here you can enter any hashtags or terms you wish to search for. You can also use Twitter's special search operators to filter out things like retweets or specific users. For this example, we'll use several search terms and restrict retweets and searches including **Azure**, which is a different Data Studio service provided by Microsoft. Figure 8.38 shows our search entry. Click the Create Trigger button.

7. After creating the trigger, you'll arrive at a screen that allows you to go to the next step. Again, there are no instructions here. To continue, click the plus button or the word That, as shown in Figure 8.39.

Figure 8.37: IFTTT Twitter triggers

Figure 8.38: IFTTT Twitter search terms

If 🐦 Then ➕ That

Figure 8.39: Click the plus button.

8. On the Choose Action Service page, select Google Sheets and click it.

9. There are only two options for Google Sheets actions: Update A Cell and Add Row To Spreadsheet. Select the Add Row To Spreadsheet option to continue.

10. On the Complete Action Fields page, you set the details for the data to collect and where it will be stored. Figure 8.40 shows the completed setup.

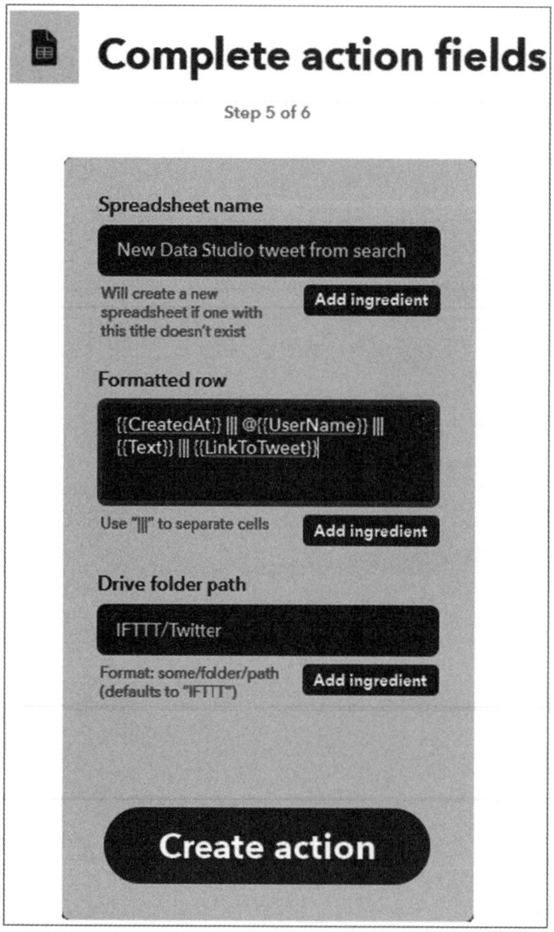

Figure 8.40: Configuring action fields

a. Change the spreadsheet name to **New Data Studio tweet from search**. IFTTT will create this spreadsheet for you.

b. Remove the three lines and the FirstLinkUrl field that follows (you don't need that field). To add different fields, click the Add Ingredient button and follow the instructions for using the three-line pattern to separate cells.

c. Change Drive Folder Path if desired. This allows you to create the spreadsheet in a folder on your Google Drive. By default, this path is set to IFTTT/Twitter, which is fine for our example. IFTTT will create these folders if they do not already exist.

d. Click the Create Action button to continue.

11. On the next screen, change the name to **Twitter Data Studio Search to Google Sheets**. If you are using the IFTTT mobile app, you have the option of receiving notifications when tweets are found.

12. Return to the IFTTT home screen and click the Google Sheets or Twitter button to see the new applet listing. Click the applet listing, and then click Settings in the upper-right corner of the screen. On the Settings screen, you can edit the trigger and action settings. You can also check on any search activity that has triggered the applet. Click the View Activity button to see recent tweets that have been captured, as shown in Figure 8.41.

Figure 8.41: Checking IFTTT applet activity

With these step completed, we should be capturing data in our Google Sheet. Unfortunately, as with most sources of data, we need to do some preparation to make sure Data Studio can read the file.

Preparing the Google Sheet for Data Studio

Whenever you pull data from a service like Twitter, you'll need to check the data formatting for use with other services like Data Studio. In this case, you must make a few adjustments to the Sheet. Follow these steps to prepare your the Sheet after it has some data in it. This should not take too long, as there are on average more than two tweets per hour using these keywords. If you are impatient, you can create a tweet yourself with the search term, and the IFTTT service usually runs every few minutes.

1. Locate and open the target spreadsheet. In our example, this is the spreadsheet called `New Data Studio tweet from search` in the `IFTTT/Twitter` folder on Google Drive.

2. We need a header row with labels for the Data Studio connector. To insert a header row, click the first row and select Insert ⇨ Row Above. Fill this row with a header for the fields: **Date**, **Source**, **Text**, and **TweetLink**, as shown in Figure 8.42.

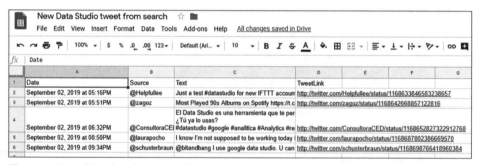

Figure 8.42: Adding headers to the Sheet

> **TIP** The date format from Twitter is not standard for Data Studio. This is due to the word "at" in the date text. Because of this, your report will only see the day and not the time, although it is clearly in the field. To work around this issue, I usually create a new column called **Timestamp**. I use a formula for the first data line in the new column and then copy that field down the entire column. This formula copies what is in the Date column but removes the word "at."
>
> ```
> =SUBSTITUTE(D2, " at ", " ")
> ```
>
> With the new field in place, Data Studio can now use the hours, minutes, and seconds if needed in a report using the Timestamp field.

Create a Data Source for the Google Sheet

Now we can make a new data source from our Google Sheet. As mentioned earlier, this particular set of search terms is very active on Twitter, so we'll have some data with which to work in a few hours. If you select fewer common terms, it may take longer to build up data. You need at least one entry in your Sheet to create a new data source.

1. Start at the Data Studio home screen. Click the Create button in the upper-left corner of the screen and select Data Source.

2. On the Google Connectors page, locate Google Sheets and click the Select button. This will take you to the Google Sheets Connector page.

3. On the Google Sheets Connector page, you should see the New Data Studio Tweet From Search Sheet in the spreadsheet list. If you don't, or if you are using another Sheets file, click Open From Google Drive and locate the file. Rename the connector, select the spreadsheet, choose the worksheet, and click the Connect button in the upper-right corner of the screen, as shown in Figure 8.43.

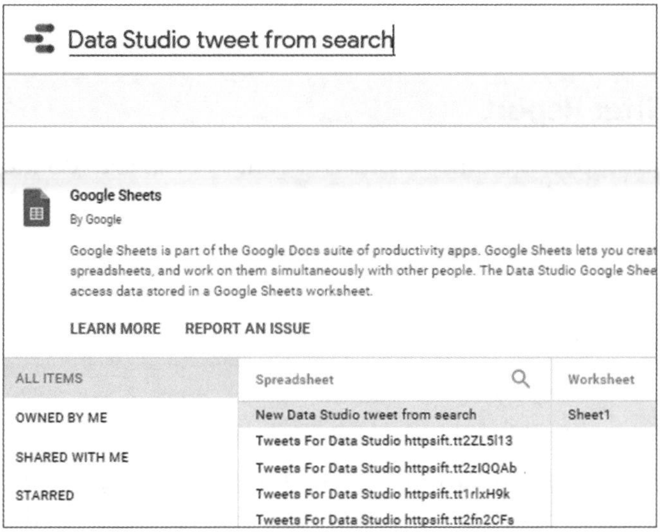

Figure 8.43: Connecting to Sheet for tweets

4. We'll create one new calculated field for our data source. This field will combine the text of the tweet with the link to the tweet for easier display in our report. Click the Add A Field button in the upper-right corner of the screen and set up the new field as shown in Figure 8.44. Click the Save button, and then return to the All Fields screen.

5. We don't have any metrics in this data source, so don't worry about the aggregation method settings. Your types should correspond to the ones shown in Figure 8.45. After checking, you can return to the Data Studio home page.

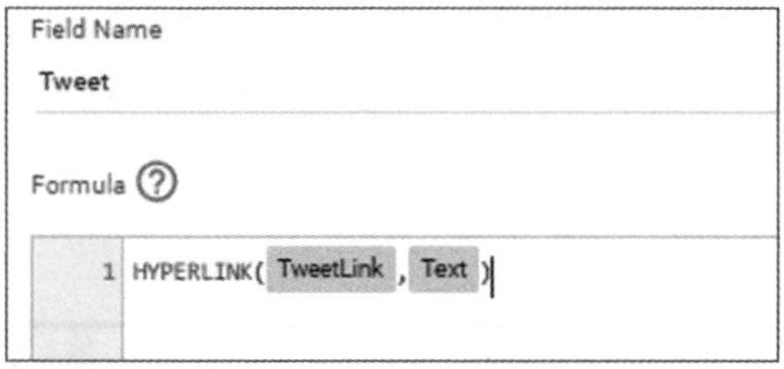

Field Name

Tweet

Formula ⑦

1 HYPERLINK(TweetLink , Text)|

Figure 8.44: Creating the Tweet link field

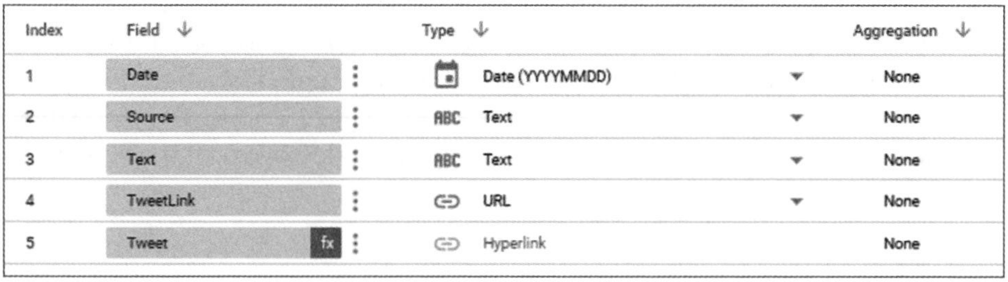

Index	Field ↓		Type ↓		Aggregation ↓
1	Date	⋮	📅 Date (YYYYMMDD)	▼	None
2	Source	⋮	ABC Text	▼	None
3	Text	⋮	ABC Text	▼	None
4	TweetLink	⋮	⊖ URL	▼	None
5	Tweet fx	⋮	⊖ Hyperlink		None

Figure 8.45: Checking the field types

Create the New Twitter Report

The requirements for this report are fairly basic. We want to be able to do the following things:

- View tweets by date and see the source of the tweet
- Go to the actual tweet
- See the number of tweets over time
- Search the tweet text
- Filter the report by source of the tweet and by date range

I have created a simple report with these needs in mind, as shown in Figure 8.46. With all of the ingredients in place, we can rebuild this report. Start from the Data Studio home page.

1. Click Blank Report in the Start With A Template section.
2. In the Add Data Source panel, you should see our new data source at the top of the list. Select the data source and click Add To Report.
3. Rename the report **Twitter Search - Hands On Data Studio Example 8.0**.
4. Select the text tool from the toolbar, and click and drag the text box into position. Add the title text. In the Text Properties tab, change the text size to 32px.

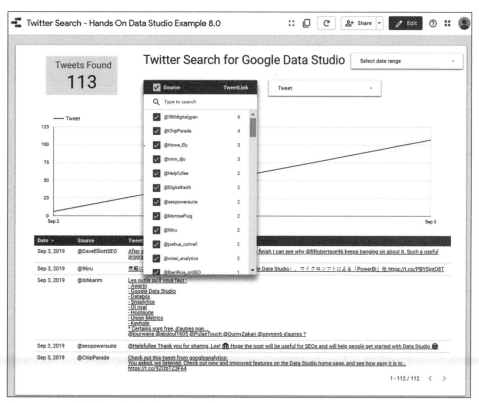

Figure 8.46: The Data Studio Twitter search report

5. Click the date range calendar icon in the toolbar and drag the control to the upper-right side of the page.

6. Click the Filter control icon in the toolbar and drag the control to position under the heading. Select the Data tab in the Properties panel. Set the dimension to Source, and set the metric to Tweet by dragging the field from the Available Fields panel. Note that you must use the drag-and-drop method to set this because it is a dimension. Set the Order drop-down menus to Metric and Descending. The configuration for the filter is shown in Figure 8.47.

7. Click the Filter control icon in the toolbar and drag the control to position it under the heading. Select the Data tab in the Properties panel. Set the dimension to Tweet. There is no need to change any other fields in this configuration.

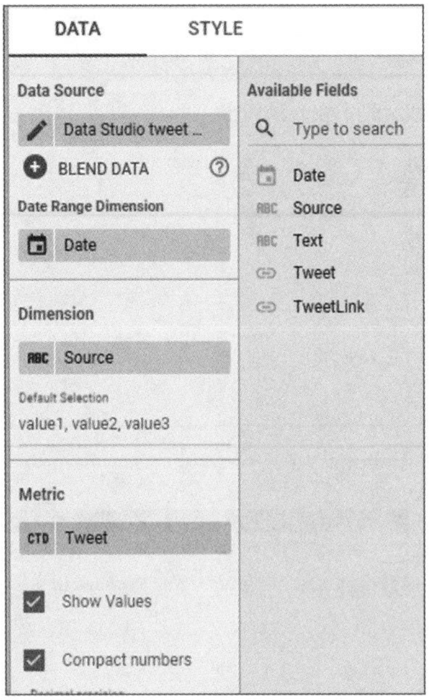

Figure 8.47: Filter control Data tab configuration

8. Use the Add A Chart drop-down menu to select the scorecard chart and size and position it in the chart. In the Configuration panel, select the Data tab and set Metric to Tweet. Hover your mouse over the field until the pencil icon appears, click it, and change the name to **Tweets Found**. Select the Style tab and change the Labels font size to 48px. Use the Metric Alignment section to set the metric name and the metric value positions to Center. Open the Background And Border Color drop-down and select a yellow color. The Style tab settings are shown in Figure 8.48.

9. Select the time-series chart from the Add A Chart drop-down menu and click and drag the box to size and position. Since there are no metric fields available, you'll see an error message, as shown in Figure 8.49. To fix this problem, select the Data tab for the chart properties. Set the dimension to Date and drag the Tweet field from the Available Fields panel to the Metric setting. Delete any extra metrics fields that show as Invalid Metric.

10. Select a basic table from the Add A Chart drop-down and drag it into position at the bottom of the report. Select the Data tab and set the dimension fields to Date, Source, and Tweet. If needed, set the Sort field to Date, Descending. Switch to the Style tab. Set the Table Labels font size to 14 (or larger for easier reading). Deselect the check boxes for Table Body and Row Numbers and select Wrap Text. Adjust the columns widths on the table as desired.

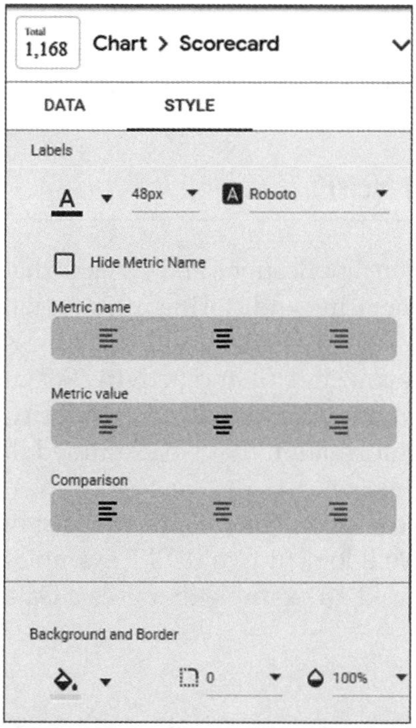

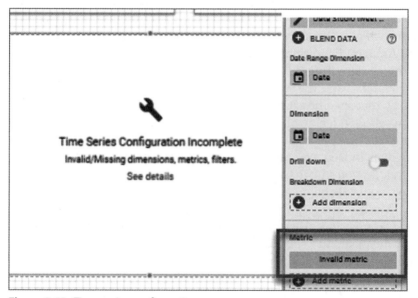

Figure 8.48: Scorecard Style tab configuration

Figure 8.49: Time-series configuration error

Since we have just built this report, there is not much to look at just yet. The time-series chart will grow over time to become more interesting. We'll see what it looks like with a full collection of data in the last section of this chapter.

Working with Data Generated for You

Data generated for you is the data that comes from applications and services that you use. Online entertainment services are generating and storing information about the videos you watch and the music you listen to. Digital health and fitness monitors gather and store information about your health and activity. Social media services create and store information about your activities, popularity, and connections. The banking and financial information that we examined in the first chapters might fall into this category as well.

In our last example, we looked at how to use a service like IFTTT to assist in gathering data from a social media service. We'll look at two IFTTT examples in this personal data section, and then we'll build an example that uses a Data Studio data source directly.

Music Service Tracking Example

Over the years, streaming music services have grown tremendously popular, with millions of users listening every day. Amazon offers one of these digital music services, called Amazon Music, as part of its Prime membership. Not only is the service available through phones and computers, but it is also available through the Amazon Echo smart speaker service.

As I sit at my desk writing this, I can say, "Alexa, play beach music," or "Alexa, play Muddy Waters," and the service will start playing a collection of songs in that style or by that specific artist.

I found myself wondering about my listening habits and if I could access a list of songs that I had played on the service, particularly ones that I liked but did not recognize. Indeed, you can connect to your personal music data through IFTTT services. As you saw in the last example, you can store your information directly into Google Sheets.

If Amazon Music is not your thing, IFTTT services can also connect to Spotify, Sound Cloud, Sonos, and other music services. The basic process is the same regardless of the particular service.

We went through a detailed example in the last section, so I will only briefly outline the steps here for how to make this connection and show you a music workbench that I created to give you some ideas for your own.

1. Connect to IFTTT; you'll need an IFTTT account.

2. Find the Amazon Alexa service and authorize access for IFTTT. Just as in the last example, once you authorize the connection, you'll have access to that service's triggers and actions.

3. Click the Explore button. Doing so will bring you to an application's discovery page.

4. Click the Make Your Own Applets From Scratch button (+).

5. Click the word This.

6. Search for Amazon Alexa and select it. This will take you to the Choose Trigger page for Alexa. There are a lot of trigger options here, as shown in Figure 8.50.

Figure 8.50: IFTTT Alexa triggers

7. Click New Song Played to add that trigger and return to the If This Then+That screen.

8. After creating the trigger, you'll arrive at a screen that allows you to go to the next step. Again, there are no instructions here. To continue, click the plus button or the word That, as shown earlier in Figure 8.39.

9. Click Action Service Google Sheets. You'll be on the Choose Action Service page. Search for Google Sheets and click it to continue.

10. Click Add Row To Spreadsheet.

11. Complete the action fields. Specify the details for the data to collect and where it will be stored. Figure 8.51 shows the completed setup. Change the spreadsheet name and folder path if desired. Click the Create Action button to continue.

Figure 8.51: Configuring Alexa action fields

12. Next, you can change the name of the Applet. You can also modify the notifications option if desired. If you leave this option on, IFTTT will send a mobile app notification for each song played. Click the Finish button to complete the setup. A confirmation screen will appear with your new applet.

13. Click the Settings button in the upper-right corner. On the Settings screen, you can edit the trigger and action settings. You can also check on any search activity that has triggered the applet. Click the View Activity button to see recent songs that have been captured, as shown in Figure 8.52.

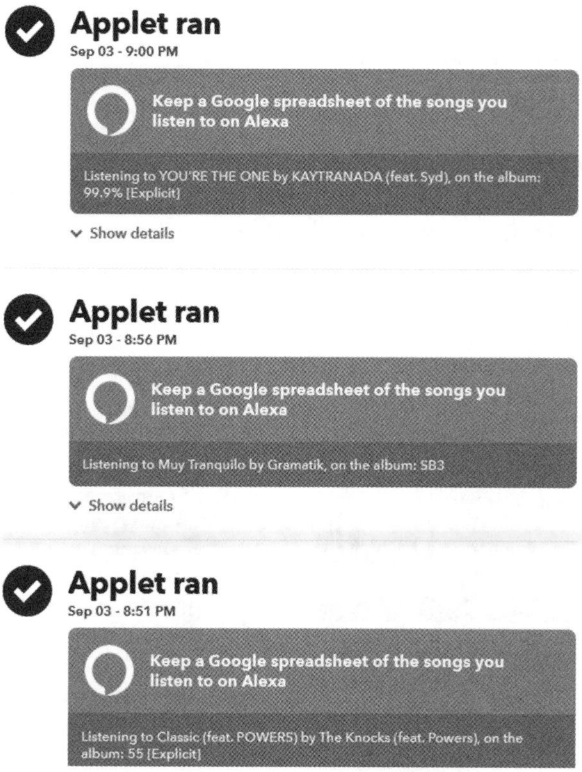

✓ **Applet ran**
Sep 03 - 9:00 PM

Keep a Google spreadsheet of the songs you listen to on Alexa

Listening to YOU'RE THE ONE by KAYTRANADA (feat. Syd), on the album: 99.9% [Explicit]

⌄ Show details

✓ **Applet ran**
Sep 03 - 8:56 PM

Keep a Google spreadsheet of the songs you listen to on Alexa

Listening to Muy Tranquilo by Gramatik, on the album: SB3

⌄ Show details

✓ **Applet ran**
Sep 03 - 8:51 PM

Keep a Google spreadsheet of the songs you listen to on Alexa

Listening to Classic (feat. POWERS) by The Knocks (feat. Powers), on the album: 55 [Explicit]

Figure 8.52: Checking IFTTT Alexa activity

14. As in the previous example, it's a good idea to run a couple of test songs first to make sure that the data is flowing into the Sheet properly. Next, you'll need to insert a header row in the Google Sheet as in the previous example. Here the fields will be **Data**, **Artist**, **Song**, and **Album**, as shown in Figure 8.53.

15. On the Data Studio home screen, click the Create button and select Data Source. Select Google Sheets from the Connectors page. Locate and select your Sheet. Rename the data source if desired and click Connect.

fx					
	A	B	C	D	E
1	Date	Artist	Song	Album	
2	October 21, 2017	America	Sandman	America	
3	October 21, 2017	America	Ventura Highway	Homecoming	
4	October 21, 2017	America	Sister Golden Ha	Shining '70s (Best Of '70s E	
5	October 21, 2017	America	Tin Man	Hits	

Figure 8.53: Adding headers to the Alexa Sheet

With your setup complete, you can start a new report to view your listening data in different ways. Let's take a look at an example of what you might do with this data. Figure 8.54 shows a workbench-style report that I created from my personal listening data.

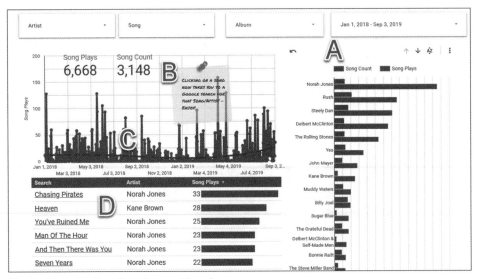

Figure 8.54: An Alexa listening workbench

You have seen how to create all the parts of this workbench-style report in previous chapters. Rather than walking through building the report again, I'll point out some of the features that were added to give this report more personal functionality:

Bar Chart   This bar chart measures both song count and song plays, which lets me easily see how much repetition I have over the songs available. The header of this chart allows the user to sort the list by Song Count, Song Plays, or Artist. In addition, the drill-down feature lets you view the metrics by album or song. In Figure 8.55, you can see the chart showing Norah Jones albums by Song Count. The chart has interactions set so that the user can easily filter by clicking the bars.

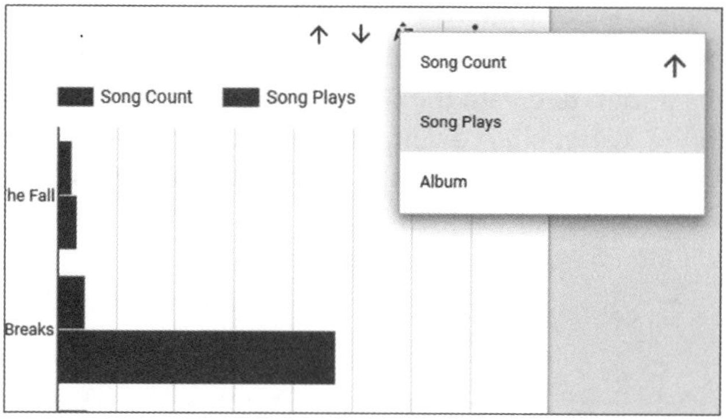

Figure 8.55: Bar chart sorting and drill down

You can set the chart to enable sorting by different fields by selecting the Enable Sorting option in the Interactions section, as shown in Figure 8.56.

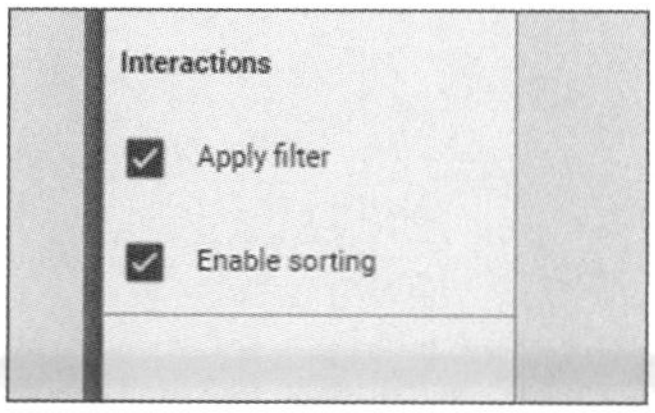

Figure 8.56: Enabling sorting on the bar chart

Pinned Note Message   This is simply a fun graphic hack. I had an image for the pinned note and simply uploaded it, as we did in previous examples. I created a text box over the image for my message and chose the Permanent Marker font. Setting the image opacity to less than 50 percent allows you to see through the image to the chart behind it. The Style settings for the image are shown in Figure 8.57.

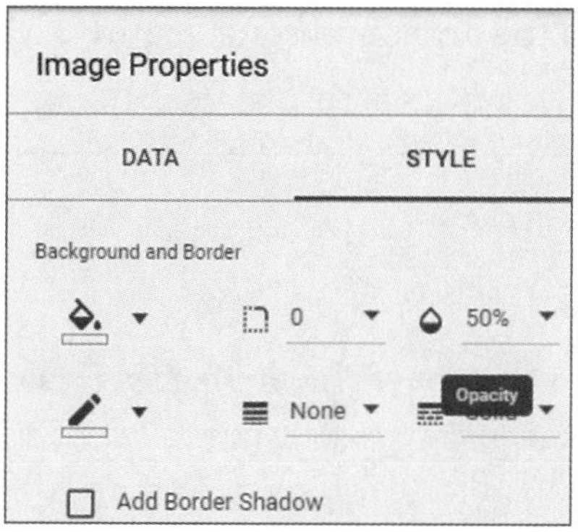

Figure 8.57: Setting Opacity in the image Style tab

Time-Series Chart   You have seen time-series charts before, but not with this particular combination of settings from the Style tab. Here we are using the Show Points option to create the dots at the peaks of the chart spikes. As you saw in the scatter chart example, the time-series chart can also use the trendline feature. The Style tab settings for this chart are shown in Figure 8.58.

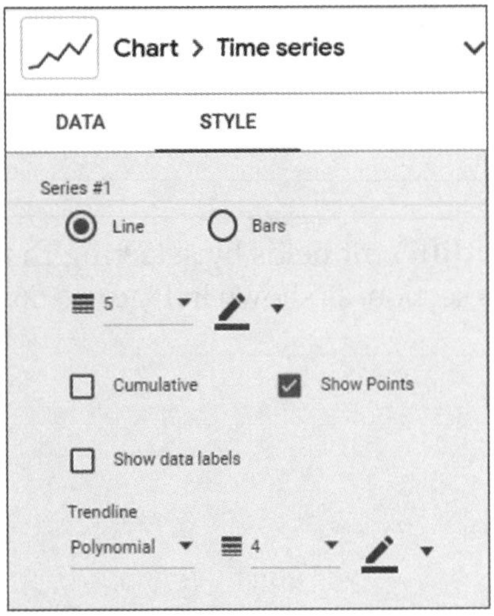

Figure 8.58: Setting points and trendline in the time-series Style tab

Detail Table   Here we have an interesting hack! This was a pretty standard table showing some song detail, but I wanted to be able to go through my song history, find an interesting song, and play it back. Since there was no way for me to do this directly, I created a new hyperlink field called Search. This is similar to the example in Chapter 6, "Using Google Search Console for Audience Insights," where we created a Google Search string to explore Search Console queries. This time, however, we're creating a query URL for YouTube with the artist and song. Figure 8.59 shows the formula for the Search field.

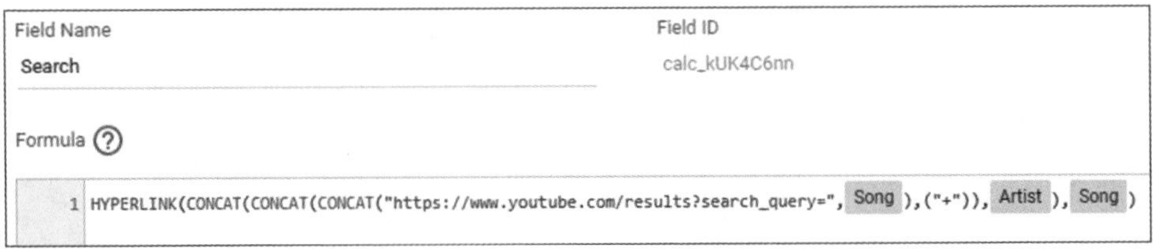

Figure 8.59: Formula for Search field for Songs

This works surprisingly well! Clicking one of these Search links for a song almost always brings back a results page with the desired YouTube video as the top result, ready to be played. A typical example is shown in Figure 8.60, where we click on the link for "Man of the Hour" by Norah Jones.

Figure 8.60: YouTube results for Search link

I might add a search for lyrics in the future. How would you build this workbench to explore your own musical tastes?

Google Fit Community Connector Example

Our last example to explore in the area of personal applications deals with health and fitness. Worldwide, more than 70 million fitness trackers were shipped in 2018. There is a plethora of personal tracking devices that can track your movement, vital signs, and even sleep patterns. See `www.statista.com/topics/4393/fitness-and-activity-tracker` to learn more.

While I am writing this, a Fitbit watch on my wrist is keeping track of my heart rate and movements. I am also slowly pedaling on an under-desk elliptical machine that sends data to my phone. Although not everyone uses a fitness tracker or measures as much as I do, you may be measuring your exercise and activity throughout the day with a smartphone.

If you want to have access to this fitness data for your own purposes and reporting, you can often use a service like IFTTT. IFTTT connects to a number of device accounts, including Fitbit, Nike+, and others. One popular service that is not supported at this time by IFTTT is Google Fit.

The Google Fit service works by measuring activity through a smartphone app that has over 10 million downloads. The app has its own basic reporting, but it is possible to access your data through a programming interface that can require a high level of programming expertise to use.

Although it is possible to build your own Data Studio connector, that is beyond the scope of this book. In this section, we'll look at retrieving Google Fit data by using a community connector. Unfortunately, most community connectors are not currently available through the standard connectors screen, so they are often overlooked.

Community connectors are built by developers and shared with the general public for use with Data Studio. Although several have been built by Google developers, they are not officially supported by Google. They are generally high quality and secure. They are kept in open-source repositories so that the developer community can inspect all the code being used to check for issues. Currently, there are some 20 connectors that can be used to access information as varied as the position of the International Space Station to data about the fictional *Star Wars* universe!

Getting a community connector up and running is not an intuitive process for a non-developer, as the documentation for the full process is scattered across several sites. In this section, we'll walk through the steps to accomplish this and make the process a bit simpler, at least for using the Google Fit community connector.

Although you can follow along with the steps to create the connector, you'll need to have the Google Fit application installed on your smartphone to get actual data for a report. Even if you don't intend to use that service, walking through this example should help you use other connectors that are available.

Community Connector Setup for Google Fit

You'll need two browser tabs or windows available in order to make this process work efficiently due to the need to copy information from one site to another. Links to these locations are also available in the Chapter 8 online resources page at www.wiley.com/go/handsondatastudio.

1. Open a browser tab or window and connect to the Google Fit source code directory. We'll be copying text from the code files from the source repository for the connector project. We'll call this **Tab A**. The page is shown in Figure 8.61. The URL for this folder is https://github.com/googledata-studio/community-connectors/tree/master/google-fit/src.

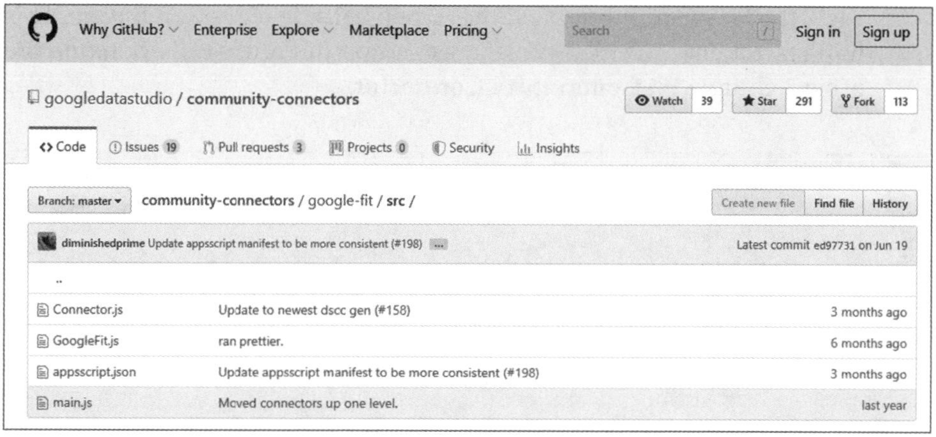

Figure 8.61: Tab A—the Google Fit source folder

2. Open a browser tab or window and connect to the G Suite Developer Hub page. You must be logged into your Google account to access this service. The Developer Hub lets you build your own projects and scripts for use with Google G Suite products. We'll call this **Tab B**. This page is shown in Figure 8.62. The URL for this site is `https://script.google.com/home`.

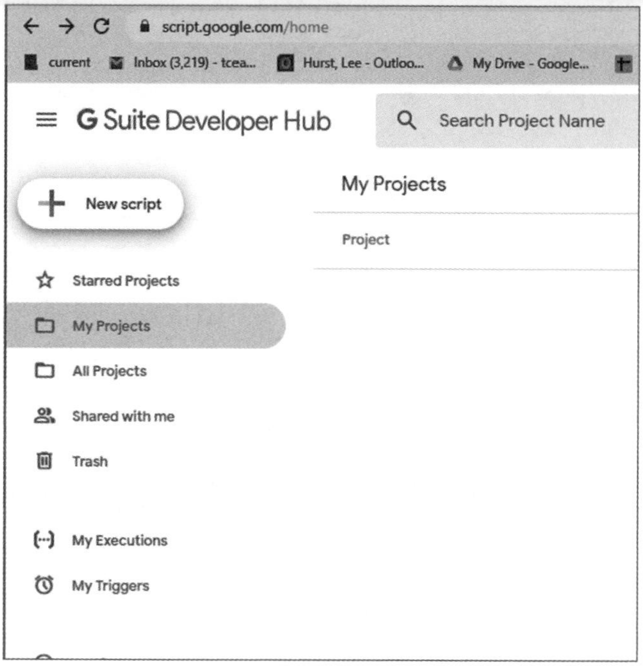

Figure 8.62: Tab B—the Developer Hub page

3. Click the New Script button at the upper-left side of the Tab B page. This will start a new, untitled project, as shown in Figure 8.63. Rename the project **Google Fit Community Connector**.

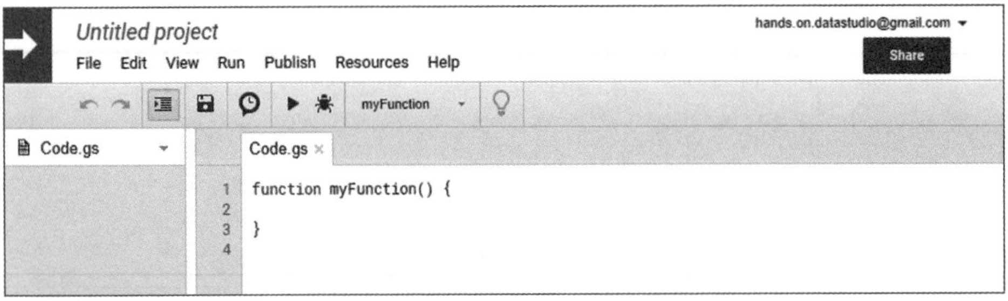

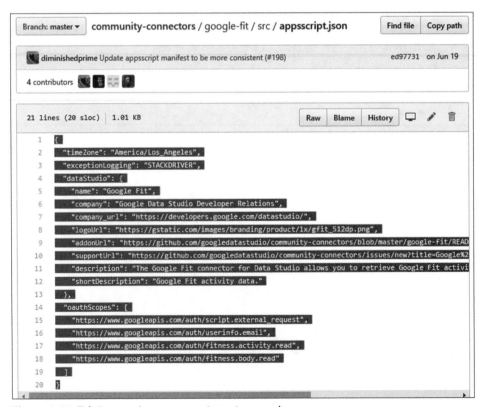

Figure 8.63: Tab B—starting a new project

4. Choose View ➪ Show Manifest File to open a new file tab on the screen called appsscript.json. We'll be pasting content into the `appsscript.json` file from Tab A.

5. Click `appsscript.json` to open the file. Select all the code text and use Ctrl+C to copy it to the clipboard, as shown in Figure 8.64.

Figure 8.64: Tab A—copying `appsscript.json` code

6. Switching back to the Developer Hub tab (Tab B), delete all current code in the appsscript.json tab and press Ctrl+V to paste the new code into the tab, as shown in Figure 8.65. Click the Save button and switch to Tab A.

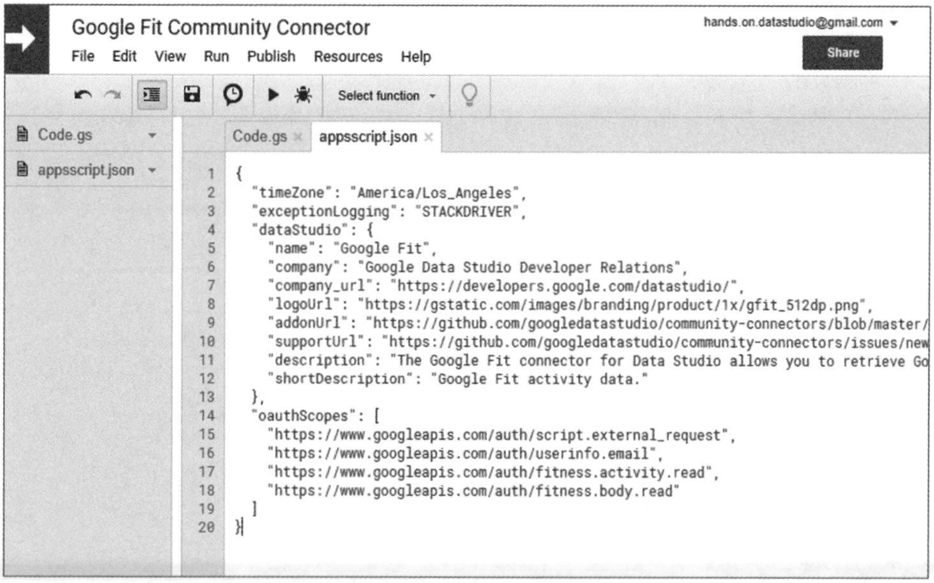

Figure 8.65: Tab B—pasting the `appsscript.json` code

7. We now need to copy all the JavaScript files and re-create them in our project. The easiest way to do this is to copy the contents of each file. Use the breadcrumb navigation on this page to return to the /src folder, select the Connector.js file, highlight all the code, and copy it to the clipboard, as shown in Figure 8.66. This is a very long file, so be sure to get all of it copied! Switch to Tab B.

8. Choose File ➪ New ➪ Script file to open the Create File dialog box. Enter the name **Connector.js** and click OK. A new tab with the name Connector.js.gs will appear with generic function code. Delete that code and press Ctrl+V to paste the new code into the tab, as shown in Figure 8.67. Click the Save button and return to Tab A.

9. You'll need to follow these same steps for GoogleFit.js and main.js. Make sure that you use the filenames with capitalization exactly as the files are listed. Figure 8.68 shows Tab B with all the files replicated. You are now done with Tab A.

10. Switch back to Tab B. Choose Publish ➪ Deploy From Manifest to open the Deployments screen. Click the line containing Latest Version (Head). A new line will appear with a link, as shown in Figure 8.69. Click the new link to go to the Connector setup page.

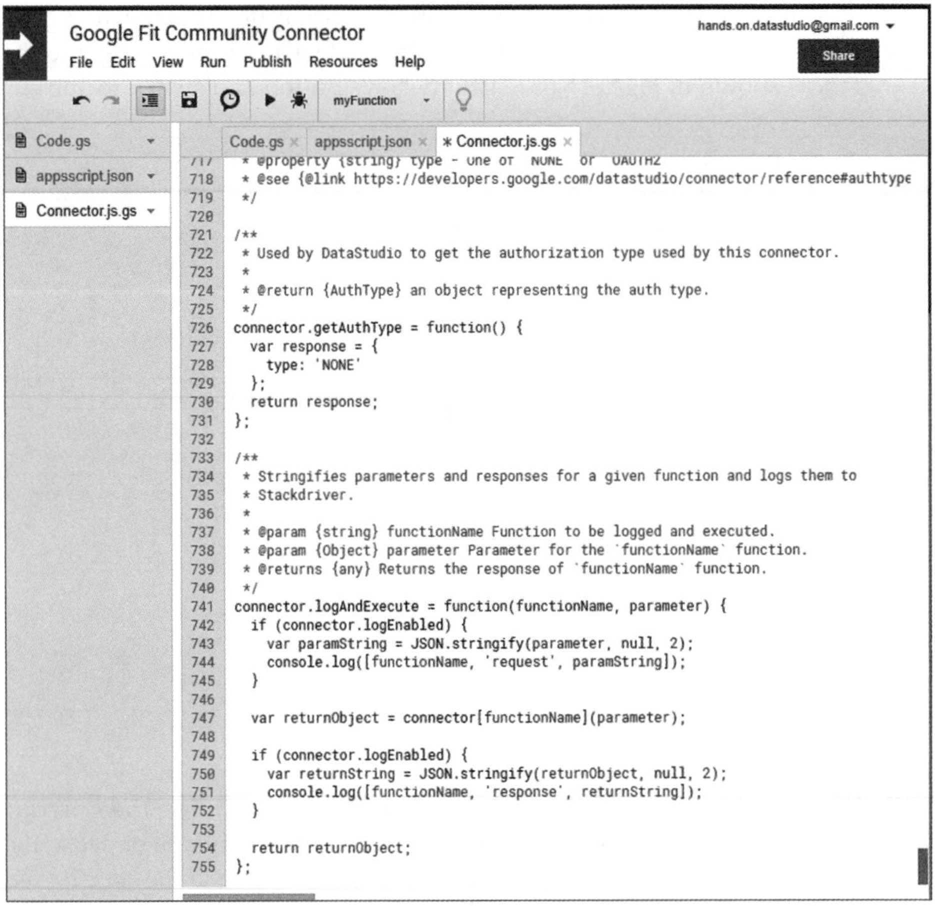

```
     Google Fit Community Connector                    hands.on.datastudio@gmail.com  ▾
                                                                              Share
     File   Edit   View   Run   Publish   Resources   Help

   ↶ ↷  ⌷  🖫  🕒  ▶ ▦    myFunction    ▾      💡

📄 Code.gs          ▾      Code.gs ×   appsscript.json ×   ✱ Connector.js.gs ×
                         717  * @property {string} type - one of  NONE  or  OAUTH2
📄 appsscript.json   ▾    718  * @see {@link https://developers.google.com/datastudio/connector/reference#authtype
                         719  */
📄 Connector.js.gs   ▾    720
                         721  /**
                         722   * Used by DataStudio to get the authorization type used by this connector.
                         723   *
                         724   * @return {AuthType} an object representing the auth type.
                         725   */
                         726  connector.getAuthType = function() {
                         727    var response = {
                         728      type: 'NONE'
                         729    };
                         730    return response;
                         731  };
                         732
                         733  /**
                         734   * Stringifies parameters and responses for a given function and logs them to
                         735   * Stackdriver.
                         736   *
                         737   * @param {string} functionName Function to be logged and executed.
                         738   * @param {Object} parameter Parameter for the `functionName` function.
                         739   * @returns {any} Returns the response of `functionName` function.
                         740   */
                         741  connector.logAndExecute = function(functionName, parameter) {
                         742    if (connector.logEnabled) {
                         743      var paramString = JSON.stringify(parameter, null, 2);
                         744      console.log([functionName, 'request', paramString]);
                         745    }
                         746
                         747    var returnObject = connector[functionName](parameter);
                         748
                         749    if (connector.logEnabled) {
                         750      var returnString = JSON.stringify(returnObject, null, 2);
                         751      console.log([functionName, 'response', returnString]);
                         752    }
                         753
                         754    return returnObject;
                         755  };
```

Figure 8.66: Tab A—copying the `Connnector.js` code

11. You'll now be on the authorization page for the connector, as shown in Figure 8.70. Change the name of the connector at the top of the page to **Google Fit Steps** and then click the Authorize button to go to the Authorization screen.

12. If you have multiple Google accounts, be sure to select the one to which your Google Fit mobile app is connected. If you do not have the app, you may continue but the connector will have no data. After selecting an account, you'll be presented with a warning screen that says "This app isn't verified." In this case, you know and trust the developer—you! Click the Advanced link to continue. At the bottom of the resulting screen, you should see a link, as shown in Figure 8.71.

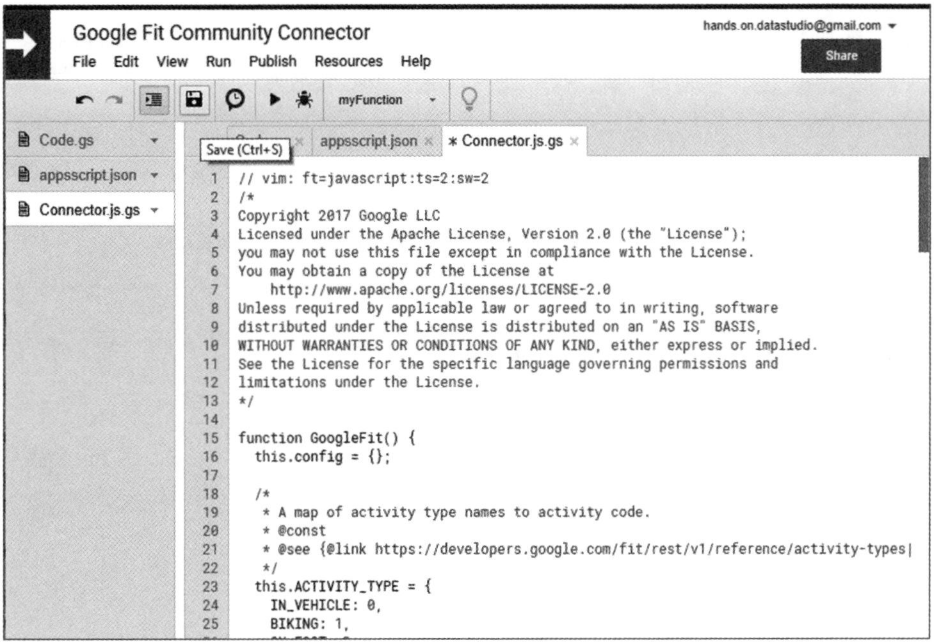

Figure 8.67: Tab B—pasting the `Connnector.js` code

Figure 8.68: Tab B—all JavaScript files replicated from Tab A

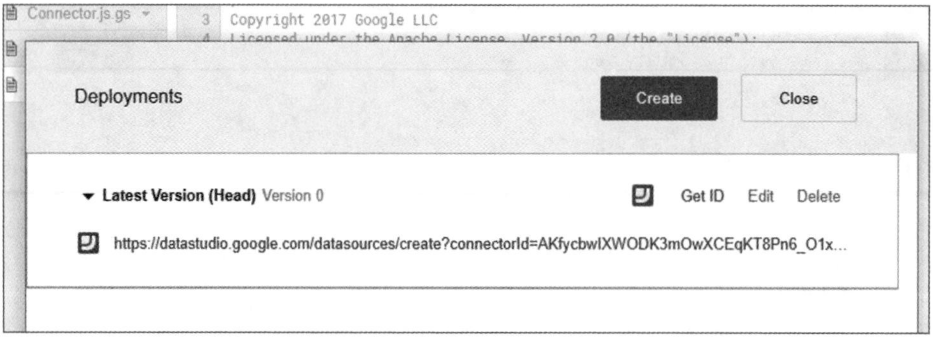

Figure 8.69: Tab B—Deployments screen with link

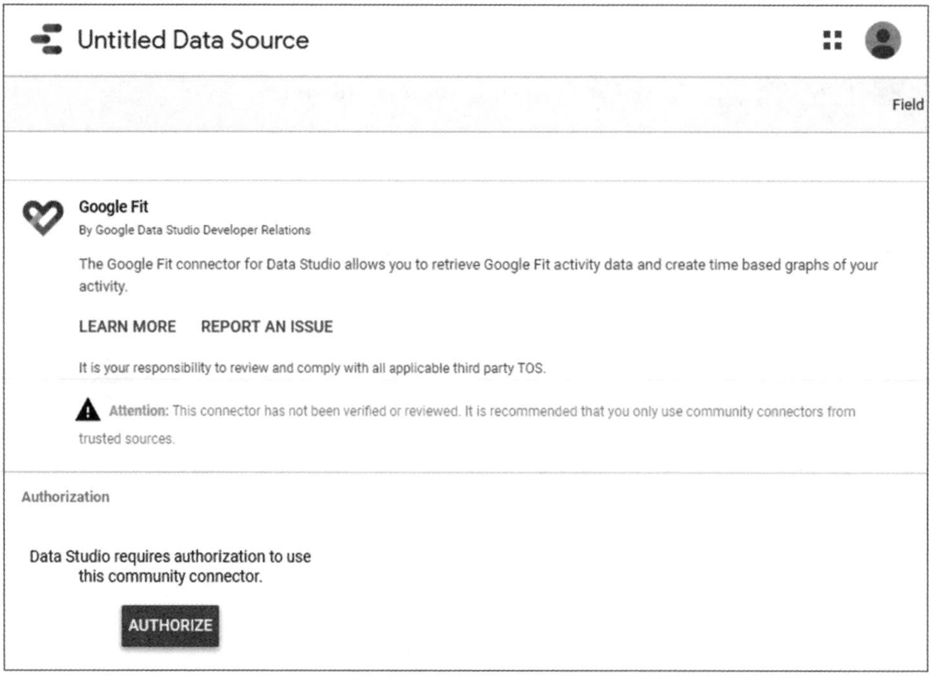

Figure 8.70: Connector authorization screen

13. Under the new message is a link: Go To Google Fit Steps (Unsafe). Click this link. There are good reasons for the stern warnings here. You should never connect your account to an app that is not verified or that is not trusted. In this case, we are using well-known code from extremely reputable sources. Developers who write their own code must go through this same process. Clicking the link will bring you to another screen that will tell you what the app needs to access on your Google account, as shown in Figure 8.72. Click the Allow button to continue.

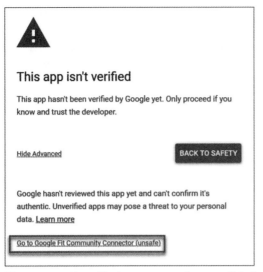

Figure 8.71: Unverified app screen after you click the Advanced link

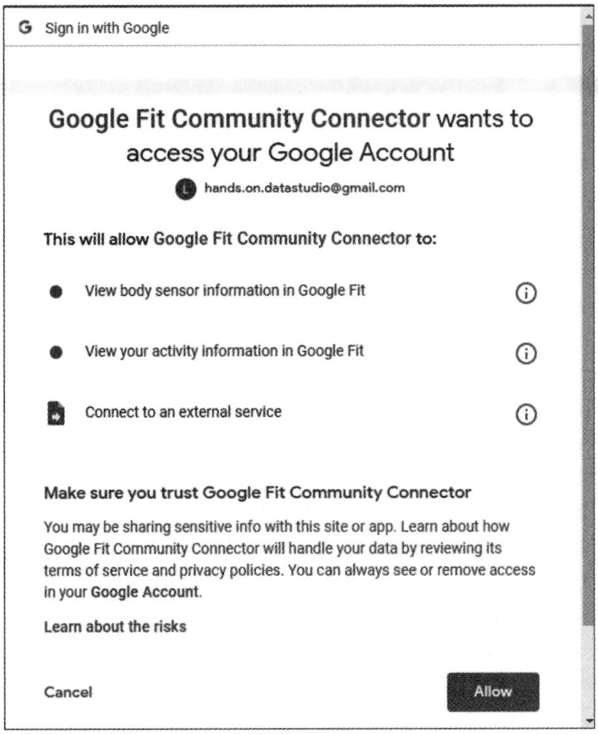

Figure 8.72: Final authorization screen

14. You should now have an option to select the type of data that you want the connector to retrieve. Click the drop-down and select Steps. Note that if you want other data in addition to Steps, you'll have to duplicate this connector and choose another data type. The Steps selection is shown in Figure 8.73. Click the Connect button in the top-right corner of the screen to continue to the fields review page.

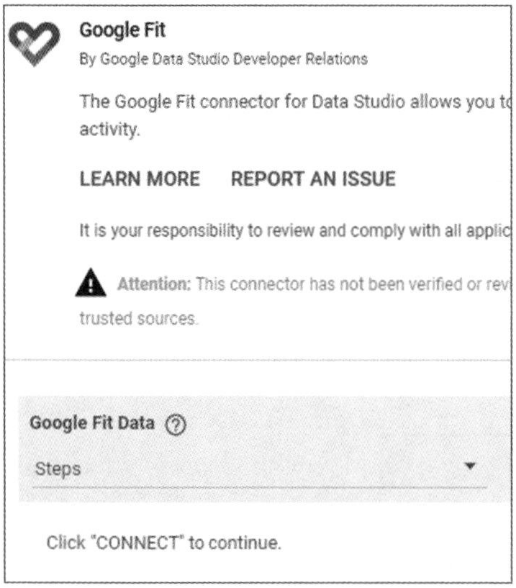

Figure 8.73: Selecting data for Google Fit

Congratulations! You made it through all the steps and now have a Google Fit connector. This connector gives you information about steps only, so if you want information about your activities, heart rate records, weight, or daily heart rate, you'll need to create a data source for each of these. Fortunately, you do not have to go through this process again once you have created the connector. The Google Fit connector will now show on the Connectors page like all others, so you can easily create additional data sources for the other parts of the Google Fit data should you want them.

Instead of building a dashboard with the Google Fit data sources, I thought it would be a good idea to look at how someone else put together their own dashboard. Every designer has a certain style, and for the sake of brevity, I keep mine simple in the examples in this book. However, this may leave you with the impression that this is the only way to design, and that is just not so.

Here is a Google Fit dashboard from David Murphy, also known as *Datasaurus Rex*. Some time ago, David created a very nice blog post and a video explaining how to use his template with your own Google Fit connectors. David has a way with graphics that makes his dashboard fun to look at. Links to his post and video are also included in the online chapter notes at www.wiley.com/go/handsondatastudio.

Figure 8.74 shows his Google Fit Dashboard.

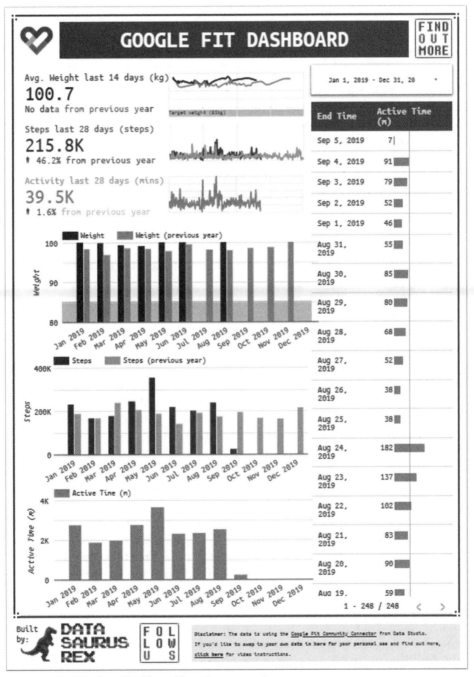

Figure 8.74: Google Fit Dashboard from Datasaurus Rex

Google Fit Data Studio Dashboard: https://datasaurus-rex.com/gallery/
google-fit-data-studio-dashboard

**Connecting your Google Fit data sources to the Datasaurus Rex Google
Fit Dashboard**: www.youtube.com/watch?v=tuNwXedZkkg

Bringing It All Together

Finally, I want to show you an example that uses created, curated, and generated data together in one report. I don't think the term "report" fully captures
the capability of many Data Studio creations. As you have seen in previous
chapters, you can build classic static reports as well as analysis workbenches
and reports that work like mobile apps.

In this example, I share a particular kind of Data Studio application that I call
an "Authority Builder." Here is the general idea:

- Bring a lot information about a niche subject together in one place.
- Add value by curating, organizing, rating, and reviewing information.
- Build searchable collections of new and historical information.
- Promote this app as a resource for the community of interest.

Sharing this kind of resource provides you with an opportunity to become
known in your field and builds your authority. This is the goal of many websites,
but I think Data Studio is particularly suited for this role.

Google Data Studio Resources is my "Authority Builder." I just call it GDSR
most of the time. It started life as a way to keep track of blog posts about Data
Studio. As my interest grew in the application, I found myself trying to keep
track of useful blog posts, bookmarking and sending myself links. Naturally, I
lost track of them and could never find what I wanted.

I started to put these references into a Google Sheet and added a subject
column so that I could remember more about the particular resource. In a minor
"eureka" moment, I realized that the place to organize these resources was in
an actual Data Studio application.

Although this approach can work in any interest area, it was particularly
suited here. First, there is some novelty value in making a resource guide about
a tool using the tool itself. Second, it provides a playground where I can push
some boundaries of the tool and use it as an example of new concepts.

Created Data

What started out as a list of a few articles on a topic evolved over time. Shortly
after building an initial version of the GDSR, I built a Google Form through

which I could easily capture the vital information about a resource. I was able to add value by providing a brief review, the audience level, how long the resource took to review, the general area and main focus of the article, and more. As you saw earlier in this chapter, this is a great way of keeping the data clean and consistent.

Although there is an element of curation here, the main focus is on creating a rich data set for each resource in the collection. As I ran across new articles, videos, templates, and such, I would enter them into my data set through my Google Form.

Over time, the resources collection has grown into hundreds of resources. Figure 8.75 shows the home page in its current form. If you visit it at any time, it may have a slightly different form as it undergoes frequent changes. You'll find a link to the GDSR application in the online notes for this chapter at www.wiley.com/go/handsondatastudio.

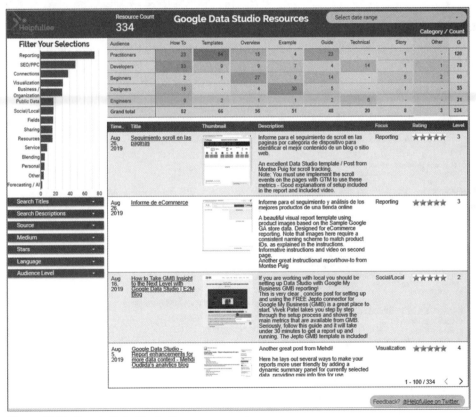

Figure 8.75: Google Data Studio Resources—main page

> **NOTE** Not everything about Data Studio is in this book! There are some features on my GDSR page that are not described in this book. It's not that these features are a secret; they just do not apply to the needs of the intended readers of this book, and I had to draw the line somewhere!
>
> Currently, there are changes to Data Studio every week, so it was important for me to cover the fundamentals that are unlikely to change over time. Interested in the latest and greatest? Check out the GDSR app!

One of the most recent changes to the GDSR corresponds directly to this chapter. Similar to our example, I decided to embed my form directly into my report. In this case, it has its own page. Although I still review all submissions, it saves time when people enter their own resources. This page is shown in Figure 8.76.

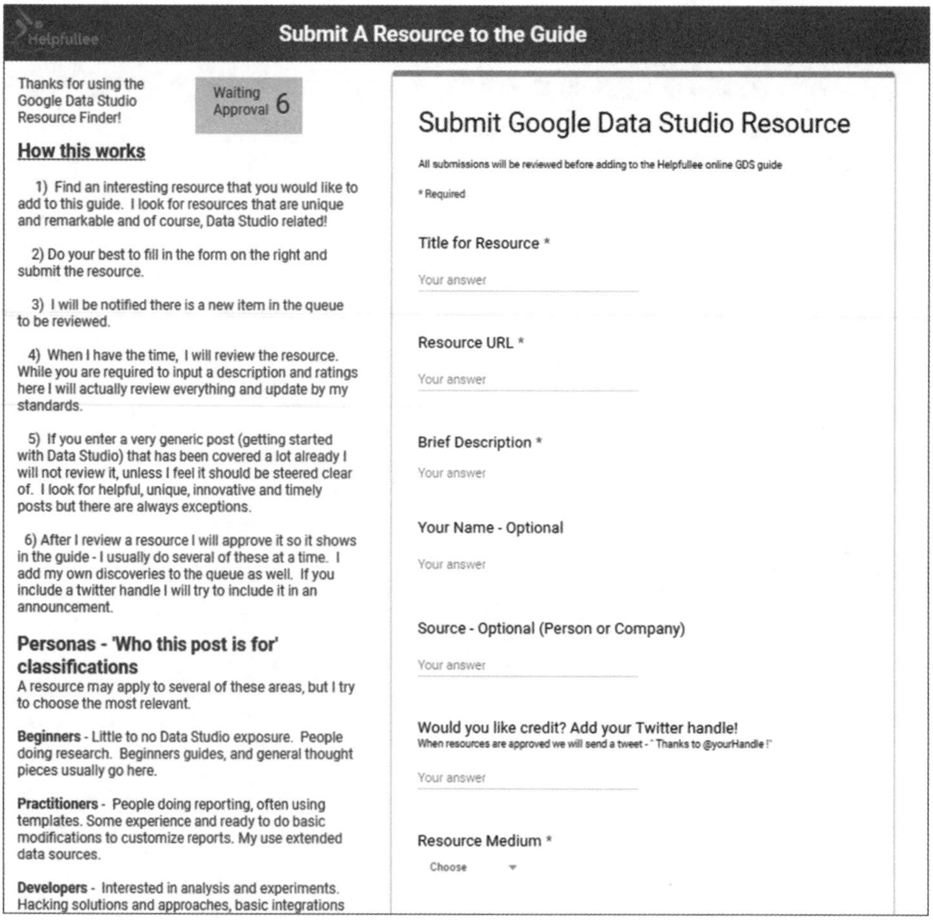

Figure 8.76: The GDSR Submit A Resource To The Guide form page

Curated Data

I discovered early on that my best source for finding new resources for my collection was Twitter. People like to announce new offerings there, but I knew that I was missing possible resources because the announcements did not show up in my feed. I started monitoring Twitter for Data Studio mentions.

Eventually, I had the idea that I could use IFTTT to capture these tweets automatically, just as we did earlier in this chapter. It was a natural step to add the tweet report to the GDSR. The current version of that page is shown in Figure 8.77.

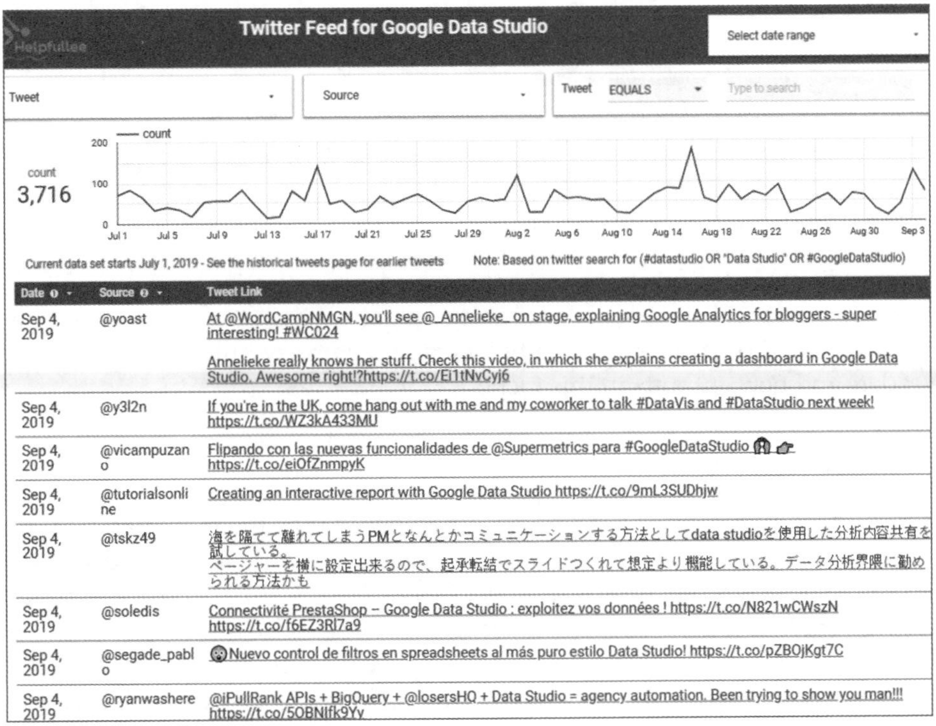

Figure 8.77: The GDSR Twitter Feed page

I found that I had a very large collection of tweets on the subject and that this affected the performance of my display. I decided to create a separate page for historical tweets. Periodically, I move some of the tweets from the Twitter feed over to another Sheet. At this time, there are over 40,000 tweets that can be searched on the subject, as shown in Figure 8.78.

You may think that a collection of tweets is not a valuable resource, but I can assure you that it is! The tweet pages don't pull in as many users as the main pages, but almost daily I personally use them for research. Not only do people tweet about new products, but they also tweet about issues they are having and their solutions.

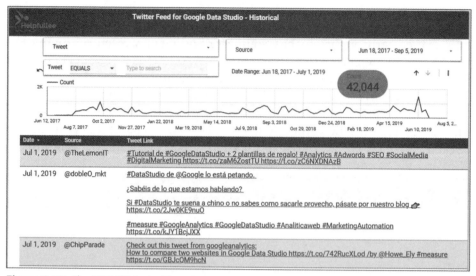

Figure 8.78: The GDSR historical tweets page

In addition, in the future I may analyze this large collection using other tools to categorize the tweets by subject area and gain even more insight into how subjects trend over time. It already lets me know, very quickly, who are the leaders and new entrants in this niche.

Generated Data

I mentioned that the tweet pages are not as popular as the main pages in the previous section. You may be wondering how I know this. One of the lesser known but incredibly useful features of Data Studio is that you can monitor the use of reports with Google Analytics!

To take this a step further, the GDSR has a page that uses the Google Analytics data source to *report on the report itself!* This is where the generated data aspect of the report plays a part. Users rarely get to see the site usage data from real sites. In addition to this report being useful to me personally, it becomes a feature of the GDSR that users can check out. Figure 8.79 shows the Analytics page.

Analytics experts may be a bit disappointed by the amount of data collected from a Data Studio report, because there is no way to measure the actual interactions on a page or modify Data Studio pages to get more data as you might do for a standard web page. Still, as you can see, there is plenty of data available to do basic analysis.

If you don't have a Google Analytics account, you now have a good reason to get one. Like the other Google tools that we've worked with in this book, Google Analytics accounts are free, and you already have everything you need to get started if you have a Gmail account.

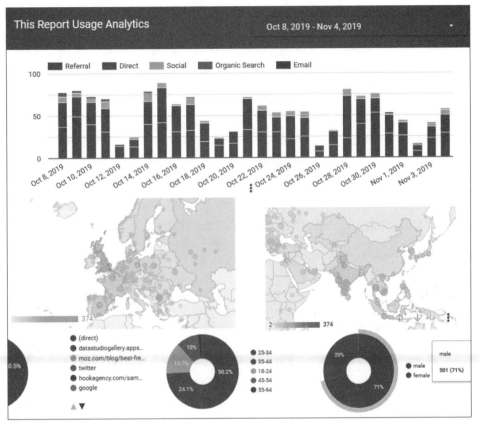

Figure 8.79: The GDSR report Analytics page

I won't go over creating the Google Analytics report here, as we already covered that information in Chapter 5, "Web Data Visualization with Google Analytics." Nevertheless, I will go step by step to show you how to create a new account, find the new tracking ID, and use it to set up tracking on your reports.

NOTE   If you plan to measure more than one report, you have three options to consider. I generally prefer option A for my own use and option C if I am setting things up for someone else.

A. Track all your reports with a single-property tracking ID and split out the data for the separate reports if desired.

B. Create a separate-property tracking ID for each report and bring them together in Data Studio if needed.

C. If you are tracking web property reports, use the same tracking ID for the website and the reports. Again, you'll have to split the data out, but this keeps the information in one place in Analytics.

1. Visit `https://analytics.google.com`. If it is your first time using Analytics, you'll get a signup page like the one shown in Figure 8.80. Click the Sign Up button, and you'll be taken to the Account setup page.

Figure 8.80: Google Analytics Sign Up page

2. Enter the Account name. A single account can be used to track multiple properties. Select the account sharing options for your personal preferences and click Next. You'll now be on the What Do You Want To Measure? page.

3. If you are daring, you can try the New Apps And Web option here, but keep in mind that at this time it is in beta. The standard web option will work just fine. Click the Next button. You'll be taken to the Property Details page.

4. Give your property a descriptive name, and specify the URL, industry category, and your time zone. You can see my setup in Figure 8.81. If you also plan to measure a website, you should use that URL. Click the Create button to continue.

Property details

Website Name

Hands On Data Studio Reports

Website URL

http:// ▾ | datastudio.google.com

Industry Category

Jobs and Education ▾

Reporting Time Zone

United States ▾ | (GMT-04:00) New York Time ▾

Figure 8.81: Google Analytics Property Details

5. Accept the terms of service agreement. You'll have to put in some information about your location (required for data protection regulations), click any applicable check boxes, and click the I Accept button to continue. The Terms Of Service agreement acceptance is only required when you add your first property to Google Analytics.

6. After agreeing to the terms of service, you'll be taken to the Tracking Code page for the property, as shown in Figure 8.82. You need the tracking ID code from this page to configure the Analytics setup in Data Studio, so copy the tracking ID from this page. In the example, it is UA-147208238-1.

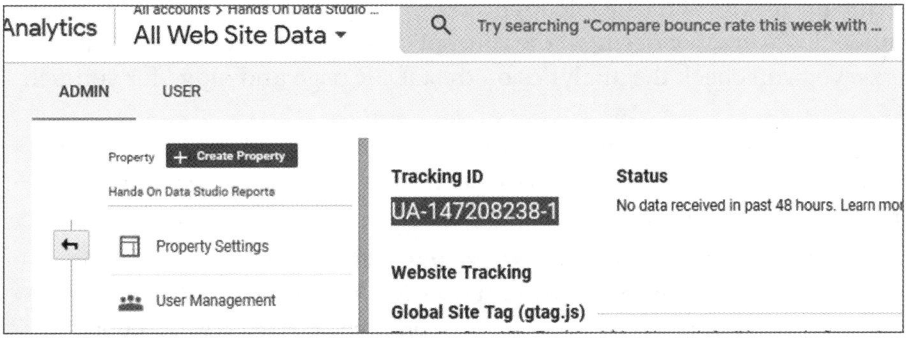

Figure 8.82: Copying the tracking ID code for Data Studio setup

7. Locate the Data Studio report on the Data Studio home screen, open it, and click the Edit button to enter edit mode.

8. Choose File ⇨ Report Settings to open the Report Settings panel on the right side of the screen. Find the Google Analytics Tracking ID field, and paste the tracking ID into this field, as shown in Figure 8.83.

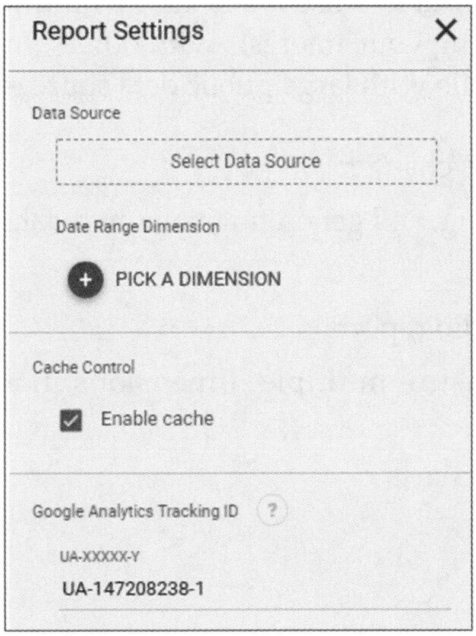

Figure 8.83: Pasting the tracking ID into Report Settings

That completes the setup, and your report will now send data to your Google Analytics account. You are now able to see report usage in Google Analytics created for your reports! If you choose to, you can even show the usage data for the report in the report itself, as I have done with the GDSR application.

TIP   If you create infographics with Data Studio, add the tracking code and share them. You can track their usage even if they are embedded in web pages on sites that you don't control! We'll cover how to embed a report into a web page as part of Chapter 9.

With our review of the GDSR application, our examples are complete for this chapter. If you are wondering if the concept of the "Authority Builder" actually works, you can check the analytics on the GDSR page and judge for yourself.

NOTE   Data Studio reports get almost no organic search traffic due to the way that Google indexes these reports. This means that almost all of the users come from referrals from other sites, social media, and repeat visits.

The volume of visits is not a lot compared to large sites, but the audience is exactly who I want to reach. Another measure of its success is the fact that I was asked if I would be interested in writing a book on the subject, and that is just what you are reading now!

Could this help you gain authority in a niche for which you have a passion? The only way to know is to try it for yourself!

Summary

Data Studio is very popular for business uses, but it is also is a flexible platform for organizing your personal data and sharing your interests with others. In Chapter 9, we'll be looking at using Data Studio with large public data sources and sharing information with communities.

These are the topics that we covered in this chapter:

- The difference between creating, curating, and generating your own data
- Using Google Forms for data capture
- Embedding Google Forms in Data Studio reports
- Using the drill-down feature to measure multiple dimensions in a single chart
- Creating and using scatter and bubble charts
- Using different types of trendlines

- Setting up an IFTTT account to assist in retrieving data
- Using IFTTT to retrieve data from social media sites like Twitter and creating a Twitter search resource
- Using IFTTT to retrieve data from your personal online services, specifically Amazon Music
- Creating reports that explore music data
- Enhancing your reports by using links to external services like YouTube.
- Setting up and using open-source community connectors using Google Fit as an example
- Working through a health and fitness tracking dashboard example using Google Fit
- Creating an "Authority Builder" to gather and share information about a niche
- Setting up a Google Analytics account and adding tracking to Data Studio reports

Going Public

In this chapter, you'll learn about public data sources that are available for you to access and use for your own reporting. We'll explore resources for public data, how to access those resources, and ways to use Data Studio to visualize that data.

Shared Data Sets

We are moving from creating information and insights for our own personal use to creating insights that we can share with a larger community. Whether that community is at a local, regional, national, or global level, there are opportunities to access data, organize it, and turn it into information for others to learn from and use.

The generation of data continues to increase, and so do public sources of data. "Open Data" initiatives have been developing over the last few years in a quest to make governments more transparent.

In addition to governments, science and health-based organizations have been putting more data in reach of those with Internet access. This sharing initiative has also spread to private businesses and organizations who can see the value of sharing some of their own research data sets.

Data set sharing is important for reproducing and checking studies. Also, the growing field of *data journalism* requires access to data sources to validate their work.

Chances are, if you are interested in a subject, particularly if it has an economic or public policy aspect, someone has compiled data and published it somewhere. Along with the individual publishers, such as government agencies and scientific groups, specialty businesses exist that provide data set services for other businesses.

As with many other Internet endeavors, the problem today is not a lack of information but the ability to find the right data for your purposes. Google has been working on making it easier for users to find data sets. In addition to falling to the special talents of Google to organize information through its search prowess, easy access to high-quality data sets tends to benefit Google's cloud services business as well.

It often requires large volumes of data and high-quality data sets to train neural networks and other artificial intelligence–related services. Google sells machine learning, pattern recognition training, and large-scale analytics data storage services. Thus, it's no coincidence that Google has been working on search services to assist users in finding data sets.

Searching for Data Sets

In September 2018, Google launched its Dataset Search service (`https://toolbox.google.com/datasetsearch`). This service is designed to surface information about data sets that are scattered across the Internet. To support this service, Google has been promoting the use of a special markup format that data publishers can use to make their contributions easier for Google to index, which makes it simpler for searchers to find what they are seeking.

The references returned by this specialty search engine usually come from one of these sources: government, research institutes and universities, data set aggregators, private businesses, and premium data services. In the examples that follow, we will omit coverage of the premium data services and focus on the free sources of data.

Although Dataset Search is still in beta as of this writing, it is a good place to start our quest to find new data sets. You'll see a simple search page with some suggested searches listed below it. If you start to type in a query—for example, **first names**—Google will start suggesting resources that you can search for directly, as shown in Figure 9.1.

Dataset Search returns results in a different way than a standard search. Results are shown on a left-side scrolling panel and details about the data set are shown on the main panel. By default, the first result is selected. This allows quick investigation of the data set description. That's a good thing, because there are more than 100 datasets related to first names alone!

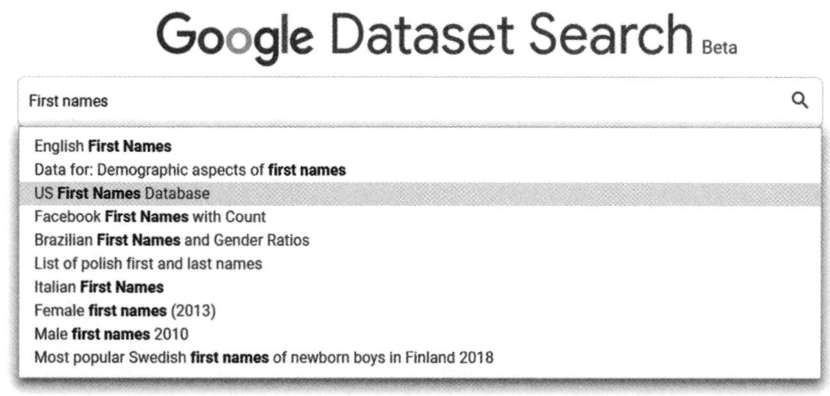

Figure 9.1: Searching for data sets related to first names

By scrolling down the list on the left side, you can get a feel for the type of data that may be in the set. Clicking a result will bring up the details in the main panel, as shown in Figure 9.2, featuring a result from Kaggle.

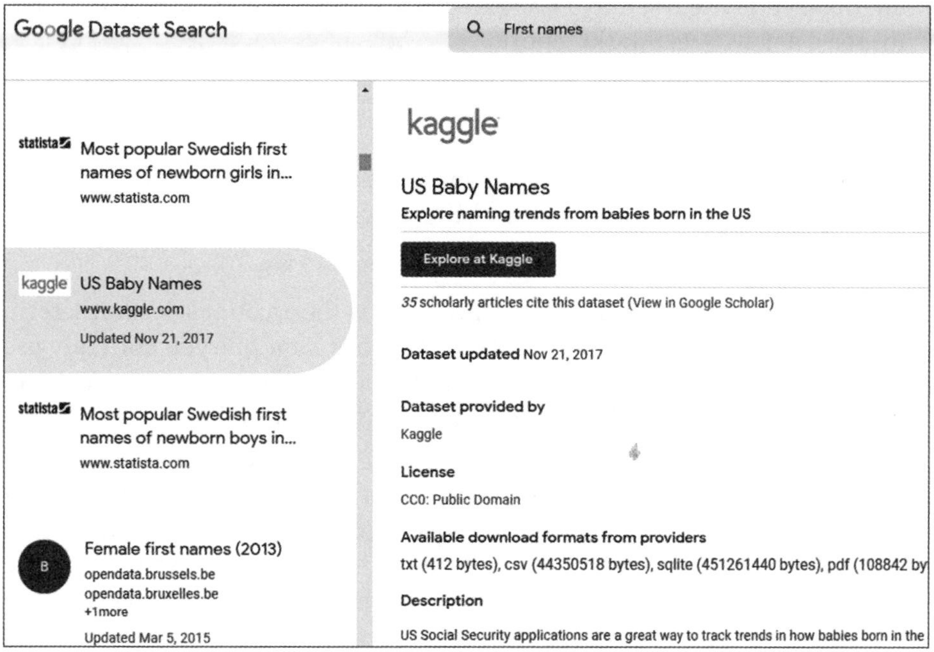

Figure 9.2: Exploring the search results

Kaggle (www.kaggle.com) falls into the category of a data set aggregator because its users collect and store data sets from many different sources on Kaggle's platform. Google Dataset Search is getting better over time, but it is still a good idea to become familiar with a couple of large aggregators since they have so many data sets and unique features.

Getting Data from Kaggle

So, what is Kaggle anyhow? Kaggle promotes itself as "Your Home for Data Science." The website, owned by Google since 2017, provides a platform used by more than a million users to create projects that are mostly related to machine learning. In addition to data set and coding facilities, they run popular machine learning contests, provide short courses on artificial intelligence, and support a job board for data science jobs.

Since this service is geared to the needs of data scientists, it may be intimidating for the typical data citizen at first glance. Although Kaggle offers many advanced services, it can still be used for basic data set storage and sharing without any special knowledge.

In this section, we'll set up a Kaggle account, find a shared data set, and use it to create a new Data Studio report.

Using a Kaggle Account

Since Kaggle is owned by Google, it should come as no surprise that you can set up an account using your standard Google credentials.

1. Begin by going to the Kaggle home page at www.kaggle.com.

2. Click the Register With Google link to open the account selection screen. Select a Google account (I suggest you use the same one you normally use to do Data Studio work if you have multiple accounts). After you select an account, you will see the Create Kaggle Account page, shown in Figure 9.3.

3. On the next screen, read the Terms Of Use And Privacy statement. After accepting, click the Create Account button to continue. You will be sent to your new Kaggle home page. This page has various announcements and messages from other users, as shown in Figure 9.4. We will use the tabs at the top of the page to go to Datasets.

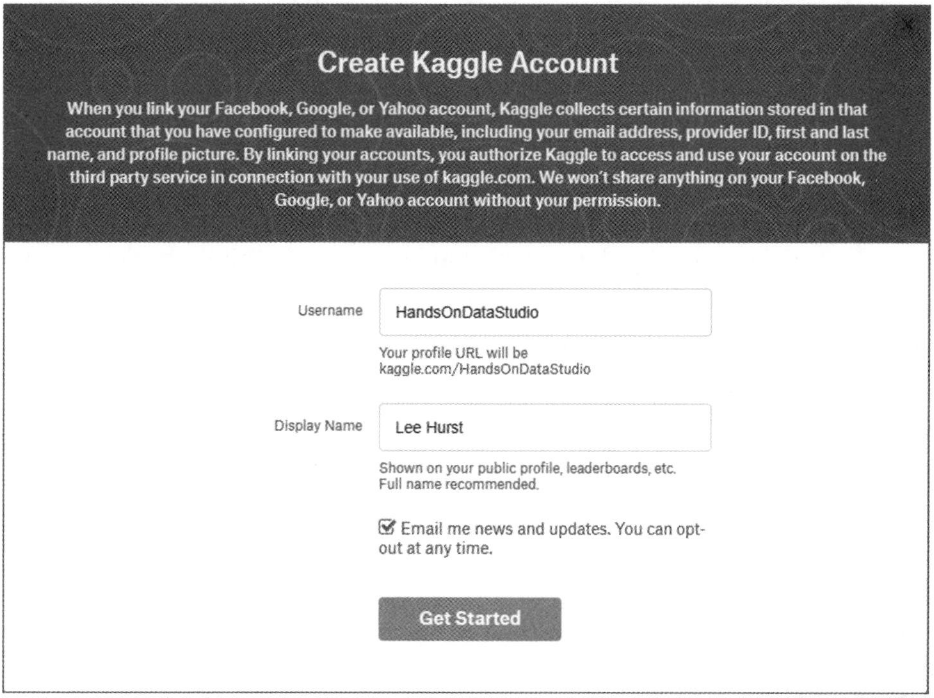

Create Kaggle Account
When you link your Facebook, Google, or Yahoo account, Kaggle collects certain information stored in that account that you have configured to make available, including your email address, provider ID, first and last name, and profile picture. By linking your accounts, you authorize Kaggle to access and use your account on the third party service in connection with your use of kaggle.com. We won't share anything on your Facebook, Google, or Yahoo account without your permission.
Username
HandsOnDataStudio
Your profile URL will be kaggle.com/HandsOnDataStudio
Display Name
Lee Hurst
Shown on your public profile, leaderboards, etc. Full name recommended.
Email me news and updates. You can opt-out at any time.
Get Started

Figure 9.3: Create Kaggle Account page

kaggle
Search
Competitions
Datasets
Notebooks
Discussion
Courses
Newsfeed
Welcome Lee Hurst
DrHB · Follow
created this topic 3 days ago
Yue Zhang replied to this
8th Place Solution
in the APTOS 2019 Blindness Detection forum
First of all I want to thank everyone who participated, shared kernels and was part of activate discussion.
PROBLEM:

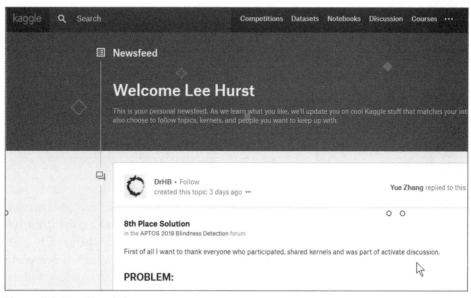

Figure 9.4: Your Kaggle home page

4. Click the Datasets tab to open the Datasets page, where you can search for various data sets. Before you search, the screen shows the most-used current datasets in the results. For our example, we will search for **UFO sightings** or simply **UFO**. The search results show the title and owner of the data set as well as some information about how long the data set has been available and the size and quality of the resource. An indicator for the popularity of the resource is shown on the right side of the screen. Generally, more-popular resources are more trusted and easier to use. The results of such a search are shown in Figure 9.5.

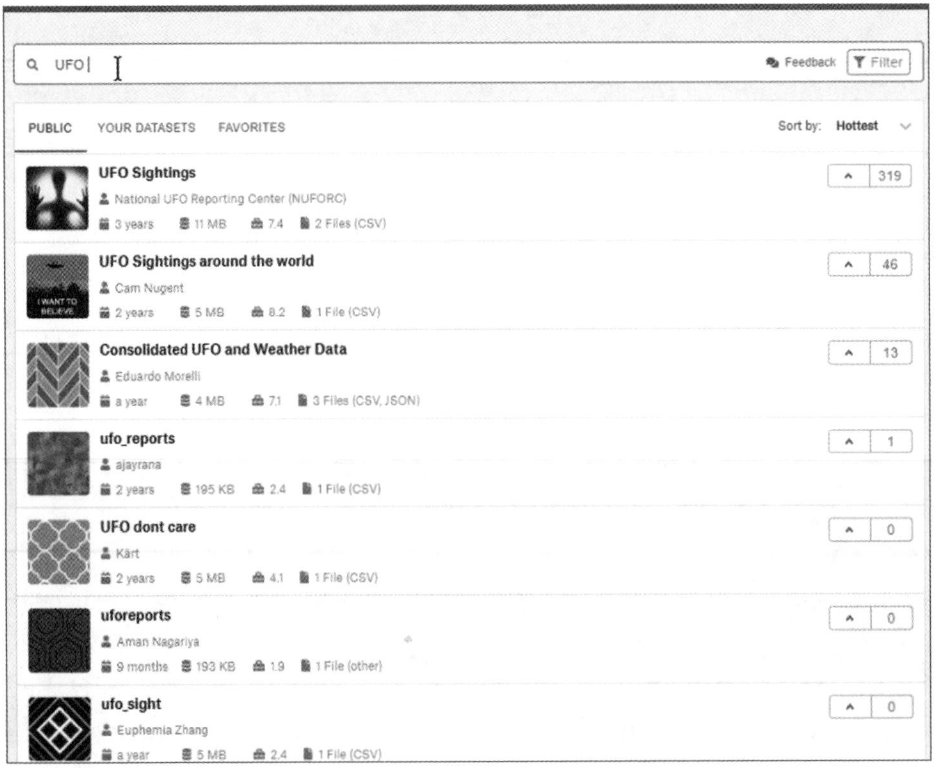

Q UFO|		Feedback Filter

PUBLIC YOUR DATASETS FAVORITES		Sort by: Hottest ⌄
UFO Sightings 👤 National UFO Reporting Center (NUFORC) 📅 3 years 💾 11 MB ⚖ 7.4 📄 2 Files (CSV)		⌃ 319
UFO Sightings around the world 👤 Cam Nugent 📅 2 years 💾 5 MB ⚖ 8.2 📄 1 File (CSV)		⌃ 46
Consolidated UFO and Weather Data 👤 Eduardo Morelli 📅 a year 💾 4 MB ⚖ 7.1 📄 3 Files (CSV, JSON)		⌃ 13
ufo_reports 👤 ajayrana 📅 2 years 💾 195 KB ⚖ 2.4 📄 1 File (CSV)		⌃ 1
UFO dont care 👤 Kärt 📅 2 years 💾 5 MB ⚖ 4.1 📄 1 File (CSV)		⌃ 0
uforeports 👤 Aman Nagariya 📅 9 months 💾 193 KB ⚖ 1.9 📄 1 File (other)		⌃ 0
ufo_sight 👤 Euphemia Zhang 📅 a year 💾 5 MB ⚖ 2.4 📄 1 File (CSV)		⌃ 0

Figure 9.5: Data set search results for UFO

5. Review the data set. Clicking the first search result, titled UFO Sightings, takes us to the Data page for that project. Here we find an informative writeup about the data set and where the data comes from originally, also known as its *provenance*. In this case, there are two data files: a complete file containing all of the collected data and a scrubbed version, where records that were missing data have been removed. For this example, we are interested in the scrubbed version listed in the Data Sources column as `scrubbed.csv`. Clicking that file shows detail such as the actual columns and their data types, as well as a preview of the file. Figure 9.6 shows this section.

| Data | Kernels (160) | Discussion (6) | Activity | Metadata | | Download (11 MB) | New Notebook | ⋮ |

Data (11 MB)   ✖

Data Sources

▦ co [scrubbed.csv]   11 columns

▦ scrubbed.csv   80.3k x 11

About this file

UFO sightings without missing / incomplete reports

Columns

📅 datetime

A city

A state

A country

A shape

duration (seconds)

A duration (hours/min)

A comments

📅 date posted

▦ scrubbed.csv (5.07 MB)   ○ ○   11 of 11 columns ▾   Views ⟋ ▦ ▯ ↧ ⦉ ✖

	📅 datetime	▼	A city	▼	A state	▼	A country	▼	A shape	▼	# durat
	10Nov06 8May14		19900 unique values		ca 12% / wa 5% / Other (65) 83%		us 81% / ca 4% / Other (3) 15%		light 21% / triangle 10% / Other (27) 70%		0
1	10/10/1949 20:30		san marcos		tx		us		cylinder		
2	10/10/1949 21:00		lackland afb		tx				light		

Figure 9.6: Detail for the scrubbed data set

6. You have several options for handling the `scrubbed.csv` file. The options are located on the right side of the detail screen, just below the column descriptions. In previous examples, we downloaded CSV files, loaded them onto Google Drive, and converted them to Google Sheets documents so that we could employ a Sheets connector in order to use the data set. While we could download a connector, Kaggle offers us a shortcut of sorts. It has incorporated Data Studio connections into Kaggle so that you can connect to a CSV file directly. This can save some time, but the first time you use this option, you will have to set up the connector. Start that process by clicking the View In Data Studio icon, as shown in Figure 9.7.

Figure 9.7: Clicking the View In Data Studio icon to connect

7. If it is your first time using the Kaggle connector, you will have to go through an authentication process. This is a one-time setup—it does not need to be repeated each time you create a connector for a Kaggle data set. After clicking the Data Studio icon, you will see the Open In Data Studio pop-up to get you started. You will need to get a Kaggle API token from your account. Right-click the Account link in this pop-up to open your account page in a new tab. The pop-up is shown in Figure 9.8.

Figure 9.8: Opening your account information from the confirmation pop-up

Switch to the browser tab for your Account page. On your account screen, scroll down to the API section. You will see a Create New API Token button, as shown in Figure 9.9.

Figure 9.9: Creating a new API token from the Kaggle account page

Click the button, and Kaggle will generate and download a file to your computer. This file is named `kaggle.json`, and it contains your username and your API key. Open the `kaggle.json` file with a text editor, and copy the key code.

8. Now that you have your API key, you can return to the Open In Data Studio pop-up and click the Confirm button. This will take you to the familiar Data Source connector setup screen. Continue the authorization process by clicking the Authorize button. A Google Account selector will appear, as shown in Figure 9.10. Select an account and click the Allow button that shows in the connection pop-up.

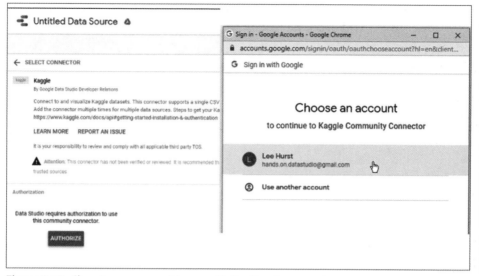

Figure 9.10: Choosing an account to use with the Kaggle connector

9. After the pop-ups have been cleared, a new form for your Kaggle credentials appears on the connector page. Enter your Kaggle username, copy and paste the key code that you copied earlier into the Token field, and click the Submit button, as shown in Figure 9.11, to continue.

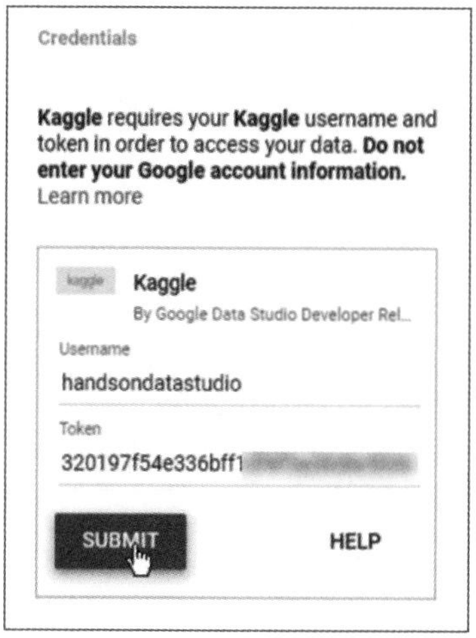

Figure 9.11: Submitting your Kaggle credentials to connect

10. Data Studio will fill in the required fields—Owner Slug, Dataset Slug, and Filename—for this connection. If these fields are not filled in for some reason, use the instructions on the page to find the field information. Change the name for this connector to **UFO Sightings - Kaggle CSV -1**,

as shown in Figure 9.12. Click the Connect button in the upper-right corner to continue. This will take you to the Field Setup page.

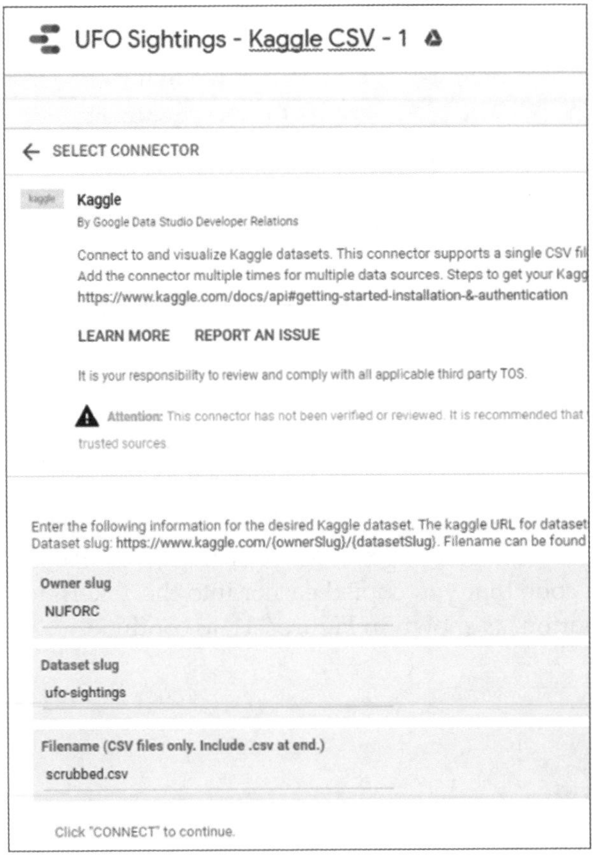

Figure 9.12: Complete connector setup

11. Some of the field types will need to be updated for use in our reports. Set the City field to Geo ⇨ City, the State field to Geo ⇨ Region, and the Country field to Geo ⇨ Country. Since we will not be needing it for our report, change the Date Posted field to Text.

12. Data Studio can plot points on a map from latitude and longitude coordinates, but it needs these values in a single field separated by a comma. To do this, click the Add A Field button in the upper-right corner of the screen. Change the name of this field to **Latitude-Longitude**. Enter the following code for the formula and click Save.

```
CONCAT(latitude, CONCAT(",", longitude))
```

Return to the fields screen. Change the type of the new Latitude-Longitude field to Geo ⇨ Latitude,Longitude.

13. Click the three vertical dots next to Datetime and select Duplicate. This will create a new field called Copy Of Datetime. Click this field to edit the name, and type **Month**. Click the Type drop-down for the field and select Date & Time ⇨ Month (MM).

The fields screen should now look like the one shown in Figure 9.13. This completes the connector and field setup. Click the Create Report button at the top right of the page to continue.

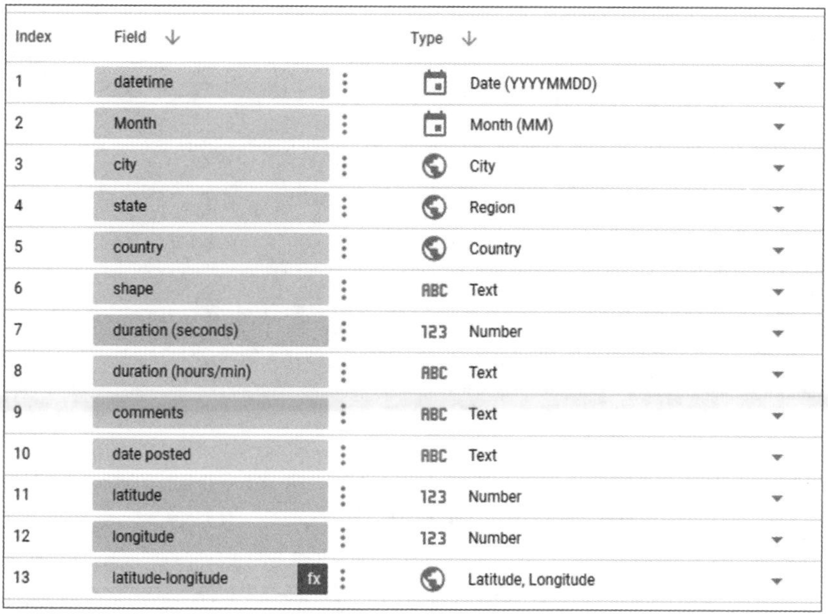

Index	Field ↓		Type ↓	
1	datetime	⋮	📅 Date (YYYYMMDD)	▾
2	Month	⋮	📅 Month (MM)	▾
3	city	⋮	🌐 City	▾
4	state	⋮	🌐 Region	▾
5	country	⋮	🌐 Country	▾
6	shape	⋮	RBC Text	▾
7	duration (seconds)	⋮	123 Number	▾
8	duration (hours/min)	⋮	RBC Text	▾
9	comments	⋮	RBC Text	▾
10	date posted	⋮	RBC Text	▾
11	latitude	⋮	123 Number	▾
12	longitude	⋮	123 Number	▾
13	latitude-longitude *fx*	⋮	🌐 Latitude, Longitude	▾

Figure 9.13: Completed fields setup

TIP In previous chapters, we created data sources and new fields before creating the report. In actual use, you probably won't know all of new fields that you will need ahead of time for report creation. If you are the owner of the data source, or you have edit rights, you can always add more fields by editing the data source while you are working on the report.

Now that you have a Kaggle connector configured, you can use it to build your reports. This UFO data set provides many options to allow you to experiment with different visualizations and layout interaction options. In this section, I will show you a workbench-type application that I designed to explore UFO sightings in the United States. This also gives us an opportunity to use a new chart type. Figure 9.14 shows the new workbench.

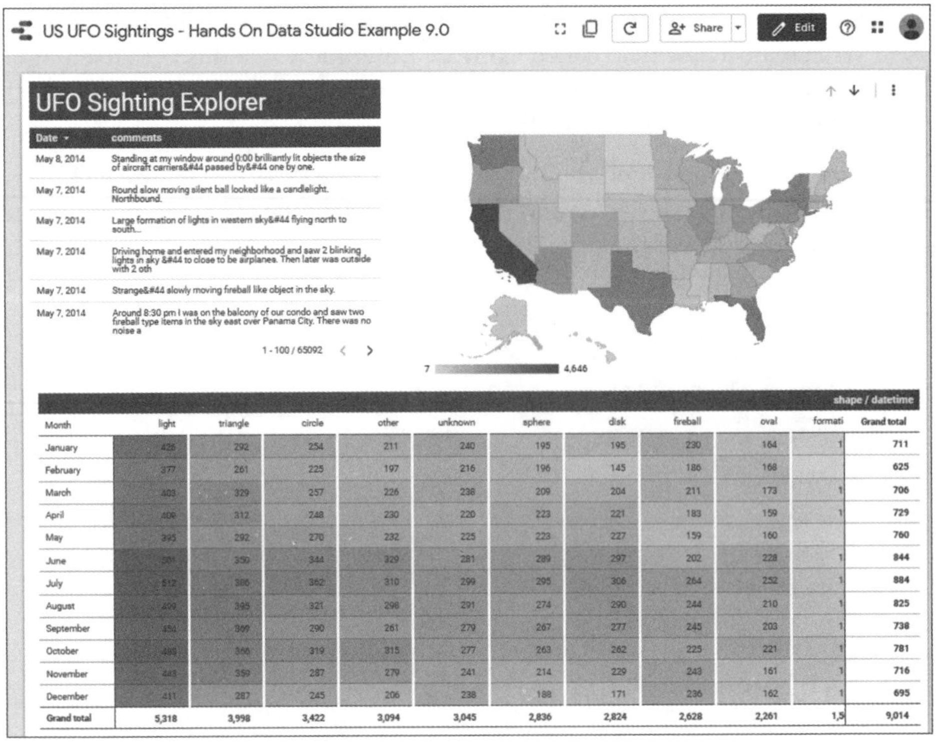

Figure 9.14: U.S. UFO Sightings Workbench

Building the UFO Sightings Workbench

Our current example employs many of the features that you have seen in our other reports. You've seen detail tables and maps with drill-down features before. In this workbench, we included a new chart type to help us navigate and zero in on particular combinations of dimensions. The new chart type is called a *pivot table*. Pivot tables are generally used to summarize large amounts of information, and in Data Studio, they can also be used as a navigation and filtering device.

We saw a pivot table put to use in Chapter 8, "Getting Personal," when we looked at the Data Studio Resources workbench. The pivot table was used to help the user narrow down the selection of resources by selecting a cell for combinations of audience and resource types. Figure 9.15 shows the table being used to filter resources to the seven items that match Developer and Example.

This method works best when there are a relatively small number of values for each dimension used in the row and column. If there are several columns or rows, the chart automatically adds slider controls to the chart to let the user explore areas that are not initially shown.

Audience	How To	Templates	Overview	Example	Guide	Technical	Story	Other
Practitioners	23	54	15	4	23	-	1	-
Developers	33	9	9	7	4	14	1	1
Beginners	2	1	27	7	14	-	5	2
Designers	15	-	4	30	5	-	1	-
Engineers	9	2	1	1	2	6	-	-
Grand total	82	66	56	51	48	20	8	3

Figure 9.15: Pivot table used to filter selections

We will briefly cover the setup for the other charts shown in the example report and cover the setup of the pivot table in more detail. Let's start the building process where we left off in the previous section. We created a blank report for editing at the end of the Kaggle data source setup process, and we are in Edit mode.

1. To make things a bit easier, we will set up filters at the beginning of the process. Select File ⇨ Report Settings to open the Report Settings panel. Set Data Source to our new Kaggle UFO data source. In the Filter section, click the Add A Filter button to open the Edit Filter settings panel. For the filter name, type **USA ONLY** and change the settings to Include Country Equal to (=) us, as shown in Figure 9.16. Click the Save button and close the Edit Filter panel.

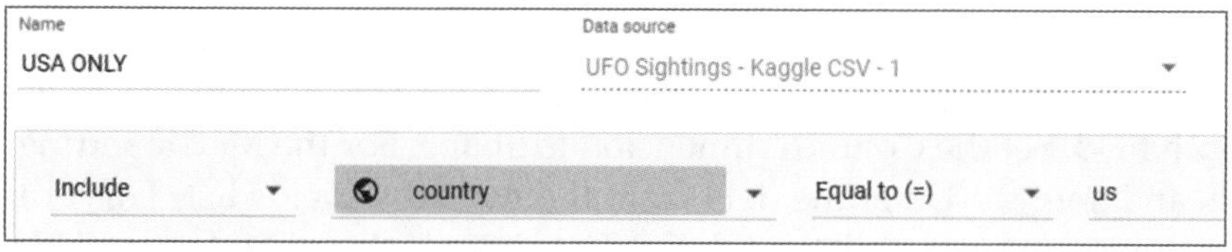

Name	Data source
USA ONLY	UFO Sightings - Kaggle CSV - 1 ▾

Include ▾	◉ country ▾	Equal to (=) ▾	us

Figure 9.16: USA ONLY report filter settings

2. Select the Untitled Report field at the top left and change the name to **US UFO Sightings - Hands On Data Studio Example 9.0**. Select the text tool from the toolbar, and click and drag the text box into place. Enter the text, and in the properties, change the text to white and the size to 32px. Set the background to blue.

3. Select a standard table from the Add A Chart drop-down, and click and drag the table into place below the header. On the Data tab for the table, set the first dimension to Datetime and change the field name to **Date**. Add the Comments field to the dimensions. Remove any Metric fields and set Sort to the Datetime field Descending. On the Style tab, under the Table Body settings, select Wrap Text and deselect the Row Numbers check boxes. Resize the columns on the table.

4. From the Add A Chart drop-down, select the Geo map and click and drag the map into position. On the Data tab for the map, set the drill-down switch to On, which will allow you to add more dimensions. Set the dimensions fields to State, City, and Latitude-Longitude. Set the default drill-down level to State. Change the Metric field by dragging the Datetime from the list of available fields. This will automatically change the aggregation of the metric to CTD, which stands for count distinct. The Zoom area should already be set to United States. Scroll to the bottom of the Data tab and check the Interactions Apply Filter box. Switch to the Style tab and set the Chart Header drop-down to Always Show. Resize the map chart if needed.

Setting Up the Pivot Table Chart

Now we will focus on the pivot table and provide more detail on how it is set up. Pivot tables have many possible configuration options, and we are looking at only one specific setup here. Google provides more documentation for pivot table options on its site at https://support.google.com/datastudio/answer/7516660?hl=en. This link and others are available in the chapter notes of the online book resources at www.wiley.com/go/handsondatastudio.

1. Choose the pivot table from the Add A Chart drop-down and click and drag the box to place it at the bottom of the page.

2. The Data tab settings for the pivot table are longer than most charts, so we'll break them up into three sections. First, set Row Dimension to the Month field. Set the Column dimension to Shape. For the Metric setting, click and drag the Datetime field from the Available Fields list. This will set the metric to count distinct dates. The setup is shown in Figure 9.17.

3. In the Totals section, select Show Grand Total for both Rows and Columns. In the Sorting section, set Row #1 drop-downs to Month and Ascending, and leave Number Of Rows set to Auto. Set the Column #1 drop-downs to Datetime and Descending, and leave Number Of Columns set to Auto. The settings for this section are shown in Figure 9.18.

4. As is often the case, you may find a row of null values in your table that are adding no value to the user. To fix this, let's add a new filter to this table to remove the null values for month. Under Pivot Table Filter, click the Add A Filter button. On the Filter picker screen, click Create A Filter to open the Edit Filter screen. Here, for Name, type **Remove Null Month**. Add the settings Exclude Month Is Null by using the drop-down fields, as shown in Figure 9.19. Click Save and return to the Data tab. Select the Apply Filters check box in the Interactions section.

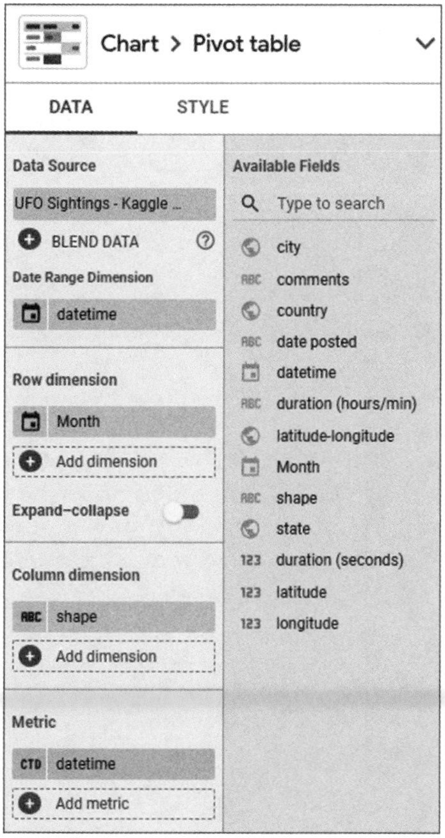

Figure 9.17: Pivot table dimensions and metrics

5. Switch to the Style tab. Locate the Metric #1 section, and from the drop-down, choose Heatmap. Use the paint bucket drop-down to change the Heatmap color to a light red. Scroll down to the Chart Header section and from the drop-down, choose Always Show.

Using the UFO Workbench

With the pivot table setup done, the example is ready to go! A sample case of what you might do with this workbench is finding the most common month and type of UFO sightings in a particular city and then reading the details for those settings. Here is a step-by-step procedure for how that would play out for my home city of Rochester, New York. Make sure that you switch to View mode first!

1. Select New York State on the U.S. map. This will filter the report for New York only.

2. Click the down arrow to drill down from state to city level. This will redraw the map to a view of New York State and show the cities as dots.

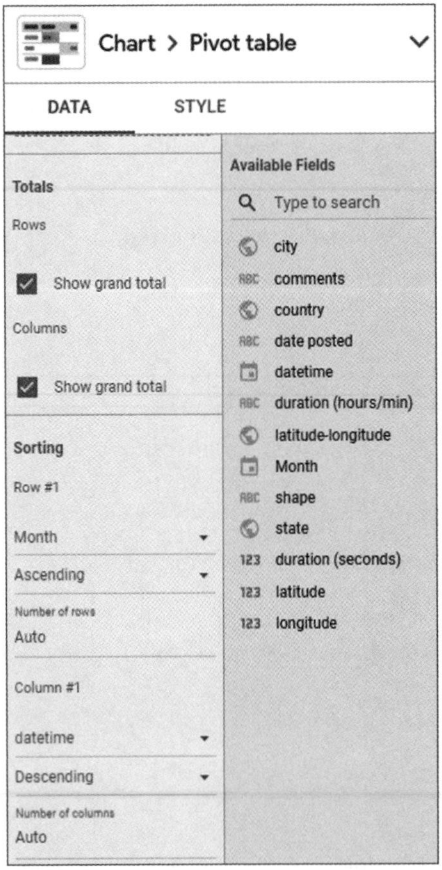

Figure 9.18: Pivot table totals and sorting settings

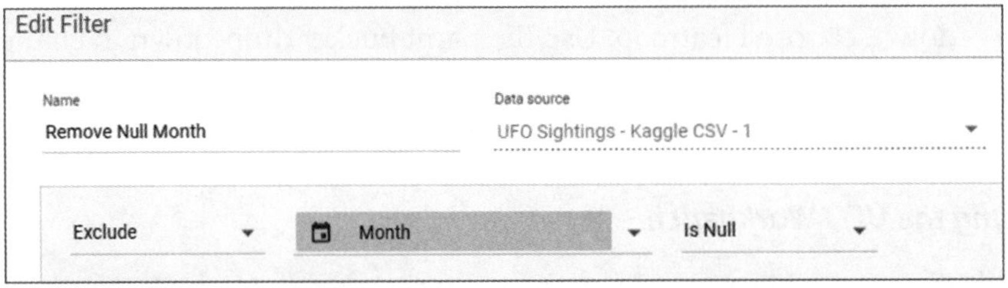

Figure 9.19: Remove Null Month filter

3. Find the dot for Rochester and click it. Rochester is located in the middle of the southern side of Lake Ontario, which separates New York from Canada. Hovering your mouse over the dots shows the city name and number of occurrences. Clicking the dot highlights it and dims the other locations as it filters the other charts. Doing this for Rochester, you see there are currently 71 comments in the detail table.

4. Use the pivot table to find the most common combination of month and UFO type. The heatmap settings make this very easy! You can see that light type in February is the most common sighting. Clicking that cell will filter the results further. You can now read the descriptions in the detail table for the five sightings.

We have gone from signing up with Kaggle to using the report based on a data set we found there. We can easily stop here and move on to the next example, but first I'd like to share one of the lesser-known options that can help you increase the responsiveness of reports.

Dealing with Performance Issues in Reports

In this Kaggle example, we relied on its connector to access the underlying data set for UFO sightings. While I was building this example, there were times when the data flow was smooth and fast and other times when the connection felt slow. In fact, sometimes the connector would time out and some charts show error messages, requiring me to reload the page. Slow applications can be disappointing for the audience, and responsiveness is a major factor that influences an audience's opinion of the usability of an application.

This speed issue is usually not apparent when using optimized connectors, like the ones from Google that handle Google Analytics. In other cases, like the third-party connectors for Google My Business and our Kaggle connector, responsiveness issues are likely to show up.

Google, of course, offers its own cloud-based services as a solution to making your reports more responsive. Their BigQuery service is designed for this kind of work, and it is indeed very responsive—even for projects with millions of records.

Although that service is quite appropriate for enterprise-level work and is becoming more accessible for smaller businesses, it may still require service charges that are more than an individual user would like to pay for their own inquiries. Fortunately, Google does offer an option that can speed up reports in many cases. Let me introduce you to the Data Studio Extract Data Connector.

Using the Extract Data Connector to Speed Up Reports

The *Extract Data Connector* is a bit of an oddball in the world of Data Studio connectors. First, if you go directly to the Data Studio Connectors page at `https://datastudio.google.com/data`, it does not show up—even if you search for it, as shown in Figure 9.20.

I believe the reason the Extract Data Connector does not show up here is because it does not connect to any particular service or source of data. Instead, this connector is designed to work with other connectors, regardless of the actual data source.

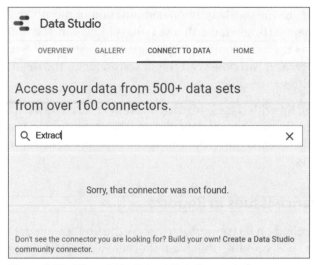

Figure 9.20: Where is the Extract Data Connector?

When you create an Extract Data Connector, you must select an existing data source to use with it. Once it's connected, you pick the fields you want from the original data source, including calculated metrics and dimensions.

After saving, the connector will extract all the data for those fields and store it for high-speed retrieval. If the connection is slow, it will take a bit of time to extract the data during setup.

The Extract Data Connector needs to communicate with the data source only once instead of repeatedly calling on the actual source while interacting with a report. Using the extracted data instead of the source makes retrieving data incredibly fast, and it makes reports extremely responsive.

If this all sounds a little too good to be true, you are very wise! There are some trade-offs that have to be considered when using an Extract Data Connector:

There is a limit of 100 MB of data for an extracted data source.   For most applications, this is not much of an issue. As an example, my collection of 40,000 tweets exports to a CSV file that is under 10 MB. If your data exceeds 100 MB, you need to look for a different solution.

The extracted data is *static*.   This means that the data does not get updated when the original source is updated. Until recently, you had to reconnect the Extract Data Connector to get updated data. Now you can set an update schedule to refresh data automatically. You can only choose to update daily, weekly, or monthly. If you need the data updated more frequently than once a day, you will need a different solution.

You may have to change aggregation methods on some of your fields.   This may actually be an advantage in cases where the original data source sets an aggregation method for a field that makes it hard to work with. The Extract Data Connector may allow you to create some calculated fields that are not possible with a standard connection.

You must have access to the original data source fields to create an Extract Data Connector.   You can only create extract data connections if you are an editor or owner of the original data source.

Creating an Extract Data Connector requires some extra steps when building a report, but it can definitely help provide a much more satisfying experience for your audience. In this last example with the Kaggle data source, we are already dealing with a static data source, and the number of fields that need to be extracted is not very large. This makes it a prime candidate for using the Extract Data Connector.

We'll set up a copy of the report and create an Extract Data Connector so that you can see the setup process. This way, you will be able to compare the performance of a report with and without the Extract Data Connector.

Start by loading the previous example, US UFO Sightings - Hands On Data Studio Example 9.0, in View mode. Remember, if you are using the premade example you will be able to copy the report, but you must have edit access to the actual data source or the report will break.

1. If needed, load your UFO report from the Data Studio home page. Switch to View mode and click the copy icon in the header of the report, as shown in Figure 9.21.

Figure 9.21: Starting the copy process

On the Copy This Report screen, accept the default data source, which should be UFO Sightings - Kaggle CSV - 1. Click the Copy Report button to continue.

2. Make sure that you are in Edit mode, and change the report title. In this case, the new report will be called **US UFO Sightings (Extract) - Hands On Data Studio Example 10.0.**

3. Choose File ⇨ Report Settings. You should see the Data Source field already set at the top of the panel. Click the current data source, as shown in Figure 9.22.

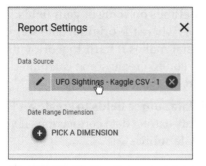

Figure 9.22: Clicking the current data source

4. Click the Create New Data Source button at the bottom of the Select Data Source panel. This will take you to the connector selection screen.

5. The Extract Data Connector will appear on this screen because we are in active edit mode. Locate the connector and select it, as shown in Figure 9.23, to go to the connector setup page.

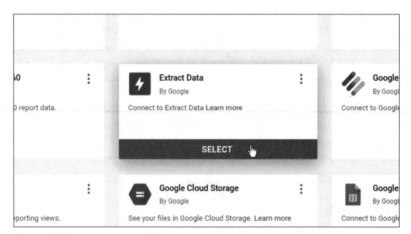

Figure 9.23: Selecting the Extract Data Connector

6. The data source setup screen is a bit different from those that you have seen before. For the Extract Data Connector, you first select a data source—UFO Sightings - Kaggle CSV – 1—will display a pop-up prompting us to add this data source to the report, as shown in Figure 9.24.

7. Rather than going to the report screen, we end up staying on the connector screen. However, there is a new panel with the fields available from the extract source as well as slots for the new data source. You will need to add all the fields that you will be using in the new connector under the Dimensions, Metrics, and Date Range on the left side of the panel. You cannot select premade filters, but you can click the Add A Filter button if you wish to create a new one.

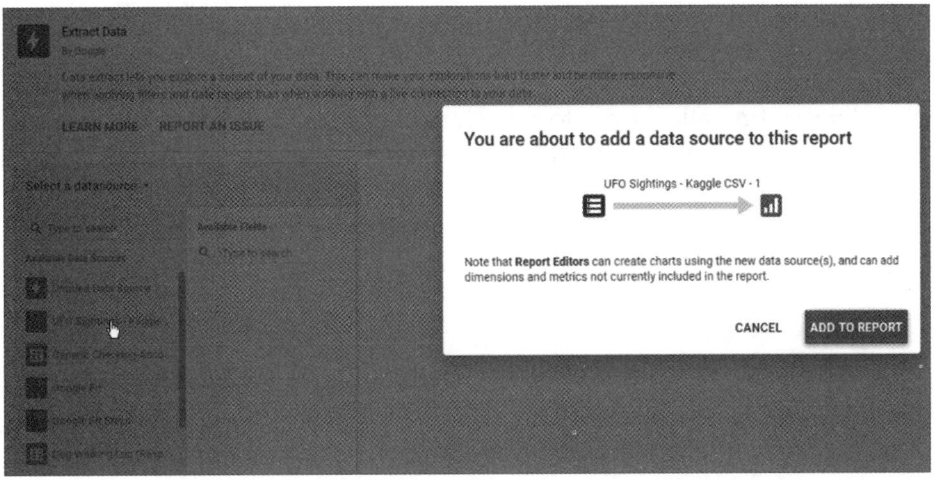

Figure 9.24: Selecting the source for the extract

You will be selecting all the original fields to be extracted. Note that this includes any calculated dimensions or metrics that you have created. This can greatly affect the responsiveness of your report because the values for these fields can be generated as the data is initially being pulled rather than being executed while the user is interacting with the report.

Figure 9.25 shows the field setup in process.

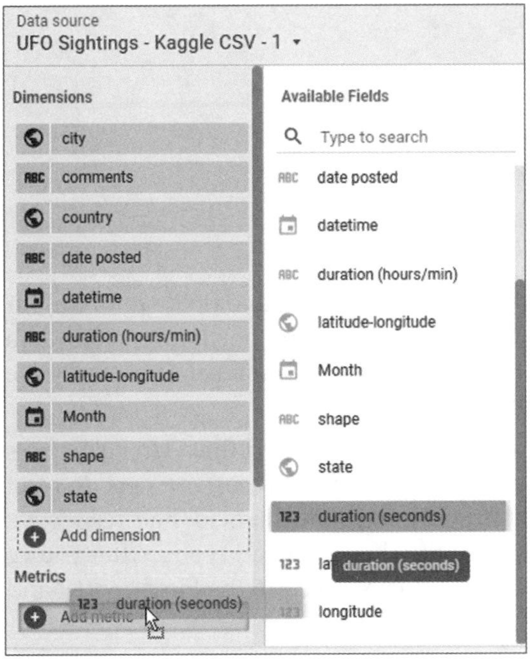

Figure 9.25: Fields set up for the Extract Data Connector

8. As you add fields on the left side, they will start showing up in a separate box on the right side called Included Dimensions And Metrics. When you are finished adding fields, you can change the Auto Update setting here. This setting allows you to refresh your extract from the original source on a daily, weekly, or monthly basis.

   In our case, we don't expect the data source to change, so we do not need to turn this function on. Click the Save And Extract button at the bottom of this panel, as shown in Figure 9.26, to continue.

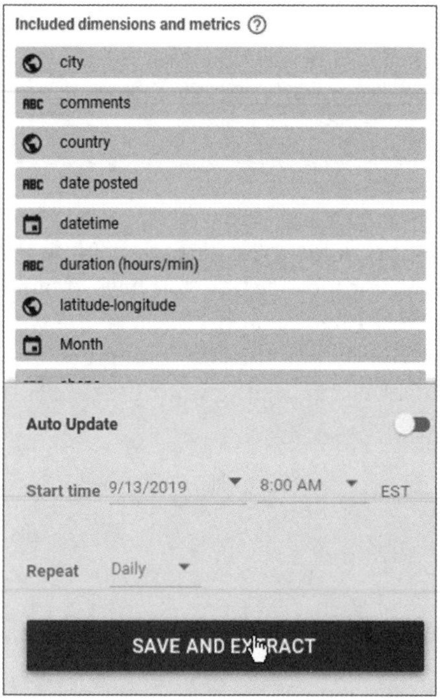

Figure 9.26: Saving settings and extracting data

9. It may take a few moments to process, but you will end up on our familiar Fields screen. This will show all the fields in the newly extracted data source and their configurations. First, change the name of the data source to **EXTRACT UFO Sightings - Kaggle CSV - 1**.

   Next, double-check the Type settings. I have noticed that Geo field types get set to text in the extract process and have to be reset. You need to reset the City, State, Country, and Latitude-Longitude fields to their respective types. Figure 9.27 shows the fields with their updated types. After you've finished your review, click the Done button to close the Fields panel and continue to the report screen.

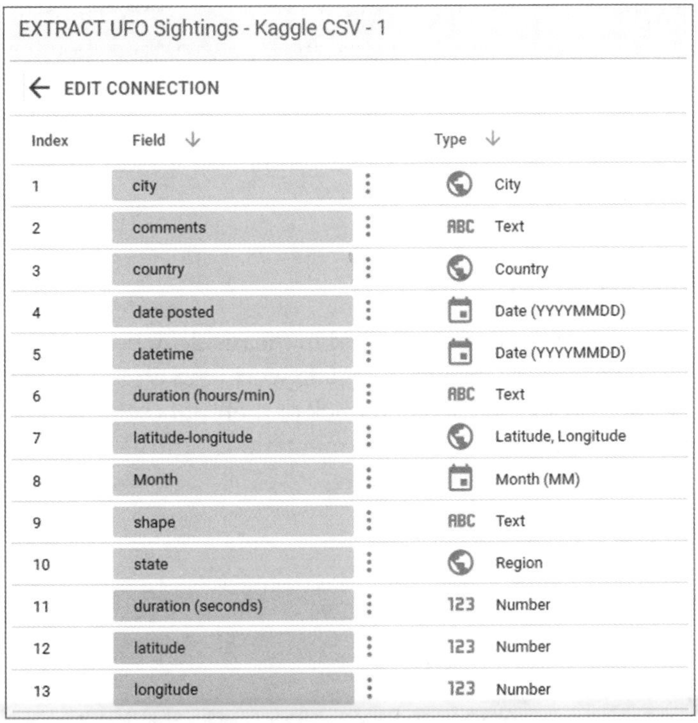

EXTRACT UFO Sightings - Kaggle CSV - 1

← EDIT CONNECTION

Index	Field		Type	
1	city	⋮	🌐	City
2	comments	⋮	ABC	Text
3	country	⋮	🌐	Country
4	date posted	⋮	📅	Date (YYYYMMDD)
5	datetime	⋮	📅	Date (YYYYMMDD)
6	duration (hours/min)	⋮	ABC	Text
7	latitude-longitude	⋮	🌐	Latitude, Longitude
8	Month	⋮	📅	Month (MM)
9	shape	⋮	ABC	Text
10	state	⋮	🌐	Region
11	duration (seconds)	⋮	123	Number
12	latitude	⋮	123	Number
13	longitude	⋮	123	Number

Figure 9.27: Updating the name and field types for the data source

10. Select File ➪ Report Settings. On the Report Settings screen, click the report-level data source and select the newly extracted data source. Next, click each chart, and in the Data tab, replace the data source with the newly extracted data source.

11. Since we have to replace all of the old data source settings with our newly extracted data source, there is no need to keep the old one connected to the report. Removing the old connector is also a good way to verify that you have replaced all the data sources correctly.

    To remove the old data source, choose Resource ➪ Manage Added Data Sources to open the Data Source Management panel, which shows all data sources connected to the report. Find the old connector and click the Remove button at the far right. You will get a confirmation box; click the Remove Data Source to complete the removal process, as shown in Figure 9.28. Click the close button to return to the report screen.

You can test the performance of both reports by going to the links included in the Chapter 9 section of the book resources page at www.wiley.com/go/handsondatastudio.

Next, we will look at another popular aggregator of datasets and a popular data visualization contest.

Name	Used in report	Status	Actions	
⚡ EXTRACT UFO Sightings - Kaggle CSV - 1 ↗ 4 charts		Working	✏ EDIT	🗑 REMOVE
▪ UFO Sightings - Kaggle CSV - 1 ↗ 0 charts		Working	✏ EDIT	🗑 REMOVE

File Edit View Insert Page Arrange Resource Help

Data source   Field editing in reports: On   ✕

Figure 9.28: Removing the original data source

data.world and Makeover Monday

Along with Kaggle, you are likely to find data.world in the results when you use Google Dataset Search. The services provided at data.world are aimed mostly at enterprise businesses that would like to keep track of their data sets and add value to them through organization and data augmentation. Figure 9.29 shows one of their results in a search for **book checkouts**.

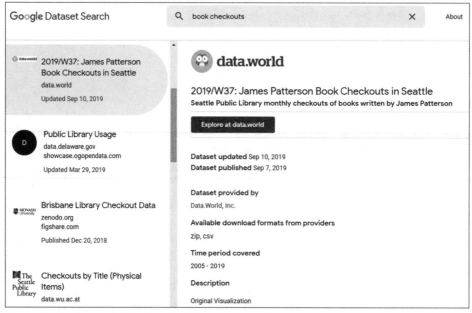

Figure 9.29: data.world result in Google Dataset Search

If you click Explore At data.world, you will be taken to a resource page for that data set, but you must be a member to view and use the files stored there. As with Kaggle, you can get a free membership login that allows you to set up a few limited-size projects and connect to their data sets. They also provide their own Data Studio connector, which allows you to connect directly to their resources.

There are a couple of interesting features that are unique to data.world. First, access to data set fields can be modified through the use of SQL queries. SQL queries allow you to manipulate fields and join multiple data sets together. SQL queries can be also be used in their Data Studio connector, which can be a major advantage when you want to combine data found in multiple files.

The other point of note is that data.world is the current home for data sets used by Makeover Monday, a free data visualization challenge, open to the public, which of course includes you! The weekly challenge provides an existing data visualization example and the data set used to create it. Participants revamp the original work with their own creations.

Makeover Monday, organized by Andy Kriebel and Eva Murray, has been running these weekly challenges since 2016. In the process, it has built an impressive collection of both data sets and visualization examples. Kriebel and Murray have even produced a beautiful book, *#Makeover Monday: Improving How We Visualize and Analyze Data One Chart at a Time* (Wiley 2018). The challenge is a consistent source for examples, guidance, and inspiration.

The Makeover Monday challenge is dominated by users of Tableau, but it is not restricted to that platform. Despite the differences between Tableau and Data Studio mentioned in the first chapter, principles of good design apply to users of all systems, and in the past year or so, some Data Studio entries have been quite popular with the reviewers.

Participating in Makeover Monday

In this section, we'll go through the basic process of checking on the weekly Makeover Monday challenge using data.world for our data set and creating a visualization that could be submitted for review.

1. Go to the Makeover Monday site at www.makeovermonday.co.uk.

2. Choose Participate ⇨ Data Sets to go to this years' data sets page. You'll see a description and links for each week's challenge resources, as shown in Figure 9.30.

3. Click the week column of the table to reverse the listing order, or scroll to the bottom of the page to find the latest data set. You can click the description of the original version for the data visualization to be made over. Click the link under the Data column for data.world. This will take you to the challenge project page on the data.world site, as shown in Figure 9.31.

4. The project page contains information about the original data visualization, the original source of the data, some suggested objectives, and links to the data sets to be used in the challenge. If you follow the discussion link at the top of the page, it will take you to a message board where participants are sharing their solutions and asking questions. Scrolling down the main page brings you to the data set section. You may not view, download, or connect to third-party applications like Data Studio unless you are a registered user.

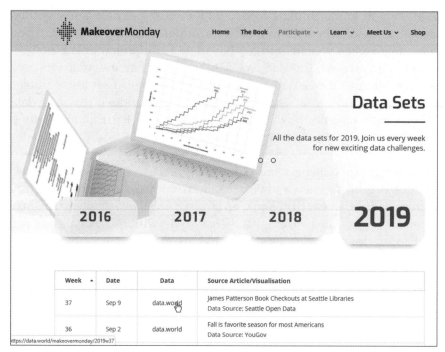

Figure 9.30: Makeover Monday data sets

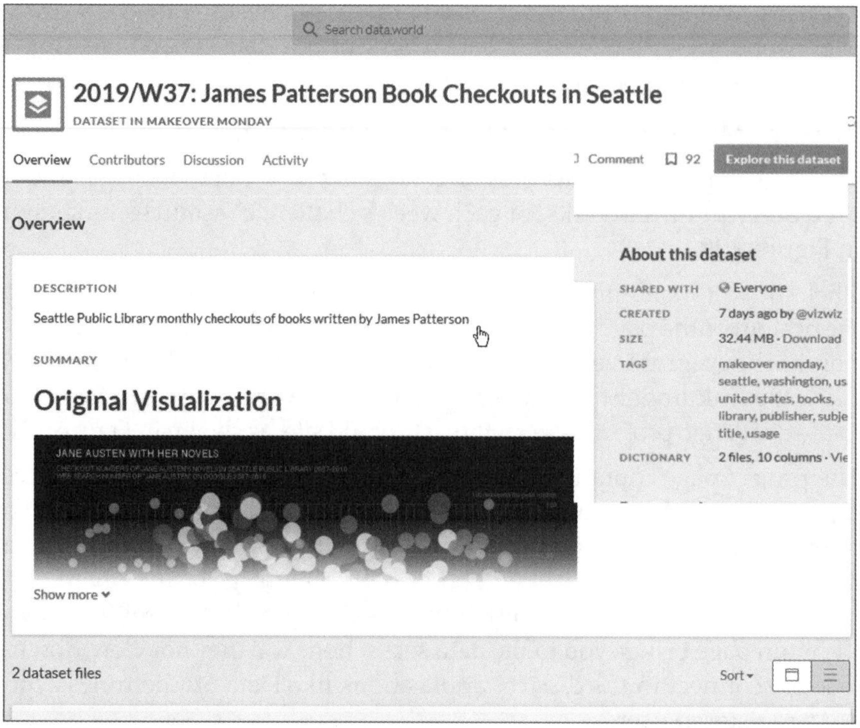

Figure 9.31: The challenge page at data.world

Clicking any of the options for the data set will result in a request for you to register unless you are already signed in. Click the down arrow and select Connect To Third-Party Apps, as shown in Figure 9.32, to get started.

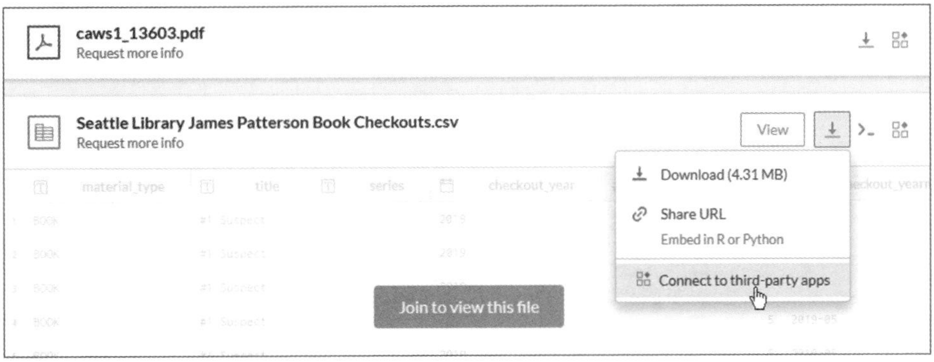

Figure 9.32: Clicking Connect To Third-Party Apps

5. If you have not registered, you will be taken to a sign-up page. You can also use the form to register, or you can use one of your other accounts. I suggest clicking the Sign Up With Google button because we will be using Data Studio connectors with this service. After selecting a Google account to use, you will be asked to give yourself a username. Do this and click the Continue button.

    You will then be presented with a screen that prompts you to create a new project. In our example, we do not need a new project, so we will skip this part by clicking the X in the upper-right corner to return to the challenge page. Now you will be able to see the data sets.

6. Since you can now see the data set, it's a good time to review it quickly. The viewer lets you see a sample of the table created by the CSV file and gives you some information about the field types and how many rows are in the data set. In this case, there are 17,918 rows.

    At this point, you might want to download the CSV file and create a Sheet on Google Drive that will become your data set, as we have done in previous examples. We have covered that before, so now click the Open In App icon instead, as shown in Figure 9.33.

7. If this is your first time through this process, you will not have registered any applications yet for integrating with data.world. You will see a pop-up with a button that offers to find integrations for you. Click the button to continue to the third-party integrations screen.

8. You will be presented with the apps page. Scroll down the page to find the Google Data Studio box and click it. This will take you to a basic description page about Data Studio. At the top of the page, click the Enable Integration button, as shown in Figure 9.34, to open the first authorization pop-up.

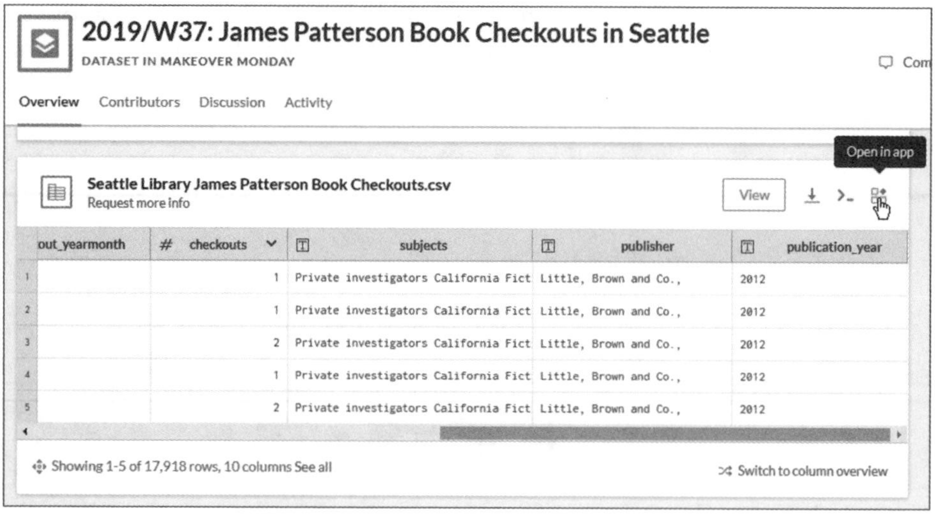

2019/W37: James Patterson Book Checkouts in Seattle
DATASET IN MAKEOVER MONDAY   ⏃ Com

Overview   Contributors   Discussion   Activity

                                                                        Open in app

📄 **Seattle Library James Patterson Book Checkouts.csv**
   Request more info   View   ↓   >_   🖥

out_yearmonth	# checkouts ∨	🔤 subjects	🔤 publisher	🔤 publication_year
1	1	Private investigators California Fict	Little, Brown and Co.,	2012
2	1	Private investigators California Fict	Little, Brown and Co.,	2012
3	2	Private investigators California Fict	Little, Brown and Co.,	2012
4	1	Private investigators California Fict	Little, Brown and Co.,	2012
5	2	Private investigators California Fict	Little, Brown and Co.,	2012

⊕ Showing 1-5 of 17,918 rows, 10 columns See all   ⋈ Switch to column overview

Figure 9.33: Clicking the Open In App Icon

Figure 9.34: Activating Google Data Studio

9. This is similar to the authorization process that you used to connect to Kaggle. The first pop-up asks you to allow Data Studio to access your data .world account. Click the Authorize Google Data Studio button to continue.

Another pop-up will appear, telling you that you have enabled Data Studio. Click the Continue To Dataset button to return to the project data set page we started on.

Scroll down the page, and again click the Open In App icon. This time, you will be allowed to select Google Data Studio for your integration, as shown in Figure 9.35.

Figure 9.35: Selecting Google Data Studio for integration

10. You will be taken to a familiar Data Source setup screen. As you saw in previous examples, you must authorize the connector once in order to use it. Click the Authorize button on this screen to continue.

    You will then be prompted to choose a Google account for this connector. Select an account, and you will be presented with another authorization screen. Click the Allow button to continue, and you will be returned to the Data Source screen. There will now be a new Authorize button on this screen; this one is designed to authorize data.world to accept the Data Studio connection. Click the new Authorize button to complete the process.

11. You will finally be presented with the data.world connect option on the Data Source screen. Here you will see a box labeled SQL Query (Max 25MB). Inside the box is the actual SQL query that the connector will use to pull data from the data set. This SQL configuration can be a major advantage in some cases, as noted earlier.

    Don't worry if you are not familiar with SQL—you won't need any skill in this area to continue. We do want to make a minor modification to the code here, however. The last line in the SQL box states Limit 5000, as shown in Figure 9.36. This could be a problem because we know that there are over 17,000 lines in our data set. Simply remove this line and then click the Connect button. Be prepared for a few minutes of waiting while the connection is being made.

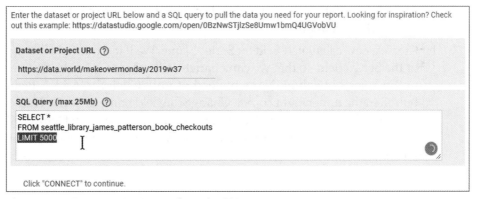

Figure 9.36: Removing Limit 5000 from the SQL query

12. Once the Fields screen appears, update the data source name and any field types that need changing. (I am naming the data source **James Patterson Book Checkouts - data.world**.) No field types should require changing, so continue by clicking Create Report. You will be reminded with a pop-up that you will be adding this data source to a report, so click the Add To Report button to continue.

13. It is usually a good idea to check your data connection by creating a simple detail table so that you can verify that data is coming through to the report as expected. In the case of the data.world connector, the simple table may take a few minutes to fill in!

14. I have found the data.world connectors to be so slow that they are almost unusable when creating a report, and they're equally slow for users of the report. Fortunately, we have the extract data method that we used in the previous example to speed things up. Let's review that process briefly here:

    a. Choose File ➪ Report Settings to open the Report Settings panel. Click the Data Source box, and click Create New Data Source at the bottom of the Select Data Source panel.

    b. On the Connectors screen, select Extract Data Connector.

    c. On the Extract Data Connector setup page, find and select the James Patterson Book Checkouts - data.world data source.

    d. Click Add To Report on the confirmation pop-up.

    e. Drag fields from the original data source to the Dimensions and Metrics sections to configure the new connector.

    f. Review the configuration, and click the Save And Extract button on the lower-right side of the panel. Be prepared to wait!

    g. Change the data source name to **James Patterson Book Checkouts (Extract) - data.world**.

    h. Create a new calculated field for Series Name. We'll use this field instead of the Series field so that we can change null values for books that are not in a series to show None instead of null. Click the Add A Field button in the upper-right corner. Change the field name to **Series Name**, and enter the case statement in the formula box, as shown in Figure 9.37. Click the Save button and return to the Fields screen by clicking the All Fields.

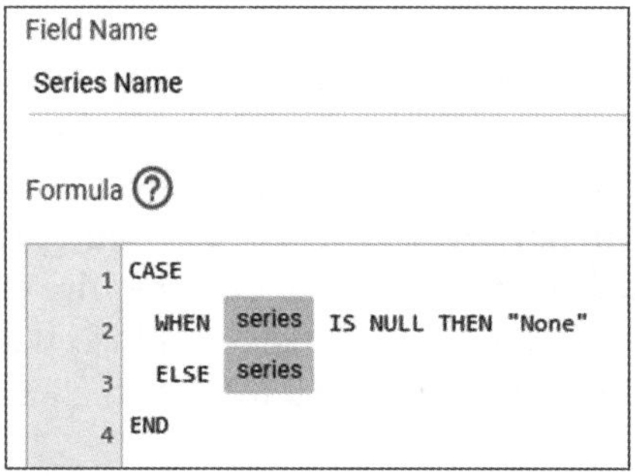

Figure 9.37: Creating the Series Name field

i. Review the Fields setup panel and change field types if needed. Click Done to close the Fields panel and continue.

15. Choose Resource ⇨ Manage Added Data Sources. You should see both the original and the extract connector here. Remove the original data source by clicking the Remove icon on the far-right side of the row. Click the close button to return to the canvas.

16. Now that you have the extract data source connected, you'll find that building a report is a much more enjoyable experience. Figure 9.38 shows the report that we built for this example. We'll review some for the new features of this report at the end of these steps.

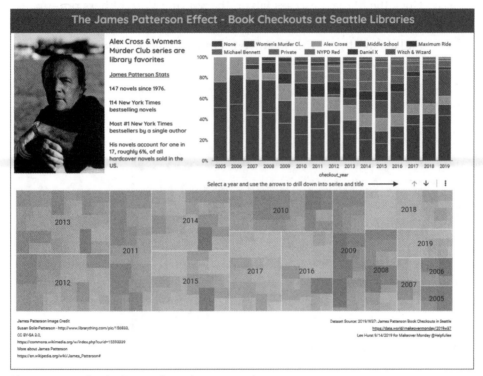

Figure 9.38: A finished report for Makeover Monday

17. We plan to share this report with the Makeover Monday Community and the public in general. To do so, we need to change the sharing settings.

a. In View mode, select the Share drop-down in the header bar and choose Get Report Link.

b. Click the Change Sharing Settings link, as shown in Figure 9.39.

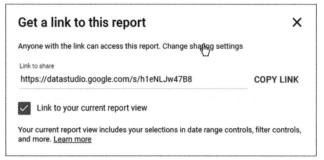

Figure 9.39: Changing the sharing settings

    c. Click the Manage Access tab on the Sharing With Others pop-up.

    d. Click the drop-down showing Off - Only Specific People Can Access and change the setting to Anyone On The Internet Can Find And View, as shown in Figure 9.40.

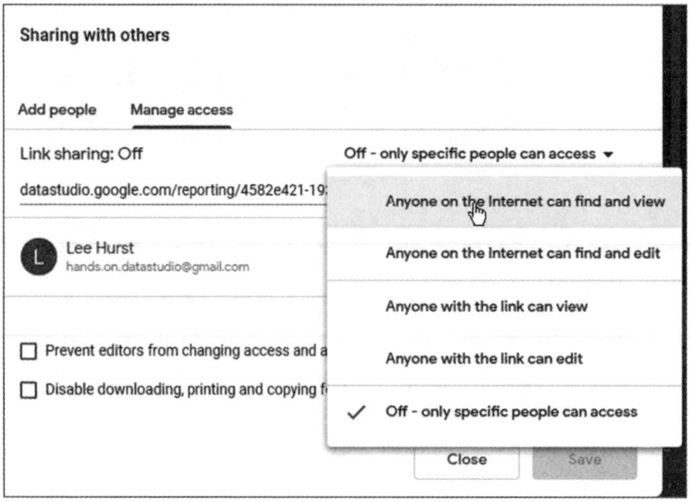

Sharing with others

Add people   Manage access

Link sharing: Off   Off - only specific people can access ▾

datastudio.google.com/reporting/4582e421-19:

                                 Anyone on the Internet can find and view

 (L) Lee Hurst
      hands.on.datastudio@gmail.com   Anyone on the Internet can find and edit

                                 Anyone with the link can view

☐ Prevent editors from changing access and a   Anyone with the link can edit

☐ Disable downloading, printing and copying f

                     ✓ Off - only specific people can access

                      Close   Save

Figure 9.40: Selecting Anyone On The Internet Can Find And View

    e. Click Save to save your sharing settings. Click the Copy button next to the link to copy the link to your internal clipboard, and then click the close button to close the pop-up. You now have the link to share!

18. In a new browser tab, return to the Makeover Monday site at www .makeovermonday.co.uk. Choose Participate ➪ Submit. The Submission page uses a basic Google Form to collect your information. Fill in your name and your Twitter handle if you wish, select the week for which you are submitting, and paste your report's share URL in the Link To Interactive Viz field.

    The last field is Link To Image. You could take a screenshot, load it on the web, and provide the link here, but Data Studio provides a much more elegant solution. Return to your report tab and make sure that you are in View mode. Click in the address bar to edit the URL, add /thumbnail to the end of the URL, and press Enter to load the page. This should produce a thumbnail URL image like the one shown in Figure 9.41.

Figure 9.41: Using a thumbnail URL for a report

Unfortunately, this thumbnail method does not work with the shorter share URL provided in the sharing settings. Copy the updated URL showing the thumbnail, return to the Submission form, and paste the thumbnail URL in the Link to Image field. Now that you are done filling in the form, click Submit.

19. You can share your report with the other participants on the Discussion page for the challenge back at data.world.

    You can also request that your report be reviewed so that you can get feedback on your creation. To do so, you need a Twitter account. If you have one, create a tweet with the following elements:

    a. Use the #MakeoverMonday hashtag.

    b. Include @VizWizBI and @TriMyData to notify the organizers.

    c. Include the #MMVizReview hashtag to indicate that you would like the report reviewed.

    d. Use your report share link in the tweet.

20. Each week, there is a webinar with professional data-visualization experts who review the submissions and make suggestions for improvements. See the page at www.makeovermonday.co.uk/webinars for a schedule and to register to view live or previous webinars.

Features and New Charts in the Example Report

Instead of a full step-by-step breakdown of our Makeover Monday example, we'll take a high-level look at some of the features and then examine the detail of the new chart types in this report.

From a high-level point of view, this report differs from our previous examples. It features more text and graphic elements designed to give the viewer more context for the information in the report. There is also more formal attribution information at the bottom of the report.

Since this is a report designed to be shared publicly, I felt it was a good idea to give credit for the image of Mr. Patterson. When searching on Google for an image to download to use, I found this image. During the download, Google provided the attribution that the owner requested for using the image.

In addition to the image credits, I provided links to the source of the data used and a link to the Wikipedia article that I used for some facts about Mr. Patterson's literary accomplishments used in the text of the report. On the bottom right is some information about me in case a viewer would like more information about the report.

Finally, there are some instructions above one of the charts that provides users with help for understanding how they can interact with the large chart at the bottom of the report. So far in our examples, we have skimped on this kind of help for the user. We'll look at ways to add helpful information in the last example in this chapter. For now, let's take a closer look at the charts included in this report.

The 100% Stacked Column Chart

First, let's look at the column chart in the report, a 100% stacked column chart, as shown in Figure 9.42.

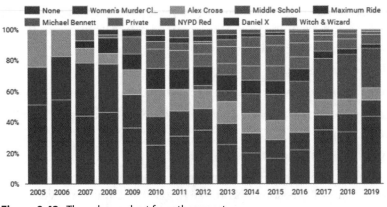

Figure 9.42: The column chart from the report

You saw stacked column charts in earlier chapters, but this is a commonly used variant. You might think of each column on this chart as an unrolled donut chart. Like a pie or donut chart, each column gives us an impression of how the parts—in this example, a book series—relate to the whole—all of Patterson's checkouts. When the year is used with a time dimension, we get a good feel over time how the percentage of a segment is growing or shrinking compared to the total.

This chart is closely related to the 100% stacked area chart. I changed the chart style here so that you can see the difference.

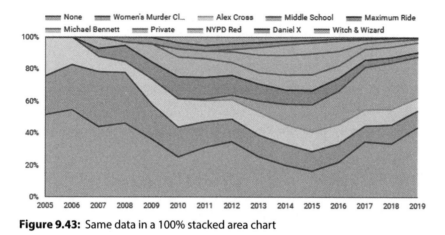

Figure 9.43: Same data in a 100% stacked area chart

There is a subtle difference for the viewer between these two versions. The area version makes the trends look more continuous, when in reality, there could be a lot of variation within a single year. The column chart version captures a bit of this distinction by separating each year into its own chart. We can still see the patterns, but the jagged jumps between years give us a clearer impression of how the data is aggregated by year.

Both of these versions give us a good feel for how the parts relate to the whole. There is a trade-off, however, and it is similar to that of the pie chart. We can see the relative amounts for each year, but we don't know what the total value is for each year. In Figure 9.44, I removed the 100% stacking property of the chart so that you can see the difference from a standard stacked column chart.

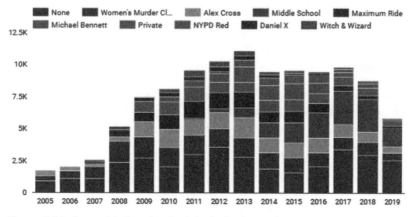

Figure 9.44: Same data in a standard stacked column chart

In the standard stacked column chart, you can see the magnitude of checkouts for each year and the relative amount for each book series. It is much harder, however, to see the relative popularity patterns that are much clearer in the 100% stacked version. Although each variant has its strong points, it is ultimately up to you as the designer to choose the chart that helps your audience gain a better understanding of the aspects of the data you are emphasizing. Of course, any of these variants will give more insight to the viewer than a series of 14 pie charts!

The following steps show how to create the 100% stacked column chart that is in the actual report. We will start with the standard stacked version so that you can see the settings differences between the two variations.

1. Starting in Edit mode, select the stacked column chart from the Add A Chart drop-down, and click and drag the chart into place on the canvas.

2. On the Data tab, adjust the following settings:
   a. Set Dimension to Checkout_year.
   b. Set Breakdown Dimension to Series Name.
   c. Set Metric to Checkouts.
   d. Set the Sort field to Checkout_year and the order to Ascending.
   e. Set the Secondary sort field to Checkouts and the order to Descending.
   f. Click Apply Filter and deselect Enable Sorting in the Interactions section.

3. Switch to the Style tab, where you have to make a few changes to the settings to make the chart match the example:

   a. In the Bar Chart section, change the number of bars from 10 to 20.
   b. Select Stacked Bars to display the 100% Stacking option.
   c. Click the 100% Stacking check box.
   d. Click the X-Axis Show Axis Title option.
   e. Change the Chart Header Visibility option to Do Not Show.

The Treemap Chart

Finally, we will look at the *treemap* chart. This is another visualization that we have not seen before. The Treemap chart was added to the standard set of visualizations in July 2019. The treemap chart from our example report is shown in Figure 9.45.

Figure 9.45: The treemap chart from the example

The treemap chart is another visualization that gives us a feel for how the parts relate to the whole. As Google explains in its online documentation, "A treemap shows your data organized into dimension hierarchies." This explanation is accurate, but it does not convey the complexity of how the treemap functions, particularly when we activate interaction properties like drill-down. Using the drill-down function hides some of the complexity of the treemap from the user.

Figure 9.46 shows an enlarged version of the chart, limited to the top 20 rows of data by book checkout amount, with the drill-down option turned off and all branch levels exposed.

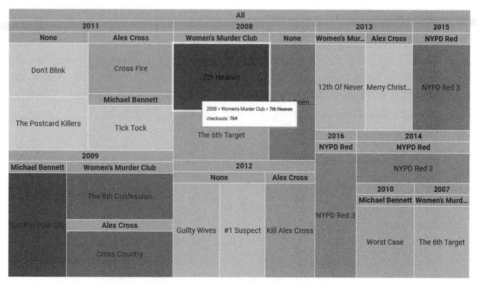

Figure 9.46: The treemap chart with branch levels exposed

From this view, we get a better idea of how the data is being displayed. The treemap does not look like a tree, but it is organized like one logically, with branches and sub-branches. Starting at the top, we have the trunk of the treemap, which is labeled All and has Years as its branches. Now we can focus on a single year's branch; for instance, 2008. The year 2008 has two branches for the book series names, Women's Murder Club and None. Following the Women's Murder Club branch shows two book titles: 7th Heaven and The 6th Target.

Hovering the mouse over 7th Heaven reveals a tooltip that shows the branch path for that box, specifically 2008 ⇨ Women's Murder Club ⇨ 7th Heaven. The tooltip also shows the number of checkouts for that combination of categories.

While this is providing the user with a lot of information, I think the truly amazing part of the treemap is that each branch and sub-branch of the chart is sized and colored to scale with all the other parts of the chart. You might want to let that sink in for a minute!

The treemap component is doing a lot of calculations behind the scenes to organize, scale, and position each part so that it fits neatly into the square shape of the chart. In Figure 9.46, our treemap is dealing only with the top 20 rows. The chart on the actual report handles the top 500 rows, and the component has an upper limit of 5,000 rows!

There are only a certain number of configurations of sections and subsections that will fit neatly into any size chart. Because of this limitation, Data Studio does not give you control over the precise order or layout of the sections. If you resize the chart, or if you filter the data in the chart from an external filter or by drilling down, the chart will reconfigure itself to fit into the chart space.

Let's look at what happens when we follow the branch path of 2008 ⇨ Women's Murder Club ⇨ 7th Heaven and use the drill-down feature. On the report, we have the branch headers turned off, so we do not see the label for All at the top of the chart. Figure 9.47 shows the branch for 2008 selected and the user about to click the drill-down arrow to the Series Name level.

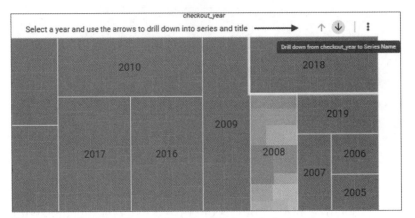

Figure 9.47: Selecting the year 2008 for drill-down to Series Name

Note that the shading inside the 2008 box is scaled and shaded to show the number of checkouts for each series, although the labels are not visible. When the user clicks the drill-down arrow, the chart will redraw itself to show only the series names in that branch. Figure 9.48 shows the result of the drill-down and selecting Women's Murder club for the next drill-down step.

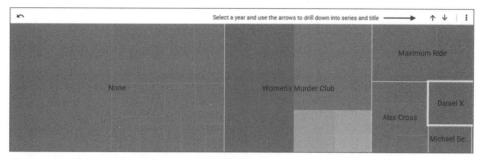

Figure 9.48: Treemap for drill down to 2008 Series Name

Here we see that the treemap has reconfigured to the Series Name level. We also have the option to drill down without making a selection first. This would create a treemap for all of the titles for 2008, but it would not be organized by Series Name. Using the drill-down, with Women's Murder Club selected, results in the treemap would be redrawn, as shown in Figure 9.49.

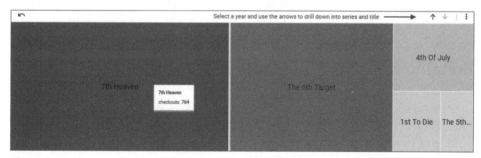

Figure 9.49: Treemap for the 2008 Women's Murder Club Series book titles

As you can see, treemaps can pack a lot of information into a very small space, particularly when coupled with drill-down interactions. Sometimes that is a good thing, but as with all visualizations, there are trade-offs to consider. While providing a lot of information through size, color, and organization, this makes the users brain work harder to process all that information. You run the risk that the user will not focus on the chart enough to get insights out of it.

When you use visualizations that capture more complexity, they tend to be more visually appealing and artistic. However, as you move toward the realm of data art, the interpretations of the visualizations become more personal and it becomes more difficult to find clear and actionable insights on which we can agree.

These steps show how to create the treemap chart that is in the actual report:

1. Starting in Edit mode, select the treemap chart from the Add A Chart drop down, and click and drag the chart into place on the canvas.

2. On the Data tab, adjust the following settings:

   a. Set the Dimension fields to Checkout_year, Series Name, and Title.

   b. Set the drill-down switch to the On position.

   c. Set the default drill-down level to Checkout_year.

   d. Set Levels to 1.

   e. Set Metric to Checkouts.

   f. Set the total rows to 500.

3. Switching to the Style tab, change these settings to make the chart match the example:

   a. In the Treemap section, deselect Show Branch Header.

   b. Change the Chart Header Visibility option to Always Show.

Now we are ready to move on to our last example in this chapter. We will tackle retrieving a real estate data set from a private commercial site.

Bringing It Home: Real Estate in Your Neighborhood

In this last section, we will use a commercial real estate site to retrieve housing data for neighborhoods. Although many sites have good visualization facilities built in, it can be worthwhile to pull the data yourself so that you can focus on the aspects that interest you the most.

The inspiration for this example comes from personal experience. I was considering moving to a different neighborhood in my city about a year ago. I enlisted a friend of mine, Dave, an experienced realtor, to help me in my search. Going out to view some open houses, I was shocked by the number of prospective buyers flocking to most properties. Buyers were in bidding wars, offering well over asking price, and purchasing homes without an inspection.

This was a vastly different market than when I had purchased a house about 10 years earlier. Consulting with Dave, he informed me that he thought the number of houses available was at the lowest number he could recall. Along with increased demand, this seemed to be causing the difficult market for prospective buyers like me.

Now I trust Dave—I know he has a lot of experience and he also loves his numbers. Nevertheless, I thought that both of us might benefit from a graphic representation that shows the current situation and how the market has changed over the past few years. I wanted to see if I could answer some of the following questions:

- Is the inventory of available houses really shrinking?

- How small is the number of available houses compared to previous year?

- Are the prices of houses increasing along with the decrease in availability?

- What is happening with the number of actual home sales? Are houses just scarce, or are they selling faster?

- Does it look like the shortage is getting any better?

- Are these general patterns across the region? How do they play out for different neighborhoods, including the one I currently live in?

I believed that a report that shed some light on these questions might be helpful for other people, and they might want information about their own local markets.

So, with my questions and the needs of my audience (mostly me!) in mind, I set out to get some answers. For this investigation, I went through the steps that we covered back in the first chapter with the cooking analogy. I will go through the steps again as we explore this topic.

Selecting the Dish to Prepare

Ideally, I would figure out exactly what kind of dish I wanted to make, then go shopping for the ingredients, and finally cook the meal. In reality, I get hungry, go to the grocery store, and buy ingredients based on what I feel like eating! When I get home, I try to put the ingredients together in a way that will be satisfying.

I will often play with the ingredients, not following a recipe, and see what I can come up with. While this is fun from time to time, I often regret not having at least some dish planned when I go shopping, because I know that even if I stray from a recipe, I will have the right ingredients to make a better meal.

I find this is very much like the real world of data visualization, particularly if we are ourselves the primary audience. We go out browsing for data, find some that looks pretty good and easy to process, and then we see what we can do with it. Again, there is value in this approach, but you get better results by starting with a plan, even if you don't follow it exactly.

Unlike with previous examples, we won't start with the finished product to use as a model. I will make a very rough sketch of how I think the report should look and keep that in mind when shopping for data.

Figure 9.50 shows a whiteboard sketch of what I think this report should look like.

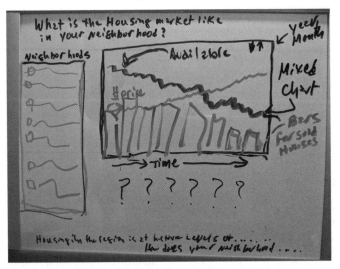

Figure 9.50: Sketch of the housing report

Admittedly, this is not much to look at, but it is enough to provide some initial direction. I have one other requirement for this report. Although I would like some interaction, I would like it to be small enough to fit on a web page. At the end of this section, I will show you a couple of simple methods for embedding your reports, giving you another way to share your insights.

Going Shopping: Hunting for Housing Data

There are a number of sources for housing information data sets. A prime source are government websites. From city to region to nation, many areas have a wealth of data available, from employment to business to housing information.

Although the data is out there, be prepared for a lengthy hunt. Even with the specialized tools for finding data sets, you will probably find yourself sifting through a lot of sources that are not what you need.

Doing a Google Dataset search for our needs turns up some government data sets on Kaggle, data.world, and some large government data stores. Unfortunately, they have some deficiencies for our needs. Some have recent data, but they don't have some of the measurements we are seeking. Some, like data .world, have comprehensive real estate data sets, but they are not very recent. A little extra digging shows that the data.world data sets come from Zillow, a large online real estate service.

It turns out that Zillow has an entire section of its website devoted to real estate research. A quick look at the site reveals that Zillow produces extensive reports and visualizations. In addition, it has a robust system for extracting real estate data for download in its Data section found at www.zillow.com/research/data.

Although some of their richest data is kept private, the publicly available information is very close to what we need for this report. Figure 9.51 shows the preparation for a download of a report.

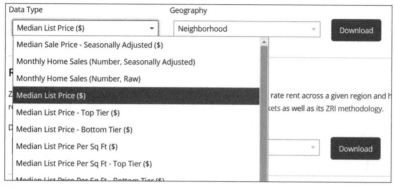

Figure 9.51: Downloading data from Zillow

A quick examination of the CSV file shows the monthly mean value of houses sold dating back to 2010 to as recently as two months ago. Although this seems pretty extensive, closer examination shows very few neighborhoods in my particular metro area. This makes the data less appropriate for this particular report. But it gives me the idea to check other real estate services and see if they have something a bit closer to what we need and to keep Zillow as a backup source if necessary.

After some more checks with the Google Dataset search, I shifted gears and went to the regular Google search looking for **real estate house price data**. After checking a few of the results, I finally landed on the data center for Redfin, another large real estate listing service.

In addition to premade reports, users can filter housing data and download it in CSV format. The first time I tried the service, I found that I was able to get extensive data for all the neighborhoods in my area.

WARNING   You must click somewhere on the data table in order to activate the download options!

Here are the steps I used to download a CSV file with local neighborhood information:

1. Go to `www.redfin.com/blog/data-center`. The main chart shown in Figure 9.52 is the service with which we will be working.

Figure 9.52: The main data selector on Redfin

2. When you go to the Redfin Data Center page, this chart appears at the top. Interestingly, the main data service is provided through a Tableau chart, so you get an opportunity to use another major data-visualization tool. There are some instructions on this page for using the service, but I found that I had to use it a few times to get the information I wanted.

    a. The default chart shows data for some selected areas. The State selector at the upper left can be used to narrow the data down to a state level. Click the State drop-down, deselect the (All) check box, search or scroll to find NY, and select its check box.

    b. Select Region Types. In our example, I want information by specific neighborhood only, but other options are available, as shown in Figure 9.53.

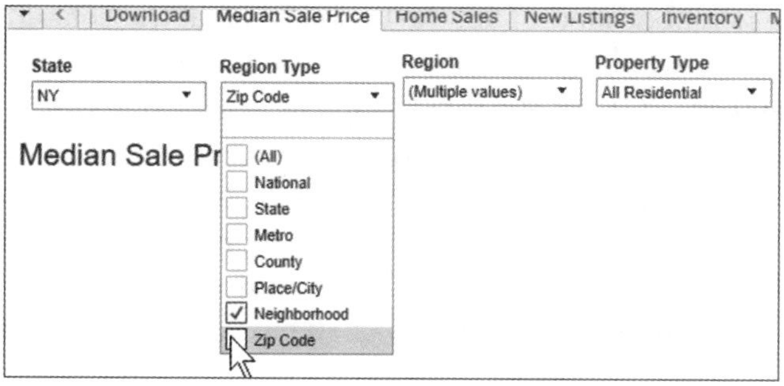

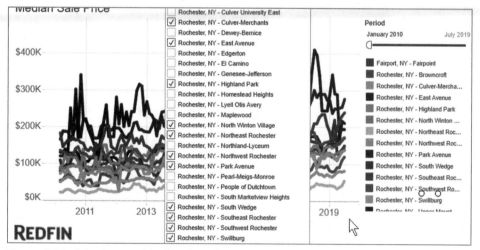

Figure 9.53: Selecting Neighborhood for Region Type

   c. Select Regions. In our case, since we selected Neighborhood as our region type, we will be able to select any or all of the regions for New York. I found the search function worked well for this. I was able to select many neighborhoods and areas in the Rochester area, as well as a couple of nearby villages. As you make your selections, the chart will update. While the style is a bit different, the functionality is very similar to the reports in Data Studio. Figure 9.54 shows the neighborhood selection in process.

Figure 9.54: Selecting neighborhoods and villages

   d. For Property Types, you can select from among several types of housing options. In this case, I selected the Single-Family Residential property type.

   e. Modify the Period setting. By default, the chart starts at January 2012. Although data is available back to 2010, it seems that this data is less complete for some neighborhoods. I left the Period slider at the default. Also, I chose not to change how the values are shown or to try to use the Seasonally Adjusted settings for this example.

3. You'll see a download icon at the bottom of the chart, but clicking it will not give you the option to download the data yet. This is the first area where you might get fooled after using the service once or twice and trying to click the download icon at this point. You will need to click the download icon, but only after finishing the other steps.

   a. Click the Download tab at the upper left of the chart. This will take you to a download review screen.

   b. Although the instructions on this page are simple, they are not quite complete—remember my warning! Click anywhere on the table to select a cell, as shown in Figure 9.55, and then click that cell again to deselect it. This activates the download functions. Now the instructions highlighted in Figure 9.55 will work!

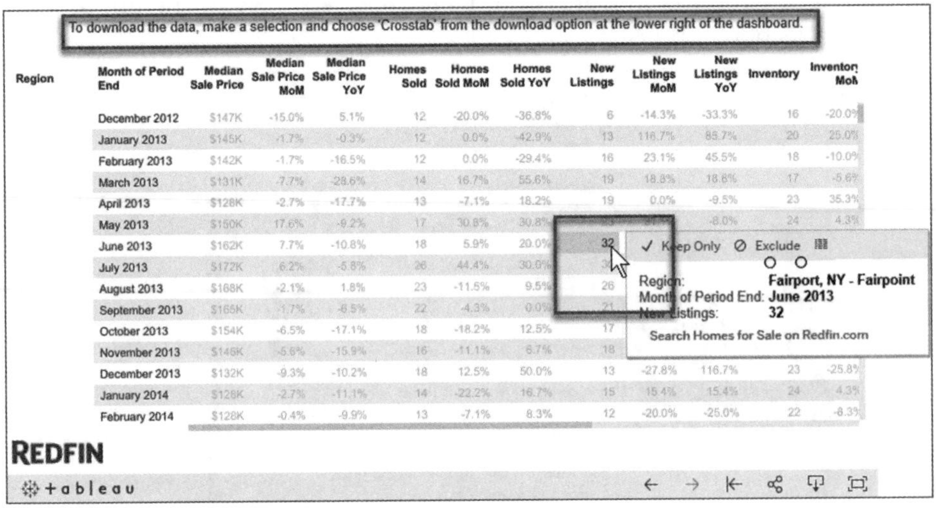

To download the data, make a selection and choose 'Crosstab' from the download option at the lower right of the dashboard.

Region	Month of Period End	Median Sale Price	Median Sale Price MoM	Median Sale Price YoY	Homes Sold	Homes Sold MoM	Homes Sold YoY	New Listings	New Listings MoM	New Listings YoY	Inventory	Inventory MoM
	December 2012	$147K	-15.0%	5.1%	12	-20.0%	-36.8%	6	-14.3%	-33.3%	16	-20.0%
	January 2013	$145K	-1.7%	-0.3%	12	0.0%	-42.9%	13	116.7%	85.7%	20	25.0%
	February 2013	$142K	-1.7%	-16.5%	12	0.0%	-29.4%	16	23.1%	45.5%	18	-10.0%
	March 2013	$131K	-7.7%	-28.6%	14	16.7%	55.6%	19	18.8%	18.8%	17	-5.6%
	April 2013	$128K	-2.7%	-17.7%	13	-7.1%	18.2%	19	0.0%	-9.5%	23	35.3%
	May 2013	$150K	17.6%	-9.2%	17	30.8%	30.8%			-8.0%	24	4.3%
	June 2013	$162K	7.7%	-10.8%	18	5.9%	20.0%	32				
	July 2013	$172K	6.2%	-5.8%	26	44.4%	30.0%					
	August 2013	$168K	-2.1%	1.8%	23	-11.5%	9.5%	26				
	September 2013	$185K	-1.7%	-6.5%	22	-4.3%	0.0%					
	October 2013	$154K	-6.5%	-17.1%	18	-18.2%	12.5%	17				
	November 2013	$146K	-5.6%	-15.9%	16	-11.1%	6.7%	18				
	December 2013	$132K	-9.3%	-10.2%	18	12.5%	50.0%	13	-27.8%	116.7%	23	-25.8%
	January 2014	$128K	-2.7%	-11.1%	14	-22.2%	16.7%	15	15.4%	15.4%	24	4.3%
	February 2014	$128K	-0.4%	-9.9%	13	-7.1%	8.3%	12	-20.0%	-25.0%	22	-8.3%

REDFIN

+ableau

Figure 9.55: Clicking the table is the secret step!

   c. Now when you click the download icon, you will see the options for Crosstab and Data, as shown in Figure 9.56. (If you skip step b, you will not have those options activated for selection.) Select the Data option.

   d. Selecting Data in the previous step activates a new data preview screen. By default, this is set to Summary data. Click the Full Data tab to see the full, non-summarized data set. Clicking the Show All Columns check box allows you to see a preview of the data formatted in columns. Click the Download All Rows As A Text File link, as shown in Figure 9.57.

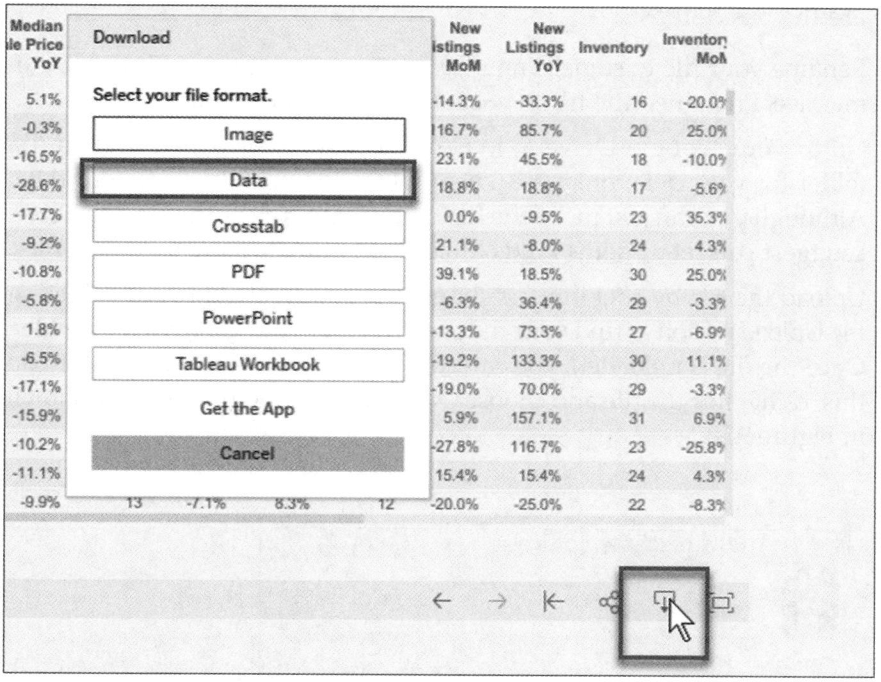

Median ile Price YoY	Download			New istings MoM	New Listings YoY	Inventory	Inventory MoM
5.1%	Select your file format.			-14.3%	-33.3%	16	-20.0%
-0.3%		Image		116.7%	85.7%	20	25.0%
-16.5%				23.1%	45.5%	18	-10.0%
-28.6%		Data		18.8%	18.8%	17	-5.6%
-17.7%				0.0%	-9.5%	23	35.3%
-9.2%		Crosstab		21.1%	-8.0%	24	4.3%
-10.8%		PDF		39.1%	18.5%	30	25.0%
-5.8%				-6.3%	36.4%	29	-3.3%
1.8%		PowerPoint		-13.3%	73.3%	27	-6.9%
-6.5%		Tableau Workbook		-19.2%	133.3%	30	11.1%
-17.1%				-19.0%	70.0%	29	-3.3%
-15.9%		Get the App		5.9%	157.1%	31	6.9%
-10.2%		Cancel		-27.8%	116.7%	23	-25.8%
-11.1%				15.4%	15.4%	24	4.3%
-9.9%	13	-7.1%	8.3%	12	-20.0%	-25.0%	22	-8.3%

Figure 9.56: Clicking the download icon and selecting Data

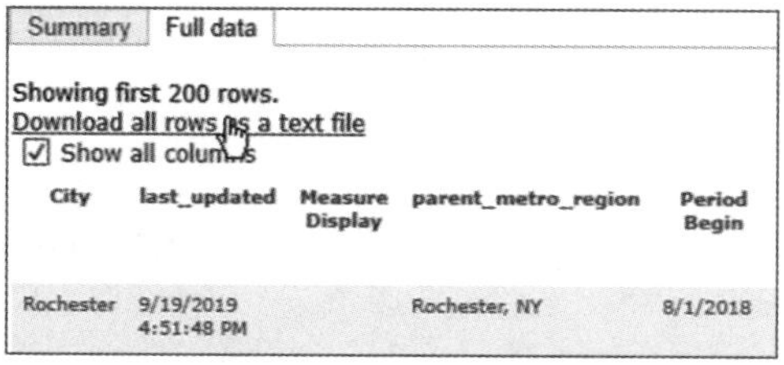

Figure 9.57: Clicking the Download All Rows As A Text File link

The downloaded file is called `data_data.csv`. We are now ready to move on to storing and processing the data file.

Unpacking the Groceries: Moving the File to Google Drive

Sticking with our cooking analogy, we need to unpack the groceries, which in our case means moving the file and storing it as a Sheet on Google Drive. Although this is the primary way to handle data sets of this size, there are other options that you may want to consider if you are working with much larger files. We will look at some of those options in Chapter 10, "Where Do You Go from Here?" For now, let's stick to the methods we first covered in detail back in Chapter 2, "Cooking with Google Data Studio."

Here are the basic steps:

1. Rename your file to something more descriptive than `data_data.csv`. In my case, I renamed the file to **`RocNeighborhoodDataA.csv`**.

2. Go to your Google Drive at `https://drive.google.com` and find a folder for your data, or create a new folder in which to store your data. Although you can just move the file to the main root of the Google Drive, I suggest you set up some kind of folder structure to store your data files.

3. Upload the file by clicking and dragging or right-clicking and selecting the Upload option to find your file and copy it to your Google Drive folder. Once the file is uploaded, you can convert it to a Google Sheet file. To do this, right-click the file and choose Open With ⇨ Google Sheets, as shown in Figure 9.58.

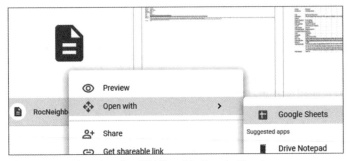

Figure 9.58: Opening the CSV file with Google Sheets

With our data file now converted to Sheets, we are ready to do some data cleaning!

Preparing the Ingredients: Fixing Data Formatting Issues

Sadly, it is a rare occurrence for a data file to be perfectly usable without some modifications. On a positive note, most of the data that we use day today has already been processed to some extent, so it could be worse. Data citizens rarely have to do as much data preparation as the people who work with data for a living. A survey (see `https://www.forbes.com/sites/gilpress/2016/03/23/data-preparation-most-time-consuming-least-enjoyable-datascience-task-survey-says/#c64cd096f637`) of data scientists revealed that data collection and preparation processes, sometimes called "data munging," account for about 80 percent of their work.

For this example, I was initially fooled into thinking that the data was ready to go once converted to a Google Sheet. After trying in vain to get some charts to work, I realized my oversight. The Median Sale Price, the primary metric in this case, was not actually a number! Although I had set it to a dollar value in the Data Source field configuration, it would not register on any chart. A closer examination shown in Figure 9.59 reveals the issue.

	M	N	O
h Mo Median Dom Yoy	Median Sale Price	Median Sale Pric M
-5.5	-32	$135K	-0.90%
-19	-148	$132K	-17.30%
-24	-12	$201K	-6.90%

Figure 9.59: The Median Sale Price is *not* a number!

Here the problem is that the data for the field uses the letter K to represent thousands. That's a pretty standard way to show a large value, and it is even shown that way in Data Studio output if the style settings for the field in a chart are set to Compact numbers. Data Studio also automatically uses the K abbreviation for thousands on the scale for graphs to save space. Apparently, Data Studio is smart enough to deal with dollar and other monetary signs, but it cannot deal with the K abbreviation for thousands!

So, we need to go back to the Sheet and modify the values for the Median Sale Price. Fortunately, this is easily done.

1. Select the entire column by clicking the row control above Median Sale Price—in this case, column N.

2. Choose Edit ➪ Find And Replace, or use the shortcut Ctrl+H, to open the Find And Replace dialog box. Enter **K** in the Find field and **000** in the Replace With field, and click the Replace All button, as shown in Figure 9.60. You should get feedback that there were many replacements; 1,472 in this example. Click Done to continue.

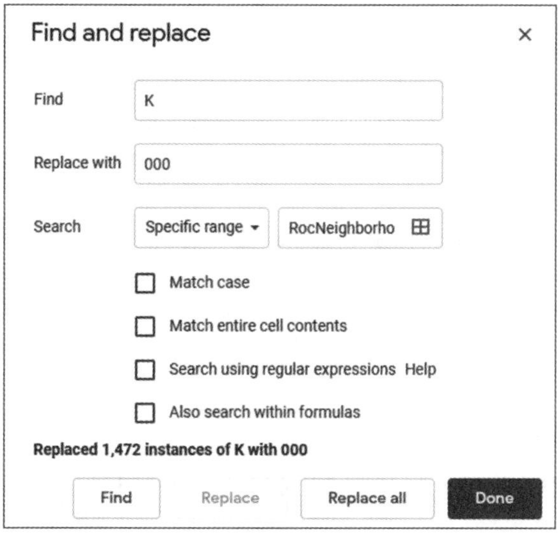

Find and replace	✕
Find	K
Replace with	000
Search	Specific range ▾ RocNeighborho ⊞
	☐ Match case
	☐ Match entire cell contents
	☐ Search using regular expressions Help
	☐ Also search within formulas

Replaced 1,472 instances of K with 000

[Find] [Replace] [Replace all] [**Done**]

Figure 9.60: Fixing the K issue with Find and Replace

3. Set the format of the Median Price column as Currency and the Period End column as a Date.

With our data preparation tasks behind us, it's time to move on to creating our data source.

Assembling the Ingredients: Connecting the Data to the Report

As you followed along throughout the previous chapters, you have seen several different variations of data connectors and their setups. As a best practice, it is a good idea to set up your data source first, and then create your report and add the data source to it. Sometimes I find it more natural simply to start the report creation and add the new data source on the fly. Usually, I will do this if I am very familiar with the data source or if I am quickly exploring data. Although I do believe creating the data source first results in fewer issues, we will walk through the other workflow so that you can see the difference. We start, as usual, at the Data Studio home page: `https://datastudio.google.com`.

1. On the Data Studio home page, click the Blank Report box in the Start With A Template section. This will bring up a new report with the Add A Data Source panel on the right side.

2. Click Create A New Data Source at the bottom of the right-side panel. This will take you to the connectors page.

3. Locate the Google Sheets connector and click Select to go to the connector setup screen for Google Sheets.

4. In our case, we are using RocNeighborhoodA as our spreadsheet. If you just created your Sheet, you may not see it listed immediately, and you can use the URL Or Open From Google Drive option to find it. My best suggestion, though, is to use the Cancel button to return to the report, take a five-minute break, and then go back to step 2. Select the Spreadsheet and the Worksheet and click Connect.

5. I named my data source **Redfin Rochester Data - Sheets 1**. Make sure that the Period End field is set to the Date type, and the Median Sale Price field is set to type Currency (USD - US Dollar ($)). Click Done and then click Add To Report at the confirmation pop-up.

Preparing the Meal: The Plan Meets Reality

In the earlier part of this section, I showed you a rough whiteboard sketch of what should be in this report. I was able to execute this plan, and the finished product for that design is shown in Figure 9.61.

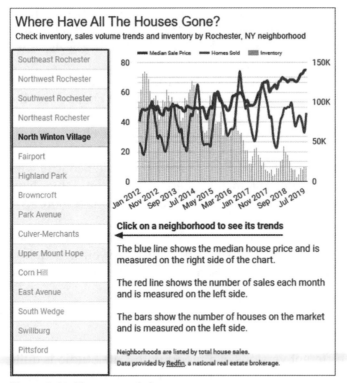

Figure 9.61: The executed plan

This example already strays a bit from the initial design. One of the issues I encountered was the way the neighborhood names were listed. In the original data, a neighborhood included the general location and the neighborhood name. For example, all of the Rochester locations were listed as seen in Figure 9.62.

v
Region
Fairport, NY - Fairpoint
Rochester, NY - Corn Hill
Rochester, NY - Park Avenue
Rochester, NY - South Wedge
Rochester, NY - South Wedge
Rochester, NY - Southwest Rochester
Rochester, NY - Southwest Rochester

Figure 9.62: Original neighborhood listing format

This might make sense if we were looking at multiple areas, but since the report was limited to the Rochester area, the extra information did not serve much purpose and just took up much needed space.

While the names could have been shortened by creating a new calculated field and a formula, I decided that it was simpler to change the actual data in the Sheet. I did so easily using the Find and Replace function in Sheets, as we did to fix the price formatting issue.

Unfortunately, this still did not solve some of the spacing issues. Due to the way that Data Studio formats the filter controls, I found it chopped off the neighborhood names. In order to get them to show correctly, I would have to stretch out the control box, which left very little space for the chart that was the main focus point.

After some formatting attempts, I decided to replace the filter control with a simple table for the names with interactive filtering turned on. Tables have much greater layout flexibility than filter controls because they have more style and formatting options.

Although this design meets the requirements, I thought it felt a bit cramped and too busy. I often find that this is the case, particularly when you are required to work with a small canvas. The initial design is good, but it could use some improvement.

The Final Design Version

Fortunately, creating different versions of a report with Data Studio is quite simple. As you saw in earlier chapters, all you have to do is copy the report and modify the copy. I find that this makes experimentation quite risk-free, as you always have the original version on which to fall back if needed.

After some consideration of the shortfalls of the original design, I decided that changing the layout of the canvas and making it longer could help the overall design. The final canvas dimensions are 500 px wide by 800 px long. While you may not have the luxury of changing a design when working for other people, when you are the final judge it gives you more latitude.

> **TIP**   Find someone who can check your work, give you feedback, and provide that service in return. Having some kind of "check buddy" can save you hours of redesign and embarrassment! I have the honor of working informally with several Data Studio experts who will often send their new work to me for a final check before releasing it to the public.
>
> Just to be on the safe side, for this example, I sent both copies of this report to my real estate friends for their opinion on which one they thought worked better. If you are going to be sharing your creations with an audience, this kind of testing is a valuable step in the process.

The final design version for this example is shown in Figure 9.63. You can access this example through the online resources for this chapter.

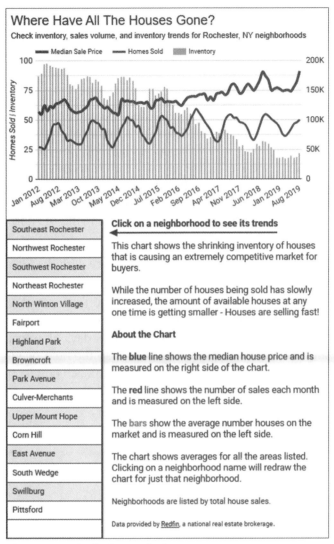

Figure 9.63: The final example design

This design has all the same basic elements of the original, yet it seems to be easier for the user to process. Simply changing the report length allowed me more room to explain what to look for in the chart. Providing a bit more whitespace and separating the chart and the interactive neighborhood table makes it easier for the viewer to process each section.

Please note the small attribution link at the bottom of the report. It is important when you build public-facing reports that you provide attribution. In this case, Redfin thoughtfully supplies their preferred wording to use when referencing data provided by their services, and I have copied that text and their preferred link here.

Here is a brief breakdown of the charts used in this report and their settings. We have not covered the combo chart in previous chapters, and the table has some style options that we haven't used yet.

Building the Combo Chart

The *combo chart* is a flexible combination of both line and column charts. The ability to show these different representations allows the designer to pack extra information into the chart. Quite often, you will need to use both the left-axis and the right-axis so that you can show metrics that have different scales in the same space. There is a trade-off, however: your viewers will have to work harder to connect the different lines and bars to their respective measurement axis. My advice is to proceed with caution in using and interpreting this kind of chart.

1. You will find the combo chart in the Line section of the Add A Chart drop-down. Select it, and then click and drag it into place. Use the Data tab to set the properties.

2. The Date Range Dimension should set automatically to the Period End field because this is the only Date field in the data source. Set the Dimension field to Period End also. By default, this will show days. However, we would like to show month and year for our chart, so the field needs to be modified. To do this, hover over the field, click the pencil edit icon, and set the properties as shown in Figure 9.64

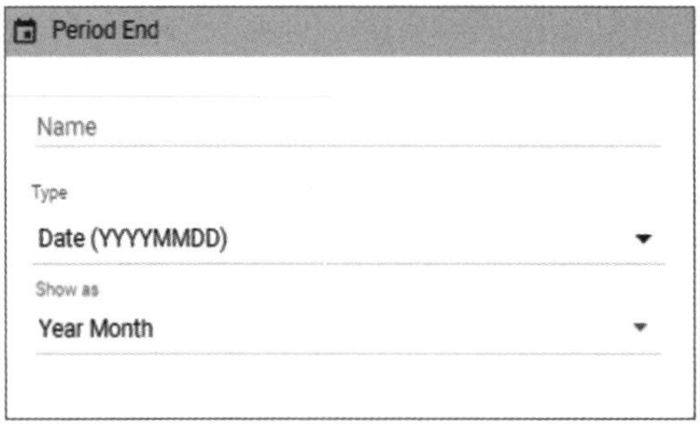

Figure 9.64: Setting dimension properties

3. Set the metric fields to Median Sale Price, Homes Sold, and Inventory in that order from top to bottom. Change the aggregation method for each one to Average.

4. Set the Sort field to Period End and the Sort Order drop-down to Ascending.

5. Configure the Series properties. Switch to the Style tab to configure the rest of the properties. Each metric will have its own set of attributes to configure.

a. For Series #1, set the type to Line, the line thickness to 4, and the line color to blue. Click the Axis To Right radio button to set the median sales price to be measured on the right-side axis.

b. Series 2 is the Houses Sold metric. Set the type to Line, the line thickness to 3, and the line color to red. Set Axis to Left.

c. Series 3 shows the Inventory metric. Here we set the type to Bars, the color to orange, and the axis to Left.

d. Under the General settings, select the Smooth check box.

e. In the Left Y-Axis section, select Show Axis Title.

f. Set Chart Header to Do Not Show.

Neighborhood Table Settings

The neighborhood selector is a streamlined table that has many features removed. This kind of setup works well when there is no room for a filter control component. Here are the settings:

1. Select Table from the Add A Chart drop-down and place it on the canvas.

2. Starting in the Data tab for the table, set the Dimension field to Region.

3. We don't need any other fields on our table, so remove any fields that are in the Metric section.

4. Set the Sort field to Homes Sold and the sort order to Descending. This will put the fields in a sensible order.

5. At the bottom of the Data tab, select the Apply Filter check box in the Interactions section.

6. Switch to the Style tab for the rest of the table setup. In the Table Header section, deselect Show Header. This will make the headings disappear to make the table cleaner and take up less space.

7. It may be hard to distinguish, but there is a slight shading difference for the rows and lines separating the table cells to make them easier to distinguish. Configure these settings with the Table Colors drop-down. From left to right, skip the header background color (we don't have a header!), set the cell border color to black, and set the odd row color to a light shade of brown using the custom color picker, as shown in Figure 9.65. If you need to use precise colors that are defined for style, specify them in the text box. The color shown here is #e9e6e4ff.

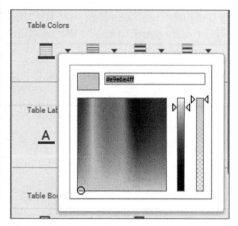

Figure 9.65: Using the custom picker to select an exact color

8. Deselect the Row Numbers and Show Pagination options.

9. In the Background And Border section, set the line color to black and the line thickness to 2, and click the Add Border Shadow check box. These settings give the table more visual definition so that it stands out more on the page.

10. In the Chart Header section, set the visibility drop-down to Do Not Show.

Now that we have completed the report, we would like to share it. In the next section, I will show you another option for sharing that we have not covered yet.

Sharing Your Dish: Embedding Reports

We have looked at some of the ways to share reports. Nonetheless, I don't feel that this book would be complete if we did not cover one final method of sharing. *Embedding* a report means adding it to an existing web page. This method of sharing opens up a new realm of possibilities. I believe that there is still a lot of untapped potential for Data Studio creators in this area.

First, it is important to recognize that when you are embedding a Data Studio report, in most cases, you are sharing that report with the world at large. There are certainly many reports that you would not want to share! Of course, there are exceptions to this; you may want to embed reports in pages on a private intranet or on a secure page that requires login.

Let's look at some of the limitations of embedding before we jump into the possible applications. Some limitations are as follows:

Embedded reports are public.   Though already mentioned, it bears repeating! A best practice is to have your web page checked by someone else, or at least check it with the "incognito" feature available in some web browsers.

Embedded reports cannot be contained.   Embedded reports can be viewed separately outside of the web page in which they are embedded. There is little to stop this possibility, as the functionality is built into the footer of a report.

Embedded reports show only one level of embedding.   By this I mean that if you have an embedded element, such as a video in your report, this will not show while the report is embedded in a web page.

Embedded reports will not work with a Data control.   As we saw in Chapter 5, "Web Data Visualization with Google Analytics," Data controls allow you to switch to other data sources on the fly for some kinds of services like Google Analytics. This means that if you create a report with a Data control in it, that control will not be visible in the report while it is embedded in the web page.

Users may be warned when clicking links.   A user following links embedded in a report may get a warning that they are leaving the website. This is a security precaution provided by Data Studio to keep people from being tricked into visiting malicious sites.

Embedding a report does not make it "responsive," even if it is embedded in a responsive page.   In this context, responsive means that a web page will reconfigure its layout in response to different size screens or resizing the screen. You can see responsive design in most web pages today by shrinking your browser size. When a certain size threshold is reached, the elements on the page reconfigure for a tablet or mobile phone optimized view. Data Studio–embedded reports can be made resizable, but they will not reconfigure layout. This means that a larger report may not look good on mobile screens.

Reuse of embedded reports cannot be restricted.   There is no way to keep an embedded report restricted to a single website. This is similar to the way that images work in web pages: anyone with a little know-how can also use your embedded report in their site.

Embedded reports provide virtually no SEO value.   This means that no matter how stunning your report or how valuable the insights, search engines such as Google cannot read or index that embedded content. Even when not embedded in a page, Data Studio reports seem to have almost no potential to bring in traffic from searches.

The limitations listed here are common for applications that are embedded in web pages, and most of these are designed to protect the security of browsers. With these limitations in mind, let's look at some of the possibilities.

Safety of Browsers   First, the limitations provide some security for users, and they don't have to be wary of using an embedded interactive report.

Increased Visibility   Data Studio reports have little search engine pull on their own, but the page in which they are embedded can be optimized to pull in search traffic, and people who would otherwise miss your creation have a better chance of seeing it.

Design Flexibility   A report that is only an inch high with a few current scorecards would not make a good report on its own, but this works great in a web page. Your page design can keep its flexibility, and updating interactive elements can be added in different sections.

Interactive Page Elements That Keep Web Users Engaged   Providing interactive visualizations is a great way to keep users on your pages and exploring your content.

Low-Cost Application Development   You may not think of Data Studio as an application development platform, but I do! Custom interactive web application development can cost a lot of money, and many small businesses cannot afford it. We will look at some examples of actual applications in Chapter 10.

Interactive Infographics   Another case is where people pay a lot of money to develop custom infographics for their websites or to promote their business. Data Studio can produce these, and they can be shared almost as easily as standard infographics.

Embedded Reports That Can Be Used in Other Sites   Although this is listed in the limitations, it's also a feature! If you create something of value, it can be shared across many sites. However, unlike a static resource such as an image, your report can be updated with new information. This means that even if a hundred sites are using your report, you can update them all with a single change to your original report or data source.

Embedded Reports That Can Be Tracked   As you saw in the previous chapter, it is simple to add Google Analytics tracking to a report so that you can see usage. In the case of embedded reports, this means that you can see every time your report was viewed, *even if it is not embedded in your site!*

Now that we have gone through why you might want to embed a report, as well as the limitations of doing so, let's see how it's done:

1. Select a report for embedding. We'll embed the report for the previous example. Keep the limitations in mind when you select a report or design a report for embedding.

2. Select your report from the Data Studio home screen and switch to Edit mode.

3. Click the Share drop-down menu at the top-right side of the report header and select the Embed Report option. You will get a pop-up with a single check box for Enable Embedding.

4. Select Embed mode and sizing. The Embed mode you select will change the text that you will copy to use on the web page for embedding. The default, shown in Figure 9.66, is Embed Code. This produces the code in the box underneath the instructions.

Paste the following into your site. The Width and Height dimensions are based on your current height and width dimensions for the report. If you change these settings, the new sizes will be reflected in the embed code. Of course, you can easily see those settings in the code itself, and you can change them directly if desired. Here is the code from the box:

```
<iframe width="500" height="800"
src="https://datastudio.google.com/embed/reporting/
62bbe6c7-4ef7-4d66-bdba-8750a5943d84/page/ufo0"
frameborder="0" style="border:0" allowfullscreen></iframe>
```

Embed Report

☑ Enable embedding

◉ Embed Code   ○ Embed URL

Paste the following into your site:

```
<iframe width="500" height="800" src="https://datastudio.google.com/embed/reporting/62bbe6c7-
4ef7-4d66-bdba-8750a5943d84/page/ufo0" frameborder="0" style="border:0" allowfullscreen>
</iframe>
```

Width (px)   Height (px)
500   800

DONE   COPY TO CLIPBOARD

Figure 9.66: Getting the embed code

If you click the other option, Embed URL, you will be presented with this URL in the box to copy:

```
https://datastudio.google.com/embed/reporting/
62bbe6c7-4ef7-4d66-bdba-8750a5943d84/page/ufo0
```

How do you know which one of these to use? It depends on the web authoring system you are using. Some systems work with the full embed code. and some can work with just the embed URL. If you are uncertain which one you will be using, simply copy both to a text file!

Use the Copy To Clipboard button to copy your selection and paste it into a text file for later use. You can always return to this screen if you need the embed code again.

5. Check the sharing settings. This is the part that trips up many people, including Data Studio experts. Just because you have enabled embedding, it does not mean that you have enabled your report to be shared! If you embed the report in a web page without changing the sharing settings, it will look just fine to you because you are the owner of the report. When someone else views the web page, however, all they will see is a big hole in the page and a message telling them that they cannot see the report. Don't let this happen to you!

   a. Click the Share button in the header to open the sharing options pop-up.

   b. Click the Manage Access tab. The default sharing setting in the drop-down is Off - Only Specific People Can Access. Click the drop-down and change the setting to Anyone On The Internet Can Find And View.

   c. You have some control over what people can do with your report once they have access to it. The first option is used to limit sharing settings to the report owner if they are working with multiple editors. Usually, you leave this deselected. The other option, Disable Downloading, Printing And Copying For Viewers, allows you to lock up your report so that it cannot be copied and people cannot download the underlying data found in charts and tables. Keep in mind that disabling users from copying does not disable them from embedding your report in their site. It does protect you from them copying the layout of your report and using their own data sources. The sharing settings are shown in Figure 9.67.

Now we come down to inserting the code into your website. How this is done will depend on the system, but here we will cover two options: Google Sites and WordPress. *WordPress* is the most popular content management system on the web. We will use the Embed Code option for that system. Google Sites is very popular in education, and as a Google account owner you have access to that system as well.

We will look at the Google Sites system first, since everyone using Data Studio has access to this service by default.

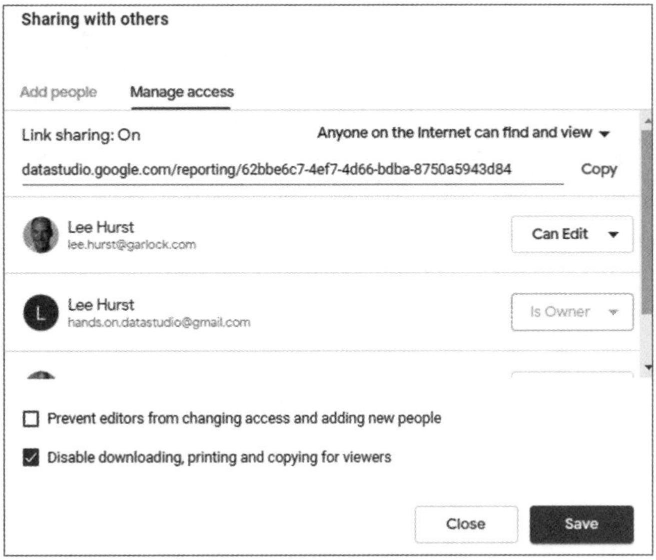

Figure 9.67: Set sharing options for embedding

TIP   Don't have access to a website? You do if you are using Data Studio, since it is also part of the standard G Suite series of applications. Google Sites is free and easy to use, but it's a limited website builder. Although it is beyond the scope of this book to teach you about Google Sites setup, it is easy to do. You can start by going to `https://sites.google.com/new`.

Embedding a Report in a Google Site

For this example, I created a simple test site for demonstration purposes. Figure 9.68 shows a page being edited.

I would like to embed the report in the space on the right side of the page. Here are the steps:

1. Double-click in the open space to open the circular editing menu with options for content that can be inserted into this space. Select the Embed option, as shown in Figure 9.69.

2. Although you have the option to embed either a URL or the embed code, Data Studio works best when you use the simple URL option. Paste your embed URL into the box, and you will see a small preview of the report, as shown in Figure 9.70. Click the Insert button to continue.

Figure 9.68: Google Site ready for report embedding

Figure 9.69: Selecting Embed from the circular editing menu

3. Stretch the embed window until the entire report is visible. With a longer report like the one we created, you may have to do this in several steps. When you have the entire report visible, the scroll bars will disappear. When you are done with your placement, click the Publish button at the top right to complete the page edits. You can then view your updated page by choosing Publish ⇨ View Published Site. Figure 9.71 shows the completed page with the report embedded.

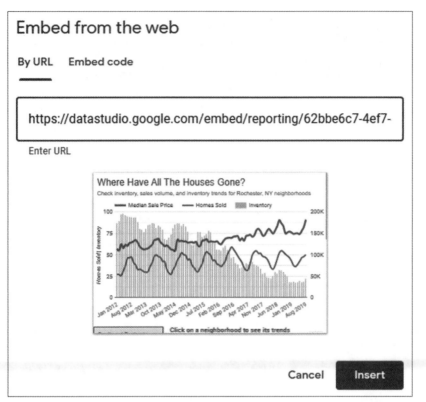

Figure 9.70: Using the embed URL for Google Sites

Embedding a Report in a WordPress Site

WordPress can be trickier to work with than Google Sites because of the multitude of plug-ins, builders, and themes that any particular site might use. Still, for most WordPress setup, the embed process is quite simple. For this example, I am using one of my personal sites that uses the Divi visual builder system. You should find that your WordPress embed process is similar.

1. Open the page for editing in your system.

2. Select the block or section in which you want to place the report.

3. Select a module or mode to insert HTML code. This is where different systems will vary. The idea here is that you must be able to enter some HTML code directly into the page. Figure 9.72 shows this process using the Divi editor. After selecting the section for the report, you insert a new Code module.

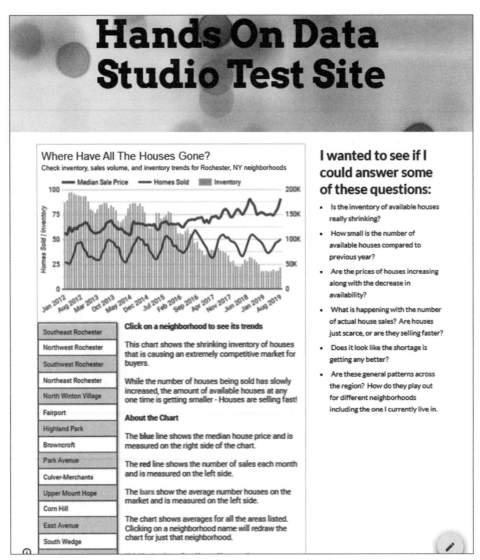

Figure 9.71: Completed Google Site with report embedded

4. Instead of using the embed URL, copy and paste the full embed code for the report into the Code box, as shown in Figure 9.73. Click Save Code and then save or update the page. If you view the page, you should now see the embedded report.

For this WordPress page, I used the same basic layout that we saw in the Google Sites example. Please bear in mind that we are keeping these pages as simple as possible for the sake of demonstration. How you design your pages is up to you. Figure 9.74 shows our WordPress page completed.

Figure 9.72: Selecting the area for the embed

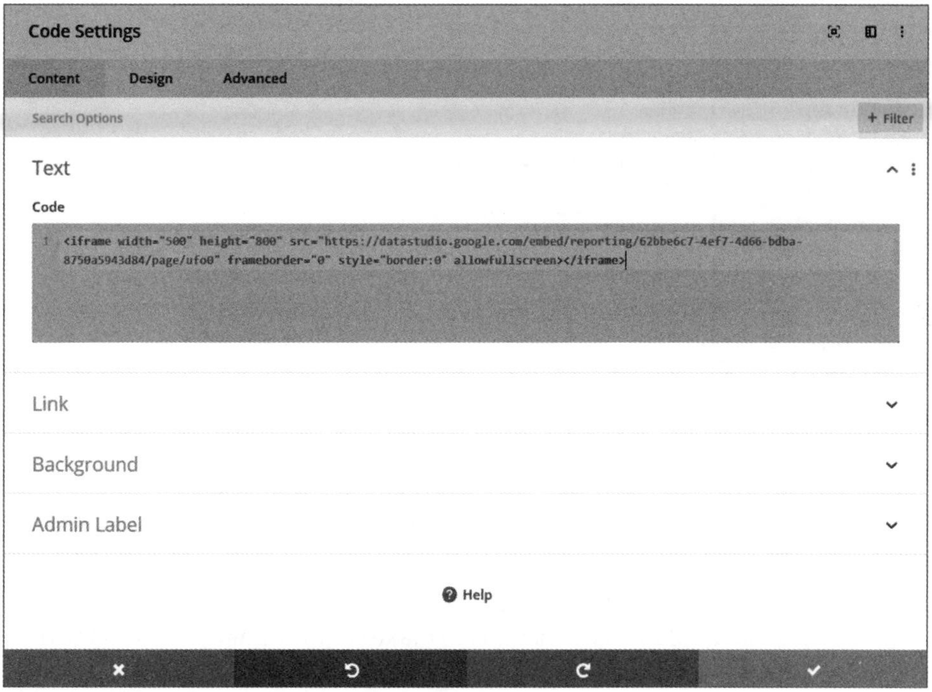

Figure 9.73: Pasting the embed code for the report

This completes the main Data Studio examples for this chapter. Before we leave the topic of working with public data, there is one common issue that we should address. This issue pertains to modifying your Google Sheets when the data comes in a summary format.

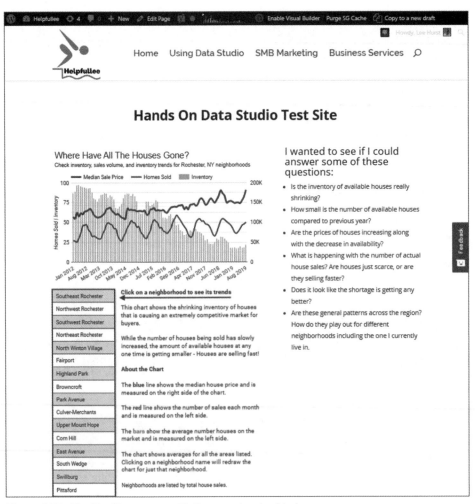

Figure 9.74: The WordPress page with the report embedded

Dealing with Pivoted Data

Often when looking for data, you will locate the ideal data set only to find that the configuration of the data makes it difficult to work with in Data Studio. As you saw in the last section, it is fairly simple to change the data format in a column, or to use the Find and Replace functions to make small changes to make the data more usable. A much harder problem to deal with is that of summarized data.

In our last example, our data was arranged in a way that made it easy for Data Studio to use. The format looks generally like Table 9.1, where I have put some example data.

Table 9.1: Neighborhood data table

DATE	DIMENSION 1	METRIC 1	METRIC 2	METRIC 3
4/30/2013	Fairport	$135,000.00	28	15
6/30/2013	Corn Hill	$132,000.00	12	10
8/31/2013	Park Avenue	$201,000.00	15	13

This is the simplest arrangement to work with. Adding extra dimensions or metrics columns does not change this general layout, and it is not a problem. This format is very "log-like," by which I mean it is likely that when the data was collected from each location, it was logged in and entered like a row on this table, where all the metrics were logged for a particular dimension value such as a neighborhood.

Although this data is convenient for machines to read, it is hard for people to extract any information out of it. Spreadsheet tools use pivot tables as a means of aggregating data in ways that the user can get some usable information. Applying a pivot to the data in our example would produce a table with the structure shown in Table 9.2.

Table 9.2: Neighborhood data table in pivot format

DATE	FAIRPORT	CORN HILL	PARK AVENUE
4/30/2013	$135,000	$135,000.00	$220,000
6/30/2013	$153,000	$132,000.00	$200,000
8/31/2013	$166,000	$201,000.00	$201,000

This allows a person to compare sales figures easily across neighborhoods for a particular date. There is nothing wrong with this per se, and as we saw earlier, Data Studio provides this functionality with the pivot table chart. Figure 9.75 shows the pivot table for this example made in Data Studio.

	Region / Median Sale Price		
Period End	Corn Hill	Fairport	Park Avenue
Aug 31, 2013	$126,000	$166,000	$201,000
Jun 30, 2013	$132,000	$153,000	$200,000
Apr 30, 2013	$144,000	$135,000	$220,000

Figure 9.75: Data Studio pivot table

Here's the problem: many data sets are not prepared in the log-style format—that is, they are available only in the pivoted format. This is an issue because it makes it impossible to generate a chart like the one in the last example from the data. This is because the dimensions columns have been removed and replaced with metric columns for each of the previously available dimension values.

I ran into this problem working with data provided by the City of London. They have a great data set, similar to the Redfin neighborhood example, which shows historical home prices by London neighborhood. The tables in the data set were already pivoted, however, so the neighborhood sales data for London had a column for each neighborhood.

If you have Microsoft Excel, you can reformat columns and rows using the Power Query functionality to "unpivot" such a table and create a new one in the log-style format. This is also possible in other data cleaning tools such as OpenRefine, but you must load the data into another tool for reformatting. Unfortunately, Google Sheets currently has no such unpivot functionality.

I decided to ask the community for help on Twitter, and I was directed to an elegant unpivot function that was found in the forums of Stack Overflow. I have not been able to thank the provider of this function directly, as the person is only identified as "The Master."

Here I will walk through the steps to add this unpivot function to your Google Sheet so that you can use it on your own data. I will be using the UK House Price Index data set, which can be found at `https://data.london.gov.uk/dataset/uk-house-price-index`. We will start with the data already converted to a Google Sheet located in a Google Drive folder.

When you first create this Google Sheet, you will find that row 2 has field ID codes that are not used in calculations. You should first remove this row as part of your data cleaning tasks.

1. Choose Tools ⇨ Script Editor to open a project with a default function, as shown in Figure 9.76.

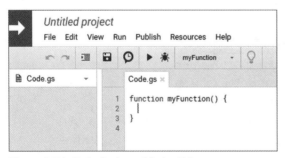

Figure 9.76: Default view of Script Editor

2. Rename the project at the top of the page to **Unpivot**. Open the drop-down menu next to the Code.gs function, select Rename, and change the name to **Unpivot**. Your screen should now look like Figure 9.77.

Figure 9.77: Setting names to Unpivot

3. Replace myFunction with the Unpivot function shown below.

```
/**
 * Unpivots the given data
 *
 * @return Unpivoted data from array
 * @param {A1:F4} arr 2D Input Array
 * @param {3} numCol Number of static columns on the left
 * @param {A1:C1} headers [optional] Custom headers for
output
 * @customfunction
 */
function unpivot(arr, numCol, headers) {
  var out = arr.reduce(function(acc, row) {
    var left = row.splice(0, numCol); //static columns on
left
    row.forEach(function(col, i) {
      acc.push(left.concat([acc[0][i + numCol], col]));
//concat left and unpivoted right and push as new array to
accumulator
    });
    return acc;
  }, arr.splice(0, 1));//headers in arr as initial value
  headers ? out.splice(0, 1, headers[0]) : null; //use
custom headers, if present.
  return out;
}
```

The function code is also shown in Figure 9.78. After replacing myFunction with the Unpivot code, save the file to continue.

```
* Unpivot.gs ×

/**
 * Unpivots the given data
 *
 * @return Unpivoted data from array
 * @param {A1:F4} arr 2D Input Array
 * @param {3} numCol Number of static columns on the left
 * @param {A1:C1} headers [optional] Custom headers for output
 * @customfunction
 */
function unpivot(arr, numCol, headers) {
  var out = arr.reduce(function(acc, row) {
    var left = row.splice(0, numCol); //static columns on left
    row.forEach(function(col, i) {
    //concat left and unpivoted right and push as new array to accumulator|
      acc.push(left.concat([acc[0][i + numCol], col]));
    });
    return acc;
  }, arr.splice(0, 1));//headers in arr as initial value
  headers ? out.splice(0, 1, headers[0]) : null; //use custom headers, if present.
  return out;
}
```

Figure 9.78: Entering the Unpivot function

4. Close the Script Editor tab and return to the spreadsheet. Create a new tab on the spreadsheet for your Unpivot table, and for the tab name, type **Average Price DS**.

5. Enter the Unpivot function in cell A1 of the new Sheet. In this case, we will be unpivoting the columns found in the Average Price worksheet and loading the unpivoted table into Average Price DS. Figure 9.79 shows the format of the Average Price worksheet.

		A	B	C	D	E	F	G	H
		Date	City of London	Barking & Dagenham m	Barnet	Bexley	Brent	Bromley	Camden
	2	1/1/1995	91,449	50,460	93,285	64,958	71,307	81,671	120,93
	3	2/1/1995	82,203	51,086	93,190	64,788	72,022	81,658	119,50
	4	3/1/1995	79,121	51,269	92,248	64,367	72,016	81,449	120,28
	5	4/1/1995	77,101	53,134	90,763	64,278	72,966	81,124	120,09
	6	5/1/1995	84,409	53,042	90,258	63,997	73,704	81,543	119,92

UK House price index Sheet ☆ ▮
File Edit View Insert Format Data Tools Add-ons Help   Last edit was made 55 min

100% ▾ $ % .0 .00 123▾   Arial   ▾   10   ▾   B I S A

fx | Date

+ ≡   Metadata ▾   By type ▾   Average price ▾   Average Price DS ▾

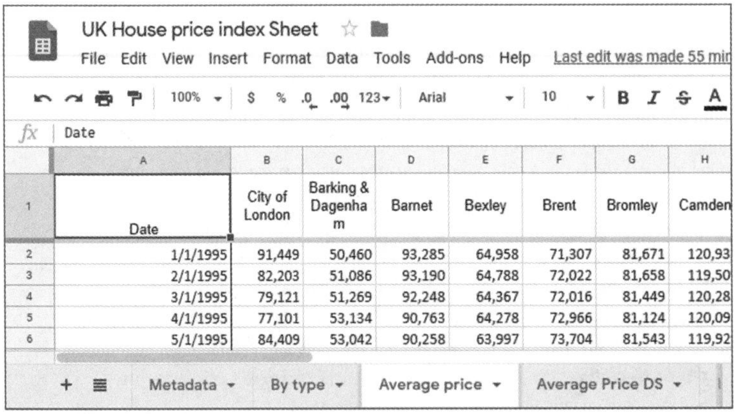

Figure 9.79: Original pivot sheet layout

Enter the following formula into the first cell of the Average Price DS worksheet:

```
=unpivot('Average price'!A:AH,1,{"Date","Area","Price"})
```

This function will run and load the unpivoted table into the blank work-sheet. Your resulting table should now look like the one in Figure 9.80.

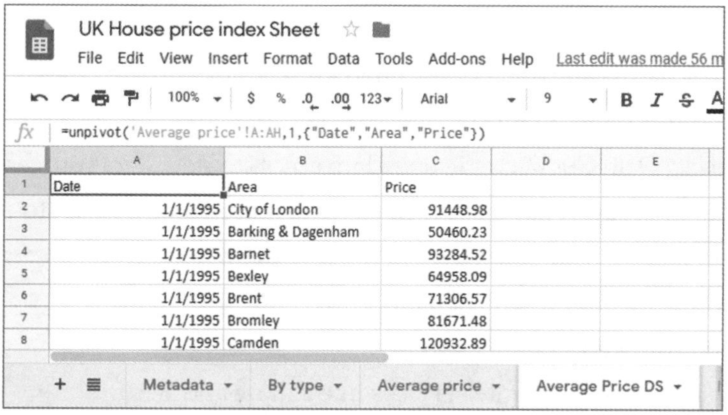

Figure 9.80: Unpivot function result

The Unpivot function turned a pivot table with 34 columns and 259 rows into a new log-style table with 3 columns and 32,935 rows! You can now connect to and use this table in your report.

Now that you have seen several publicly accessible data sources and how to use them, our examples for this chapter are complete.

NOTE   As mentioned in Chapter 1, "Data Studio and the Data Citizen," Data Studio is constantly being developed. When I was writing this chapter, Data Studio intro-duced a new feature called *optional metrics*. You may see it in some of the Data tab images for our chart setups. Using this feature, you may be able to take advantage of the pivot-style layout. It provides a drop-down menu on a chart, where you can select metrics that the user can choose, similar to a filter control for dimension values.

Optional metrics will let the user compare things like different neighborhood sales histories on the same chart. While you can do this to a certain degree with a breakdown dimension and a filter control, the optional metrics will give the user better control over what they see on a chart if the option is enabled and configured.

As of this writing, this new feature was purposely left out because there were some bugs in the implementation and it could not be demonstrated with confidence.

Summary

The amount of data that is available for anyone to use is growing daily. Data sets for your interest area may exist, but they may be difficult to locate. We covered several ways to find interesting data sets, and we used some of the larger services to find different ways to access that data for reporting. Finally, we covered some ways to reformat data that you may find into a more usable format. Here are some of the areas that we covered in this chapter:

- Google Dataset Search and how to use it
- The Kaggle service and how to connect to data sets stored there
- Setting up and using pivot tables
- Using the Extract Data Connector to speed up access to slow data sources
- The Makeover Monday visualization challenge and how to participate
- Connecting to data sets on data.world and using their connectors
- Setting up and using a 100% stacked bar chart
- Setting up and using a treemap chart
- Finding data sets from corporate services like Zillow and Redfin
- Designing a report for embedding
- Limitations and features of embedding reports in web pages
- Setting up and using combo charts
- Embedding reports in popular website systems
- Unpivoting data in Google Sheets

I hope that this tour of publicly accessible data encourages you to do your own data analysis in the areas that interest you—for your own pleasure and the betterment of your community.

CHAPTER 10

Where Do You Go from Here?

In this final chapter, we'll cover possible next steps in your journey and development. We'll look at some of the more advanced features of Data Studio, from data handling to visualizations to the wild areas in development. The directions you pursue are up to you.

Helping Your Audience See the Light

When you build reports and applications for your own use, you'll have little need for additional information on the screen. At this point, you already know what to look for in your reports. This is not the case for other people using or interacting with your Data Studio applications.

It is not often that our visualizations will speak clearly for themselves. If you are not available to explain the significance of what the user is seeing, your insights can easily get lost on the audience that you seek to inform.

I've divided the use of additional information into two broad types: annotations and instructions. *Annotations* are used to give context and point to the insights that you are trying to highlight. Instructions help users of your application apply the interactive features to find insights of their own.

First, we'll take a look at ways to annotate your charts.

Annotation Ideas for Static Reports

If you are producing a static report—for example, one without interactive date settings that shows a snapshot of what you want to communicate—you have many options for annotation. You can use graphic elements and text to guide the user to the parts of the report on which you would like them to focus. Some of them can also be used with interactive reports, but you need to take care if the user is able to change time ranges, because your charts will change but the graphic elements will not update their locations. Let's look at some elements you can use for this kind of annotation.

Annotating a Time-Series Chart

Back in Chapter 6, "Using Google Search Console for Audience Insights," we looked at reporting from Google Search Console. In one section, I focused on the mystery of a very large spike in impressions for my website, and we looked at the ways to investigate such anomalies. While that made a good story, all of the explanation for the spike was missing from the report we were using!

In this example, I have copied the report from Chapter 6 and removed the Date Range control, making the report static. Figure 10.1 shows an annotation added directly to the time-series chart.

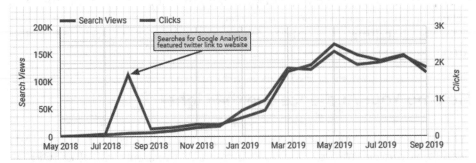

Figure 10.1: Explaining anomalies in the time-series chart

The viewer of this report can now clearly see the reason for the spike in search views. This annotation was done fairly simply using the Line tool to draw an arrow and a text box. Following are the modifications to the text box that I used to get the effect shown in Figure 10.1:

1. Click and drag a text box to the canvas and fill it with text. The Text Properties panel appears on the right side of the screen.

2. Set the font size to 10px, and change the text alignment to centered.

3. In the Background and Border settings, use the paint bucket drop-down to select the background color. Use the pencil drop-down to select the outline color.

4. The Padding settings are used to fine-tune the appearance of your text. In this case, we set the line height to 8px, the left and right padding to 0px, and the top padding to 4px.

This kind of annotation is fairly easy to create and is very flexible. The arrow element can be connected to the text box so that if the box is dragged, the arrow will stretch to point to the same location.

Another common way to highlight sections of a chart and provide additional information uses semitransparent shading to bring attention to specific time periods. We'll use some shading and text to provide an explanation for the steep increase in search views and clicks shown on the chart.

Figure 10.2 shows the use of shading and text to help the user understand the impact that publishing blog posts has on search views and clicks for the website. Here we use a light gray semitransparent rectangle element to show periods of publishing and lack of publishing.

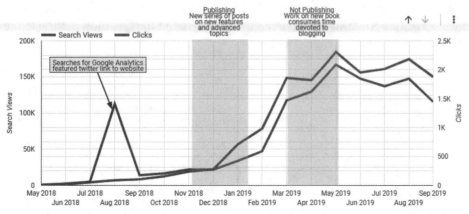

Figure 10.2: Using shading and text for annotation

Here are the instructions for the rectangle box that I used to get the effect shown in Figure 10.2:

1. Create a new rectangle by selecting the rectangle icon from the toolbar and clicking and dragging to the canvas.

2. By default, rectangles are the color dictated by the theme, and the default theme makes these a bright blue color. In the Rectangle Properties panel, use the paint bucket drop-down to set the color to a medium gray. Click the droplet icon to change the transparency level from 100% to 30%.

3. Size and position the rectangle box.

4. Add a descriptive text box above the rectangle.

So far, the annotations that we have provided have been fairly standard. Next we'll look at some that are more unique to the Data Studio platform.

Adding Descriptive Text

First, it is often quite useful to have a longer section of text to provide more information to the user and help make the report stand on its own so that the user does not have to refer to external descriptions.

We have used text boxes already, and it is easy to see how they can be extended into longer sections of text. Data Studio has one feature for text boxes not found on many other platforms. Text boxes include the option to make the text scrollable. This allows you to add as much descriptive text to the report as you need without having to worry about running out of space.

To demonstrate this feature, I have copied some text from Chapter 6 and pasted it into a text box on the report. To make the text scrollable, locate the Overflow settings in the Text Properties panel and change the setting from Overflow to Hidden. The Hidden setting hides the text outside the frame of the text box until the user scrolls down, as shown in Figure 10.3. Leaving the Overflow setting to the default would cover the chart below it.

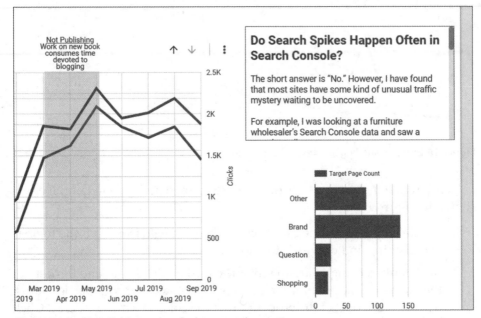

Figure 10.3: A scrollable text box for long text descriptions

If you are using a scrollable text box, keep in mind that the user has only a small window to view the text, so you may want to reformat the text for easier reading.

Embedding Other Elements

Data Studio has some robust embedding features that allow you to embed other types of content and media into your report. In Chapter 7, "Viewing Local Organization Data from Google My Business," we used the embed feature to add a Google Form to the Dog Walking report so that we could add our own data.

Although you can embed most web content that is available to share in this way, you may only use a URL to embed the content; you do not have the ability to use HTML code for this feature. Most Google G Suites products can be embedded in your report, including Sheets, Slides, and Docs.

You can also embed video content, such as YouTube videos, directly in the report. This feature greatly extends your ability to tell a story about the data and further help your audience.

To embed external content in your report, follow these steps:

1. Many types of content allow sharing. Remember, though, that you want to use a regular URL—not embed HTML code. In the case of YouTube videos, click the Share button and copy the URL instead of using the Embed option.

2. While you are in Edit mode in your report, click the Embed icon and then click and drag the Embed box onto the canvas as you do for other elements.

3. On the Data tab of the URL Embed Properties, paste your URL into the External Content URL field. Figure 10.4 shows a YouTube video being embedded into the report.

Keep in mind that there are limitations to embedding. If you are embedding your report into a web page, content embedded in that report may not be visible. In addition, make sure that your embeds of Google Drive content have the correct sharing options set. Again, it's always a good idea to test your report with the same permissions your audience has to check what they will be seeing!

Annotation Ideas for Interactive Reports

When your report is static, you have all kinds of options for annotation. This changes a bit when your report is dynamic and interactive. In some cases, you may want to add information about particular dates or occurrences that will show up directly on a time-series chart.

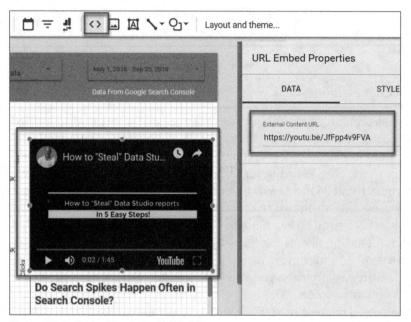

Figure 10.4: Embedding a YouTube video

Although Data Studio has not provided a direct way to do this, some hacks allow you to show some information on charts and as dynamic text. A bit later in the "Data Blending" section, you'll see another way to do this. For now, however, we'll concentrate on the simpler solutions in this section.

For the following example, we'll add two fields that will provide additional information about when specific pages were published on my website. We have covered field creation in previous sections, so I'll simply show the specifications here. First, we start with the Blog Post field that will be used as a metric on the charts:

```
Field Name: Blog Post
Formula:
CASE
   WHEN Date = "20180824" THEN 1
   WHEN Date = "20181012" THEN 1
   WHEN Date = "20181229" THEN 1
   WHEN Date = "20181104" THEN 1
   WHEN Date = "20190116" THEN 1
   WHEN Date = "20190211" THEN 1
   ELSE 0
END
```

The field definition for Blog Post creates a new metric that registers a value of 1 for each of the dates listed. You can also create one-off date metrics this way by creating a field with only one date in the CASE statement. This clever workaround was documented by Nick Hood at Data Runs Deep in Australia. You can read more about it here:

```
https://datarunsdeep.com.au/blog/simple-annotations-google-data-
studio-time-series-charts
```

Once the Blog Post metric is defined, you can use it in your time-series charts. It's not a perfect solution, because you'll need to use the right-side metric to scale the markers correctly, and this creates a scale on the chart that is hard to explain to the user. Although you can remove the scales on the y-axis of the chart, there is no control to remove only the right-side y-axis. You can work around this by placing a rectangle element over the right-side y-axis to hide it from the user, as shown in Figure 10.5. I intentionally made this rectangle semitransparent so that you can see the placement.

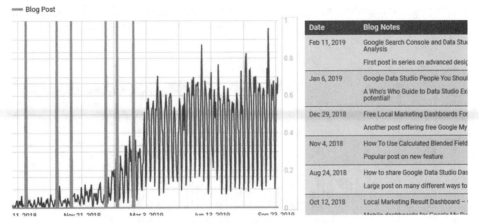

Figure 10.5: Dynamic annotation fields in a chart and table

Now we'll define a Blog Notes field that will be used as a dimension. The formula code is very similar in form to the Blog Post field.

```
Field Name: Blog Notes
Formula:
CASE
  WHEN Date = "20180824" THEN "How to share Google Data Studio
Dashboards and Reports \n\n Large post on many different ways to share"
  WHEN Date = "20181012" THEN "Local Marketing Result Dashboard - GMB
Data Studio Example \n \n Mobile dashboards for Google My Business"
  WHEN Date = "20181104" THEN "How To Use Calculated Blended Fields In
Data Studio \n\n Popular post on new feature"
  WHEN Date = "20181229" THEN "Free Local Marketing Dashboards For Small
Business  \n\n Another post offering free Google My Business dashboards"
  WHEN Date = "20190106" THEN "Google Data Studio People You Should
Know \n\n A Who's Who Guide to Data Studio Experts - lots of sharing
potential! "
```

```
  WHEN Date = "20190211" THEN "Google Search Console and Data Studio for
SEO Questions Analysis \n\n First post in series on advanced design and
analysis"
  ELSE ""
END
```

In the Blog Notes field, we provide a text description for each date. Note the use of \n\n in the quoted text. \n is a special character combination that Data Studio will interpret as a request to add a line break to the text as it displays in tables. Using \n\n creates a blank line, and it can help with formatting the text for easier reading.

Now that we have our annotation fields set up, let's look at how they can be used. Figure 10.5 shows the time-series chart from our Chapter 6 example, and it has an added table to show the blog notes.

Both the chart and table components are connected to the Date Range control for the page. If the date range is changed to show year-to-date, the table and chart update in the way that you would expect, as shown in Figure 10.6.

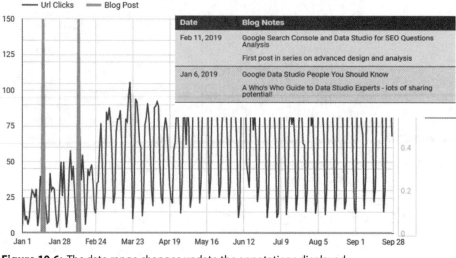

Figure 10.6: The date range changes update the annotations displayed.

Here are the setup details for the time-series chart:

1. Click and drag a time-series chart to the canvas and position it.

2. Configure the Data tab for the chart. In this case, we are using Date for the dimension. We set URL Clicks and Blog Post as the Metric fields.

3. Configure the Style tab for the chart. Locate Series #2, which represents the Blog Post field, and set Axis to Right.

The Blog Notes table is fairly simple, but to get it to display as shown, you must apply a filter to the table. This filter removes rows where the Blog Notes field is blank. Here is the table and filter setup:

1. Click and drag the table chart from the Add A Chart drop-down and position it on the canvas.

2. Configure the Data tab for the table. Set the Dimension fields to Date and Blog Notes. Remove any Metric fields and set the Sort field to Date.

3. While still on the Data tab, select Add A Filter in the Filter section to open the filter definition screen. Set the name to **Blog Notes Filter** and the field Exclude Blog Notes Equal to (=). By leaving the Value field blank, this filter will exclude all blank blog notes entries from the table.

4. Configure the Style tab. You can set your table colors to those of your choosing or leave them alone. I like using alternating colors because I think it makes the rows easier to differentiate. Deselect Row Numbers and Show Pagination, and select Wrap Text in the Table Body section.

Providing Detailed Instructions for Users

Currently, Data Studio does not provide tooltip-like pop-ups for standard graphic elements or filter controls. This is too bad, because that method is fairly universal and saves space on the page. Of course, even if tooltips were available, they could go only so far in guiding a user through the use of combinations of filters and suggestions for what to look for in the visualizations.

I developed some complicated schemes to show pop-ups with helpful messages, but they were difficult to develop and maintain. They also required covering some parts of the report with invisible components that blocked user interaction with the elements they covered. Fortunately, the Data Studio community has developed several good alternatives for this need that are much easier to implement than mine.

This section shows an example of a report that simulates instruction layers added to the Search Console example report. To make the faux layering work, we'll be employing the same methods that we used in Chapter 7 when we created a mobile app report with buttons to move from one page to another.

The most efficient method for implementing this type of layering is to duplicate the main report page, create separate layer pages, and then create the links on the report page that will trigger the instruction layers to appear. We'll follow that order here. We start off with a copy of our Chapter 6 example report.

1. After copying the report, switch to Edit mode and rename the report. Next, create a duplicate of the report page by choosing Page ➪ Duplicate Page. You now have a duplicate of the main report page. We'll use this page as the instruction layer.

2. First, we create a single instruction box so that we can work on the style that will be used on all the other boxes. After creating the first one, we copy and modify it so that all the boxes have a consistent style. Figure 10.7 shows the completed layer page that we'll use for displaying the instructions.

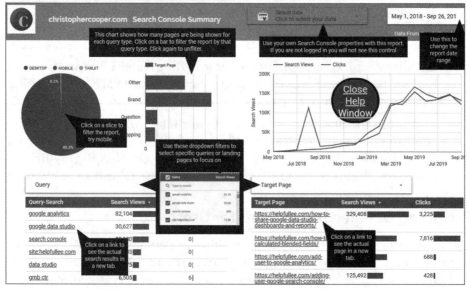

Figure 10.7: Completed instruction layer page

To make the black text box, we create a simple text box and set the background to black and the text to white. The pointer part of the text box is just that—we use the Line tool to create a short, wide arrow shape; color it to black to match the text box; and position it. This makes a very flexible callout box! Figure 10.8 shows a close-up of the callout arrow connected to the box.

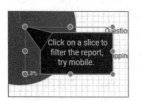

Figure 10.8: Constructing the callout box

In the Line Properties for the arrow, set the line color to black and the width to 22. We set the line end to Pointer and specified a custom size of 33.

3. Copy the first box and arrow and then modify the text and position to create the other callout boxes. In the example, you can see a number of different-sized boxes and arrow directions. These are all copies of the original box resized, with the arrow shifted and rotated as needed.

4. Create the return link, the large red button sitting over the time-series chart. Follow the instructions from Chapter 7:

   a. Create a text box, and change the corner rounding in the Properties settings.

   b. Modify the background, text, and outline colors.

   c. Highlight the text and click the link button. Click in the link field and select the page "First" to select the main report page.

For this example, we'll create another page for a detailed description explaining the big traffic anomaly seen in August 2018 for search views. As before, we begin by returning to the main report page in Edit mode.

1. Create a duplicate of the report page by choosing Page ➪ Duplicate Page. You now have a duplicate of the main report page. We'll use this page as the detail description layer. Figure 10.9 shows the newly completed detail page.

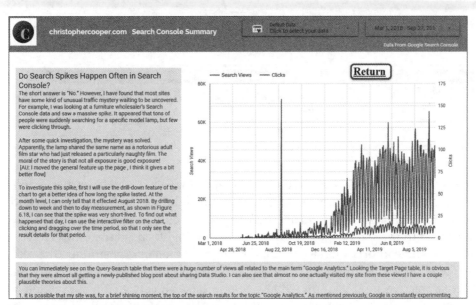

Figure 10.9: Completed detail layer page

2. We want only the main time-series chart, so select and delete all the other elements and chart components on the page.

3. Stretch the chart and change it to view the time period by days instead of months in order to make the spike in search views a bit more dramatic. Then, create the text box on the left and the one under the chart. For my example, I copied text from Chapter 6 explaining the cause for the spike. I opted for a different background color for the text boxes to create a slightly different style from the main page.

4. As in the previous layer example, create a text box with rounded edges and add a link that goes back to the first page of the report.

Now it's time to turn our attention back to the main report page. Figure 10.10 shows the completed page with information icons.

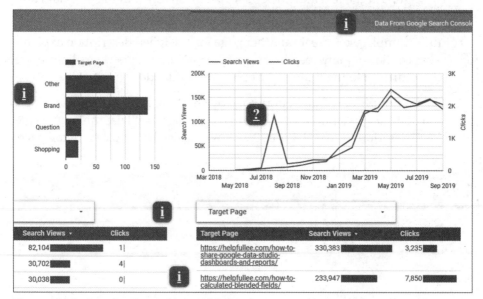

Figure 10.10: Completed main page with link icons

I added one question icon on the chart that links to the detail layer discussion. To create these icons, I created text boxes, changed the font style and size, and then changed the background and outline properties. Finally, I linked the single character in the text box to the other pages. Again, I focused my efforts in creating a single information icon first, and then I copied and positioned the rest.

These icons are simple, and they get the job done, but I admit they are not the most attractive. Find your own that suit your taste and style. You are invited to check out the resources for this chapter to explore some links with more ideas on creating information links and annotations. You can find the chapter links on the Resources page at www.wiley.com/go/handsondatastudio.

Next we'll look at a way to add charts to your reports that are not included in the standard Data Studio set of charts.

Community Visualizations

Data Studio is developing new features at a furious pace. During the writing of this book, a new visualization, the *treemap*, was added to the standard list of charts, and several charts had their capabilities enhanced. Although the standard charts cover a lot of possibilities, they by no means cover all the possibilities for expressing data in visual ways!

To solve the desire for different chart types, Data Studio built in the ability to add external visualizations to your reports. The Community Visualizations option gives you access to other widgets created by the developer community. Some of these are developed internally at Google, and some are developed by external developers.

I've had the opportunity to try several recently developed visualizations, but most have not yet been added to the official gallery for general public use. There is currently a push by Google to encourage more development and submission of visualizations, so we can expect to see more in the future.

In this section, I'll walk you through adding a community visualization to a report. We'll begin with a blank report started with a data source. In this case, we'll use the UFO reports data source that we used in Chapter 8, "Getting Personal." To begin, we create a pie chart to show the relative amounts of reported UFO shapes.

1. Open the data source connected to the report for editing. To do so, click the existing pie chart while in Edit mode, which shows the data source connected to it at the top of the Data tab. Clicking the pencil icon opens the data source to the Fields screen.

2. To use community visualizations, an owner of the data source must change the setting. After access has been turned on, other editors using the data source can also use the community visualizations. You'll find the setting at the top of the Fields panel, as shown in Figure 10.11. Once you have turned on the access setting, click the Done button to return to the canvas.

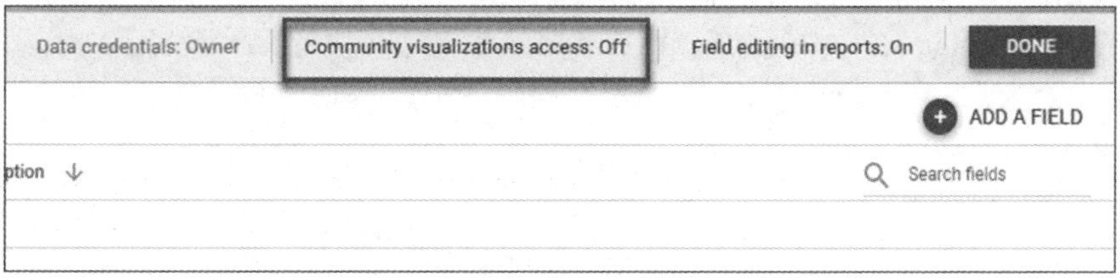

Figure 10.11: Setting community visualization access

3. Click the Community Visualizations icon on the toolbar. A menu of featured visualizations and a form to add a specific visualization by ID appear. Select the Sunburst chart by Yulan Lin, as shown in Figure 10.12.

Figure 10.12: Selecting a community visualization chart

4. Configure the Data tab for the chart. The Sunburst chart is similar to the pie chart, except it will handle multiple dimensions as well as a metric. Set Dimensions to Month and Shape and set the metric to count the number of comments.

5. Configure the Style tab for the chart. In my case, I changed the line color to black, but you can change to a limited number of preset color schemes.

The final chart appears next to the standard pie chart. The Sunburst chart shows the month of the year and the count of UFO shapes when you hover your mouse over a segment, as shown in Figure 10.13.

Keep your eyes open for community visualization additions and improvements in the near future. I've seen several terrific animated visualizations that may soon be available through this service. Animated charts will add entire new dimensions to your visualizations. Of course, in addition to using community visualizations, you can create and share your own. To find out about the latest advances in this area and learn more about development, visit `https://developers` `.google.com/datastudio/visualization`.

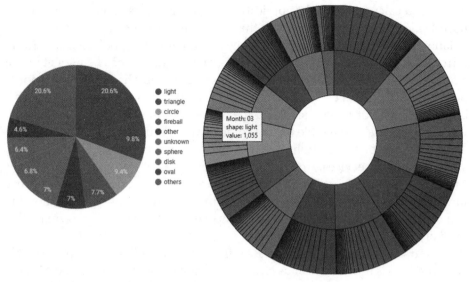

Figure 10.13: Completed Sunburst chart

Data Studio as an Application Development Platform

In this section, we'll take a brief look at a different way of using Data Studio. I will make the case that Data Studio is a good, although limited, platform for building web applications. True, the tool was designed primarily for data visualization, but that description could cover a lot of different uses depending on how broadly you use the terms *data* and *visualization*.

The largest area of potential is in the development and distribution of data widgets. These are limited-scope, embeddable applications that depend on a simple data source. The following is a very modest example.

Consider the simple web application, built with Data Studio, shown in Figure 10.14. Although my graphic design friends might find this a bit basic, it is a fully functioning application, ready to be embedded in a web page.

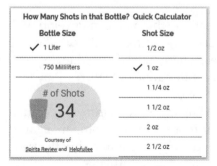

Figure 10.14: A basic data widget

This is a calculator type of application; the user selects some options, and a useful calculation is performed. In this case, it is actually the illusion of a calculation that is happening. This widget was created long before Data Studio introduced calculated fields. So, how is the calculation done? The widget uses a simple three-column Google Sheets table as its data set. The columns are Bottle Size, Shot Size, and # of Shots. The rows in the table consist of every possible combination of bottle, shot size, and the correct number of shots. The "calculation" is the value in the table for the combination of filter values.

Calculator-type applications like this one are common on the web. They provide all kinds of services, from estimating how much it will cost to repair your car to life insurance costs to how much a nanny will cost per week. Not every kind of calculator can be easily replicated in Data Studio, of course, but many can be. The ability to use calculated fields extends the capability to create this kind of application much further.

Of course, my programmer friends will point out that listing all the possible combinations is nowhere near as efficient as figuring out a formula and actually making a calculation. They would be right, but does it really matter? Table rows are cheap, and in the case of Google Sheets and some other data sources, they are actually free! Who cares if you have to use 10 or 10,000 rows in a spreadsheet? The result is the same.

There are some limitations for creating this kind of lookup calculation, of course. As you add options, the number of possible combinations that you would have to list can increase dramatically. In situations where you can select only one item in each dimension, you can figure out how many rows you would need by multiplying the number of options for each dimension together.

In this example, I had two bottle sizes and six shot glass sizes, so I needed only 12 rows to cover all the combinations.

The major limitation for using Data Studio for a calculator, however, is the lack of direct user input. As of this writing, there is no way for users to put in their own value, like the cost of the bottle, and have Data Studio calculate how much a shot will cost. Still, this leaves you with a wide range of possibilities with which to work.

There are two other major types of applications that you can develop with Data Studio. First, you can create selectors. *Selectors* are found all over the web also. You can find them in most online stores, where they are used to help you narrow down product selections based on a combination of features. Any long list with several features is fair game for a selector.

Another common type of application is a comparator. A *comparator* is similar to a basic selector, but the user selects two or more things to compare against each other. Again, products are a primary target for comparators, but there are many other applications, such as comparing statistics for athletes.

In addition to these major application types, there are others that are less common. I once created an adventure game using Data Studio. It was not great, I admit, but the idea can be used for more practical uses like guided selling applications or simple diagnostic applications.

Limitations of Data Studio Widgets

Before we look at the reasons why you might want to use it, let's look at more limitations of using Data Studio for application development.

There is no way to make use of user input, except in search boxes.   This is the main issue listed in the previous section. The user has options to make selections only.

You are limited to embedding your application in web pages or running them in the Data Studio interface.   Unlike when we're developing a JavaScript application, we don't have the option to seamlessly make the application part of the page. Data Studio embeds may take a bit of time to load, so they may not show up immediately on the page.

You cannot measure activity inside a Data Studio report.   There is no simple way to determine how many times a user clicked a particular selection or used a certain filter.

You cannot see elements that are embedded in a Data Studio report that is itself embedded in a web page.   For instance, if you have a video that is embedded in the report, the video will not show in the report if it is embedded in a page.

Once you embed a widget in a web page, there is no way to stop someone else from doing the same.   When you embed a widget in a page, there is no simple way to hide the code used to embed it. This is not unique to Data Studio; it is just the way embedding works.

You'll be limited to the controls available in Data Studio.   Some components, like the filter controls, may not be optimal for every application. Although you have a lot of latitude for design, there are limitations to how much control you have over some components' size and design.

The Case for Embedded Data Studio Widgets

Even with those limitations, I am very optimistic about using Data Studio for developing applications. Here are the reasons why:

Valuable Content for Websites   Infographics cost hundreds to thousands of dollars to develop, but organizations are willing to pay this much because infographics provide lasting value. What is better than an infographic?

Well, an interactive infographic! It is hard to overstate the value of applications like product selectors, interactive guides, and updating progress charts. Enabling your viewers to interact with widgets increases viewers' engagement and time spent on a website.

Speed and Cost of Development   Custom application development is not in the budget for most small organizations, and the effort to learn how to program is just not possible for most small business owners. The shots calculator took very little time to design and develop. It could have been created with a technology like JavaScript, but doing so would involve custom development that would take much longer and require hiring a developer. Such custom applications may be too much for a small business or organization to develop.

Ease of Modification   Developers of custom applications are often not available when you want updates. With Data Studio, you don't need special programming skills to update or modify the layout. For most applications, there is no need for any special database skills, such as SQL knowledge, to maintain or update the data either.

Sharing of Editing Responsibilities   You can share your application with a developer without exposing your actual data sources or your content management system, or you can share the data-updating responsibility without giving access to the application.

Ease of Maintenance   Many application technologies are "free" but require hosting, maintenance, and security updates. Plug-ins for popular content management systems like WordPress must constantly be updated to keep ahead of security requirements. With Data Studio, updates are automatic and there is no hosting requirement!

Scalability   This is where I think things get really interesting! Sure, the shots calculator is cute, but imagine if 1,000 different sites embedded it on their pages. If a change is made by the owner, all of those instances are *updated instantly*! The widget creator doesn't have to worry about distribution or updating all those users.

Ease of Customization   Let's say that one of those 1,000 sites doesn't want the standard shots calculator—they want one with their logo on the shot glass. How long do you think it would take to simply copy the report, paste the image on the shot glass, and give them the new URL for embedding? All of the instances are still running on the same data sources, so the requirements for customization are minimal.

Usage Information   In Chapter 8, you saw how your reports can be connected to Google Analytics so that you can see actual audience usage. This is true for embedded widgets as well. So, this means that if you had 1,000 sites embed your widget, you would get visibility to their use on all 1,000 sites! You won't get information about the site in which the widget is embedded, other than the name of the site, but you'll get usage information about how many visits each instance of your widget gets, along with some of the other metrics that Google Analytics provides.

Data Studio may not be the right tool to use in some cases, but there are many cases where it can be used successfully. Data Studio can provide your audience with some utility while you are creating an integrated application for your site.

Widgets-in-the-Wild

The shots calculator example is more than a demo created for this book—it lives on a website that features liquor reviews, on a page that discusses the topic of bottle and shot glass size. You may not think this little widget would make much of a difference, but people spend 218 percent more time on this page than the site average.

On the less entertaining side of things, let's talk about fluid sealing for rotating shaft machinery. If you need a bearing isolator with specific properties, you may find what you need on the page shown in Figure 10.15.

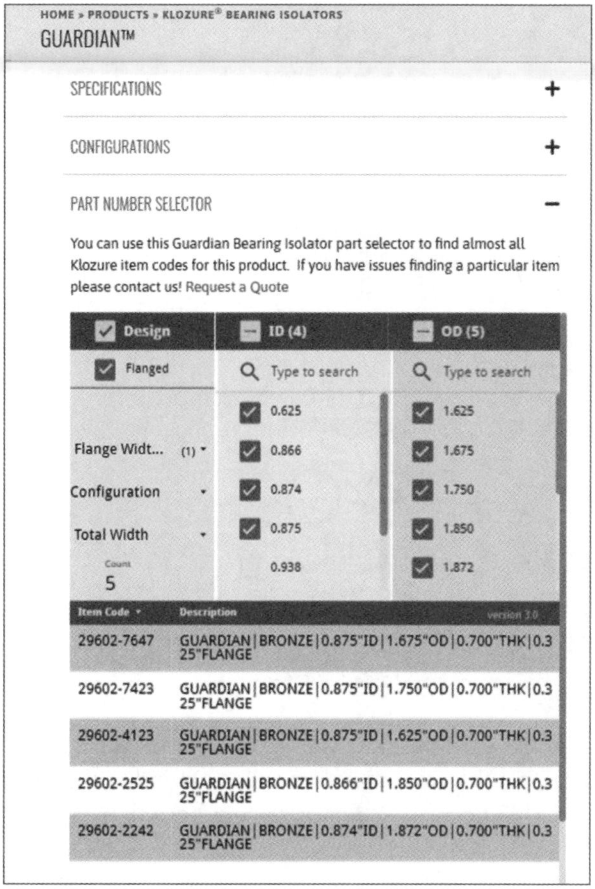

Figure 10.15: A Data Studio part finder

This simple product selector fits snugly in the page, where it helps the audience find the right product to order out of more than 2,500 options. This model works well on manufacturing sites where providing a full store-type experience is not appropriate or is cost prohibitive but product selection is needed.

As noted earlier, one of the strengths of Data Studio for widget development is the ability to scale distribution. Although this widget lives on the manufacturer's site, they could offer this widget to their distributors, providing the same product selection on their sites, quality-controlled and updated by the manufacturer, with no additional development cost or maintenance overhead.

The last example of widgets-in-the-wild comes from a site devoted to mountain bikes. The site, Bike Chaos (www.bikechaos.com), uses Data Studio embedded reports extensively. Figure 10.16 shows a bike comparison page that uses three separate reports to compare more than 700 different bikes side by side.

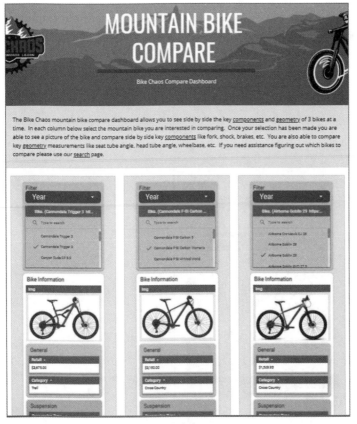

Figure 10.16: Comparing mountain bikes

In addition to comparisons, the site has extensive searches provided through Data Studio embedding. Figure 10.17 shows a selector page where you can sort through the extensive collection using the filters, which includes price ranges. Clicking a bike image here takes you directly to the manufacturer's page for that model.

Figure 10.17: Finding the right mountain bike

Now that you have some ideas for applications, we can turn our attention to using bigger data sources and data storage options, as well as how you can combine different data sources in your reports through data blending.

Exotic Ingredients and Your Pantry

In this section, we'll explore different directions you might take regarding data sources and storing your data sets. The first area to examine will help you expand what you can do with the data sources to which you already have access.

Data Blending

Connecting data sources together is a major capability of Data Studio you should know about and consider using if you delve into more advanced areas of analysis and reporting. We'll cover it here for the sake of completeness.

Data Studio enthusiasts reading this book will probably wonder why I left this subject out of other sections and only briefly cover it near the end of this book. The main reason for this is that data blending is, well, tricky!

First, let's examine why you might want to join two sets of data together:

Combining Metrics from Different Sources to Total Them   A common issue in the world of Google Analytics is that a person may have more than one website or multiple analytics profiles that they want to show totaled.

Combining Data from the Same Data Source   The most common case here is comparing the same data over two date ranges, using a chart to show the difference in the value between the two periods. Although the compare time period function on most charts lets you do this to a certain extent, it does not let you store the differences in a separate field.

Augmenting Your Report with External Data   A simple example is connecting weather information to sales data to see if there is a correlation.

Data Studio uses *data blending* to join data sources together. For those familiar with databases and SQL, the blending method used here is a left-outer join. For those unfamiliar with SQL and databases, this won't make a bit of sense! Let's just say that there are several methods to join tabular data, and each one of them has its own characteristics. At this time, Data Studio uses this particular method only.

I will walk you through a typical example here. I want to combine the sessions metric from two of my Google Analytics properties so that I can see the sessions for each property on the same time-series chart. There are several ways that I might do this, but Data Studio has some methods to make data blending a bit simpler for users who would like to use the feature without too much setup.

Let's start with a simple report page to which we have connected a Google Analytics data source, as we did back in Chapter 5, "Web Data Visualization with Google Analytics." We'll call the first data source **Source A**.

1. From the Add A Chart drop-down, select the time-series chart and position it on the page. The default metric for Google Analytics is Sessions, so this should display as the metric on the chart, but if necessary, change the metric to **Sessions**.

2. Select the chart and use Ctrl+C and Ctrl+V to copy and paste the chart. Position it next to the original.

3. Connect the second data source to the new chart. We'll call the second data source **Source B**. On the Data tab of the new chart, click the Data Source field, which is currently set to Source A. This will open a panel where you can select a data source. Select your second Google Analytics data source and confirm that you want to add this data source to the report. Your new chart should update with the new data from Source B.

4. Using the mouse, select one chart by clicking it and include the second chart in the selection by pressing the Ctrl key while clicking the second chart. With both charts selected, right-click between them to open a context menu. Figure 10.18 shows both charts and the context menu.

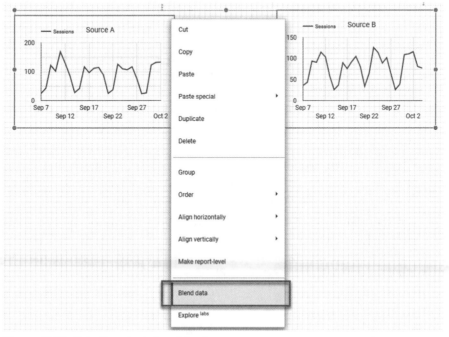

Figure 10.18: Selecting charts for a blend

5. Choose Blend Data from the right-click menu, and Data Studio creates a new chart by blending the data sources from the original charts. If you do not need the originals, you can select and delete them. Figure 10.19 shows the new chart and the Data tab configuration.

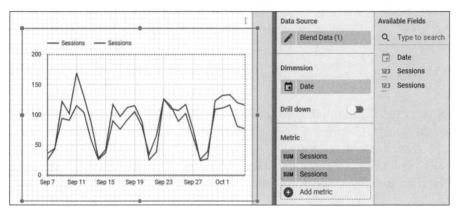

Figure 10.19: Blended chart and properties

6. Data Studio helps you by performing the blend, but there are still some things that you'll want to update. First, note that the table now has two lines for sessions, which is what we want, but they are both called Sessions. Second, the newly blended data source is given a very generic name, in this case Blend Data (1). If you create a new blended chart, say for pageviews, a new blended source will be created called Blend Data (2). If you create several charts this way, it will be easy to get these data sources mixed up. In this case, we'll open the blended data source properties so that we can rename the Sessions fields and the data source for clarity and reuse. Figure 10.20 shows the updated blend configuration.

a. Click the pencil icon on the Blended Data (1) source found in the Data Source field of the Data tab for the chart. The Blend Data properties open.

b. Change the names of the Sessions fields so that they can be distinguished from each other. In this case, we'll call them **Sessions A** and **Sessions B**. You can do this by clicking the field and editing the names.

c. On the right side of the screen, you'll see a listing of the included dimensions and metrics. This is where you can change the data source name. Change the name, in this example to **Blend A B Sessions**, and click Save. Finally, close the panel using the close button.

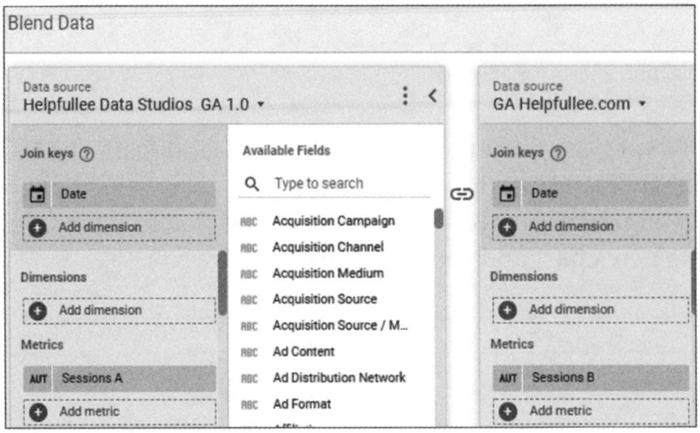

Figure 10.20: Blend data properties configuration

With our fields renamed, the blended chart can now show the Sessions for both data sources clearly. We have one last task to perform with this chart: we want to show the total sessions for both data sources combined instead of individually. To do this, we need to create a blended calculated field. Unlike with regular data sources, you cannot define a new field directly in the data source.

You must create new calculated fields for a blended source directly on the chart in which they will be used. This is another reason for renaming the Sessions fields on the blended data source: if they have the same name, they become very difficult to work with. To create a new Total Sessions field for the chart, follow these steps:

1. Add a metric by clicking the Add Metric button in the Metric area of the charts' Data tab.

2. At the bottom of the panel that opens, click the Create Field button.

3. Assign the new field a name—we'll call it **Total Combined Sessions**. In the Formula box, we must add Sessions A and Sessions B together to get the total. Because of the way aggregation takes place in Data Studio, you'll want to set up your formula this way: **SUM(Sessions A) + SUM(Sessions B)**.

4. Click the Apply button to add the field to the chart. Figure 10.21 shows the configuration and the chart updated with the new field.

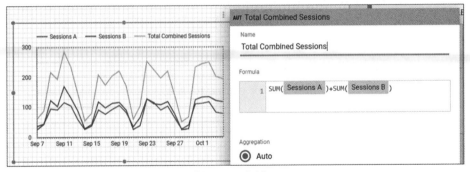

Figure 10.21: Our new Total Combined Sessions field

5. If you just want to show just the Total Combined Sessions, delete the other two metrics from the Data tab. Figure 10.22 shows the final chart version.

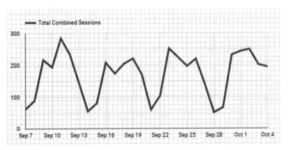

Figure 10.22: Final Total Combined Sessions chart

> **TIP**   As stated earlier, Data Studio Blending can be tricky! It is very easy to get unexpected results or to try to blend the unblendable! As I help users, I find that blending is by far what causes them the most trouble. This is a rapidly evolving area in Data Studio, so it is a good idea to have current references handy to help you if you run into trouble. Check out the Chapter 10 notes for references to the latest resources at www.wiley.com/go/handsondatastudio.

File Upload

Throughout this book, we've made heavy use of Google Sheets as a place to store the data for our reports. While Sheets will probably be your primary location to store your own data, there are other options. Data Studio provides standard connectors for a number of sources, including MySQL databases. For those of you needing something in between Google Sheets and a custom database, there is the File Upload service.

The *File Upload service* may be a good choice for your data set storage, but it has some quirks. Here are some of the pros and cons to consider before using this method:

Pros

- Store up to 1,000 data sets.
- Upload files 100 times a day for each data set.
- Each file can be up to 100 MB in size.
- You have 2 GB of total storage.
- Files are stored in the cloud with no storage costs, and you do not need to set up a cloud account.
- Files uploaded are treated as a data set. You can append to an existing data set by uploading a new file.
- You can manage uploaded files through the Data Studio Connector or through Google Cloud services if you want, and the files you upload are available to other cloud services.
- It is a good way to get a gentle introduction to Google Cloud services.
- Data Connector access is reasonably fast.

Cons

- Multiple files uploaded to a data set are appended to the set, not merged. This means that you have to be careful about duplicating records if you're uploading a file to an existing data set.

- The File Upload service handles only CSV-formatted files, and it is very strict about how special characters, such as commas and quotes, are treated in the data.

- Header rows can have only letters, numbers, or underscores; they must start with a letter or an underscore; and they are limited to 128 characters.

- You cannot have line breaks in your data except at the end of a line.

- Data must be UTF-8 encoded. If you are exporting data from Microsoft Excel or other tools, it may not be in the correct format. I have had numerous issues with this restriction, because many things don't transfer well to this format.

Although the promise of free data set storage is enticing, this option is appropriate only for very clean, uniform data. The uploading of a file, getting errors, fixing issues, and trying again can get frustrating quickly. A single bad character in the file will cause it to be rejected with errors.

If you decide to use this method, you'll find it a bit different from other ways of storing data sets. You start by creating a data source and managing the file upload and management as part of that process. Here are the steps:

1. From the Data Studio home screen, click the Add button and select Data Source. This will take you to the Connectors screen.

2. You'll find the File Upload connector in the Google Connectors section. Select the connector, and you'll be taken to the Connector setup page.

3. Upload a new file to create a new data set. If you already have data sets, they will show up here. Click the Click To Upload Files button to find a file on your system, or drag a CSV file into the upload box, as shown in Figure 10.23.

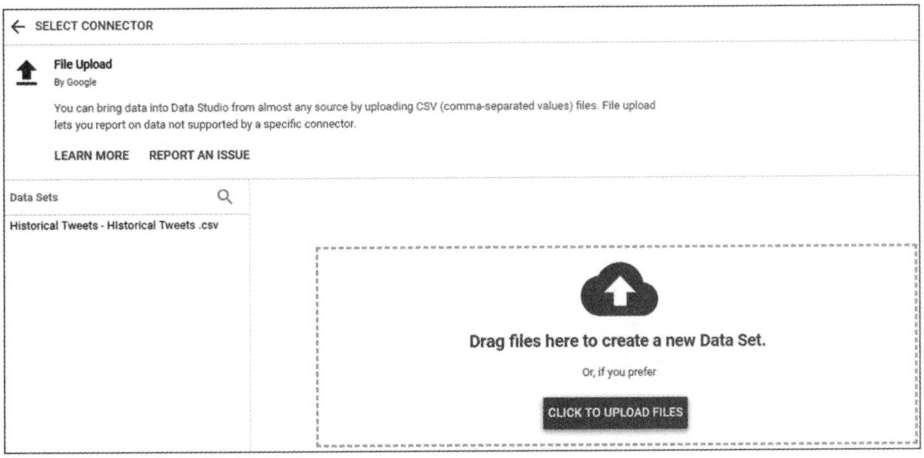

Figure 10.23: Ready to upload a new CSV file

4. After you upload a file, the connector will take a few moments to process the file. If you have errors in your file, you'll be notified at this point and be provided with details on which lines to check. If your file is processed without errors, the results will display with details about the new data set, including the file size. At this point, you may also add more files to the data set, provided that they are in exactly the same format. Added files will be appended to the data set. When you are done here, click the Connect button to go to the Fields configuration screen. Figure 10.24 shows the results of uploading a new CSV file.

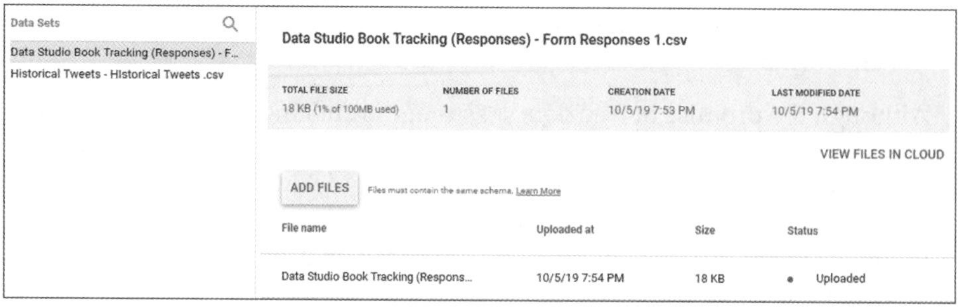

Figure 10.24: File uploaded successfully

With these steps completed, your File Upload data source is ready for use! You can edit the data source from the main Data Studio home page, or while in a report, edit the data source and return to the connection screen from the Fields page. Note the View Files In Cloud option on this page. Clicking this button will take you to the Google Cloud Platform, where you can see how your file is being stored. You can explore the rest of the Google Cloud platform from this point. Google Cloud services are well beyond the scope of this book, but we'll look at another option available on this platform next.

BigQuery for Big Data

I believe one of Google's main reasons for giving away a powerful service like Data Studio is to drive adoption of their cloud platform services. If you think that this sounds far-fetched, you may not be familiar with just how lucrative the cloud computing market is. Many people are unaware that Amazon, while famous for its e-Commerce platform, actually derives the majority of the company's profit from their cloud platform, Amazon Web Services (see `www.cnbc .com/2019/02/12/how-amazon-makes-money.html`).

The other players in the cloud services market, including Google, Microsoft, IBM, and Oracle, would all like to catch up to Amazon in selling cloud services. Getting people familiar with their platform through applications like Data Studio plays well into Google's goals.

One of the premier Google cloud offerings that is becoming an introduction to their cloud offerings is called *BigQuery*. This is a service "that enables interactive analysis of massive datasets working in conjunction with Google Storage." When Google says "massive" data sets, it's not exaggerating. And it is very, very fast. Perhaps it should be no surprise that this service works very well with Data Studio.

> **NOTE**   How fast is BigQuery? Of course, the answer depends on how you are measuring it. The answer also depends a lot of configuration. Analysis queries are also being sped up, in some cases, by a special new "BI Engine." In some circumstances, this feature may be invoked on your Data Studio reports when you are using the service.
>
> But how fast is it? Queries on tables with billions of rows are executed in seconds. When the BI Engine is connected, the speed of queries is less than a second!

I believe that we'll see increasing numbers of people beginning to use Google platform cloud services as more massive data sets become available to the public and as the price for such services drops. One reason I have not covered this service in detail is that there may be costs involved, depending on how it is used. While BigQuery is a premium service, Google provides a free "sandbox," which is available for individuals to use right now without even providing their credit card.

The sandbox provides 1 terabyte a month of query capacity and 10 GB of free storage. Any tables that you create in the sandbox have a retention period of 60 days. This is a great way to explore the capabilities of the service.

Using BigQuery is well beyond the scope of this book, but I'm going to walk you through the steps of connecting to BigQuery, opening one of their large public data sets, and using the Data Studio Explore feature. The public data sets are free to explore, and they give you the opportunity to try out the BigQuery Data Studio services without having to load your own information.

To give this example some focus, let's see if we can quickly find the venue with the longest average duration time for all Major League Baseball games for the 2016 regular season. The data set we'll use is pretty large—it has more than 760,000 records!

1. Start by going to `https://console.cloud.google.com/bigquery`. If it is your first time using the service, you'll be asked to log in and agree to the terms of service. Then, you'll be taken to your BigQuery page.

2. In order to use the service, you need to create a new project. Click the Create button at the top right of the screen.

3. A default project name will be generated for you. You may use this or provide your own, as shown in Figure 10.25. Click the Create button to open the Sandbox page.

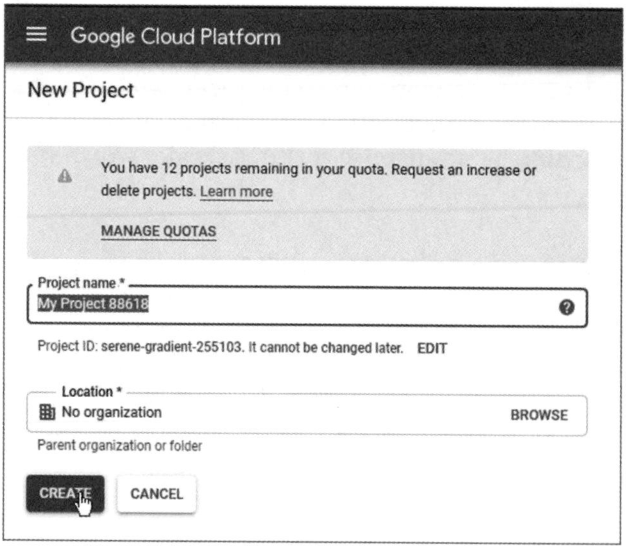

Figure 10.25: Name your BigQuery project.

4. On the left side of the screen, from the Add Data drop-down, choose Explore Public Datasets, as shown in Figure 10.26. This will take you to the Marketplace Datasets page.

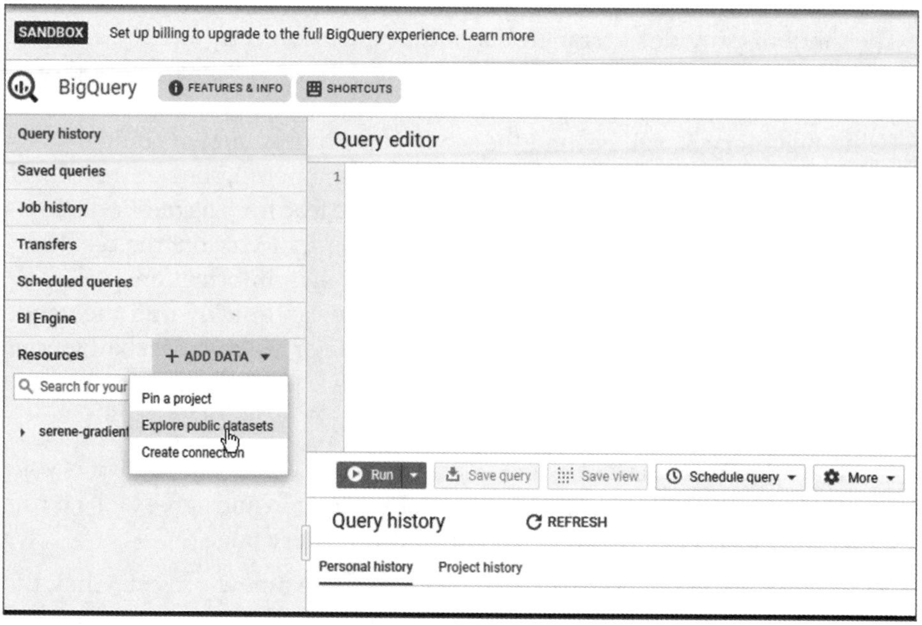

Figure 10.26: Choosing Explore Public Datasets

5. As you can see, we have quite a few public data sets available to explore. In this example, we are using the MLB 2016 Pitch-by-Pitch data set. Locate this data set on the screen and select it. This will return you to the Sandbox page, and you'll now have access to all the public data sets in the scroll pane on the left side of the screen. The data set marked Baseball will be highlighted, and a description of the data will appear in the center of the screen.

6. Click the data set to expand the selection to show the tables contained in that set. As shown in Figure 10.27, select the games_wide table. This will bring up the schema for that table, which lists the fields and their types. You can also click the Details and Preview tabs to see different views of the table data.

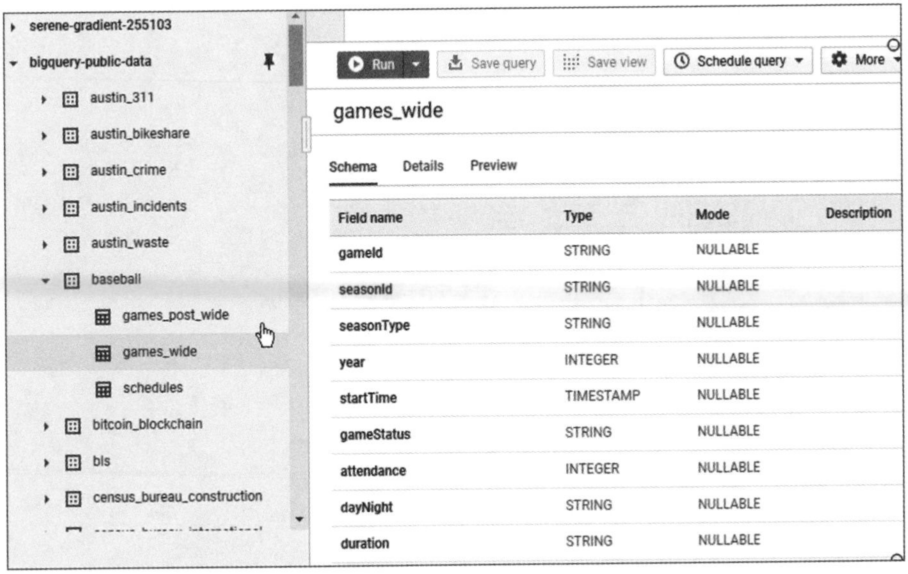

Figure 10.27: Selecting a data set table

7. At the far right of the page, you'll see a set of table options. From the Export drop-down, select Explore With Data Studio, as shown in Figure 10.28. This will open a new browser tab with the Data Studio Explorer.

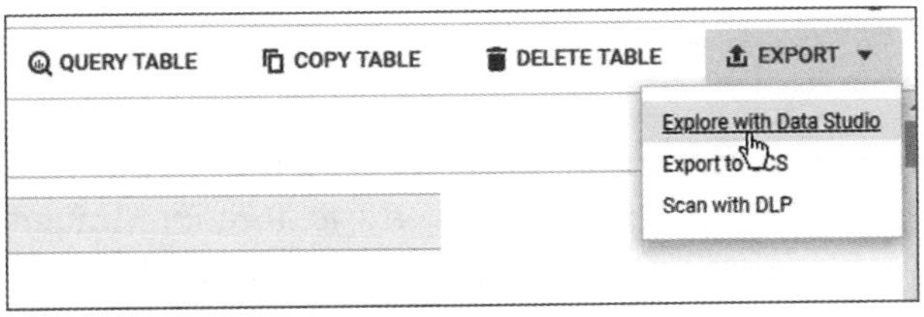

Figure 10.28: Selecting Explore With Data Studio

8. The Explorer screen is similar to the normal Data Studio report editing page, but it is simplified. You have only a basic canvas, charts, and selectors with which to work. The Explorer screen is very responsive, and data updates very quickly. A default table will fill the canvas when you first bring up the screen. Delete this table by clicking the ellipsis at the top-right of the table and selecting the Delete option. Next, select the geo map chart from the Add A Chart drop-down, as shown in Figure 10.29.

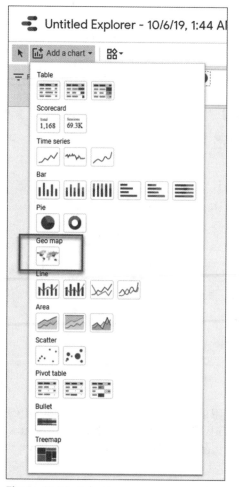

Figure 10.29: Selecting a new geo map chart

9. Your new map may start with a configuration error. To fix this, in the Data tab, set Dimension to venueCity. Next, change the metric to durationMinutes from the available fields. By default, the aggregation method for this field is Sum. Edit the field on the chart and set Aggregation to Average.

10. Switch to the Style tab. Set the max color to red and the min color to blue. Figure 10.30 shows the settings and the map with the updated colors.

Figure 10.30: Updated color scale for the map

If you were to hover over the largest point on the map, you would see that the city with the highest average duration for baseball games was Phoenix, Arizona, and the highest duration was 202.65 minutes.

At this point, you can click the Save button, which will allow you to return to this Explorer screen from the Data Studio main page. Once the report is saved, you can also copy the chart and paste it into an existing report, or you can create a new report with the chart by clicking the Share button. In addition, the new data source for BigQuery is created automatically, so you can use it in other reports.

We gained extra speed from the BI Engine, which loads results into high-speed memory for reporting. You can tell if the BI Engine has operated on a chart because it shows a small lightning bolt symbol at the upper right of the header for the chart. If you have been following along and tried this example, you'll find that the Explorer and the charts that it creates are very responsive, despite the large size of the data set.

Community Connectors

In Chapter 8, you had some exposure to community connectors. We used the code provided by the developer community for the Google Fit service to create our own connector. The next level of complexity and mastery is to program and build your own connectors.

Granted, building your own connectors, and later sharing them with others in the community if you wish, is a big departure from building simple reports! However, should you be so inclined to take up the challenge, Google provides numerous reference guides and tutorials to help you build your own connectors for services to suit your own needs.

As a data citizen, you have the ability to access data your way, with your own tools.

The Latest Dishes: New Developments and Releases

During the writing of this book, there were more than 20 announced Data Studio updates! I can't guarantee what the future holds for this tool, but if past years have been any indication, Google will support it with continued development and community outreach.

You can find the latest release notes for Data Studio at https://support.google .com/datastudio/answer/6311467. You'll find posts by enthusiasts to help you master these new features, as well communities of users ready to help. You'll find more Data Studio resources in the Chapter 10 references at www.wiley.com/ go/handsondatastudio.

Summary

In this chapter, we looked at directions that you might pursue for further development and growth with Data Studio. We covered the following topics:

- Annotating static reports with graphic elements to highlight important points of interest
- Annotating methods for dynamic reports using calculated metrics
- Using multiple pages to simulate tooltips to help users navigate complex reports and provide instructions
- Embedding other media such as videos into reports
- Using community visualizations to extend report capabilities
- Using Data Studio as a platform for developing data widgets and online applications
- Reviewing the basics of data blending and combining multiple data sources
- Using the File Upload connector for storage of large CSV file-based data sets
- Introducing BigQuery as a tool for working with large data sets and using Data Studio to explore the Google Cloud Platform public data sets

There is no end to the potential for improvement when it comes to using a tool like Data Studio. Practicing your skills in both report development and analysis will help you grow as a communicator and as someone skilled at deriving valuable insights from data.

This book covered the fundamentals of finding and creating data sets and using them with Data Studio to create visualization applications for personal and business use and for the larger community. In some respects, we have traveled a great distance—yet in some ways, we have remained grounded in the fundamentals of reporting and data visualization. The goal of this book is to provide you with the fundamentals so that you can pursue your own goals and use data and tools for your own purposes.

It is my hope that this book helps you in your journey to go from data to information and insight in order to drive meaningful action and impact in your personal, business, and public life. Use the tools and resources to take control and claim your role as a responsible data citizen.

Index